Jesus and His Jewish Parables

Theological Inquiries

Studies in Contemporary Biblical and Theological Problems

General Editor
Lawrence Boadt, C. S. P.

PAULIST PRESS
New York • Mahwah

Jesus and His Jewish Parables

Rediscovering the Roots of Jesus' Teaching

Brad H. Young

PAULIST PRESS
New York ● Mahwah

Library of Congress Cataloging-in-Publication Data

Young, Brad.
Jesus and his Jewish parables / Brad H. Young.
p. cm.
Bibliography: p.
Includes index.
ISBN 0-8091-3031-9 (pbk.) : $13.95 (est.)
1. Jesus Christ—Parables. 2. Parables, Jewish. 3. Rabbinical literature—Relation to the New Testament. 4. Bible. N.T. Gospels—Criticism, interpretation, etc. I. Title.
BT375.2.Y66 1989
226′.806—dc19 88-29975
CIP

Published by Paulist Press
997 Macarthur Boulevard
Mahwah, NJ 07430

Printed and bound in the
United States of America

CONTENTS

TO MY TEACHER AND FRIEND,
PROFESSOR DAVID FLUSSER

♦

"Our rabbis say: Let not the parable be lightly esteemed in your eyes, since by means of the parable a man can master the words of the Torah."

Song of Songs Rabba 1:1,8–9

♦

INTRODUCTION: PARABOLIC TEACHINGS AND THE PROBLEM OF HERMENEUTICS

According to the gospels, Jesus told numerous parables. While the story parables that Jesus tells seem deceptively simple, they have confused and confounded scholars, theologians and the lay reader for centuries. Although scholars have been quick to criticize the church fathers for their free allegorical interpretation of the parables, few academic studies have been able to bridge the chasm of time, history and culture that separates us from Jesus the parable teacher and prevents us from making connection with the original setting of these story illustrations. Was the original audience of the teacher from Nazareth confused by his parables? How is it possible to step into the shoes of the ancient people of Israel and really listen to the parables?

From the early works of the church fathers to the most recent publications on the parables of Jesus, often one area of study is neglected or totally ignored. The fact is that story parables only appear in Jewish literature and in the gospels. Yet few works have investigated the relationship between early rabbinic parabolic teaching and the vivid illustrations of Jesus. The sages of ancient Israel were profound teachers and their use of the parable can also aid our understanding of the parabolic illustrations of Jesus. The work at hand is a pioneering quest which will try to bridge the chasm between the world of Jesus and the modern interpreter. Many methodological problems must be carefully treated to critically examine the parables of Jesus in comparison to rabbinic parables. Nonetheless it is impossible to hear the parables if we do not use all the available sources to rediscover their historical context.

Hence the use of parables, examples and illustrations in instructive materials is a popular and an effective didactic method that has found a place in antiquity as well as in the present. Moses Maimonides (Rambam) began his famous treatise *The Guide for the Perplexed* with a discussion of what he called the prophetic parable. In fact one of the main purposes of this portion of his work was " . . . the explanation of very obscure parables. . . . "[1] Paradoxically, while many parables may be described as teaching aids that aim to clarify and to illustrate, they are nevertheless often difficult to interpret or even obscure as Rambam has described them.[2] Few interpreters, from ancient times to the present, have been able to agree on an acceptable hermeneutic that can be applied to the parable.

Agadic teaching has always been popular among the people and the intended audience appreciated and understood the parables.[3] R. Meir was noted for dividing his teaching into three parts—one third halachah, one third agadah and one third composed of parables.[4] The Mishnah laments that parabolic teachers ceased after R. Meir died.[5] R. Meir was noted for having a collection of three hundred fox parables of which unfortunately only few have survived.[6] Rashi provides an example of an early interest in parabolic instruction when he discusses the parable of the fox who outwitted the wolf in his commentary on the talmudic text that discusses R. Meir's use of parables.[7] The early interest in parables did not resolve the hermeneutical issues concerning their interpretation.

Like rabbinic parables, Jesus' parables have aroused interest and puzzlement among interpreters for centuries.[8] Parables comprise a significant portion of the extant teaching discourses preserved in the synoptic gospels. In fact, the parables make up about one third of all of Jesus' instruction.[9] How can the Jesus of history be adequately grasped without dealing with his parabolic instruction? The problem of rediscovering the original meaning of Jesus' parabolic teaching is compounded because the parables can only be understood when viewed in relationship to their historical situation.[10] Once these parables were divorced from their original Jewish milieu they became more difficult for interpreters to understand. They were obscured by being interpreted from the standpoint of a new setting far removed from Jesus by history, language, culture and an entirely different religious orientation.

The parables of Jesus are intimately related to the religious heritage, culture, language, agricultural life and social concerns of the Jewish people during the Second Temple Period. J. Jeremias expressed the opinion that Jesus was the first Jewish teacher to use parabolic instruction[11] and J. Neusner has suggested that the parable is a later rabbinic didactic technique that was not used until after the destruction of the Temple. Neusner writes, "Pharisaic-rabbinic traditions contain few, if any, parables (these are all late)."[12] On the one hand, Jeremias' approach tends to drive a wedge between Jesus and the Jewish background to the gospel teachings, and on the other hand, Neusner's speculation[13] ignores the evidence of the gospels which should be viewed to a certain extent as containing examples of early Jewish instruction before the destruction of the Temple, even if the preservation and transmission of the traditions within Jewish and Christian circles are not always exactly parallel. Jesus' parables in the gospels indicate that other contemporary Jewish teachers employed the parable as a didactic mode during the Second Commonwealth even if the evidence is somewhat fragmentary.

Even if Jesus was not the first parabolic teacher, his masterful use of the parable helps to account for his phenomenal popularity and success. Indeed, he was a master of the agadah. Jesus' parabolic teachings captured the imagination and the heart of the people. Jesus made extensive use of parables. Parables appear far more frequently in Jesus' teaching than in the teaching of the Tannaim or even the more agadic teaching of the Amoraim.[14] As Pinchas Lapide has observed, "Rabbi Yeshua of Nazareth would apparently have agreed with Rabbi A. J. Heschel, who wrote: 'Halakhah deals with details . . . Aggadah inspires'."[15] A passage from the Talmud supports this analysis of the agadah. R. Abahu and R. Chiya b. Aba were both giving lectures, the Talmud records. R. Abahu gave an agadic discourse and R. Chiya b. Aba gave a halachic lecture. The people abandoned the exposition of R. Chiya b. Aba to listen to R. Abahu's agadic lecture.[16] Apparently, the people found R. Abahu's discourse more interesting because of its agadic content. Not everyone could have appreciated or understood the technicalities of halachic instruction but agadic teaching had wide appeal that could speak to the less educated and yet often would also engage the mind of the scholar on a deeper level that the uninitiated would not fully comprehend.

Jesus' parables inspired the people. His parables do not moralize or provide platitudes; instead they function to convey a message. For instance, few lectures can succeed to expose the inconsistency of hypocritical criticism as well as the humorous parabolic saying about the beam and the splinter (Matthew 7:3–5; Luke 6:41–42).[17] Likewise, few expositions can express the concept of forgiveness quite as well as Jesus' parable of "The Unforgiving Servant" (Matthew 18:21–35). The parable communicates the force of forgiveness, between the individual and the offender, and also between man and God. The parable allows the listener to conceptualize the relationship being taught in concrete terms. If a picture can express a thousand words, then a parable can express a thousand expositions. Parables can concisely convey religious complexities in remarkable simplicity.

The terms *parabolē* in Greek and *mashal* in Hebrew require some qualification. Rambam speaks of prophetic parables and discusses their interpretation[18] but his understanding of the parable would comprise many more sayings than the story examples that will be considered in the present work. Dov Noy employs the term "story parables" without giving any definitions.[19] Nevertheless it becomes clear what Noy means by this term from his collection of R. Simeon bar Yochai's parables. Noy is referring to story illustrations. But the word *mashal* has a wider range of meanings. Etymologically, L. Koehler and W. Baumgartner have derived the Hebrew word *mashal* from the Akkadian root *masalu* which means "be resembling, be like." They also mention the *Old-South-Arabic* root which means "image."[20] In rabbinic literature the terms *mašhal* or *matlā* have various connotations as C. Thoma noted. "*Mašal/matlā* kann ja neben Gleichnis auch den Spruch, das Sprichwort, die Metapher, den Vergleich und eine hermeneutische Regel bedeuten."[21] Beyond the basic meaning of resemblance, in biblical Hebrew the word *mashal* can denote a riddle or an allegory (i.e. Ezekiel 17:2ff),[22] a parallelism or an oracle of comparisons (i.e. Numbers 23:7,18; 24:3f), a proverb or wise saying (i.e. Proverbs 10:1)[23] and even a by-word (i.e. Job 17:6).[24] In rabbinic literature the meaning has been enlarged to include story parable illustrations along with proverbs[25] or even simply verses.[26] The work at hand will deal primarily with the story parable illustrations. These illustrative examples were related to the rubric *mashal* at a later period as an extension of the basic meaning of resemblance or comparison.

The Greek word *parabolē* apparently is derived from the verb *paraballō* which means "*set beside* or *parallel with*" or "*compare* one with another."[27] In the Greek mind before the composition of the New Testament, the word *parabolē* denoted something parallel or a comparison, a likeness or even a wise saying.[28] The LXX translators of the Hebrew scriptures rendered the Hebrew word *mashal* by the Greek word *parabolē* twenty two times.[29] This is by far the most accepted translation of the word *mashal* which was translated by *paroimia* only three times.[30] Philo uses the word *parabolē* as meaning a comparison when he likens the world to a brick in his discussion of Genesis chapter eleven.[31] The author of the epistle to the Hebrews, the only other book of the New Testament which contains the word *parabolē* other than the synoptic gospels, employs the term as denoting a symbol, a figure or a type (Hebrews 9:9; 11:19). Curiously enough, neither the word *mashal* nor the expression *parabolē* (in the LXX) ever appears as meaning a story parable in the Old Testament even though several items like Nathan's reproof (2 Samuel 12:1–4), Jotham's fable (Judges 9:8–15) or Isaiah's vineyard (Isaiah 5:1–7) are remarkably similar to parables in rabbinic literature and in the synoptics. Scholars who accept Jülicher's methodology may consider these examples from the Hebrew scriptures as allegories and not parables, but the likenesses between these illustrations and story parables are inescapable. Although these stories are not described by the rubric parable in the biblical text, for all intents and purposes they are indeed parables.[32]

The fable is another medium of comparison which is closely related to the parable. In fact Rabbi Meir's three hundred fox illustrations would probably be nearer to the fable than to the story parable. Theon Aelius of Alexandria described the fable as being λόγος ψευδὴς εἰκονίζων ἀλήθειαν, that is, a "fictitious story picturing a truth."[33] The fable usually makes use of animals. The fabulist employs his animal cast metaphorically, attributing human emotions, reasoning and behavior to his characters. The object of the fable is much more frequently designed to teach worldly wisdom or a lesson of common sense rather than moral principles. The fable is an ancient and widely used form of communication which was known among the Sumerians of the second millennium B.C.E.[34] The fable appears in early Greek literature (Hesiod, *Opera et Dies* 202-210) and was later popularized in anthologies (cf. Babrius, Phaedrus and Avianus). The fables are generally attributed to Aesop (cf. Diogenes Laertius 5.80)[35] but they were widely used by rhetoricians and writers and also it would seem reasonable that even the unlearned would have enjoyed using these entertaining anecdotes. By way of contrast, instead of animals that behave like people, story parables usually contain human characters which are cast into a drama with a more or less realistic setting. Exaggerations and surrealistic elements may be employed in the parable. These elements keep the listener's attention and sometimes shock the audience by inserting an extraordinary action opposed to accepted convention and normal custom into an ordinary everyday life situation. Parable telling is far more than storytelling because it is intimately related to the context of the parabolist's message. The parable illustrates a truth by using a comparison and its message often has moral implications. The abstract is made concrete. So while the parable and the fable are somewhat similar in function and structure they have an entirely different form and composition. Comparative study of the fable and parable will produce only fragmentary results because of their very distinct differences.

The story parables were always intended to elucidate and to illustrate. Nevertheless, perhaps because the meaning of the parables was not always clear to the evangelists and redactors of the gospels,[36] they sometimes treat the parables as esoteric teaching. As noted above, the word parable is sometimes used in connection with a riddle and this may have contributed to this misunderstanding.[37] When the meaning of a parable is not immediately clear, Jesus gave an explanation (e.g. Matthew 13:18–23; Mark

4:13–20; Luke 8:11–15). Sometimes these explanations of parables have been rejected as secondary. Rabbinic parables often have an interpretation, and though every example must be considered individually one cannot take the liberty of rejecting all the explanations as later additions. The parables are not understood without them. Hence a difficult to understand parable should not be considered secret teaching. The lack of clarity may be due to the unknown occasion of the illustration or because its interpretation has been lost or replaced. Moreover once the parable had been removed from its original Jewish setting from the Second Temple Period, it became much more difficult to analyze. Sometimes the interpretation provided in the gospel text may be suspect (cf. Matthew 13:36–43) but this kind of technique which makes use of parable and interpretation is well known in rabbinic literature. The purpose of the parable was to instruct and *not* to conceal Jesus' message.

Of course the use of the Greek word *parabolē* in the synoptic gospels must also be carefully analyzed in any discussion of the meaning of the term in the teaching of Jesus. The word appears primarily in phrases used by the evangelists to introduce an illustration or a saying. It appears forty-eight times in the synoptics—seventeen times in Matthew, thirteen times in Mark, and eighteen times in Luke. Matthew, Mark and Luke use the word *parabolē* seven times in parallel one to the other. Matthew and Mark use it together three times where it does not appear in Luke. Each evangelist uses it independently of the other synoptic gospels—Matthew five times, Mark one time, and Luke eleven times. Did Jesus ever introduce his story parables by using the noun *mashal* (*parabolē* in Greek)? Did Jesus employ this term as meaning a saying or a proverb?[38] One must carefully analyze the gospels to determine what text reflects the earlier sources of the evangelists. In some cases it seems that the use of the word *parabolē* as an introductory formula for the story parables in the gospels texts was an innovation which was made at a later stage of the tradition. However as Flusser has suggested, Luke preserves a saying which seems to be derived from the early Greek translation of the Semitic sources of the synoptics.[39] After the Parable of the Sower, the disciples approach Jesus and ask him the interpretation of the parable (Luke 8:9) to which Jesus responds (Luke 8:11), ἐπηρώτων δὲ αὐτὸν οἱ μαθηταὶ αὐτοῦ τίς αὕτη εἴη ἡ παραβολή . . . ἔστιν δὲ αὕτη ἡ παραβολή. The text can be reconstructed into Hebrew, ... וישאלוהו תלמידיו מה הוא המשל? ויאמר המשל הוא.[40] So while the word *parabolē* was used secondarily by each of the evangelists and the redactors of the gospels, it is possible that the source of this proliferation stemmed from the *Vorlage* of the synoptics.

In most of the instances where the term *parabolē* appears, it forms a part of a transitional sentence that betrays evidence of redaction. Seldom can these transitional sentences be reconstructed into the idiomatic Hebrew that characterizes the best sources of the extant gospel narratives. However caution must be taken. Here it is at least necessary to mention the possibility that the Hebrew undertext of the gospel narratives may have used the term *mashal* in the sense of a story parable as well as a saying or proverb (Luke 4:23). The Greek phrase ἔλεγεν δὲ καὶ παραβολὴν πρὸς αὐτοὺς appears with slightly different wording three times in Luke (5:36; cf. 6:39; 12:16).[41] It could be reconstructed into the phrase ואמר להם משל or even into biblical Hebrew ויאמר להם משל.[42] No one should be dogmatic on these points. These proposed Hebrew reconstructions are not without their problems as the phraseology itself is not fully paralleled in the Hebrew used during the period. Did these phrases appear in the earliest Hebrew sources for the life of Jesus?[43] While a definitive answer is difficult, if it would be in the affirmative it could explain the later redactors' proliferation of the term in secondary contexts. At any rate, the majority of these introductory preambles were probably inserted into the gospel narratives at a later stage of the tradition and utilized as connecting phrases to join the parables to their individual contexts.[44]

Interestingly enough, like Jesus' parables, secondary introductory formulas appear to have been augmented to many rabbinic parables. In the homiletical midrash Pesikta Derav Kahana where several manuscripts have been preserved, the introductory formulas like משל למה הדבר דומה frequently do not appear in the better readings.[45] This can also be seen in the available textual evidence of other midrashim. Sometimes scribes felt a certain amount of freedom in making minor changes like adding an introductory formula or changing a phrase like "The Blessed One" to "The Holy One Blessed be He." Probably many parables originally began with only the Hebrew word "to" (-ל), which meant "this may be compared to" or more simply "like." Philo uses a similar construction with the Greek word *hōsper* when he writes, "Then *like* on a ship crew . . . " (*Con. Ling.* 22). This should be compared to the gospels (i.e. Matthew 25:14). The usage in the gospel would reflect the Hebrew word for "like" or "as" (-כ). Story parables have been introduced by a variety of formulas and T. Guttmann has collected numerous examples.[46] Some parables started with a simple imperative like "Look at the fig tree . . . " (ἴδετε; Luke 21:29) or similar idioms like "Go out and see . . . " or "Go out and learn from . . . " which appear in rabbinic literature.[47] The introductory phrases of specific parables will be discussed as an on-going part of this work. In any case it can be seen how the preambles which introduced a story parable became standardized.

Even if the word *mashal* was ascribed to Jesus' story parables at a later time, the term itself is certainly apropos. The story parable is a resemblance or a likeness.[48] The *Old-South-Arabic* root which means image[49] is very close to this meaning because an image may be compared to the original in order to determine the accuracy of the resemblance. S. Loewenstamm has called attention to an Assyrian text in which the king is said to resemble or be in the very image of the deity (*mushshulu,* from *mashalu*), "The shadow of the god (is) a free man. [And] the shadow of a free man (is) a slave. The king: He is li[ke] the image of a god."[50] The grammarian and exegete from Narbonne, David Kimche (1160?–1235?), connected the idea of man being created in God's image with the concept of man's reign over God's creation on the basis of the Hebrew root *mashal* which appears in the causative conjugation in Psalm 8:9.[51] Thus man was created in the image of God and he rules over God's creation. A similar understanding is also reflected by Saadiah Gaon (882–942).[52] In any case, one sees the close connection between the image and the original which formed the basis for making the likeness. This has led some scholars to call the biblical *mashal* a model, exemplar or paradigm.[53] Cohen has argued that the Akkadian verb *telu* which means to tell or to express is derived from the Akkadian noun *teltu.* Furthermore, the noun *teltu* is the "Akkadian interdialectal equivalent" of the Hebrew noun *mashal.*[54] A *mashal* is telling or describing a likeness. What is the interaction between the image and the illustrand? What relationship is being compared? How does the story parable function to convey a message? Interpreting this interrelationship between the comparison *(mashal)* and the object *(nimshal)* of the parable is the core of the hermeneutical question. Actually the etymological considerations are of secondary significance because the meaning of the mashal was determined in later times as the story parable became an accepted didactic technique in oral and written tradition.

These brief introductory remarks leave many questions unanswered, but hopefully some of these issues can be clarified after further consideration of specific story parables. In the work at hand an inductive approach to the meaning of a story parable must be pursued without a detailed analysis of the wider connotations included in the definition of the Hebrew term mashal. An inductive approach allows research into the wider range of meanings of the term which are so important for a proper understanding of the development and emergence of the parable as a well defined pedagogic technique. Also the qualification of the relationship between the illustration, single or multiple *tertia comparationis* and the illustrand must first be studied inductively. The story parable and the problems of its interpretation and its development as a literary genre will be analyzed, as it appears both in the synoptic gospels and in Jewish literature. Are Jesus' parables indeed related to rabbinic parables? Only exploration and experimentation with the extant materials can determine whether a comparative approach to the parables both in talmudic literature and in the gospels can be a useful and effective hermeneutical methodology.

Comparative study must deal not only with contrasts and comparisons but also must consider each literature separately as independent works. After a brief look at the present state of scholarship in regards to parabolic research, the parables of Jesus and selected parables from Jewish literature must be studied in light of their own individual contexts.

Notes

1) Shlomo Pines, trans., *The Guide for the Perplexed* (Chicago: Chicago University Press, 1963), p. 12 and M. Friedländer, trans., *The Guide for the Perplexed* (London: George Routledge, 1928), p. 4.

2) Ibid. See also Jerome who said that only the apostles understood Jesus' parables, "After the parables which he spoke to the people which only the apostles understood. . . . " *Matth.* 13:53–54, in A. Klijn and G. Reinink, *Patristic Evidence for Jewish-Christian Sects* (Leiden: Brill, 1973), pp. 216–217. This idea is already reflected in the Epistle of Barnabas XVII, 2, "For if I write to you concerning things present or things to come, you will not understand because they are hid in parables."

3) Compare the story concerning R. Abahu and R. Chiya B. Aba in b. Sotah 40a and cf. A. Feldman, *The Parables and Similes of the Rabbis* (Cambridge: Cambridge University Press, 1927), pp. 19–20.

4) B. Sanhedrin 38b. See W. Bacher, *Agada der Tannaiten* (Strassburg: Karl T. Trübner, 1903, reprint 1965), vol. 2, pp. 6–7, idem, *Agadot Hatanaim* (Jerusalem: Devir, 1919), volume 2, part 1, p. 3. See also the section of this work, "Parable, Agadah and Tradition," note 78.

5) M. Sotah 9:15.

6) B. Sanhedrin 38b–39a.

7) See Rashi's text on b. Sanhedrin 38b–39a. This text has been discussed by Zebi Hirsch Chajes, *The Student's Guide through the Talmud,* translated by J. Schachter (New York: Feldheim, 1960), p. 217. Compare with Rabbi Berechiah Hanakdan's 117th fox fable which is discussed by Haim Schwarzbaum, *The Mishle Shu'alim (Fox Fables) of Rabbi Berechiah Ha-Nakdan* (Kiron: Institute for Jewish and Arab Folklore Research, 1979), pp. 550–555. See also Ben Edwin Perry, *Babrius and Phaedrus* (Cambridge, Massachusetts: Harvard University Press, 1975), p. 538, Phaedrus, number 593.

8) C.H. Dodd, *The Parables of the Kingdom* (Glasgow: Collins, 1961), pp. 13–14.

9) A.M. Hunter, *Interpreting the Parables* (London: SCM Press, 1981), p. 7. Not only do the parables make up a significant amount of the materials preserved and attributed to Jesus, but Dodd has also observed, "There is no part of the Gospel record which has for the reader a clearer ring of authenticity." Idem, *The Parables,* p. 13.

10) Recently there has been a move away from the historical method of parable research. Ernst Fuchs, Bultmann's student and successor at Marburg, sees the parables as "language events" *(Sprachereignisse)* that enter the life situation of the hearers and challenge them to make a decision; idem, *Zur Frage nach dem historischen Jesus* (Tübingen: J.C.B. Mohr, 1965), pp. 136–142, 379, 424–430; idem, *Hermeneutik* (Bad Cannstatt: R. Müllerschön Verlag, 1958), pp. 212–219. Robert Funk feels that it is demeaning to call a parable a mere teaching device because they press the hearer "to choose between worlds." Cf. idem, *Language, Hermeneutic and Word of God* (New York: Harper and Row, 1966), pp. 161–162. Dan O. Via has emphasized that the parables must be considered as literary aesthetic creations that have a universal application to the human situation, idem, *The Parables: Their Literary and Existential Dimension* (Philadelphia: Fortress Press, 1980), pp. 24–25. For a discussion about the school of parable research known as the new hermeneutic and those who have tried non-historical approaches, see Warren Kissinger, *The Parables of Jesus a History of Interpretation and Bibliography* (Metuchen, New Jersey: The Scarecrow Press, 1979) pp. 173–230. See also Paul Ricoeur, "The 'Kingdom' in the Parables of Jesus," *Anglican Theological Review* LXIII (1981), pp. 165–169 who has accepted this approach. Some of these studies have resulted from a pessimism regarding the reliability of the available resources for reconstructing the historical situation and therefore avoid consideration of the philological tools and historical sources that pave the way for an honest and critical evaluation of the evidence. This point is crucial. To what extent can the parables be studied as aesthetic objects once they have been removed from their historical setting? How can one apply a parable to the proper human situation after it has been divorced from its *Sitz im Leben* by language, culture, religion, two thousand years of history and a completely different conceptual world? There is no easy way out. The historical and philological tools are essential for understanding the parables in their original context before their message can be properly applied to a contemporary setting. All the evidence must be carefully evaluated. After the historical groundwork has been laid, then modern researchers are in a better position to make application of the parables to the human situation. The parables do have a timelessness that transcends their strict historical setting but this setting must be clearly understood in order to grasp the full impact of a parable's message today.

11) J. Jeremias, *The Parables of Jesus* (London: SCM Press, 1972), p. 12. Here Jeremias claims, "Jesus' parables are something entirely new." But Jotham's Fable and Nathan the prophet's rebuke in the Hebrew

Scriptures are remarkably similar to Jesus' parables even though the word parable is not used to describe their word pictures (Judges 9:7–15; 2 Samuel 12:1–4).

12) Jacob Neusner, "Types and Forms in Ancient Jewish Literature: Some Comparisons," *History of Religions* XI (1972), p. 360 and p. 368. Nevertheless in an appendix to Neusner's *A History of the Mishnaic Law of Purities Part XIII Migvaot* (Leiden: E.J. Brill, 1976), pp. 224–226, Robert Johnston has cited some examples that would considerably modify Neusner's stated position. The fact that Johnston's article "Parables among the Pharisees and Early Rabbis" has appeared in this appendix to Neusner's own book may indicate that Neusner himself could be reconsidering or has changed his view.

13) Of course, Johnston, in his short article "Parables among the Pharisees and Early Rabbis," cites several sources and T. Guttmann discusses some early parables; see *Hamashal Betakufat Hatanaim* (Jerusalem: Abir Yaakov, 1949), pp. 13, 23–24. Guttmann makes the mistake of attributing parables belonging to the Houses of Hillel and Shamai to the great leaders themselves. He also fails to note Johanan ben Zakai's parable in b. Shabbat 153a. Sometimes his references are not accurate but his work is still useful. Part of this whole question is related to the reliability of attributions in rabbinic literature. Neusner has recently discussed some of the criteria for determining the traditions in the Mishnah; idem, *Judaism the Evidence of the Mishnah* (University of Chicago Press: Chicago, 1981), pp. 14–22. The most systematic treatment of the whole question was carried out by W. Bacher, *Tradition und Tradenten* (Leipzig: Gustav Fock, 1914, reprint Berlin: Walter de Gruyter, 1966). Bacher's work is still of great value. Since many of the rabbinic sources were compiled in later periods, the reliability of the source of a quotation has great importance. M. Smith, Neusner's mentor, has great reservations concerning the attribution in ancient sources: "In general, good sayings went about the ancient world looking for good Fathers, and it often happened that they found several." Idem, "The Jewish Elements in the Gospels," *Journal of Bible and Religion* 24 (1956), p. 94. Nevertheless, the rabbis were noted for their meticulous preservation of tradition and students were required to cite a reference according to the Tradent (even conflicting opinions must be properly preserved; see Ch. Albeck, *Mevo Lamishnah,* Tel Aviv: Devir, 1979, p. 84; cf. Avot 6.6; b. Megilah 15a; b. Chulin 104b; b. Nidah 19b; m. Eduyot 1.3; b. Shab. 15a, b. Ber. 47a, b. Bek. 5a, b. Erub. 53a, Avot 2.8, 3.8; cf. J. Bowker, *The Targums and Rabbinic Literature,* Cambridge: Cambridge University Press, 1969, p. 49 and B. Gerhardsson, *Memory and Manuscript,* Copen-

hagen: C.W.K. Gleerup, 1964, pp. 122ff). No doubt inconsistencies and inaccuracies can be found in the sources but this is not sufficient reason to be overly pessimistic concerning every attribution of each tradition. Sometimes an authority may simply make reference to an earlier source that has its own prehistory. Compare for instance the often cited example of Hillel's version of the golden rule which also appears in Tobit 4:15 and in Arm. Ahiqar 8:88 (see J.M. Lindenberger, "Ahiqar," Charlesworth, ed., *The Old Testament Pseudepigrapha,* vol. 2, p. 490; see also note 67). Similar sayings were known in antiquity (cf. Leviticus 18:19; Diogenes Laertius 5:21 on Aristotle and see A. Dihle's study, *Die Goldene Regel,* Göttingen: Vandenhoeck und Ruprecht, 1962). This does not negate the possibility that Hillel probably made use of the rule even if the logion did not originate with him. Every individual tradition must be carefully analyzed. While caution must always be taken, the credibility of an attribution should be questioned primarily in cases where there is sufficient evidence to doubt its reliability, such as a faulty text, linguistic considerations, the same saying attributed to multiple authorities in various sources, inconsistencies in a chain or sequence of tradents, an out of character remark in a tendentious text or other internal and external factors. Some of these considerations may be subjective and must be weighed in individual cases. Each must be verified on the basis of its own merits. Often the credibility of an attribution can be further established (or discredited) by a careful study of the parallels. Besides Bacher's monumental work cited above *(Tradition und Tradenten)* A. Hyman's *Toldot Tanaim Veamoraim* (Jerusalem: Boys Town Jerusalem Publisher, 1963) and Bacher's agadot series are essential tools.

14) A. Feldman, *The Parables and Similes of the Rabbis Agricultural and Pastoral* (Cambridge: Cambridge University Press, 1927), pp. 5–6. Feldman observes that the Amoraim employ more allegory than the Tannaim. See also Joseph Klausner, *Jesus of Nazareth* (London: Allen and Unwin, 1927), pp. 264f. See also references cited in note 12 above.

15) Pinchas Lapide, "Hidden Hebrew in the Gospels," *Immanuel* 2 (1973), p. 31.

16) B. Sotah 40a and cf. note 3 above.

17) The same saying with some minor stylistic differences appears twice in the Talmud. In the tractate b. Arakin 16b, the saying is attributed to R. Tarfon (circa 100) and in b. Baba Batra 15b the same saying is attributed to the Amora R. Yochanan (circa 260). See P. Billerbeck, *Kommentar zum Neuen Testament aus Talmud und Midrasch* (München: C.H. Beck, 1978), vol. 1, p. 446.

18) Shlomo Pines, trans., *The Guide for the Perplexed,* p. 12.

19) Dov Noy, "Mishle Melakim Shel Rashbi," *Machanayim* 56 (1961), p. 74.

20) L. Koehler and W. Baumgartner, *Lexicon in Veteris Testamenti Libros* (Leiden: E.J. Brill, 1958), p. 575. See also F. Brown, S.R. Driver and C. Briggs, *A Hebrew and English Lexicon of the Old Testament* (Oxford: Clarendon Press, 1974), p. 605, and E. Ben Yehuda, *Milon Halashon Haevrit Hayashanah Vehachadashah* (Jerusalem: Hotzaah leor, 1959), vol. 7, pp. 3386–3391. Compare Chaim Cohen, "Eduiyot Akadiyot Chadashot Legabe Hamuvan Vehaetimologiyah Shel Hamunach 'Mashal' Bamikra," Benyamin Uffenheimer, *Sefer Zikaron Leyehoshua Grintz* (Tel Aviv: Hakibutz Hameuchad, 1982), pp. 315–324. The meaning of likeness can be illustrated well by the *nifal* form of the verb *mashal,* e.g. Psalm 28:1, 49:13,21; 143:7; Isaiah 14:10.

21) C. Thoma, "Prolegomena zur einer Übersetzung und Kommentierung der Rabbinischen Gleichnisse," *Theologische Zeitschrift* (1982), p. 514. On the rabbinic parables, see now the important work of C. Thoma and S. Lauer, *Die Gleichnisse der Rabbinen Erster Teil Pesiqta deRav Kahana (PesK)* (Bern: Peter Lang, 1986), pp. 12–81.

22) See also Psalm 78:2; Ezekiel 21:5; 24:3. Here Ezekiel's narrative (Ezekiel 17:2) is described by both the term parable and the word riddle. Without a knowledge of the historical background, the text is impossible to understand. The riddle is an allegorical brain teaser and it is generally agreed that the great eagle (Ezekiel 17:3) represents the Babylonian king who exiled Jehoiachin in 597 (2 Kings 24:11f; Jeremiah 24:1, 29:2). He replaced Jehoiachin (the top of the young sprouts in verse 4) with Zedekiah (the seed of the land in verse 5). But Zedekiah was not true to the great eagle and turned to another great eagle (verse 7), Hophra the pharaoh of Egypt. The unclear imagery of the parable has to be explained. Ezekiel explains the passage and makes application in the continuation of the narrative. See G.A. Cooke, *The Book of Ezekiel the International Critical Commentary* (Edinburgh: T. and T. Clark, 1970), pp. 181ff.; and C. F. Keil and F. Delitzsch, *Commentary on the Old Testament Ezekiel, Daniel* (Eerdmans: Grand Rapids, 1978), vol. 9, pp. 236ff.

23) See also 1 Samuel 10:12, 24:14; Ezekiel 12:22–23; Proverbs 1:1, 25:1, 26:7–9, Job 13:10; Ecclesiastes 12:9. The apocryphal book of Ben Sira provides some further examples. Not all of Ben Sira's Hebrew undertext has been discovered and it is not always clear if the Greek version is based upon the extant Hebrew fragments. In these sections where no Hebrew text is available, the Greek word *parabolē* was connected with wise sayings (e.g. Ben Sira 1:24; 20:20,27; [21:16? Sinaiticus by a corrector, see J. Ziegler, *Septuaginta—Sapientia Iesu Filii Sirach,*

Göttingen: Vandenhoeck & Ruprecht, 1965, p. 223]; 38:33). One of the Geniza Manuscripts shows that this meaning of sagacious sayings was ascribed to the Hebrew word *mashal* and then translated into Greek by the word *parabolē* (Ben Sira 3:29). The word *mashal* is also rendered by the Greek word *paroimia* (Ben Sira 6:35) which usually was employed to translate the Hebrew word for riddle, *chidah* (Ben Sira 8:8; 39:3; 47:17). Also the name of the biblical book Proverbs was rendered into the Greek as *paroimiai* by the translators of the Septuagint (see also Proverbs 1:1).

24) Compare Tobit 3:4. See also Deuteronomy 28:37; Psalm 44:15, 69:12; 1 Kings 9:7; 2 Chronicles 7:20; Ezekiel 14:8; Jeremiah 24:9.

25) See Bacher, *Die exegetische Terminologie der jüdischen Traditionsliteratur* (Darmstadt: Wissenschaftliche Buchgesellschaft, 1965, reprint from Leipzig, 1899–1905), vol. 1, pp. 121–122 and vol. 2, pp. 120–121, idem, *Erke Midrash* (Jerusalem: Carmiel, 1970), vol. 1, p. 84; vol. 2, pp. 231–232. The Aramaic word *metla* is used as a proverb in Pesikta Derav Kahana, 4 (Mandelbaum, p. 59) Bacher, *Die exegetische Terminologie,* vol. 2, p. 122. Cf. Luke 4:23; 6:39.

26) See Pesikta Derav Kahana 4:3 (Mandelbaum, p. 62) and compare the midrash in Pesikta Derav Kahana with Josephus *Ant.* 8,2,5 (8:44) and Song of Songs Rabbah 1:11.

27) H.G. Liddell and R. Scott, *A Greek-English Lexicon* (Oxford: Clarendon Press, 1968), p. 1304. Philo employs the verb to show a comparison or a likeness. Virtue is parallel to the threshing floor mentioned in Exodus 22:6, "Virtue he likens (παραβέβληκε) to the contents of the threshing floor. . . . " (Philo, *Legum Allegoriae* III:249). See also F.W. Gingrich and F.W. Danker, *A Greek-English Lexicon of the New Testament and Other Early Christian Literature,* second edition from Walter Bauer's fifth edition (Chicago: University of Chicago Press, 1979), p. 611.

28) H.G. Liddell and R. Scott, *Lexicon,* p. 1305; F.W. Gingrich and F.W. Danker, *Lexicon,* pp. 612–613.

29) E.C. dos Santos, *An Expanded Hebrew Index for the Hatch Redpath Concordance to the Septuagint* (Jerusalem: Dugith Publishers, 1976), p. 124.

30) Ibid.

31) Philo, *De Confusione Linguarum,* 99.

32) Compare 2 Samuel 14:4–24 and Ecclesiastes 9:13–18 which also have similarities to the story parable.

33) Theon, *Progymnasmata* (chapter 3), cited by B.E. Perry *Babrius*

and Phaedrus, pp. xix–xx. See also H. Schwarzbaum, *The Mishle Shu'alim,* p. i. Schwarzbaum discusses the definition of a fable but does not make a differentiation between a fable and a parable.

34) H. Schwarzbaum, *The Mishle Shu'alim,* pp. xviiif.

35) Herodotus mentions Aesop as the fable writer. He is reported to have been a slave and to have belonged to Iadmon (Book II.134).

36) Cf. Luke 4:23. This proverb, "Physician, heal yourself," was known in various forms (Genesis Rabbah 23:4; Leviticus Rabbah 5:6; cf. Billerbeck, vol. 2, p. 156; cf. Babrius, Fable 120; Matthew 27:40; b. Baba Metzia 107b). Another saying that is close to a proverb is found in Luke 6:39 (Matthew 15:14). This proverb concerning the blind is paralleled in Plato, *Republic* 8, 554, B (Paul Shorery, *The Republic,* Loeb, vol. 2, pp. 274–275). The next saying, "A disciple is not above his teacher" (Luke 6:40; Matthew 10:24–25), also appears in b. Berachot 28b (cf. parallels in Billerbeck, vol. 1, p. 578).

37) The riddle was difficult to understand without an explanation (see note 22). Cf. Ezekiel 21:5 where the parable teller is viewed as presenting difficult to understand examples. A similar situation may be seen in Ben Sira 39:2–3. See Wrede, *The Messianic Secret,* p. 57.

38) The word parable in Luke 4:23 (and possibly in Luke 5:36, 6:39 and 12:16) seems to have appeared in the earlier source(s) of the synoptics and could have given rise to the proliferation and secondary use of the word *parabolē* in other contexts (e.g. Luke 8:4,9,10,11?; 12:41; 13:6; 14:7?; 15:3?; 18:9; 19:11; 20:9,19; 21:29?; Mark 3:23; 4:2,10,11,13,30,33,34; 7:17; 12:1,12?; 13:28; Matthew 13:3,10,13,18, 24,31,33,34,35,36,53; 15:15; 21:33,45?; 22:1; 24:32). The idea that the parables contain esoteric teaching concealed from the multitudes and revealed to the disciples is also a secondary aspect in the redaction of the gospel texts (cf. Matthew 13:1–17) and parallels; cf. W. Wrede, *The Messianic Secret* (London: James Clarke, 1971), pp. 55 ff. Noteworthy are the remarks of Abraham Ibn Ezra (1164–1089) who commented on the parables as lines of communication that are designed to illustrate the character of God, "The Torah and the Sages have spoken of the Creator in human terms, as parables and examples so that the ear can hear what it can hear, and all that is said in the Torah and the Prophets on the honor of God is just to make it easy on the ear." Quoted from M. Orfali, "Anthromorphism in the Christian Reproach of the Jews in Spain (12th–15th Century)," *Immanuel* 19 (1984–85), p. 72, and the words of Abraham Ibn Ezra were noted by W. Bacher, "Materiex pour servir a l'Histoire de l'exegese biblique en Espagne," *REJ* 17 (1888), p. 281.

39) See Flusser, *Die rabbinischen Gleichnisse,* p. 247.

40) Cf. also Flusser's discussion and reconstruction, *Die rabbinischen Gleichnisse,* pp. 247f and pp. 265–281.

41) Concerning Luke 12:16 one should consult the variant reading in Θ and part of family 1 where the *kai* is inserted after the *de.* The *kai* could have been deleted as superfluous at an early stage of the textual transmission. Without further evidence caution must be taken on this point. The word *legon* which comes at the end of this introductory formula would denote a very strong biblical Hebrew style when (re)translated into Hebrew: ויאמר להם משל לאמר . . . .

42) The question of *vav* consecutive and the semitized Greek of the synoptics needs further research. R.L. Lindsey feels that the *vav* consecutive was a characteristic of the pre-synoptic Hebrew *Vorlage* (private conversation). See also David Flusser, "Lukas 9:51–56—Ein Hebräisches Fragment," *The New Testament Age Essays in Honor of Bo Reicke* (Macon: Mercer University Press, 1984), vol. 1, pp. 165–179 and especially p. 169. As David Flusser pointed out (private communication), the *vav* consecutive also appears in rabbinic literature (cf. b. Kidushin 66b).

43) The question of the original language of the sources of the gospels in general and the parables in particular will be discussed further in the chapter on the synoptic problem and at the end of the next chapter on modern parable research.

44) The discussion ahead on the synoptic problem will deal with the various stages of the development of the gospel traditions.

45) Cf. the critical edition prepared by Bernard Mandelbaum, *Pesikta de Rav Kahana* (Jewish Theological Seminary of America: New York, 1962). Mandelbaum provides a list of 69 parables in his index that appear without an introduction and often other manuscripts have inserted an introductory preamble.

46) T. Guttmann, *Hamashal Betakufat Hatanaim* (Abir Yaakov: Jerusalem, 1949), pp. 7–12. Not all of his examples apply to the story parable. See also Feldman, *The Parables and Similes of the Rabbis,* p. 15, note 1.

47) Cf. Eliyahu Zuta, p. 175, p. 182, p. 185. The phrase "Go out and see . . . " is used to introduce a story that illustrates honor for father and mother (b. Kidushin 31a; b. Avodah Zara 77b; cf. Pesikta Rabbati 23–24, Friedmann, p. 123b and j. Peah chap. 1, hal. 1, 15c where the phrase does not appear). The phrase occurs frequently in tannaitic midrashim; cf. Bacher, *Die exegetische Terminologie,* vol. 1, p. 75 and vol. 2, pp. 80–81, idem *Erke Midrash,* vol. 1, p. 51; vol. 2, pp. 201–202. Nevertheless

the evidence for determining the original introductory formulas of the story parables is at best fragmentary and caution must be exercised. The expression *idete* in Luke 21:29 seems to have introduced "The Parable of the Fig Tree," and this may be a clue for introductions to other similar illustrations.

48) Perhaps one of the best ways to illustrate this meaning is to see passages in the Hebrew Scriptures where the verb is used in the *nifal,* i.e. Psalm 28:1; 39:13,21; 143:7; Isaiah 14:10.

49) See note 20.

50) S. Loewenstamm, "Chaviv Adam Shenivra Betzelem," *Tarbitz* 27 (1957–58), pp. 1–2 and idem, "Beloved is Man in that he was created in the Image," *Comparative Studies in Biblical and Ancient Oriental Literature* (Neukirchen, Vluyn: Neukirchener Verlag, 1980), pp. 48–50 and there see also note 5.

51) F. Talmage, *Sefer Haberit* (Jerusalem: Bialik Institute, 1974), p. 32. The author is indebted to David Flusser who first called his attention to these texts. An interesting fact comes to light when Radak is studied in comparison to Ekphantos, namely that Radak makes use of this hellenistic text (or its source, or both drew from a common tradition; see Stobaios 3,9,51; H. Thesleff, *The Pythagorean Texts of the Hellenistic Period,* Finland, Acta Academiae Aboensis, 1965, p. 89 and p. 362; cf. Talmage *Sefer Haberit,* p. 32). The problem of etymology of the Hebrew *mashal* and its double meanings, "to rule" and "to resemble," has been discussed by Cohen, p. 316. The Assyrian texts cited by Loewenstamm and David Kimche's suggestion concerning Psalm 8:5–8 may help to clarify the creation story. Man is created in the image of his Creator in the sense that man has dominion over his creation. Kimche suggests that man resembles God not in the physical sense but in the rule and authority that he has been given. This chain of command God-man-creation recalls Ephesians 5:23–24, 1 Corinthians 11:3 and Didache 4:11.

52) See J. Kafah, *Perushe Rabenu Saadiah Gaon Al Hatorah* (Jerusalem: Mossad Harav Kook, 1976), pp. 12–13. David Flusser called the author's attention to this passage.

53) W. McKane *Proverbs* (Philadelphia: Westminster, 1970), p. 26. Cited by Cohen, p. 318.

54) Cohen, pp. 319–320.

THE PARABLES AND THEIR INTERPRETERS: MODERN PARABLE RESEARCH

Much has been written on the parables of Jesus. A study of the great amount of literature which has accumulated on parabolic teaching will reveal that few scholars can agree on how to properly interpret the individual elements, the form, the structure and certainly not the message of the parables. Here a new approach to the parables is advanced which recognizes the essential need to study the teachings of Jesus in light of early Jewish thought and sources. This perspective to the parables cannot avoid linguistic analysis or critical comparative research. Here we will examine the influential works of A. Jülicher and P. Fiebig. C.H. Dodd and J. Jeremias have reopened discussion on the parables and Jesus' approach to the eschatological future. D. Flusser has made significant progress in dealing with the text of the gospels and their relationship to rabbinic literature. Finally I must make some observations concerning the original language of the parables. Philological study will certainly aid interpreters in recovering the original thrust of the message of the parables. The present select survey of parable research will ask why so many current studies on the parables ignore the best parallel sources we have for the study of Jesus' parables.

Parables have had a long history of interpretation from the period of the redaction of the gospel narratives and the early church fathers to the present. Moreover rabbinic parables have by no means escaped commentary and discussion which can be exemplified by the great Jewish exegetes like Rashi (Rabbi Shlomo Yitzchaki, 1105–1140), Abraham Ibn Ezra (1089–1164) and Rambam (1135–1204).[1] The church fathers for the most part were detached from the Jewish world[2] and show little interest in or knowledge of Jewish literature, but pioneers[3] like John Lightfoot did do early comparative studies of rabbinic texts and the New Testament. He originally composed his commentary in Latin (1675). This work was translated into English in 1684 and was reissued in 1859. The popularity of Lightfoot's treatment of the material can be seen by the fact that the 1859 edition has recently been reprinted (1979). In his search for parallels, Lightfoot often cited the Talmuds and also made use of relatively later rabbinic sources without careful historical methodology. Not only did he have to rely on poor, uncritical and unscientific editions of the sources, but he also from time to time misreads the texts which he cited.[4] Still one cannot help but be impressed by Lightfoot's pioneering efforts considering the time in which he was writing. Although Lightfoot's anti-Jewish prejudices are not in the least bit suppressed, he did help to create an interest in the comparative study of rabbinic materials and the New Testament. These biases had a counterproductive effect on his research as well as cultivating mistaken impressions that led to intolerance. Moreover the mere study of parallels can often be misleading. The parables of Jesus would have to wait much longer before a truly serious and comprehensive consideration of rabbinic parables and their relevance to the gospel texts would be produced.

Jesus' parables are survivors of a long history of capricious and whimsical hermeneutical treatments that have often distorted their message. Nevertheless the parables have survived intact and are well preserved in the textual traditions of the synoptic texts. Adolf Jülicher is often attributed with the distinction of being the initiator of modern parable research.[5] Jülicher will be remembered primarily because of his strong and systematic attack against the ever popular allegorical method of parable hermeneutic.[6] Adolf Jülicher's predecessors like H.A.W. Meyer (1858) or even A.B. Bruce (1882) warned against allegorizing.[7] Jülicher was unrelenting in his persistence to eliminate the allegorical approach. His near exhaustive treatise *Die Gleichnisreden Jesu* (first volume, 1886; second volume, 1899) is probably the most influential work ever written about the parables and its impact is certainly still felt today.

While the allegorical approach can also be exemplified by

some modern popular exegesis, the church fathers have been known for their notorious allegorization of the parables.[8] Augustine provides the well known and extreme example of the type of approach which Jülicher attacked and which would surely lead to questionable results. In treating the parable of "The Good Samaritan" (Luke 10:29–37), Augustine discerns special meaning for each detail of the story. The "certain man" is identified as Adam, and Jericho stands for the moon which represents man's mortality. The Samaritan in the parable represents Jesus himself. Incidentally as one can easily see his interpretation is based upon a rudimentary knowledge of Hebrew. The inn signifies the church and the apostle Paul is considered to appear in Jesus' story as the innkeeper.[9] Similarly the founder of Latin Christianity, Tertullian, solves his exegetical problem concerning the parable of "The Lost Coin" by applying the allegorical method. His question regarded the interpretation of the "drachma" whether it symbolized a lost heathen or a Christian who had fallen from the faith. Tertullian finds a solution:

> . . . albeit it had been 'lost' in a house, as it was in a church; albeit found by the aid of a 'lamp' as it were by aid of God's word. Nay, but this whole world is the one house of all; in which world it is more the heathen who is found in darkness, whom the grace of God enlightens, than the Christian who is already in God's light.[10]

In determining that the lost coin of Jesus' parable represents a pagan and not a Christian, Tertullian fights fire with fire by creating a new allegorical interpretation to displace one which he found objectionable. Thus, he succeeded to support his own opinion; however it is highly questionable whether the new allegory is any more credible than the former. Indeed, this hermeneutical method only distorted and obscured the original meaning of Jesus' parables and enabled the interpreter to use the text to prove practically whatever he desired.

Jülicher and Fiebig

Jülicher's work did much more than merely attack the allegorical method; it opened a new era of research. The first volume of this work categorized and defined rubrics like parable, allegory, metaphor and simile. This volume has been widely acclaimed, and even Paul Fiebig, Jülicher's contemporary and most outspoken critic, employs Jülicher's terminology. As has often been pointed out, most of Jülicher's categorization has been influenced by Aristotle (i.e. *Rhetoric* 2.20; 3.4). The aim of a parable is to prove a single point and therefore it cannot contain any allegorization or more than one point of comparison between the *Bildhälfte* and the *Sachhälfte.*[11] Surprisingly while Jülicher's analysis in his first volume was greatly praised, the strict application of this method in his second volume has been sharply criticized and subsequent Jülicherians have not always been consistent in towing the line on the one moral approach to every parable.[12]

Jülicher minimized the importance of rabbinic parables and only gave them a superficial treatment. Perhaps he felt that it was impossible to ignore them entirely because they did resemble the parables of Jesus. In any case he did mention two parables from talmudic literature, one of which was attributed to the Amora, R. Zeira, and the other, "The Parable of the Field and the Sharecroppers" (Exodus Rabbah 27:9) which could be compared and contrasted to parables from the gospels (i.e., Matthew 20:1–16 and parallels and Matthew 21:28–32).[13] Jülicher's point is that the rabbinic parables are inferior and that their parabolic teaching is beset with pedantry and the dust of academic discussion, in contrast to the fresh full of life parables of Jesus.[14] A. Feldman may be responding to Jülicher's somewhat biased judgment when he wrote his book, which he entitled *The Parables and Similes of the Rabbis Agricultural and Pastoral* (1924). Concerning critics of the rabbinic parables, Feldman noted, "When, e.g. the popular character of the N.T. parables and their powerful appeal to the masses is contrasted with the alleged heavy professorial nature of Rabbinic similes propounded to the students in the academies of learning, a most erroneous impression is evidently entertained of the whole object of Aggadic literature. These critics have failed to grasp the spirit which animated those Rabbi-preachers, the spiritual descendants of the Prophets and poets of the Bible. . . ."[15]

Jülicher's observations about rabbinic and gospel parables are neither documented nor based on even a cursory examination of the evidence preserved in all the sources of post-biblical Jewish literature. The basic problems of comparative research escaped Jülicher and he fails to distinguish between gospel literature, which is *sui generis,* and the talmudic corpus, a tradition which has a different *raison d'être.* In spite of Jülicher's knowledge of literary analysis and his love for category he does not deal with talmudic literature or the relationship between rabbinic parables and their context.[16] His brief mentions of rabbinic literature were primarily aimed at disqualifying the Jewish sources and their relevance for comparative study.[17]

Paul Fiebig was Jülicher's most outspoken and articulate critic. On the one hand, Jülicher minimized the importance of rabbinic parables, and on the other hand, Fiebig maximized the connection between Jesus' parables and their rabbinic counterparts. While Jülicher claimed that each of Jesus' parables had only one point of comparison, Fiebig maintained that like rabbinic parables, Jesus' parables had multiple points of comparison and are not free from allegory. Fiebig's earlier work,[18] *Altjüdische Gleichnisse und die Gleichnisse Jesu* (1904), was much more than a corrective to Jülicher's strict one point approach, because Fiebig collected fifty-three parables from the *Mekilta Derabbi Ishmael* (including similes and metaphors), translated them and discussed their relationship to the parables of Jesus. Fiebig sees Jesus' parables as being similar in form and content to the rabbinic parables and therefore a comparative study is indispensable, "Es handelt sich ja doch bei einer konfrontierung der neutestamentlichen mit den talmudischen Gleichnissen ebenso sehr um die Form als um den Inhalt."[19]

Nevertheless Fiebig feels obliged to offer his value judgment and discusses how very superior Jesus' parables are in comparison to those of the rabbis.[20] This makes his work much less scientific and distorts the study of the parables as literary forms by entering into the realm of apologetics. Fiebig's work lacks a certain depth and perception, and one feels that Fiebig's polemical correctives to Jülicher are foremost in his mind.[21] In 1912, Fiebig published another book on the parables entitled, *Die Gleichnisreden Jesu im Lichte der rabbinischen Gleichnisse des neutestamentlichen Zeitalters ein Beitrag zum Streit um die "Christus-*

mythe" und eine Widerlegung der Gleichnistheorie Jülichers.[22] Here Jülicher even finds honorable mention in the complete title of Fiebig's book. Fiebig noted Jülicher's ignorance of the foundational philological, cultural and religious Jewish background to Jesus' teaching, "Für Jülicher ist der Talmud eine terra incognita. Für Jülicher ist Mischna, Tosephta usw. ein leere Name. . . . "[23] He sees a great danger in ignoring the Jewish sources and in forgetting that Jesus was a Jew living in the environment of the Jewish people during the days of the Second Temple. One cannot approach the text from the modern mindset:

> Die Ausdrucks- und Denkweise der Juden der Zeit Jesu, soweit sie hebräish-aramäish reden, ist charakteristisch verschieden von unserer Denk- und Redeweise. Sieht man dies nicht, so steht man fortwährend in Gefahr, die Evangelien, die doch von geborenen Juden der Tannaitenzeit herrühren, misszuverstehen.[24]

Fiebig's criticisms of Jülicher went far deeper than merely citing rabbinic parallels and showing that these sources were closer to the historical Jesus than Aristotle. He posed the question: Had Jülicher converted Jesus into a modern German philosopher or professor who developed a revolutionary systematic approach to religious thought in the realm of abstract ideas? Fiebig pointed out:

> Jesus war kein Philosoph. Nirgends finden wir bei ihm abstrakte Ausführungen, wissenschaftliche Abhandlungen und ähnliches. Ebensowenig waren die Apostel oder die Evangelisten Philosophen. Ihre ganze Bildung, ihre Ausdrucks- und Denkweise trägt den Stempel jüdischer Eigenart an sich, die man nur verstehen kann, wenn man beachtet, wie der Hebräer, wie der Orientale, der Aramäer, der Syrer, der Araber redet und denkt. Der echte Jude und Orientale denkt konkret, anschaulich, nicht abstrakt. Er denkt nicht schulmäßig, schematisch, philosophisch, systematisch, sondern volkstümlich, lebendig, lebhaft, unsystematisch, haftet mit seinem

> Ausdruck am Einzelnen, schaut im Einzelnen, Konkreten das Allgemeine an, empfindet das Allgemeine, ist aber weder fähig noch gewillt, es in Worte zu fassen und zu Theorien zu verarbeiten.[25]

While all of Fiebig's generalizations here may not be conclusive, his basic corrective comments concerning the historical and cultural framework that can enlighten the parabolic teaching of Jesus are certainly justified. But whether Fiebig is disagreeing with Jülicher or attacking Arthur Drews' book *Die Christusmythe*[26] or just pointing out the mistakes made by Weinel[27] or by Deissmann,[28] he will always be remembered as a corrector. He was never able to define or to develop his own methodology adequately, nor did he succeed in any great degree to influence his contemporaries.[29]

Dodd and Jeremias

C.H. Dodd and J. Jeremias represent the current historical and critical approach to the parables of Jesus even if a great deal of their methodology is based upon the groundwork laid by their predecessors. The nineteenth century protestant liberalism, as represented by leaders like F. Schleiermacher (1768–1834) and A. Ritschl (1822–1889) who stressed the moral and ethical teachings of Jesus founded upon an experimental "God-consciousness,"[30] provoked a reaction from J. Weiss in his famous *Die Predigt Jesu vom Reiche Gottes* (1892).[31] Weiss challenged the idea that the kingdom of God is present in the hearts of men who obey the ethical teachings of the scriptures and that this kingdom can be realized in an ideal society where men live up to these standards advocated by the so-called Ritschlian school represented by such eminent leaders as W. Herrmann (1846–1922) and Adolf von Harnack (1851–1930). Weiss desired to re-establish the historical background to the kingdom of God and understood Jesus' use of the term as an eschatological concept. The entire question will be more thoroughly considered in the section of the present work which deals with the parables of the kingdom.

Albert Schweitzer's work also contended that Jesus' moral

instruction had been overemphasized to the great neglect of his eschatological teaching which was the primary thrust of the historical Jesus' message. While Weiss was primarily involved in academia, Schweitzer developed his theory and popularized it among a wider audience of Christians within and beyond academic circles. Dodd took up this stream of thought in his book, *The Parables of the Kingdom.* Jesus' proclamation of the coming kingdom was a warning of the imminent eschatological crisis. In fact the hermeneutical questions that deal with the parables and the kingdom of God motif are inseparably interrelated.[32] Certainly no one would deny that many of Jesus' parables treat the kingdom theme even if this idea has been secondarily proliferated in the redaction of the gospel narratives.

Dodd maintained that he could rediscover the original meaning of the parables by reconstructing their original "setting in life." Of course Dodd is merely recognizing the problem described by the form critics when he observed that sometimes a parable has to be removed from the artificial context given to it in the gospel texts.[33] Then if possible one must endeavor to recover the parable's original setting. Dodd's work suggests hypothetical settings which recast gospel scenes—Jesus being confronted by unsympathetic inquirers, Jesus being questioned by eager disciples, or Jesus prophetically warning the people of a future eschatological crisis. In some ways this approach somewhat enlivens or breathes fresh life into the illustrations of Jesus and projects them in a moving picture. Not surprisingly, Dodd's method has gained credence and popularity.

Jeremias must be credited with further developing the approach and making his own contributions to it. He basically accepted Dodd's re-creation of the *Sitz im Leben* of the parables, but adds the necessary critical and technical tools mandatory for reconstruction of the original form of the parables. Jeremias carefully treated the problem of the Semitic background of the parables and its significance.[34] He properly understood the far-reaching implications that linguistic analysis of the original language of the parables had upon their interpretation. However, he never questioned Dodd's basic contentions concerning an imminent eschatological crisis that was fermenting and soon to come upon the earth.[35] In fact, this end times theme becomes quite clear and strong in both Dodd's and Jeremias' works.

The main thrust of Jesus' eschatological message is in need of reinterpretation. One can only question to what extent this hypothetical situation can be imposed upon so many of Jesus' parables. Is Jesus to be perceived as an end times radical proclaiming imminent catastrophe? While not neglecting the eschatological aspects of Jesus' teaching, it must be observed that much of his great ethical instruction deals with practical issues of everyday life. Jeremias rightly emphasized that the parables of Jesus must be understood in light of all that can be known concerning his message.[36] But if Dodd and Jeremias have wrongly understood the central theme of the parables, then Jesus' career is only obscured by an obsession to create an eschatological crisis. Perrin, who was one of Jeremias' outstanding students, has continued to base his interpretation of the parables upon the same theory. He criticized Jülicher's interpretation of the parables of the "Unjust Judge" and the "Importunate Friend at Midnight." According to Perrin's analysis, Jülicher mistakenly applied these parables to constancy in prayer. Perrin attributes this interpretation to the German liberalism of Jülicher's era.[37] From the work of Dodd and Jeremias, Perrin learns that these parables relate to being steadfast during the future crisis which was soon to occur.

On the contrary, we must question whether the theme of constancy in prayer proposed for these parables is formulated primarily from the atmosphere of German liberalism. In fact, one might venture to observe that if anyone is introducing a new and foreign concept into the central message of these two parables, it is Perrin and his predecessors. Prayer is a primary concern in Jesus' teaching as well as in early Jewish thought.[38] These two vivid illustrations encourage Jesus' listeners to pray expectantly. The unjust magistrate figure makes use of the familiar rabbinic hermeneutical principle of *argumentum a minori ad maius* (קל וחומר). If an evil judge will be moved by persistence, how much more will the compassionate God respond to steadfast prayer. Certainly Jesus' first audience grasped the irony of the second illustration. No self-respecting oriental would refuse a friend hospitality—even at midnight. It is opposed to all the rules of custom and culture. Neither will God neglect to be attentive to those who seek him earnestly in prayer. Nothing unusual or incongruous with the historical Jesus emerges from this theme. The gospels record, "Ask, and it shall be given you; seek, and you shall find; knock, and it shall be opened unto you" (Matthew 7:7; Luke 9:11; cf. Matthew 6:5–15; Luke 11:2–4, 25).

Jeremias claims that the theme of the eschatological crisis is inherent in Jesus' parabolic saying, "Agreement with One's Accuser" (Matthew 5:25–26; Luke 12:57–59).[39] He notes the different contexts of the evangelists: "Luke emphasizes God's eschatological action, Matthew, the disciple's conduct."[40] However, the argument based on context is at best misleading. Here Jeremias contends for Luke's arrangement. Probably neither the context of Matthew nor that of Luke should be considered more trustworthy. The entire arrangement of the synoptics seems largely artificial and it is hazardous to interpret the parables solely on matters of their placement within each evangelist's framework. The placement of a parable may aid in understanding how the evangelist viewed the parable. Nevertheless, a distinction rightly should be made between the evangelist's interpretation and the original intention of Jesus.

Yet Jeremias suggests that Matthew's understanding of this parable as pertaining to "the conduct of life" is a gross misinterpretation. For Jeremias, it is inconceivable that this parable could be literal. Concerning this question, he adds, " . . . there is no denying that the reason for such a direction sounds perilously near triviality."[41] The researcher must critically examine even the finest scholars. It may be questioned whether this instruction as it relates to procedure in everyday life is indeed trivial. On the contrary, not only is it practical, but it is also sound. Anyone who has been involved in litigation must realize that legal matters or courtroom scenes are not idle concerns. Just the opposite is true, especially in courts where justice may not always be served. However, because this interpretation is too literal, Jeremias argues, "Jesus lives in the expectation of the great catastrophe, the final πειρασμός (Mark 14:38), the last crisis of history which His death will introduce."[42] Hence Jeremias imposes the urgency of the coming final catastrophe upon the parable but it may be questioned whether this theme was expressed as the original message of the illustration.

Other occasions may have precipitated the development of this illustration. An exegetical interest may be discerned, as perhaps this parable is related to the biblical passage, "Do not go hastily to argue *your case:* otherwise, what will you do in the end when your neighbor puts you to shame?" (Proverbs 25:8). Jesus warns against going too hastily before a tribunal in order to plead one's case against the prosecution. The pragmatic advice is simple. It is far preferable to make harmony with your accuser than to go before a judge where the outcome of the claim is uncertain. Moreover it is not necessary to view the saying within the strict limitations of a lawsuit in the courtroom but as an approach to life. The text seems to be closely related to another dominical saying, " . . . if anyone would sue you and take your coat, let him have your cloak as well; and if anyone forces you to go one mile, go with him two miles. Give to him who begs from you, and do not refuse him who would borrow from you" (Matthew 5:40; Luke 6:29–30). In other gospel texts, Jesus addresses the dynamic force of forgiveness and reconcilement (Matthew 18:23–35). Do these dominical sayings teach the somewhat radical concept that acts of self-denial can actually precipitate God's redemption in an evil and unjust world? In any case a solution which emphasizes the human relationship between the accused and the accuser seems to be nearer to the existential force of the more practical interpretation of Jesus' parabolic saying. Reconciliation between man and his brother is not far from the original message of this dramatic illustration. However, to force the theme of an end of the world catastrophe upon this parable goes against the grain of its content and obscures its very practical everyday application.

C.G. Montefiore perceived the implications that can be drawn for Jesus' illustrative story in light of rabbinic literature. The motif conveys to Montefiore this message, " . . . one must be reconciled with one's neighbour quickly so as not, perchance, to have to appear before God unreconciled with one's neighbour. God only forgives those who have forgiven, or who have sincerely sought reconcilement with their neighbour."[43] This instruction is paralleled in the teaching of Israel's sages and is probably related to the concept of compromise.[44] Though one's judgment at the time of death possibly could be in the background, is an eschatological theme implied? Man is directed to forgive, make peace with his accuser and not to continue with attitudes of resentment. The theme echoes the directive concerning the Day of Atonement which prescribes that God cannot pardon offenses between an individual and his neighbor until genuine rapprochement has been implemented between the conflicting parties.[45] This is not the only possible application of Jesus' parable.[46] Nonetheless, the suggestion that the gospel parable was warning of an impending catastrophe seems unlikely.

Jeremias' tendency to overestimate the eschatological emphasis in the message of Jesus can be further illustrated by his treatment of the Disciples' Prayer. When dealing with the petition τὸν ἄρτον ἡμῶν τὸν ἐπιούσιον δὸς ἡμῖν σήμερον (Matthew 6:11; Luke 11:3), Jeremias reconstructs the original "Aramaic" text on the basis of Jerome's reference to the *Gospel of the Nazarenes* where a variant reading appears for the difficult word *epiousion.*[47] Even A. Deissmann noted the difficulty presented by this obscure Greek word which Origen (*De Orat.* 27:7) himself said was unknown in Greek.[48] Jerome says that the text of the *Gospel for the Nazarenes* contains the variant מחר for the Greek, *epiousion.*[49] This reading would cause the request to be translated, "Give us tomorrow's bread today." Jeremias comments, "As a matter of fact, in late Judaism *maḥar,* 'tomorrow,' meant not only the next day but also the great Tomorrow, the final consummation."[50] Besides the fact that Jeremias' reference to "late Judaism" is less than specific, the reading itself is not without serious problems. In the first place, Jerome's evidence is questionable. When citing from the *Gospel of the Nazarenes,* Jerome sometimes seems to contradict himself and the variant readings he notes appear to have an interpretive tendency. Instead of "into the holy city," the Jewish gospel contains the reading "Jerusalem" (Matthew 4:5), which is an explanatory comment that would hardly be necessary for a Jewish Semitic-speaking readership. Also the reading that changes the difficult statement concerning the tearing apart of the temple's veil (Matthew 27:51; cf.

parallels) to a story about the collapse of the temple's lintel could possibly be based on the reference in Josephus' *Jewish War* (VI.293–300). Any reading derived from this source must be carefully scrutinized. Unfortunately this source has not survived. Due to the tendentious nature of these fragmentary quotations, one must be extremely cautious in accepting an alternate reading from Jerome's references without firm internal or external evidence.

Perhaps an even greater problem with this proposed reading is the quite awkward reconstruction that results. Combining the words "bread" and "tomorrow" together into the construct state in order to formulate a phrase which would be idiomatic in either Hebrew or Aramaic is very difficult. It would seem that the phrase לחם מחר or לחמן לדמחר (Jeremias' reconstruction) would sound strange if not bizarre to a native speaker because of stylistic considerations. Moreover we must question whether the words of the *Gospel of the Nazarenes* should be interpreted as originally meaning "the bread of tomorrow" which would give hope to a despairing group of Christians longing for better times in a future age. The text does not necessarily have to be interpreted eschatologically. At least, it is possible that the alternate reading *machar* may simply be another translation or interpretation of the Greek word *epiousion.*[51]

Two other objections could be raised in regard to the variant reading from the *Gospel of the Nazarenes.* The most obvious objection is based on philological and textual grounds. First, this reading cannot explain the appearance of the Greek word *epiousion,* because the word *machar* would be no problem whatsoever for a Greek translator who would simply render it with *aurion* which is well attested in the gospels and Acts. In fact the Hebrew word *machar* is translated by *aurion* forty-eight times in the Septuagint and was its Greek equivalent.[52] No, one would expect that a more difficult Semitic idiom would lie behind the obscure word *epiousion.* This is the second objection to Jeremias, namely that such a Hebrew phrase does appear in Proverbs 30:8c, " . . . the food [bread] which is needful for me." The Hebrew phrase *lechem chuki* which occurs in Proverbs might not have been entirely clear to a Greek translator.[53] If the Greek word *epiousion* is to be understood as *epi* and *ousia* which can mean "necessary for existence,"[54] then it is very near to the meaning of the Hebrew phrase לחם חקי which in the Aramaic targum was translated by לחמא מסתי ("the bread that is enough for me") and less literally in the Septuagint by σύνταξον δὲ μοι τὰ δέοντα καὶ τὰ αὐτάρκη. This indicates that the Vulgate's translation of Matthew 6:11, *supersubstantialem,* preserves the correct understanding of the Greek word *epiousion.* Luke's version, "each day" (Luke 11:3), seems to be an adaptation from Matthew's source. Flusser noted that the extreme position of reliance on God for one's provision for "this day" is reflected in a saying of Hillel.[55] The Hebrew phrase את לחם חוקנו תן לנו היום is probably very near to *ipsissima verba* of Jesus and it could be translated, "Give us today our necessary bread." An eschatological meaning seems therefore remote. Considering the life of Jesus (Matthew 8:20; Luke 9:58) and his message (Matthew 6:25–34; Luke 12:22–31) in light of the background of early Jewish thought (Psalms of Solomon 5:18–21),[56] the simple humble petition for daily necessities is consistent with the data known about Jesus' life and career as depicted in the gospel texts.

No one should minimize the importance of Dodd's and Jeremias' contributions. The historical and critical approach which they have used to analyze the gospel texts of the parables suggested that it was possible to bridge the chasm that separates the modern researcher from the *Sitz im Leben* of Jesus. Their work made distinctions between the historical situation of the compilers of the gospels, their sources and what can be known concerning the life and teachings of Jesus. However for the most part their research bypassed the question of rabbinic parables and their relationship to the parables of Jesus. Jeremias claimed that Jesus was the first Jewish teacher to use parables and thereby caused a polarization between the parables of rabbinic literature and the parabolic teaching of Jesus. Even though this is true, he resorted to the evidence of rabbinic parables on occasion in order to elucidate the texts of the gospel parables.

Flusser

The similarities between the parables of Jesus and those of rabbinic literature have been recognized by many of the researchers who have written about parables. Nonetheless the importance of these resemblances have often been minimized and few scholars have been willing to explore the possible usefulness of comparative study. It seems that some of the scholarly scruples might be connected to the chronological problems concerning the time difference between the composition of rabbinic texts and the gospels, and other hesitations may have been derived from apologetic interests. Perhaps Fiebig's criticism of Jülicher, namely that his specialization as a New Testament scholar did not include a general knowledge of rabbinic literature would also hold true for many modern New Testament researchers as well. Many of the specific problems concerning comparative study of the parables have been treated in a brave new approach advocated by Flusser. In a Hebrew article from his book, *Jewish Sources in Early Christianity,* and also in the first volume of his epoch-making book, *Die rabbinischen Gleichnisse und der Gleichniserzähler Jesus,* Flusser has developed an approach which analyzes the parables motifically as a literary genre.[57]

Flusser skillfully demonstrates the continuity of motifs which appear in parabolic teaching. While not minimizing the significance of parallels between rabbinic parables and Jesus' parables, Flusser's work goes far beyond the scope of Fiebig's work of discovering parallels and attempting either to account for their existence or to show that one parable is superior to its cognate. Flusser shows that parabolic teaching is the combining of specific known motifs. These are interwoven together in order to illustrate a relationship between the parable and the object of the illustration. A masterful parable teacher draws from a ready repository of illustrative expressions and word pictures which function to communicate a particular message.[58] It is the skillful interweaving of these motifs and their relationship to the object or theme being illustrated that determines the parable's success. Jesus' parables on the one hand, and the rabbinic parables on the other, contain similar illustrative motifs wich show a continuity of expression in parabolic teaching. Apparently Jesus' audience was familiar with this popular style of agadic instruction.[59] While this does not absolutely prove beyond the shadow of a doubt that parables were widely used in the agadic teachings of Jesus' contemporaries because of the fragmentary state of the evidence, it seems more likely that the gospels preserve remnants of early Jewish instruction rather than the beginnings of a new *Gattung.* In any case Flusser's work suggests that much can be gained by a comparative study which listens to the message of each parable and analyzes it according to its structure and various storytelling components. Flusser's work also carefully analyzes the Greek text of the synoptic gospels which is essential for the interpretation of the parables.

Similar themes may be expressed by different motifs. Flusser noted the theme of the "wise and the foolish" and shows how different motifs were utilized to communicate a similar relationship. Flusser compares this idea which takes the form of the wise and foolish virgins in Jesus' parable (Matthew 25:1–13) with the rabbinic parable of the king's wise and foolish servants. In the rabbinic parable, both the wise and the foolish servants were given garments. The prudent servants ironed, folded and stored the garments properly. The foolish used the garments at work. When the king requested the servants to return the articles of clothing, the wise were prepared and the foolish were not ready. This parable is used to explain the verse of scripture which teaches, " . . . the spirit will return to God who gave it" (Ecclesiastes 12:7). The parable is an exhortation to be prepared for the time when a man's spirit will return to God.[61] Hence we discover a contrast in descriptive language which characterizes the difference between the wise servants and the foolish ones.

Jesus' parable also contains the theme of the wise and the foolish. The wise maidens were prepared with lamps ready for the return of the bridegroom. The foolish virgins had failed to take the necessary preparatory measures. They were rejected by the bridegroom. Another example of the theme of the wise and the foolish can be culled from the midrash Leviticus Rabbah 56:8, only in this example the figures are two tenants who present requests to the householder. The prudent tenant communicates his capabilities as a manager. He tells the landlord that the farm is in great condition but that he could use more finances. The unwise tenant, on the other hand, emphasizes his problems and needs to the landlord. The landlord is willing to invest more than requested in the land of the capable tenant. Other illustrations of this theme are plentiful (e.g. Matthew 7:24–27). These examples suffice to demonstrate that the same theme may be presented differently by various illustrations culled from the rich heritage of parabolic teaching. The parable teacher creates the desired effect by giving the story its emphasis. Thus, Jesus' parable of the ten maidens' significance is related to the unexpected or unknown time of the Son of Man's coming. In the king parable discussed above, the rabbis are concerned with man's preparation for the unknown time of death.

Moreover, Flusser points out that two similar motifs may be presented to express different themes. He cites the famous saying of R. Tarfon, R. Akiva's colleague, "The day is short and the task is great and the laborers are idle . . . and the master of the house is urgent" (Avot 2:15).[62] Flusser compares this parable with the logion of Jesus, "The harvest is plentiful, but the laborers are few; therefore beseech the Lord of the harvest to send out laborers into the harvest" (Luke 10:2; Matthew 9:37–38). Three common motifs are presented in both similes: the plentiful harvest and the great task, the shortage of workers and the idle laborers, and also the Lord of the harvest and the master of the house. However, the motifs have a different significance. Flusser observes that the rabbis would have seen a reference to the study of the Torah in the words of R. Tarfon (cf. b. Kiddushin 41b).[63] Jesus' saying, on the other hand, refers to the expansion of his movement of spiritual renewal. In addition, Flusser points out that the words, "the day is short and the task is great," are paralleled in the ancient writings of the Greek writer Hippocrates (fifth century B.C.).[64] Thus, similar word pictures are represented in three different contexts. While the comparative language of these motifs are parallel, the meaning and message conveyed is unique and must be interpreted in light of each specific context.

The Interpretation of the Parables

The interpretation of the parables of Jesus and their rabbinic cognates present many difficult problems. A comprehensive approach is necessary. The Greek text of the synoptics must be critically studied and the interrelationships of the gospel narratives must be evaluated philologically. The rabbinic parables provide the key to unlock the deeper meaning of Jesus' parables and comparative research can be of great value. The simplistic approach of trying to prove that the rabbis are dependent upon Jesus or vice versa is counterproductive. For practical purposes the search for who influenced whom will be an exercise in futility. However it is possible to study the parables of Jesus in light of their rabbinic cognates when the parables are viewed as a unique genre. Naturally the historical and critical problems connected with the study of rabbinic literature cannot be avoided. Neither can the study of the gospels ignore the complex questions surrounding their compilation.

Earlier attempts to show the sublimity of Jesus' parables over the parables of the rabbis were not only unscientific, being based upon the value judgments of the researcher, but also were detrimental for the study of parabolic teaching in general. The discovery of parallel parables is not always as helpful for understanding parabolic instruction as is the elucidation of various common motifs in the realm of a well-defined literary type. The parables of Jesus, like those of Israel's sages, are derived from the common environment of the rabbinical world of instruction. The illustrative motifs and examples are drawn from a common stream. The details and the everyday life situations in the sometimes exaggerated or paradoxical reality of the parable have to be interpreted by the message and by the theme of the parable itself.[65] As Safrai once pointed out, the parables not infrequently describe the life of the wealthy and royalty, something far removed from the poor existence of many agricultural workers that made up the majority of the audience who listened to the storyteller.[66] Other parables deal with life closer to home. The classic type of parable that appears in homiletical midrashim warrants special attention and additional research. The way that a parable teacher combines, interchanges, and develops the various components of his illustration will bear some traits of originality. Often the process of interweaving various motifs and formulating a story parable was designed to illustrate a specific theme and not to entertain. In the case of Jesus and the rabbis, the purpose is often to illustrate certain aspects of the relationship between a man's life and his relationship to his Creator.[67]

Flusser has also raised the question concerning what he considered to be the earlier "classic" type of parable. This type of parable illustrates a principle which is often related to a moral or ethical issue and it is less likely to be directly connected to a biblical text. The exegetical parables are more closely connected to a scripture text. To some extent they have been proliferated in talmudic literature and seem to have developed from the more popular anecdotes and story illustrations of the classic variety. The spontaneous illustrations used by Jesus are certainly close to this classic type of parable and can aid in recognizing and interpreting this type of parable when it appears in a text. Jesus does not seem to use the parable as an exegetical mode but later rabbis were quick to recognize the utility of parables in interpreting holy writ. The mashal became one of thirty-two principles of scriptural interpretation attributed to R. Eleazer ben Jose Hagalili.[68]

Another aspect of this whole question has been mentioned by Clemens Thoma.[69] Thoma discusses Flusser's book *Die rabbinischen Gleichnisse* and comments on the parables in *Pesikta Derav Kahana.* The classic variety of parables appear quite frequently in texts that have been called the homiletical midrashim. Generally speaking these midrashic works are not yoked to the biblical narratives in verse by verse exposition like Genesis Rabbah or the Mechilta (though Genesis Rabbah and the Mechilta certainly do display a freedom to go far beyond a literal verse by verse commentary and not infrequently contain collections of earlier *derashot*). Midrashim like *Pesikta Derav Kahana* and *Pesikta Rabbati* which contain homiletical materials from Sabbath and festival sermons stylized with *petichtot,* anecdotes, collections of agadic materials and halachic matters are similar but different from the more expositional rabbinic works. To what extent the homiletical midrashim contain and made use of earlier sources will continue to be a matter of scholarly investigation but it has become generally recognized that a midrash frequently is a composite of complexes of earlier source materials. *Tanna Debe Eliyahu* is more properly speaking an ethical treatise, but it also contains a number of what may be considered classic parables which the darshan weaves into the fabric of his treatment of some of the great ethical, theological and practical themes of the Jewish faith outside the strict framework of a single biblical text. All the historical and critical questions of each midrashic work must be carefully considered in any treatment of the parables, but the homiletical midrashim and their classic type of parables should not be excluded from the comparative study of early parabolic teaching.

The foregoing treatment of selected works from the scholarly investigation of parabolic instruction is by no means complete as others have surveyed parable research more fully.[70] An exhaustive discussion of the research of early parabolic teaching has not been the aim here. The school of the so-called "new hermeneutic" has not even been treated, primarily because its methodology is occupied more with the application of the universal meaning of the parable and less with the basic historical issues.[71] Here brief notice has been made of the contributions of both Jülicher and Fiebig. Interestingly the hermeneutical questions surrounding the comparative study of Jesus' parables and those from talmudic literature had already developed into a live issue of controversy at the dawn of the modern era of parable investigation. Jülicher's work has had immense influence and Fiebig's correctives have been inconsequential in the scholarly works that followed, perhaps in part because of Fiebig's somewhat problematic presentation. Dodd, and Jeremias after him, have brought the kingdom of heaven controversy to the fore and have tried to recreate the original *Sitz im Leben* of Jesus' parables. Nonetheless, with the exception of Flusser's pioneering efforts and major contributions, very little work has been done in the area of comparative studies since the Bultmannian era. The results of Flusser's associative method of research suggest that a great deal is yet to be done in the area of rabbinic and gospel parables. Nevertheless the relationship between the parables of Jesus and their cognate meshalim from talmudic literature is an area of research which has been largely ignored. A trend can be discerned however that expresses a renewed interest in rabbinic parables and their relationship to the gospel narratives.[72] This is a very complicated field of investigation that requires a careful consideration of the philological and textual questions related to the synoptic problem on the one hand and the chronological and literary problems presented by the study of talmudic literature and rabbinic meshalim on the other. The present work will deal with some of these foundational and technical problems which will hopefully pave the way for further comprehensive research in the future.

The Original Language of the Parables

Philology is an essential tool in the study of the origin and development of the gospel texts and therefore it is important to discuss the original language of parabolic teachings and its impact upon the interpretation of the parables of Jesus. Much has been written concerning Jesus' mother tongue and the original language of the gospels and Acts.[73] Years before the discovery of the Dead Sea Scrolls, G. Dalman suggested that Jesus spoke Aramaic and many have been influenced by his work.[74] Nevertheless much of the evidence which he adduced was later discredited by the fact that the targumim he employed to reconstruct the language of Jesus were derived from a later period. One might question the unqualified use of a translated source for exemplifying the spoken language of a people in a given period. Only non-translational passages can be admitted as evidence and it is difficult to determine whether these sections actually represent the language spoken during the period. C. Torrey also made use of Aramaic phrases from the targumim, and it should be pointed out that many if not all of the alleged "Aramaisms" are also well documented in Hebrew.[75] Jeremias felt that some of the verbal differences in the synoptic gospels could have developed from different Greek translations of the same Aramaic text.[76] M. Black, M. Wilcox, J. Fitzmyer and G. Vermes have theorized an Aramaic *Vorlage.*[77]

One must differentiate between literary activities and the spoken language of the period.[78] Black conceded, "In comparison with the extensive Hebrew discoveries, only a small number of Aramaic texts have so far come to light at Qûmraṇ."[79] In fact the scrolls dealing with everyday life of the sect like the *Manual of Discipline* were also composed in Hebrew. It is hard to imagine that the sect would have written this treatise in a language that would be difficult for its initiates or members to understand even if the literary nature of the scroll makes it highly unlikely that it could accurately represent the spoken language of the people. The language of the biblical commentaries, the thanksgiving hymns, and the letter believed to have been written by the founder of the sect *Miktzat Meaaseh Torah* were also composed in Hebrew and a number of the phrases from Hebrew scrolls have been paralleled in the gospels.[80] While all of these problems cannot be discussed at length, several studies have supported the position that Jesus spoke Hebrew and that the gospels are derived from a Hebrew source. These claims have been corroborated by the Papias tradition.[81] E.Y. Kutscher writes, "... it was in Judea, the heart of the Jewish state of the Hasmoneans, that MH [Mishnaic Hebrew] had existed as the spoken language for centuries, side by side with Aramaic."[82] The fact that Mishnaic Hebrew was indeed a spoken language as M. Segal maintained has been further supported by the discovery of the Hebrew Bar-Koseba letters which in Kutscher's words "... did not originate in scholarly circles but dealt with mundane matters that had to do with their military and administrative background."[83] No one can easily dismiss the possibility that the gospel could have been composed originally in Hebrew. Without dealing with this important question in depth, the work at hand is based on the premise that the extant gospel texts are derived from a Semitic undertext which was close in linguistic characteristics to Late Biblical Hebrew and Mishnaic Hebrew. One must keep in mind that the traditions of the early tannaitic sages are preserved in Mishnaic Hebrew and that the Aramaic language was used later by the Amoraim.[84]

On the question of the original language of the parables, the situation is much less ambiguous. Rabbinic parables are preserved in Hebrew.[85] Segal even noted texts written in Aramaic that change languages. The narrative is Aramaic until a parable is cited. The parable is related in Hebrew. Then the narrative returns to the Aramaic.[86] Sometimes the language of characters in a Hebrew parable is Aramaic. This adds color to the story illustration. It also gives credence to the view of a language situation where people understood both Aramaic and Hebrew. Perhaps the

Aramaic speaking characters are meant to be depicted as simple people (sometimes animals) who are ignorant and do not know Hebrew.[87] Are these characters supposed to represent non-Hebrew speaking diaspora Jews from the land of exile? Perhaps these characters are representative of the non-Jewish population which would not have spoken Hebrew. In any case, since the linguistic medium of rabbinic parables was Hebrew, it is only reasonable and at least a high probability that Jesus also employed Hebrew in telling his story illustrations and that they would have been recorded and preserved in the Hebrew language.

Notes

1) See Rashi on b. Sanhedrin 38b–39a and Rambam, *The Guide for the Perplexed,* trans. Shlomo Pines, p. 12 and see here the "Introduction," notes 1 and 37 and cf. also Ibn Ezra's commentary on Genesis 29:12.

2) Only Jerome ever mentions the names of any rabbis, in *Esaiam* 8, 11–12 (LXXIII, p. 116). This passage is cited by A.F.J. Klijn and G.J. Reinink, *Patristic Evidence for Jewish Christian Sects* (Leiden: Brill, 1973), pp. 220–221 and discussed by R. Pritz, *Nazarent Jewish Christianity* (Leiden: Brill, 1988), pp. 58–62.

3) I.e. Campegius Vitringa, *De Synagoga Veteri* (Franeker: J. Gyzelaari, 1696); Christian Schöttgen, *Horae hebraicae et talmudicae in universum Novum Testamentum* (Leipzig: F. Hekel, 1733–1742, two volumes) and Johann G. Meuschen, *Novum Testamentum ex Talmude et antiquitatibus Hebraeorum Illustratum* (Leipzig: J.F. Braun, 1736). Cf. R.M. Johnston, "Parabolic Interpretations Attributed to Tannaim" (Unpublished doctoral dissertation: Hartford Seminary, 1977), pp. 3f. Also see G.F. Moore, "Christian Writers on Judaism," *Harvard Theological Review* 14 (1921), pp. 197–254 and J.W. Doeve, *Jewish Hermeneutics in the Synoptic Gospels and Acts* (Assen: Van Gorcum, 1954), pp. 1–15.

4) For instance, Lightfoot cites Maimonides, *Mishnah Torah,* chapter 1, as containing the phrase "fishers of the law." This is said to be parallel to Matthew 4:19 where the expression "fishers of men" appears (cf. Mark 1:17). However the passage actually reads "principles of the law" and not "fishers of the law" (*Mada Halachot* Chapter 1:12). Lightfoot misread דייגי תורה for דיני תורה; cf. Lightfoot, *A Commentary on the New Testament from the Talmud and Hebraica* (Grand Rapids: Baker Book House, 1979), vol. 2, pp. 88–89.

5) Norman Perrin, "The Modern Interpretation of the Parables of Jesus and the Problem of Hermeneutics," *Interpretation,* 25 (1971), pp. 131–132. See also James C. Little, "Parable Research in the Twentieth Century I. The Predecessors of J. Jeremias," *The Expository Times,* 87 (1975), p. 357.

6) Ibid. See also W. Sanday, "A New Work on the Parables," *The Journal of Theological Studies* 1 (1900), pp. 161–180.

7) H.W.A. Meyer, *Kritisch exegetischer Kommentar über das Neue Testament* (Göttingen: Vandenhoeck und Ruprecht, 1858), vol. 1, p. 449. Cited by G.V. Jones, *The Art and Truth of the Parables* (London: SPCK, 1964), p. 3. A.B. Bruce, *The Parabolic Teaching of Christ: A Systematic and Critical Study of the Parables of our Lord* (New York: A.C. Armstrong and Son, 1908 reprint from 1882), i.e. pp. 278–279. Bruce's work has also been discussed again by W.S. Kissinger, *The Parables of Jesus, a History of Interpretation and Bibliography* (Metuchen, New Jersey: The American Theological Library, 1979), pp. 67–71.

8) See Kissinger, *The Parables of Jesus,* pp. 1–33.

9) C.H. Dodd, *The Parables of the Kingdom* (Glasgow: William Collins, 1961), pp. 13–14. Dodd quotes from Augustine's *Quaestiones Evangeliorum* II, 19.

10) Tertullian, "On Modesty," Chapter VII, A. Roberts and J. Donaldson, *The Ante-Nicene Fathers* (Grand Rapids: Eerdmans, 1965), vol. 4, p. 80.

11) A. Jülicher, *Die Gleichnisreden Jesu* (Darmstadt: Wissenschaftliche Buchgesellschaft, 1969), vol. 1, pp. 112ff.

12) Eta Linnemann accepts Jülicher's one point approach but admits that it is possible that "Jesus also composed one or two allegories *alongside* the similitudes and parables." See idem, *Parables of Jesus Introduction and Exposition* (London: SPCK, 1977), p. 8. Linnemann herself seems very doubtful that Jesus used allegories but cites "The Parable of the Wedding" (Matthew 22:10–14), "The Parable of the Sower" (Mark 4:3–9 and parallels), "The Parable of the Tares Among the Wheat" (Matthew 13:24–29), "The Parable of the Dragnet" (Matthew 13:47f), and also "The Parable of the Wicked Husbandmen" (Mark 12:1–12 and parallels) and "The Ten Virgins" (Matthew 25:1–13) as possible allegories. Matthew's parable of the wedding is a secondary reshaping of Luke's parable of the great supper (Luke 14:15–24). She doubts the authenticity of the interpretations of the parables. Nevertheless, the fact that she allows for the possibility that Jesus employed allegories along with parables shows a weakening in Jülicher's methodology. Dan Via has also questioned Jülicher's methodology in his chapter, "Parable and Allegory,"

where he concludes, "There is more than one important element in a parable, and all of these features must be given consideration . . ." *(The Parables their Literary and Existential Dimension* (Philadelphia: Fortress Press, 1980), p. 25. N. Perrin accuses Jülicher of developing " . . . a manifesto of nineteenth-century German theological liberalism" (idem, "Modern Interpretation of the Parables," pp. 132–133). Perrin accepts Jülicher's approach but rejects the application of it. Jülicher has by no means escaped scholarly rebuttal, e.g. Jeremias, *The Parables of Jesus* p. 19; C.H. Dodd, *The Parables of the Kingdom,* p. 22; R. Stein, *An Introduction to the Parables of Jesus* (Philadelphia: Westminster, 1981), pp. 51–58.

13) Jülicher, *Gleichnisreden,* vol. 1, pp. 169–172. This is not to say that Jülicher ignored rabbinic teaching entirely; see Johnston, "Parabolic Interpretations," p. 11 and note 5.

14) Jülicher, *Gleichnisreden,* vol. 1, pp. 170–173.

15) A. Feldman, *The Parables and Similes of the Rabbis Agricultural and Pastoral* (Cambridge: Cambridge University Press, 1927), p. 19.

16) Jülicher does mention the agada for polemic reasons: "In der Hagada redet halb Israelit, halb der Rabbi, in Jesu Parabeln redet allein der Israelit . . . der wahre ewige Jude." Idem, *Gleichnisreden,* vol. 1, p. 173.

17) On the one hand he criticized agadic literature for being too rabbinic and on the other hand he tried to adapt the rabbinic parable concerning the giving of the Torah and the sharecroppers into his own scheme of parable interpretation (Jülicher, *Gleichnisreden,* vol. 1, pp. 171–172). Jülicher discovered this parable from A. Wünsche, *Neue Beiträge zur Erläuterung der Evangelien aus Talmud und Midrasch* (Göttingen: Vandenhoeck & Ruprecht's Verlag, 1878), p. 250. One cannot help but wonder if Jülicher might have arrived at different conclusions had he been better acquainted with rabbinic literature.

18) Paul Fiebig, *Altjüdische Gleichnisse und die Gleichnisse Jesu* (Tübingen: J.C.B. Mohr, 1904).

19) Ibid, p. 3.

20) Ibid, pp. 162–163. See also I. Abraham's penetrating discussion of the relationship between rabbinic parables and gospel parables where he also treats Fiebig's work, *Studies in Pharisaism and the Gospels* (New York: KTAV Publishing House, reprint 1967), first series, pp. 97ff.

21) Johnston noted, " . . . he [Fiebig] proceeds to set out an annotated list of fifty-three items (perhaps coincidentally corresponding to the fifty-three parables of Jesus treated by Jülicher in his second volume?) which,

while not all exact parallels to New Testament parables, he believes to be instructive. One may note that the collection was far from homogeneous with respect to form and genre, including simple similes as well as narrative *meshalim.*" Johnston, "Parabolic Interpretations Attributed to Tannaim," pp. 31–32.

22) Paul Fiebig, *Die Gleichnisreden Jesu im Lichte der rabbinischen Gleichnisse des neutestamentlichen Zeitalters ein Beitrag um Steit um die "Christusmythe" und ein Widerlegung der Gleichnistheorie Jülichers* (Tübingen: J.C.B. Mohr, 1912). The title of this work clearly betrays Fiebig's polemic motives.

23) Fiebig, *Die Gleichnisreden,* p. 121.

24) Ibid, p. 122.

23) Ibid, p. 126.

26) Arthur Drews, *Die Christusmythe* (Eugen Diederichs Jena, 1910). The work was translated into English by Joseph McCabe, *The Witnesses to the Historicity of Jesus* (London: Watts and Co., 1912).

27) Fiebig attacks Weinel for making the same mistakes that Jülicher had made, idem, *Die Gleichnisreden,* pp. iiif. One cannot help but think that Fiebig could have been more successful if he had devoted more efforts in dealing with the texts than in polemicizing.

28) Fiebig, *Die Gleichnisreden,* p. 122. In many ways Fiebig's criticisms of Deissmann are justified but Fiebig did not really treat the evidence adduced by Deissmann. However it may be doubted whether Deissmann ever adequately treated the question of the Jewish background. Deissmann did however admit that " . . . within the New Testament there are portions of which 'the original language' was not Greek but Semitic." A. Deissmann, *Light from the Ancient East* (Grand Rapids: Baker Book House, 1978), p. 64. While he affirms that an "Aramaic" gospel once existed (ibid., p. 65), Deissmann seems to minimize the influence of the Semitic background to the text.

29) Fiebig was not disregarded by all as can be illustrated by E. Nourse's article, "Parable (Introductory and Biblical)," which appeared in Hasting's *Encyclopaedia of Religion and Ethics,* vol. 9, pp. 629–630. Nourse observed, "Only recently have the rabbinic parables been made the subject of scientific investigation. But sufficient has been done by Bugge, Lagrange, and especially Fiebig to make it certain that hereafter the exegesis of the parables of Jesus must be based upon and start from a knowledge of the significance and use of the parable in the Rabbinical schools." Nevertheless few have built upon Fiebig's pioneering efforts.

30) F. Schleiermacher, *The Christian Faith* (Edinburgh: T. and T.

Clark, 1902), p. 723. For a discussion of Schleiermacher's influence on parable research, see W. Kissinger, *The Parables of Jesus a History of Interpretation and Bibliography,* pp. 84–85.

31) J. Weiss, *Die Predigt Jesu vom Reiche Gottes* (Göttingen: Vandenhoeck & Ruprecht, 1892); the work was translated into English by R. Hiers and D. Holland, *Jesus' Proclamation of the Kingdom of God* (Fortress Press: Philadelphia, 1971). Weiss' thesis is treated more extensively in the section of the present work which deals with the parables of the kingdom.

32) Cf. N. Perrin, *Jesus and the Language of the Kingdom Symbol and Metaphor in New Testament Interpretation* (Fortress Press: Philadelphia, 1980), pp. 97–98. See the chapter in the present work entitled, "The Parables of the Kingdom of Heaven."

33) C.H. Dodd, *The Parables of the Kingdom,* pp. 84ff. Cf. also the recent study, Bernard Brandon Scott, "The King's Accounting: Matthew 18:23–34" *Journal of Biblical Literature* 104 (1985), pp. 429–442, who noted the problem, "A major problem confronting the interpretation of Jesus' parables is their preservation in contexts created by others" (ibid, p. 429).

34) J. Jeremias, *The Parables of Jesus* (London: SCM Press, 1972), pp. 25ff. Jeremias proposed that Jesus spoke Galilean Aramaic instead of Hebrew. This question will be treated later. One must also question Jeremias for thinking that the variations in the wording of the synoptics was caused by different translators. In the chapter on the synoptic problem the different stages of the gospel tradition are outlined more fully. Here it must be pointed out that most of these differences are probably better understood as entering the texts during redaction after the gospel tradition had been translated.

35) Jeremias, *The Parables,* p. 112.

36) Ibid, p. 115.

37) N. Perrin, *Jesus and the Language of the Kingdom* (London: SCM Press, 1976), p. 96.

38) Cf. Matthew 6:5–15; 7:7–11 and Luke 11:1–4, 9–16. A similar idea is expressed in early Jewish thought in the parable attributed to Samuel the Little in Taanit 25b (cf. Bacher, *Die Agada der Tannaiten,* vol. 1, p. 371). See also my work *The Jewish Background to the Lord's Prayer* (Center for Judaic Christian Studies, 1984). Why search for deep eschatological meaning in these texts that speak about prayer?

39) Jeremias, *The Parables,* pp. 43f. Cf. Dodd, *The Parables of the Kingdom,* pp. 101–103.

40) Jeremias, *The Parables,* p. 44.

41) Ibid, p. 43.

42) Ibid, p. 44.

43) C.G. Montefiore, *The Synoptic Gospels* (New York: KTAV, reprint, 1968), vol. 2, p. 62 and also idem, *Rabbinic Literature and Gospel Teachings* (New York: KTAV, reprint, 1970), p. 40.

44) Many passages could be cited to illustrate this theme (cf. Billerbeck, vol. 1, pp. 284–287). For instance see the midrash, *Seder Eliyahu* where the darshan urges true reconcilement between each individual involved in a disagreement (שעשה מריבה עם חבירו, M. Friedmann ed., *Seder Eliyahu Rabbah,* Jerusalem: Wahrmann Books, 1969, pp. 105–106, Chapter 18). Then the text from Proverbs (25:8), cited above, is quoted and applied to a situation where agreement between adversaries is needed. Then the darshan adds that one must be prepared to give account for oneself, even before the heavenly tribunal. The concept of compromise is expressed in tannaitic literature. See the view of R. Joshua ben Korcha who felt that arbitration was a *mitzvah* and the opinion of R. Simeon ben Menasya who affirmed the principle of compromise (tos. Sanhedrin 1:2ff; b. Sanhedrin 6b; jer. Sanhedrin chap. 1, hal. 1, 18b; Sifre Deut. 17, Finkelstein, pp. 28f) and see M. Elon, "Compromise," *Encyclopaedia Judaica,* vol. 5, cols. 857–859. Flusser first noted the connection between Jesus' parable and compromise in rabbinic literature.

45) M. Yoma 8:9, "For transgressions that are between man and God the Day of Atonement effects atonement, but for transgressions that are between a man and his fellow the Day of Atonement effects atonement only if he has appeased his fellow" (Danby's translation).

46) John Lightfoot, *A Commentary on the New Testament from the Talmud and Hebraica* (Grand Rapids: Baker Book House, 1658, reprinted in 1979), vol. 2, p. 115. Lightfoot writes, "The words, therefore, of the verse have this sense: 'Does your neighbour accuse you of some damage, or of money that is due him? And are ye now going in the way to the bench of three to commence the suit? Compound with your adversary, lest he compel you to some higher tribunal, where your danger will be greater.'"

47) J. Jeremias, *The Lord's Prayer* (Philadelphia: Fortress Press, 1980), pp. 23ff; and Jeremias' *The Prayers of Jesus* (Philadelphia: Fortress Press, 1978), pp. 100ff.

48) A. Deissmann, *Light from the Ancient East* (Grand Rapids: Baker Book House, 1980), p. 78, note 1. See also M. Black, *An Aramaic Approach to the Gospels and Acts* (Oxford: Clarendon Press, 1977), pp. 203ff; Walter Bauer, *A Greek-English Lexicon of the New Testament and*

Other Early Christian Literature revised and augmented by F.W. Gringrich and F.W. Danker (Chicago: The University of Chicago, 1979), pp. 296–297; and B. Metzger, "How Many Times Does 'Epiousios' Occur Outside the Lord's Prayer?" *The Expository Times,* 69 (1957), pp. 52–54.

49) Jerome, *Comm. on Mat.* for Matthew 6:11 and *Comm. on Ps. CXXXV;* see P. Vielhauer, "The Gospel of the Nazareans," in E. Hennecke and W. Schneemelcher, ed., *New Testament Apocrypha* (London: SCM Press, 1973), vol. 1, pp. 139–153; M.R. James, *The Apocryphal New Testament* (Oxford: Clarendon Press, 1980), pp. 4f; and R. Cameron, *The Other Gospels: Non Canonical Gospel Texts* (Philadelphia: Westminster, 1982), pp. 97–102.

50) Jeremias, *The Lord's Prayer,* pp. 23–25.

51) Cf. Vielhauer, "The Gospel of the Nazareans," pp. 139–146 and note 49 above. See Klijn and Reinink, *Patristic Evidence for Jewish-Christian Sects,* pp. 214–215, for it seems that Jerome interpreted the words of the Hebrew gospel like Jeremias, " . . . which means, the bread which you will give us in your kingdom, give us to-day." The saying does not make sense in the context of the Disciples' Prayer. Nonetheless compare the text, "Your teacher Joshua did not expound it thus but rather He that serveth God and His territory shall be satisfied with His bread of the future world . . ." which appears in Genesis Rabbah 82:8 (Albeck, p. 986) and cf. Billerbeck, vol. 2, p. 484. In this text the idiom, "shall be satisfied with His bread of the future world" is closely related to the context of the entire passage. It is certainly to be differentiated from the saying, "Give us our bread for tomorrow," which seems to be another interpretation of Matthew's difficult Greek text.

52) See Elmar Camilo dos Santo, *An Expanded Hebrew Index for the Hatch-Redpath Concordance to the Septuagint* (Jerusalem: Dugith Publishers Baptist House, 1976), p. 109.

53) Cf. Brad Young, *The Jewish Background to the Lord's Prayer* (Austin: The Center for Judaic-Christian Studies, 1984), pp. 23–27; and David Flusser, "Have You Ever Seen a Lion Laboring as a Porter?" *Studies in Bible and Jewish History Dedicated to the Memory of Jacob Liver,* ed. Benyamin Uffenheimer (Tel Aviv: Tel Aviv University Press, 1971), pp. 331–334.

54) See Walter Bauer, *A Greek-English Lexicon of the New Testament and Other Early Christian Literature* revised and augmented by F.W. Gringrich and F.W. Danker, p. 297 and H. Liddell and R. Scott, *A Greek-English Lexicon* (Oxford: The Clarendon Press, 1976), p. 1274, and also notes 48 and 52 above.

55) See note 52 above.

56) Cf. Adolph Büchler, *Types of Jewish-Palestinian Piety from 70 B.C.E. to 70 C.E.* (London: Jews College, 1922), pp. 134–135. See also note 53 above.

57) David Flusser, *Yahadut Umekorot Hanatzrut* (Tel Aviv: Sifriyat Poalim, 1979), pp. 150–209; idem, *Die rabbinischen Gleichnisse und der Gleichniserzähler Jesus* (Bern: Peter Lang, 1981); and see also Flusser's comments on the panel discussion concerning J. Petuchowski's article ("The Theological Significance of the Parable in Rabbinic Literature and the New Testament," *Christian News from Israel* No. 2 [10] vol. 23, 1972, pp. 76–86) in "A Panel Commentary on Petuchowski's discussion of the Parable," *Christian News from Israel* No. 3 (11) vol. 23 (1973), pp. 147–148. Cf. J. Duncan M. Derrett's articles on the parables, many of which have been reprinted in his work, *Law in the New Testament* (London: Darton, 1970).

58) Flusser, *Yahadut Umekorot Hanatzrut,* p. 159.

59) Ibid, pp. 202f.

60) "This may be compared to a mortal king who distributed royal apparel to his servants. The wise among them folded it up and laid it away in a chest, whereas the foolish among them went and did their work in them. After a time the king demanded his garments: the wise among them returned them to him immaculate, [but] the foolish among them returned them soiled. The king was pleased with the wise but angry with the foolish. Of the wise he said, 'Let my robes be placed in my treasury and they can go home in peace'; while of the foolish he said, 'Let my robes be given to the fuller, and let them be confined in prison.' Thus too with the Holy One, blessed be He: concerning the bodies of the righteous He says, 'He entereth into peace, they rest in their beds;' (Isa. 57:2) while concerning their souls He says, 'yet the soul of my Lord shall be bound up in the bundle of life with the Lord thy God' (1 Sam. 25:29). But concerning the bodies of the wicked He says, 'There is no peace saith the Lord, unto the wicked;' (Isa. 48:22) while concerning their souls He says, 'and the souls of thine enemies, them shall he sling out, as from the hollow of a sling' (1 Sam. 25:29)." b. Shabbat 152b.

61) Flusser, *Yahadut Umekorot Hanatzrut,* pp. 169–170.

62) Ibid, p. 205.

63) Flusser, *Yahadut Umekorot Hanatzrut,* p. 205; idem, *Die rabbinischen Gleichnisse,* pp. 141ff. Citing Derenbourg, the great nineteenth century orientalist, also Bacher made note of the similarity between R. Tarfon's saying (Avot 2.15f) and that of Hippocrates, W. Bacher, *Die Agada der Tannaiten,* vol. 1, p. 349, note 2. Flusser recognized the relationship of these sayings to the gospels (Matthew 9:37f and Luke 10:2).

64) See Flusser's chapter, "Ursprung und Vorgeschichte der jüdischen

Gleichnisse," in *Die rabbinischen Gleichnisse,* pp. 141–160. This has also been discussed by J. Jacobs, "Aesop's Fables among the Jews," *The Jewish Encyclopedia,* vol. 1, pp. 221f. See also S. Lieberman's comments in *Tosefta Ki-fshutah Order Nashim,* part 8, pp. 983f. Cf. H. Schwarzbaum, *The Mishle Shu'alim (Fox Fables) of Rabbi Berechiah Ha-Nakdan a Study in Comparative Folklore and Fable Lore* (Kiron, Israel: Institute for Jewish and Arab Folklore Research, 1979), pp. i-lv. Compare Luke 4:23 with Babrius' fable no. 120, "Physician Heal Thyself," in B.E. Perry, *Babrius and Phaedrus* (Cambridge: Harvard University Press, 1975), p. 157 and see parallels Gen. R. 23.4 (Albeck, p. 225), b. Baba Metzia 107b, Lev. R. 5.6 (Margulies, p. 118); cf. Billerbeck, vol. 2, p. 156. Fitzmyer also called attention to yet another variation of this saying from Euripides, *Frag.* 1086, "'A physican for others, but himself teeming with sores,'" idem, *Luke I–IX,* p. 535.

65) Flusser, *Yahadut Umekorot Hanatzrut,* p. 157.

66) Private communication.

67) Flusser, *Yahadut Umekorot Hanatzrut,* p. 207.

68) H.G. Enelow, *The Mishnah of Rabbi Eliezer* (New York: The Bloch Publishing Company, 1933) and S. Lieberman, *Hellenism in Jewish Palestine* (New York: The Jewish Theological Seminary of America, 1962), p. 68; H.L. Strack and G. Stemberger, *Einleitung in Talmud und Midrasch 7. Auflage* (München: Verlag C.H. Beck, 1982), p. 38; compare also the discussion in J.W. Doeve, *Jewish Hermeneutics in the Synoptic Gospels and Acts* (Assen: Van Gorcum, 1954), pp. 60ff.

69) C. Thoma, "Prolegomena zu einer Übersetzung und Kommentierung der rabbinischen Gleichnisse," *Theologische Zeitschrift* (1982), p. 526. See now C. Thoma and S. Lauer, *Die Gleichnisse der Rabbinen Erster Teil Pesiqta deRav Kahana (PesK)* (Bern: Peter Lang, 1986).

70) W.S. Kissinger, *The Parables of Jesus a History of Interpretation and Bibliography;* see also the three articles by J. Little, "Parable Research in the Twentieth Century I. The Predecessors of J. Jeremias," *The Expository Times* 87 (1976), pp. 356ff; idem, "Parable Research in the Twentieth Century II. The Contributions of J. Jeremias," *The Expository Times* 88 (1977), pp. 40ff; idem, "Parable Research in the Twentieth Century III. Developments since J. Jeremias," *The Expository Times* 88 (1977), pp. 71ff; N. Perrin, *Jesus and the Language of the Kingdom* (Philadelphia: Fortress Press, 1976), pp. 89–193; idem, "The Modern Interpretation of the Parables of Jesus and the Problem of Hermeneutics," *Interpretation* 25 (1971), pp. 131–148; and R.M. Johnston, "Parabolic Interpretations Attributed to Tannaim," Unpublished doctoral dissertation, The Hartford Seminary Foundation, 1978, pp. 1–123.

Cf. also E. Baasland, "Zum Beispiel der Beispielerzählungen zur Formenlehre der Gleichnisse und zur Methodik der Gleichnisauslegung," *Novum Testamentum* 28 (1986), pp. 193–197 and 200–202.

71) See note 10 above in the "Introduction."

72) See Johnston, "Parabolic Interpretations," p. 105. This trend is actually more of a recognition of neglect; see for instance the appendix in A.M. Hunter's popular book, *Interpreting the Parables* (London: SCM Press, 1964), pp. 113–116. One cannot help but note the apologetical aspect of Hunter's treatment, "Nor can the candid reader fail to note how much more vital, dramatic and compelling are Christ's parables. To compare Jesus as a maker of parables with the rabbis is like comparing Shakespeare with the minor dramatists of his time. In the art of parable he has no peer, and none of the rabbis dare even challenge comparison" (p. 116). Again no significant research is done concerning the function of the parable in the context of midrashic literature. See also note 59 above and cf. Roger David Aus, "Luke 15:11–32 and R. Eliezer ben Hyrcanus's Rise to Fame," *Journal of Biblical Literature* 104 (1985), pp. 443–469.

73) For a working bibliography on this and related questions, cf. Ch. Rabin, "Hebrew and Aramaic in the First Century," *The Jewish People in the First Century* (Amsterdam: Van Gorcum, 1976), vol. 2, pp. 1007–1039. M. Black, *An Aramaic Approach to the Gospels* (Oxford: The Clarendon Press, 1977); M. Wilcox, *The Semitisms of Acts* (Oxford: The Clarendon Press, 1965); F. Zimmermann, *The Aramaic Origin of the Four Gospels* (New York: KTAV, 1979); E. Schürer, revised and edited by G. Vermes, F. Millar and M. Black, *The History of the Jewish People in the Age of Jesus Christ* (Edinburgh: T. and T. Clark, 1979), vol. 2, pp. 20–28; while much of the Aramaic letters, scrolls and inscriptions that have been discovered in recent years are referred to in this survey, the importance of the Hebrew materials are minimized; A. Abott, *Clue a Guide through Greek to Hebrew Scripture* (London: Adam and Charles Black, 1900); H. Birkeland, *The Language of Jesus* (Oslo: Avhandinger utgitt av Det Norske Videnskaps-Akademi, 1954); J. Grintz, "Hebrew as the Spoken and Written Language of the Second Temple," *The Journal of Biblical Literature* 79 (1960), pp. 32–47; idem, *Perakim Betoldot Bayit Sheni* (Jerusalem: Marcus, 1969), pp. 79–101; D. Bivin and R. Blizzard, *Understanding the Difficult Words of Jesus* (Arcadia: Makor Foundation, 1983), pp. 19–103; R. Martin, *Syntactical Evidence of Semitic Sources in Greek Documents* (Missoula: Society of Biblical Literature, 1974) and on word cf. also with Galen Marquis, "Word Order as a Criterion for the Evaluation of Translation Technique in the LXX and the Evaluation of

Word-Order Variants as Exemplified in LXX-Ezekiel" *Textus,* edited by E. Tov, (Jerusalem: Magnes, 1986); E.Y. Kutscher, *Hebrew and Aramaic Studies* (Jerusalem: Magnes Press, 1975), pp. 27–70; E.Y. Kutscher, *A History of the Hebrew Language* (Jerusalem: Magnes Press, 1982); M.H. Segal, *A Grammar of Mishnaic Hebrew* (Oxford: The Clarendon Press, 1978); J. Klausner, *Historiyah Shel Habayit Hashani* (Jerusalem: Achiasaf, 1954), pp. 103ff; A. Bendavid, *Lashon Mikra Velashon Chachamim* (Jerusalem: Davir, 1967); and cf. E. Ben Yehuda, "Prolegomena," *A Complete Dictionary of Ancient and Modern Hebrew* (Tel Aviv: Sefer, 1948) pp. 80ff. See also the important studies by Randall Buth, "Hebrew Poetic Tenses and the Magnificat," *Journal for the Study of the New Testament* 21 (1984), pp. 67–83; idem, "Luke 19:31–34, Mishnaic Hebrew and Bible Translation," *Journal of Biblical Literature* 104 (1985), pp. 680–685. Of course these bibliographical materials are by no means exhaustive. Each source provides more references. Two questions have to be asked: What languages were spoken and understood by the Jewish people during the Second Temple period? In what language was the earliest records of Jesus' life and teachings preserved? Hebrew was understood and spoken during the period and as D. Flusser pointed out (private conversation), even if Jesus may have said something in Aramaic, his words would have been preserved and transmitted in Hebrew. (Mark of course seems to be interested to add color to his narrative by adding some Aramaic phrases.) Finally careful consideration of the linguistic evidence from the synoptic gospels points to a Semitic undertext which only verifies the Papias tradition which refers to a text written in the *hebraidi dialekto* ("Hebrew language," Eusebius, *Hist. Eccl.* III, 39; Loeb vol. 1, p. 296).

74) G. Dalman, *The Words of Jesus* (Edinburgh: T. and T. Clark, 1902) and idem, *Jesus Jeshua* (New York: KTAV, reprint, 1971); see also R.L. Lindsey, "A Modified Two-Document Theory of the Synoptic Dependence and Interdependence" *Novum Testamentum* 6 (1963), pp. 246f.

75) C.C. Torrey, *Our Translated Gospels* (London: Hodder & Stoughton, 1936). Torrey seems to have derived some of his examples by looking up Greek passages from the gospels in the Septuagint and then checking the Hebrew text of the Bible against the Aramaic Targum. This does not indicate whether a text is a Septuagintalism, an Aramaism or a Hebraism. Many if not all of the claims he makes to prove an Aramaic *Vorlage* of the gospel narratives would also hold true for a Hebrew undertext as well.

76) See Jeremias, *The Parables of Jesus,* pp. 25ff.

77) See note 72 above. This presupposition is the basis of much research; J. Fitzmyer, *The Semitic Background of the New Testament* (Missoula: Scholar's Press, 1974); G. Vermes, *Jesus the Jew* (Glasgow: Fontana, 1977); idem, *Jesus and the World of Judaism* (Philadelphia: Fortress Press, 1984). Cf. J. Fitzmyer, *The Gospel According to Luke I–IX* (Garden City: Doubleday, 1983), pp. 116ff; Fitzmyer is very cautious about proposing an Aramaic original and suggests that the Semitisms may actually have resulted from Luke's residence in Syrian Antioch, " . . . the source of such [Aramaic] interference could be Luke's origin in Syrian Antioch, where he lived as an *incola,* speaking the Aramaic dialect of the indigenous natives of that country, though he was also educated in the good Hellenistic culture of that town. A Palestinian background of some material cannot be ruled out" (p. 116).

78) See note 72 above. Flusser (private communication) called attention to a passage from the *Letter of Aristeas* (11), where Demetrius reported, " . . . in the country of the Jews they use a peculiar alphabet (just as the Egyptians, too have a special form of letters) and speak a peculiar dialect. They are supposed to use the Syriac tongue, but this is not the case; their language is quite different" (R.H. Charles, *Apocrypha and Pseudepigrapha of the Old Testament,* vol. 2, p. 95; see J. Thackeray's edition, pp. 552–553 in H.B. Swete, *An Introduction to the Old Testament in Greek,* New York: KTAV, reprint, 1968, first printed in 1902, and see R.J.H. Shutt, "Aristeas to Philocrates," J.H. Charlesworth, ed., *The Old Testament Pseudepigrapha,* vol. 2, p. 12). Flusser suggested that people mistakenly thought that the Jewish people spoke Aramaic because this was the language they used in communicating with non-Jews as a carry-over from the influence of Imperial Aramaic which was widely understood. The other language referred to is of course Hebrew which was used by the Jewish people among themselves. Another passage seems to confirm that Hebrew was known by the Jewish people, " . . . your law shall be translated from the Hebrew tongue which is in use amongst you into the Greek language . . ." (*Letter of Aristeas,* 38, Charles, *Apocrypha and Pseudepigrapha of the Old Testament,* vol. 2, p. 99; Thackeray, op. cit., p. 558; R.J.H. Shutt, "Aristeas to Philocrates," J.H. Charlesworth, ed., *The Old Testament Pseudepigrapha,* vol. 2, p. 15). The language of the Jews is the language of the Torah.

79) Black, *An Aramaic Approach* (third edition), p. 39.

80) Cf. Kutscher, *History of Hebrew,* pp. 112–113. See E. Qimron and J. Strugnell, "An Unpublished Halakhic Letter from Qumran," *Biblical*

Archaeology Today (Jerusalem: Israel Exploration Society, 1985), pp. 400–408 and see the authors' condensed report with the same title, *The Israel Museum Journal* 4 (1985), pp. 9ff.

81) Eusebius, *Ecc. His.*, III, 39, 16 (Loeb, p. 296). Cf. S. Pines, *The Jewish Christians of the Early Centuries of Christianity according to a New Source* (Jerusalem: The Israel Academy of Sciences and Humanities, 1966), pp. 16–18 and p. 23.

82) Kutscher, *History of Hebrew,* p. 116.

83) Ibid, p. 117 and see also J.T. Milik, *Discoveries in the Judaean Desert Les grottes de Murabba'ât* (Oxford: Clarendon Press, 1961), vol. 2, p. 70.

84) See M.H. Segal, *A Grammar of Mishnaic Hebrew,* pp. 3–5, " . . . the Tannaim are, as a rule, made to speak in MH [Mishnaic Hebrew], even in ordinary conversations, and with women and children" (p. 4). It is true that a number of sayings attributed to Hillel have been preserved in Aramaic, but it must be remembered that Hillel was an immigrant from Babylon. Many of these same sayings are also known in Hebrew. Other traditions have sometimes also been preserved in parallel versions with both Aramaic and Hebrew. Here it is impossible to enter into the discussion of which tradition is a translation and which is the source text, but let it suffice to say that each individual case has to be considered.

85) Flusser, *Die rabbinischen Gleichnisse,* p. 18. See also preceding note.

86) B. Baba Kama 60b and b. Taanit 5b, cited by Segal, *A Grammar of Mishnaic Hebrew,* pp. 4–5 and see b. Sotah 40a. Safrai (private communication) also pointed out that the prayers and halachic formulations are also preserved in Hebrew. Even if a question was discussed in Aramaic, the halachah was transmitted in Hebrew.

87) This suggestion was originally forwarded by Safrai (private communication).

THE PARABLES AND TALMUDIC LITERATURE: PARABLE, AGADAH AND TRADITION

The earliest parables were designed to be told. It was only at a later period that they were preserved in written form. They belong to the agadah whose most basic meaning is storytelling.[1] Of course agadah is much more than telling a story, but this aspect of agadah is important when one tries to understand the problems of the development of parabolic teaching in the context of ancient Judaism. The earliest parables were meant to be given extemporaneously as a part of oral instruction and only later did they become fixed within the framework of written traditions.

The Dead Sea Scrolls describe the custom of the sect to have someone expounding the teachings of scripture continually.[2] Josephus, Philo, rabbinic literature as well as the New Testament speak about the proclamation of the Torah on festivals, Sabbaths and informal occasions.[3] This practice of what S. Safrai has termed "actualizing" the word must have been conducive to the development of parabolic teaching and would have preceded and accompanied the crystallization of these traditions into writing.[4] The gospels remain some of the earliest witnesses to parables in the spontaneous instruction attributed to Jesus, though these too were committed to writing. In fact story parables only appear in the gospels and in rabbinic literature. Parables took shape as artistic creations in oral teachings before they became a literary genre. Agadic teachings can aid in recapturing the atmosphere in which parables became a popular pedagogic technique.[5]

Parables have an adaptability that allows them to be used by different parabolists and applied to quite diverse situations.[6]

Rabbinic literature has preserved a rich repository of parables many of which are remnants of earlier classic parabolic instruction and others which were developed and applied to new contexts during the creative processes which produced talmudic literature. The gospels represent a literary tradition that is not entirely paralleled in talmudic literature. Nevertheless, parables make up a significant portion of both the synoptic gospels and rabbinic literature. Probably on a scale comparing the number of parables to the volume of material, the parables are much more frequent in the gospels than in rabbinic literature. This is just an indication of the problem. Parables are a unique literary genre which appear in diverse kinds of literary traditions and which must be researched in the individual context of each tradition. Careful systematic research in this area must avoid the danger of "parallelomania" and seek to interpret the parable in the context of rabbinic literature and in the context of the gospel.[7]

The aim of this work is to analyze the parable as it develops in agadic teachings and becomes an integral literary genre within similar but diverse traditions and then to view some of the hermeneutical questions concerning parabolic teaching from a new perspective. But before we begin an inductive examination of select rabbinic parables in the context of their sources, it will be helpful to consider some of the basic stylistic features of Jewish meshalim.

Stylistic Characteristics of Rabbinic Parables

The definition and description of the stylistic features of Jewish parables will be an ongoing endeavor in the continuation of this work. At this juncture, a few summary observations can be advanced. Many of the illustrations that will be examined betray a common structure and form. Perhaps one of the best ways to describe parabolic instruction is to compare the parable to a mini-play.[8] We will discover that rabbinic parables usually contain introductory formulas. The introduction to the parable may be only one word or a longer phrase to capture the audience's attention and to arouse their curiosity (discussed in the introduction above). Before the first act of the mini-production, usually one is introduced to the main characters of the cast. The cast of the play may consist of a king, a householder, sons, servants, daughters or ordinary people.[9] After the introduction and the naming of the cast, the drama begins.

Once the director starts the action several scenarios or dramatic combinations are possible. Often the first act merely sets the stage by explaining the setting and the situation of the story. The second act generally introduces the crisis. The listeners are kept in suspense until the crisis is resolved. Often it is the conflict that provides the cohesion for the parable. The conflict connects the introduction and the cast to the action that follows and it invites the listener to interact with the plot of the story. It is not unusual to discover elements of shock that traumatize the action as the plot of the story thickens. Following the solution of the crisis in act three, rabbinic parables often elucidate the intended application of the mini-play.

The applications are often introduced by the Hebrew word *kach* (thus), which then paves the way for a brief explanation of the points of comparison between the mashal and the nimshal. In rabbinic parables, the application may be accompanied by biblical verses which further strengthen the main theme of the illustration or reinforce the connection between the various tertia comparationis and the *Sache* illustrated by the parabolic language. Actually this was the aspect of rabbinic parables that most troubled Jülicher because he thought that this application within rabbinic parables turned the story into an allegory.[10] Jülicher maintained that a true parable is never allegory but always has one main theme. While one may be inclined to agree with Jülicher that a parable is usually told to illustrate one main theme, it is doubtful whether points of comparison between the *Bild* and the *Sache* turn the parable into an allegory. In fact this is probably a very important nexus between the parables of Jesus and rabbinic parables which has often been overlooked by interpreters. The question of allegory in parabolic teachings will be examined at the end of this chapter.

Story parables generally do not have long and involved plots. Nonetheless the conflict of the story may be quite intense even if the resolution of the crisis in the parable is forthcoming in a direct manner. Somewhat like select advertisements on television, parables have to capture the attention of their audience, present the evidence and get to the point in an imaginative way that will drive home the theme being illustrated. The concise parable of "The Prince and His Nursemaids" exemplifies the form and structure of rabbinic parables as mini-dramas which functions to communicate a message.[11] The parable is introduced by a prolegomenon, it colorfully presents the members of the cast and develops the interesting plot of the story with its paradoxical conflict. The message of the parable becomes clear at the turning point of the drama and the parable's conclusion. This is the common narrative form and structure of this genre of literature.

THE PRINCE AND HIS NURSEMAIDS

> A parable, to what may the matter be compared? To a king who had a young son. He entrusted him to two nursemaids. One occupied herself with harlotry and the other with witchcraft. The king commanded them to give his son milk but not to teach him their ways. Thus the Holy One blessed be He warned Israel concerning the Egyptians and the Canaanites, "Do not learn from their ways," and He said, "Train up a child in the way he should go, and when he is old he will not depart from it" (Prov. 22:6).

The parable is introduced by the Hebrew phrase, משל למה הדבר דומה למלך, "A parable, to what may the matter be compared? To a king . . ." The parabolist introduces the colorful members of his cast, the king, his young son, and the questionable nursemaids. The conflict of the mini-drama centers around the fact that one nursemaid is a prostitute and the other is a witch. Why would a king turn over his young son to the care of such problematic nursemaids? The king instructs them to perform their tasks as nursemaids but not to teach his son their evil ways. Hence we encounter the paradox and the element of shock that prepares the audience for the turning point in the parable. The prince with all his advantages is receiving care from a witch and a prostitute! The strong surrealistic element of shock in the illustration captures the audience's attention. The lady who occupied herself with harlotry is identified with the Egyptians and the one who practiced witchcraft is related to the Canaanites and signifies idolatry.[12] In some ways this parable may have served as an explanation to account for the fact that the people of Israel failed to observe the Torah and consequently were exiled. They had been influenced to some degree from their experience with the Egyptians and with the Canaanites. The message of the parable becomes clear after the stage has been prepared and the action of the drama has been set in motion. The turning point and application of the parable comes with the Hebrew word כך (thus). The parabolist makes the shift from the mashal to the nimshal, "Thus the Holy One blessed be He warned Israel concerning the Egyptians and the Canaanites, 'Do not learn from their ways!'" The literary form of the parable as a mini-drama with characters, plot and action is patent and can certainly be compared to the gospel parables.

Parable and Midrash

The Hebrew word midrash is a technical term that has a wide range of meanings. The work at hand cannot aspire to discuss the definition of midrash fully. Others have treated the question.[13] Here it must be sufficient to make a few summary observations. From the biblical period, the Hebrew word דרש has been connected with interpretation of tradition (e.g. Ezra 7:10). It can describe an intensive investigation of the meaning of each aspect of the text. The *pesharim* discovered among the Dead Sea Scrolls exemplify this keen interest in biblical interpretation and the term מדרש התורה already appears in the sect's treatment of Isaiah 40:3 (Manual of Disciple 8:14–15). In rabbinic literature the term can signify study, halachic decisions, biblical interpretations, sermons, instruction or homiletical discourses. In modern times the term midrash has been associated with a particular corpus of literature. This literature contains halachic discussions, studies of biblical passages, consideration of hermeneutical problems as well as collections of homiletical discourses. The accumulation of these various sources which were fused together into the framework of various themes or interpretations of biblical texts underlines the importance of understanding individual elements of midrashic literature.

Though the parable should by no means be confined exclusively to midrashim because they appear in many contexts throughout talmudic literature, story parable illustrations appear quite frequently in midrashic texts many of which are representative of early Jewish homiletical instruction. Our investigation will deal more with the parable as a literary genre within select midrashic texts though a number of parables that deal with halachic matters and more basic questions of man's relationship to God and his neighbor will also be considered. It is always necessary to contextualize the parable and to interpret it according to its function within the framework of the source from which it is derived. Some of these texts are closely connected to biblical interpretation and others are composed of various homilies linked together around different themes. What was the purpose of parabolic instruction in the context of the text in which it appears?

Mechilta Derabbi Ishmael

The Mechilta Derabbi Ishmael is one of the so called Midrashe Halacha. However the word halachah is somewhat misleading because these texts contain a great deal of agadah. The Mechilta for example contains much more agadic teaching than strictly treatments of halachic questions[14] and not surprisingly numerous parables. The Mechilta is recognized as one of the earliest midrashim even though it was not known by its present name until a later time.[15] The agadic teachings in this midrashic collection presents two intriguing and inter-related questions: To what extent do these *derashot* actually preserve early homilies of the sages? If the answer to this inquiry is affirmative then one must ask the second question: In what ways have these traditions been reshaped and adapted in the literary stages of the transmission?[16] In many ways it is impossible to answer these questions entirely satisfactorily. Nevertheless one can discern the role that parables played in the development of the sages' instruction.

THE MECHILTA DERABBI ISHMAEL (HOROVITZ, P. 59)

In this passage from the Mechilta two parables are cited; one is attributed to R. Eleazar b. Azariah and the other to R. Simeon bar Yochai. This text has numerous parallels.[17] The occasion of the parable attributed to R. Eleazar b. Azariah demonstrates how parabolic instruction was used in exposition. According to the context, several of the disciples had gone to Yavneh for the Sabbath. Because R. Joshua was not present to participate in the discussion or to hear the teaching of the Torah on the Sabbath at Yavneh, he asked who had been there to deliver the lesson. The answer was R. Eleazar b. Azariah. What follows is a description of R. Eleazar b. Azariah's discourse and the parable which he was said to have utilized in his homily.

> Once the disciples spent the Sabbath in Jabneh. R. Joshua, however, was not there on that Sabbath. When the disciples came to visit him, he said to them: "What new lesson did you have in Jabneh?" They said to him: "After you, master." He then said to them: "And who was there for the Sabbath?" They said to him: "R. Eleazar the son of Azariah." Then he said to them: "Is it possible that R. Eleazar the son of Azariah was there for the Sabbath and did not give you anything new?" So they said to him: "He brought out this general idea in his exposition of the text: 'Ye are standing this day all of you . . . your little ones,' etc. (Deut. 29:9). Now what do the little ones know about distinguishing between good and evil? It was but to give the parents reward for bringing their children, thus increasing the reward of those who do His will. This confirms what has been said: 'The Lord was pleased for His righteousness' sake'," etc. (Isa. 42:21). Then R. Joshua exclaimed and said to them: "Is not this a new teaching? Behold, I am nearly eighty years old, and I never had the good fortune to get this teaching until this day. Blessed are you, our father Abraham, in that Eleazar the son of Azariah is a descendant of yours. Surely the generation in which

> there is an Eleazar b. Azariah is not to be considered orphaned." Then they said to him: "Master, he also brought out this general idea in the exposition of the text: 'Therefore, behold, the days come, saith the Lord, that they shall no more say: "As the Lord liveth, that brought up the children of Israel . . ." but: "As the Lord liveth that brought up and that led,"' etc. (Jer. 23:7–8). One can illustrate it by a parable.

This is the context of R. Eleazar b. Azariah's parable. This passage indicates that it was customary to have someone expound the Torah on the Sabbath at Yavneh. The excitement of study and discovery emerges from R. Joshua's exclamation concerning the discourse delivered by R. Eleazar b. Azariah. R. Joshua's younger disciples had not fully appreciated the significance of the homily. Here it seems that the word sermon or homily is appropriate. R. Eleazar b. Azariah is said to have, "brought out this general idea in his exposition" (כלל זה דרש).[18] Hence it seems that what is preserved in this tradition are excerpts from R. Eleazar's sermon which he delivered at Yavneh on the Sabbath. Apparently a Sabbath message was the accepted custom.[19] His homily included a parable used to illustrate the biblical verse from Jeremiah 23:7–8, "Therefore, behold, the days are coming, says the LORD, when men shall no longer say, 'As the LORD lives who brought up the people of Israel out of the land of Egypt,' but 'As the LORD lives who brought up and led. . . ."

THE MAN WHO DESIRED CHILDREN

> One can illustrate it by a parable. To what can it be compared? To the following: One was very desirous of children. After a daughter had been born to him, he would swear by the life of the daughter. When again a son was born to him, he left off swearing by the daughter and swore only by the life of the son.

The parable of this exposition is taken out of the everyday life of the people. Of course in oriental culture, the birth of the son was considered to be more important than that of the daughter. The parable is by no means elaborate and is closely connected to the biblical verse it illustrates. The expression, "As the LORD lives," was considered to be an oath (Jeremiah 23:7–8). Hence the man swears in the parable. The rest of the verse is also reflected in the parable. The second redemption will take precedence over the deliverance of the people of Israel from Egypt in much the same way as a man swears by the child which is more precious. This parable is followed by another illustration in the name of R. Simeon bar Yochai. Two parables employed to illustrate a single point is not at all infrequent in rabbinic literature.[20] Often as here, the two parables will be attributed to two different authorities. However in the parallels to this passage, the first parable does not appear and the attribution to R. Simeon bar Yochai in the second illustration is absent. Only here is this parable attributed to R. Simeon.

THE TRAVELER AND HIS PERILS

> R. Simeon b. Yochai says: One can illustrate it by a parable. To what can it be compared? To the following: One was traveling along the road. He encountered a wolf and was saved from him. So he kept on telling the story of the wolf. Then he encountered a lion and was saved from him. So he forgot the story of the wolf and kept on telling the story of the lion. He then encountered a serpent and was saved from him. So he forgot the story of the wolf and kept on telling the story of the serpent. So it is with Israel. Later troubles cause the former ones to be forgotten.

The second parable reinforces the first. It emphasizes the aspect of deliverance somewhat more than its predecessor.[21] The tremendous importance of the redemption of Israel from Egypt can be superseded by God's miraculous deliverance from present and future troubles. Both of these parables are used to illustrate the same point. God has miraculously delivered Israel, and in order to make this truth come alive, in his sermon the preacher uses a colorful parable that describes the perilous dangers that a traveler might encounter. Hence this early homily, described in the Mechilta as being delivered at Yavneh, employs the parable in order to illustrate the story of the exodus and at the same time gives the description of God's redemption from the past a present application.

The Mechilta Derabbi Ishmael (Horovitz p. 125)

The parable of the blind and the lame who guard the king's orchard is perhaps the best known parable that appears in rabbinic literature.[22] The colorful illustration has a number of parallels. In the Mechilta, the occasion of the story is a conversation between Antoninus (Marcus Aurelius?) and R. Judah the Prince.[23] R. Judah is asked a theological question concerning the judgment and he responds with this vivid illustration. In this passage from the Mechilta, the illustration is employed in the exposition of the biblical text which describes the deliverance of the people of Israel from Pharaoh. The horse and the rider were both cast into the sea together. The illustration is introduced: "What would God do? He would make the man ride upon the horse and thus judge them together, as it is said: 'The horse and his rider hath He thrown into the sea.'" What follows is presented as an excerpt from a conversation between R. Judah and Antoninus.[24]

THE LAME AND THE BLIND

> Antoninus asked our Teacher, the Saint: "After a man has died and his body ceased to be, does God then make him stand trial?" He answered him: "Rather than ask about the body which is impure, ask me about the soul that is pure." To give a parable for this, to what is this like? To the following: A king of flesh and blood had a beautiful orchard. The king placed in it two guards, one of whom was lame and the other blind," etc. closing with, "and afterwards, 'that He may judge His people'" (Ps. 50:4).

The parallel in the Babylonian Talmud is more complete (cf. the longer text of the Mechilta in a number of manuscripts and the Mechilta Derabbi Simeon bar Yochai). The entire story concerning how the lame and the blind conspired together to obtain the fruit which they were guarding is described in the Talmud.[25]

THE LAME AND THE BLIND

> Antoninus said to Rabbi: 'The body and the soul can both free themselves from judgment. Thus, the body can plead: The soul has sinned, [the proof being] that from the day it left me I lie like a dumb stone in the grave [powerless to do aught]. Whilst the soul can say: The body has sinned, [the proof being] that from the day I departed from it I fly about in the air like a bird [and commit no sin].' He replied, 'I will tell thee a parable. To what may this be compared? To a human king who owned a beautiful orchard which contained splendid figs. Now, He appointed two watchmen therein, one lame and the other blind. [One day] the lame man said to the blind, "I see beautiful figs in the orchard. Come and take me upon thy shoulder, that we may procure and eat them." So the lame bestrode the blind, procured and ate them. Some time after, the owner of the orchard came and inquired of them, "Where are those beautiful figs?" The lame man replied, "Have I then feet to walk with?" The blind man replied, "Have I then eyes to see with?" What did he do? He placed the lame upon the blind and judged them together. So will the Holy One, blessed be He, bring the soul [re]place it in the body, and judge them together, as it is written, "He shall call to the heavens from above, and to the earth, that he may judge his people: He shall call to the heavens from above"—this refers to the soul; "and to the earth, that he may judge his people"—to the body.'

Already G.F. Moore called attention to the fact that this illustration is paralleled in Indian literature and he suggested that this was the origin of the parable.[26] The same story is repeated by the fourth century church father Epiphanius where it is cited as a quotation from the prophet Ezekiel's apocryphon concerning the resurrection.[27] Some scholars have tried to connect this document with one of the two books of Ezekiel mentioned by Josephus.[28] The first would be canonical Ezekiel and the other could be identified with the fragmentary references to the so called Apocryphon of Ezekiel in patristic literature. Insufficient evidence precludes certainty in this matter. Nevertheless one cannot help but consider this suggestion as quite reasonable although any resolution of the question must be based on much more than a handful of quotations in secondary literature.[29] Not only does this parable appear in Indian sources,[30] in Epiphanius' reference to the Apocryphon of Ezekiel as well as references to the motif in the Greek Anthology (IX:11–13b),[31] but also it has a number of parallels in rabbinic literature.[32]

The parable seems to have been widely circulated and its colorful story line must be one of the contributing causes of its popularity. The parable is not complete in all the manuscripts of the Mechilta and some of the better manuscripts simply insert the word "etc." after the introduction to the parable. Margulies suggested that this parable was so well known that the scribe felt that it would be superfluous to repeat it in the text.[33] Of course the other possibility is that a later scribe inserted the parable into the text of the Mechilta because he was acquainted with the illustration from other sources. This possibility is much less likely as the parable in the Mechilta seems to be independent of the text's wording in the parallel rabbinic accounts and it does have strong textual attestation.[34] Thus it appears that the parable was abbreviated by a later scribe(s) who copied the text of the Mechilta.

The illustration is important not only because it throws light on the development of early parabolic teaching but also because it is a point of intersection between cultures and theological speculation.[35] The question concerning the bodily resurrection and the judgment of the soul was intriguing to the minds of Israel's sages.[36] As is well known, during the days of the Second Temple, the subject of the resurrection had become a point of controversy between the Pharisees and the Sadducees which can be documented from the New Testament as well as from other early contemporary sources.[37] In Buddhagosha's *Visuddhimagga,* the interdependence of mentality and materiality is discussed. It is in this context that the parable appears in the *Visuddhimagga.*[38] In a different milieu, it was the question concerning the resurrection and the judgment of the body and the soul which influenced Epiphanius to include the reference in his compendium of heresy refutations. Moore's initial suggestion that the parable was derived from Indian thought seems sound, though this question must be thoroughly researched by authorities in ancient Indian literature and its sources.[39] The theological question dealt with in this parable occupied the interest of a number of cultures in late antiquity which is indicated by the circulation of the motif. In talmudic literature, the longer story in the Apocryphon of Ezekiel appears in the streamlined form and structure of the rabbinic parable. Here the channels (Jewish, non-Jewish; Hellenistic, non-Hellenistic) through which this parable was transmitted into the literature of ancient Israel are less important than its function in the context of the midrash.

In the Apocryphon of Ezekiel the king is preparing a wedding feast for his son.[40] The wedding feast motif is a common theme in other rabbinic parables but interestingly enough it does not appear in any of the parallels from talmudic literature. This parable also appears in Midrash Tanchuma, Leviticus Rabbah, and the Mechilta Derabbi Simeon bar Yochai.[41] In the Midrash Tanchuma the parable comes as an explanation of the verse, "Say to the people of Israel, If any one (נפש) sins unwittingly . . ." (Leviticus 4:2). This biblical passage is also cited in Leviticus Rabbah and in the Yalkut. The Hebrew word for soul *nefesh* is the connecting word in the midrash. The darshan explains how the soul that sins will be judged with his body. Midrash Tanchuma adds the detail that the king sought guards who would not be able to steal his fruit and thus chose a blind man and a lame person. This is probably a later aggrandizement.[42] The parable is preserved anonymously in Midrash Tanchuma. In Leviticus Rabbah it is attributed to R. Ishmael and the parable is cited in I. Al-Nakawa's *Menorat Hamaor* in the name of R. Simeon.[43] In the Mechilta Derabbi Ishmael as well as in the Mechilta Derabbi Simeon bar Yochai and the Babylonian Talmud, the context of the parable is R. Judah the Prince's answer to Antoninus' inquiry. These sources connect Psalm 50:4 with the conclusion of the story, "He calls to the heavens above and to the earth, that he may judge his people." This interpretation is also reflected in Midrash Hagadol (cf. Midrash Tannaim), "R. Simlai says, 'How do you know that there is not a portion of the Torah in which the resurrection of the dead does not appear, but we are not able to interpret it? It was said, 'He calls to the heaven above,' this means to bring the soul, 'and to the earth' this means to bring the body. Afterward, he judges it together with the body (עִמּוֹ instead of עַמּוֹ, Psalm 50:4)'."[44] Thus at the resurrection of the dead, the body and the soul are reunited to be judged together.

Not all agreed with this interpretation. Compare the statement of R. Eleazar, "All that is in heaven was created out of heaven, and all that is on earth was created out of the earth." R. Joshua disagreed and maintained, "All that is in heaven and on earth was created from nought but heaven."[45] In fact in the continuation of the passage from Leviticus Rabbah, a different opinion is expressed by R. Chiya.[46] The tradition is paralleled in Midrash Hagadol where it is attributed to R. Levi.[47] Several manuscripts of Leviticus Rabbah also attribute this second opinion to R. Levi.[48] According to R. Chiya (R. Levi), only the soul will be held responsible and the body will not be judged. In order to prove his point, he tells a parable. Hence here is an example where one parable is used to argue one side of an argument and then another parable is employed to prove the opposite side.

THE PRIEST'S DAUGHTER AND THE *TERUMAH*

R. Chiya taught: This may be compared to a priest who had two wives, one the daughter of a priest, and the other the daughter of an Israelite, and handed to them dough of *terumah,* and they rendered it unclean. Said he to them: 'Who made the dough unclean?' Each said that the other had made it unclean. What did the priest do? He let the daughter of the Israelite alone, and began taking to task the daughter of the priestly family. Said she to him: 'My lord priest, why are you letting the daughter of the Israelite alone, and taking me to task? Have you not handed it [i.e. the dough] to both of us alike?' Said he to her: 'She is the daughter of an Israelite, and is not trained [in the laws appertaining to *terumah*] from her father's house; but you are so trained from your father's

> house, and for this reason I am leaving her alone, and taking you to task.' Even so will it be in the time to come. The soul and the body will be standing for judgment. What will the Holy One, blessed be He, do? He will let the body alone, and take the soul to task. The latter will say before Him: 'O Lord of the Universe, we have sinned both of us as one; why dost Thou let the body alone, and take me to task?' He will answer her: 'The body is from the lower [earthly] regions, from a place where they sin, but thou art from the upper [celestial] regions, from a place where they do not sin. Therefore do I let the body alone, and take you to task.'

The Mechilta alludes to this argument when R. Judah says, "Rather than ask me about the body which is impure, ask me about the soul that is pure."[49] This aspect of the issue is made clearer in the Midrash Hagadol. It does not cite the first parable about the lame and the blind. However the second illustration does appear and the conclusion of the text emphasizes the distinction between the "pure" and the "impure."[50] This should be connected to the Mechilta where the same terminology is used. The mention of the "pure" (soul) and the "impure" (body) alludes to the second argument which states that only the soul will be judged. This treatment is very closely connected to the parable which speaks about the priest with two wives. The wife who was the daughter of a priest was expected to be more cautious in matters of purity than the second wife who was the daughter of a common Israelite (non-priest).

The function of the parables in these texts is very instructive. They are used to argue both sides of an issue concerning the resurrection of the dead and the judgment of the soul. On the one hand, the tradition has been preserved in written form with its parallels in various texts. On the other hand one can easily recognize the live discussion that preceded the composition of these parables in writing.

Sifra: Torat Kohanim

Sifra is another of the works referred to as Midrashe Halacha. It contains a mixture of both agadah and halachah but deals with numerous halachic questions as it provides comment on the book of Leviticus.[51] This midrashic work contains fewer parables than the other early tannaitic texts from this collection of Midrashe Halacha. One could note that the Mishnah and the Tosefta also do not preserve as many parables in relation to the volume of material as some of these other more agadic midrashim. While agadah seems to be the area where parabolic teaching was more widely proliferated, one can observe how the parable functioned to interpret the biblical text and to deal with the complexities of the halachah in daily life.

SIFRA ON LEVITICUS 1:2 (WEISS, 4D)

The exegesis of the book of Leviticus was of great interest and according to tradition it was the first book that a child studied.[52] The first parable to be considered here is one that deals with the interpretation of the biblical text.[53] It explains the second verse of Leviticus which begins to describe the sacrificial system of ancient Israel: "The LORD called Moses, and spoke to him from the tent of meeting, saying, 'Speak to the people of Israel, and say to them, When any of you brings an offering to the LORD, you shall bring your offering of cattle *(behemah)* from the herd or from the flock . . .'" (Leviticus 1:1–2).

THE SERVANT AND HIS MASTER'S COMMAND

> "An offering to the LORD" (Leviticus 1:2). The word animals *(behemah)* from this verse can mean all living things that are referred to as animals, "These are the living things which you may eat among all the beasts *(behemah)* that are on the earth" (Leviticus 11:2). But it says "from the herd or from the flock," (Leviticus 1:2). He may not present it, but if he does it must be fit. A parable to one who was told by his master, "Go and bring me wheat." But he went and brought him both wheat and barley. Thus he added to his command, as it says, "from the herds and from the flocks you shall bring offerings." However, here the only meaning of the term animals *(behemah)* is herds and flocks. To what may it

be compared, to one who was told by his master, "Do not bring me anything but wheat." If he brings anything in addition to the wheat, he will have transgressed the command of his master.

In many ways these two examples which function together to clarify a particular halachic question are borderline parables. However one discerns two simple illustrations which both contain a master, a servant who is given a command and the action that results. But these brief parabolic examples are cited merely to elucidate a text from the Torah. They employ a hermeneutical principle outlined in the beginning of this midrash. This rule of interpretation is referred to as "the general and the specific" (כלל ופרט). This aspect of the text has been explained by Z. Rapoport and further explored by L. Finkelstein.[54] The general term "animals" *(behemah)* is limited by the more specific terms that follow—namely "from the herds and from the flocks." The parables have been used to demonstrate this point and clarify a possible ambiguity in the biblical text. This seems to be a literary usage of the parable.

SIFRA ON LEVITICUS 20:21 (WEISS, 93b)

This parable is another example of an illustration based upon the biblical text. A similar parable appears elsewhere in Sifre Deuteronomy (section 43), but one discerns a number of differences.[55] Here the parable is merely a picture that depicts the verse from Leviticus 18:28.[56]

THE PRINCE'S STOMACH

"Lest the land vomit you out, when you defile it . . ." (Leviticus 18:28). The land of Israel is not like other lands because it will not tolerate transgressors.[57] They tell a parable, to what may the matter be compared? To the son of kings who was fed something which his stomach could not bear. He vomited it up. Thus it is with the land of Israel which cannot tolerate transgressors. Thus it was said, "Lest the land vomit you out, when you defile it, as it vomited out the nation that was before you" (Leviticus 18:28).

The parable is closely connected to the interpretation of the biblical verse. In fact, already in the passage from Leviticus which employs this coarse expression, "the land vomited out its inhabitants" (18:25), one discovers that the darshan in Sifra explains the literal meaning from the text using parabolic language, "*Like* a man who vomits up his food."[58] The parable illustrates the significance of the land, the people and the law in Jewish thought. In fact, later the text of Sifra records, "Every Israelite who dwells in the land of Israel receives upon himself the yoke of the kingdom of heaven."[59] The land was defiled by its former inhabitants and they were expelled. The people of Israel must observe the commandments. Transgression by the inhabitants of the land will lead to exile.[60]

Sifre Numbers

Epstein pointed out that the interpretation of the Torah in this collection of midrashic works known as the Midrashe Halacha is representative of the "Talmud" that was employed by the Tannaim.[61] Hence the interpretation of the biblical text and its relationship to halachic matters in everyday Jewish life naturally were of supreme importance to the Tannaim. The hermeneutical principles adopted to interpret the Torah would affect many aspects of daily life.[62] Like the Mechilta, Sifre Numbers is comprised of a considerable amount of agadah. These portions of teaching can provide insights into early rabbinic exegesis as well as homiletical orations.

SIFRE NUMBERS 131

This portion of Sifre Numbers deals with the interpretation of the verse, "While Israel dwelt [sat down] in Shittim the people began to play the harlot with daughters of Moab" (Numbers 25:1).[63] The discussion that follows this passage revolves around principles of interpretation. Sifre Numbers describes the argument between Rabbi Akiva and Rabbi. According to the parallel in the Yalkut Shimeoni and a Vatican manuscript of Sifre Numbers, Rabbi is Rabbi Meir.[64] The verbal identity of this parallel from the Yalkut is very close to the text in Sifre Numbers and this seems to be an indication that the Yalkut Shimeoni was quoting another version of Sifre Numbers. Friedmann accepted the attribution to R. Meir and there seems little reason to question it because of the chronological considerations. In this passage, Rabbi Akiva supports his argument by telling three imaginative parables. Here is the context of the parables.

> "And Israel sat down in Shittim and the people began to commit whoredom" (Numbers 25:1). Wherever in Scripture [the words] "they sat down" occur, it is connected with moral degradation; for instance: "And the people sat down to eat and to drink, and rose up to play;" or (Gen. 37:25): "And they (Joseph's brethren) sat down to eat bread (before selling Joseph)." R. Akiba says: "Every section in Scripture is explained by the one that stands next to it." Said R. [Meir]: "There are sections which are close to one another and yet as distant as is the East from the West in subject matter. For instance, we read (Ex. 6:18): "Behold the children of Israel will not listen to me." [And, as if in answer to this] God said unto him (Moses): "They will listen to my voice" (Ex. 3:18). On the other hand, we read (Lev. 21:9): "And the daughter of any priest, if she profane herself by playing the whore . . . shall be burnt with fire," and immediately following it we read (v. 10): "And if the high priest," etc. (and there is no connection at all with the preceding verse)." [Said R. Akiba: "There is a connection], for when a priest's daughter is burnt for immorality, a high priest is, so to speak, burnt with her." Here is a parable . . .

The argument concerns the hermeneutical principle employed by R. Akiva, "Every section in Scripture is explained by the one that stands next to it" (כל פרשה שהיא סמוכה

לחברתה למודה הימנה). Bacher pointed out that R. Eleazar used this principle before R. Akiva but that R. Akiva incorporated it into his more developed system of biblical interpretation.[66] Akiva is well known for his stress on the importance of each aspect of the biblical narrative. He would even consider the significance of *scriptio defectiva* as opposed to *scriptio plena* or any kind of word duplication or repetition in a text—many of which were mere linguistic characteristics of biblical Hebrew. This approach has often been contrasted to R. Ishmael who maintained that the words of the Torah are to be interpreted as the words of men.[67] R. Meir objects to R. Akiva's methodology. He maintains that some passages adjacent to one another may not be related and provides prooftexts to make his contention clear. The entire question is important for the study of scripture and could have far-reaching effects on halachic matters. R. Akiva is prepared to argue his point and takes R. Meir's last prooftext as his point of departure.

R. Meir had maintained that the text, "And the daughter of any priest if she profane herself by playing the harlot . . . shall be burnt with fire" (Leviticus 21:9) was not connected with the following verse, "And if the high priest . . ." (Leviticus 21:10). R. Akiva maintained that there is a connection because by executing the priest's daughter one is also preventing her from bearing children—one of whom could even have been the high priest himself. This aspect of the question emerges from his parable. The argument is a strong one in the thought of the sages who taught that one who takes the life of a man destroys an entire world.[68] Therefore the parable is much more than a discussion of hermeneutics but also has profound moral implications and shows R. Akiva's approach toward the value of human life and the requirements of virtuous conduct. R. Akiva artfully argues his position by three parables.

THE CENTURION WHO BECAME A DESERTER

Here is a parable. To what may it be compared? Unto a centurion who had served his term but failed to enter his primipilate[69] (to which he would have been promoted in due time), and fled. The king sent after him, and when he was brought back, the king commanded

> that the head of the deserter be cut off. Before the execution, the king said: "Fill a vessel with golden denarii and carry it before him, and say unto him: 'If you had behaved like your colleagues, you would have received the vessel of golden denarii, and [preserved] your soul, but now, you have lost both your soul and your money!' So also with the daughter of a priest who has played the harlot; the high-priest goes in front of her and says to her, 'If you had behaved in the way which your mothers had behaved, you may have been found worthy to become the ancestress of a high-priest in like manner.[70] But now you have lost both yourself and your honor!'" Thus these two sections, "And the daughter of any priest . . ." (Lev. 21:9) and "The priest who is chief among his brethren . . ." (Lev. 21:10), are brought together.

The parable is the result of the discussion of the meaning of scriptural passages and their proper interpretation. It is important to understand clearly the context of this discussion because one discerns several points of comparison between the parable and the illustrand. Unlike most rabbinic parables, the king figure in Akiva's illustration does not represent God. This is also the case in Jesus' parable concerning the cost of discipleship (Luke 14:31–33). Here the king is compared to the high priest. The priest's daughter who went astray (from Leviticus 21:9) is identified in the parable with the centurion who abandoned the king before he received his position in his primipilate. Both receive the sentence of execution. R. Akiva then connects the high priest with the king who gives the sentence. Hence R. Akiva has employed the parable to prove that there is a reason for these two verses to be located next to each other. According to Sifre, he uses two other parables to strengthen his argument. Whether all three of these parables originate with R. Akiva or are the result of the compilation of the midrash in its literary stage is difficult to determine with absolute certainty.

THE KING WHO WAS RECONCILED WITH HIS WIFE

> Similarly it says (Hos. 1:9): "For ye are not my people," and [immediately afterwards] it says (1:10): "And the

> number of the children of Israel shall be as the sand of the sea, which cannot be measured nor numbered; and it shall come to pass that in the place where it was said unto them: 'Ye are not my people [there it shall be said unto them, ye are sons of the living God].'" What connection is there between these verses? It is like unto a king who, being angry with his wife, sent for a scribe to come and write for her a bill of divorce. [But] before the scribe arrived the king was again reconciled with his wife. Said the king [at the arrival of the scribe]: "Should the scribe go back as soon as he has come, without having done anything?" Therefore he said to him: "Come and write that I have doubled her dowry." Thus it was said, "For ye are not my people," (Hos. 1:9) and "the number of the children of Israel shall be as the sand of the sea" (Hos. 1:10).

This parable is used to illustrate the relationship between two adjacent verses that seem to contradict one another. Again one can see some points of comparison. The king is God and the queen is Israel. The use of these motifs was widespread in the parabolic teaching of Israel's sages.[71] One might ask if the scribe here could be representative of the prophet—but care must be exercised in taking the representative elements of the illustration too far. The parable is a colorful illustration and reinforces the point of the previous parable. The third and final parable is also based upon verses from Hosea.[72]

THE GENERAL AND THE REBELLIOUS PROVINCE

> Similarly it says (Hos. 13:16): "Samaria must be condemned, for she hath rebelled against her God," and [immediately afterwards] it says: "Return, O Israel, upon the Lord thy God" (Hos. 14:1) What is the connection? Here is a parable. To what may it be compared? Unto a province which rebelled against its king. The king sent out a general with orders to devastate that province. That general was experienced and coolheaded. He said to them (the rebellious province):

> "Take heed! Otherwise I will do unto you as I have done unto this province and its allies, and unto that colony and its allies." Thus it was said: "Samaria must be condemned, for she has rebelled against her God," (Hos. 13:16) and [immediately afterwards]: "Return, O Israel" (Hos. 14:1).

The final illustration in this threesome is somewhat similar to the previous one. Two contradictory verses are explained. Even though Samaria is condemned one finds a call to repentance which opens the possibility for forgiveness. The king in the parable sends a general to the rebellious province. Somewhat like a prophet of doom, the general warns the people what will happen if they do not submit to the king. Thus the rebellious people who deserve to be punished are given another chance to repent.

This cluster of parables attributed to R. Akiva in Sifre Numbers are cited after the verse "While Israel dwelt [sat down] in Shittim the people began to play the harlot" (Numbers 25:1). The midrash states that whenever the text describes the people as sitting down, it refers to some kind of moral degradation.[73] R. Akiva's remarks are pertinent to the discussion because the words "While Israel sat down" are situated next to the phrase, "the people began to play the harlot." Hence R. Akiva's arguments which are employed to counter R. Meir's objection are formulated in imaginative parables. These parables and the conclusions based upon this approach are accepted into Sifre Numbers without additional criticism.

Other questions remain to be asked. Were these parables originally connected to this discussion on Numbers 25:1 or were they more likely cited on another occasion and later transferred to a new context? Even though this question is difficult to answer with certainty, it should be noted that these parables would have been suitable in other contexts as well. Of course many references appear in rabbinic literature concerning the exegetical approach of R. Akiva and these parables deal with his methodology in interpretation of the biblical text. In a famous passage, R. Ishmael accuses R. Akiva of devoting too much attention to each word and detail of the text. As Safrai has pointed out, the differences between R. Akiva and R. Ishmael are connected to their respective teachers.[74] R. Akiva was influenced by his master, R. Nahum Eish Gimzo. According to tradition, R. Akiva served his master twenty-two years during which time they studied the meaning of every occurrence of the untranslatable Hebrew particle *et* (את) in the Torah.[75] The Torah is divine and no word or particle was to be viewed as superfluous.[76] These three imaginative parables from Sifre Numbers demonstrate how well R. Akiva could defend his position. The evidence from the literature indicates that he was a dramatic preacher and certainly had a significant influence on the formation of Jewish halachah.[77] One should point out that parabolic instruction was most certainly an integral part of his dynamic teaching. Moreover as has been noted above, his most illustrious disciple, R. Meir, was known to have three hundred fox parables (fables) even though only a small number of them have been preserved.[78] R. Akiva is also known to have taught in Fox parables (e.g. b. Berachot 61b).[79] Again, his famous fox parable was a reply to the complaint of another colleague. During the persecution when Jews were forbidden to study Torah, R. Akiva continued teaching in spite of the dangers. Pappus b. Judah cautioned him and asked if he were not afraid of the consequences of his activities. R. Akiva responded to this question with an illustration:

THE FOX AND THE FISH

> I will explain to you with a parable. A fox was once walking alongside of a river, and he saw fishes going in swarms from one place to another. He said to them: From what are you fleeing? They replied: From the nets cast for us by men. He said to them: Would you like to come up on to dry land so that you and I can live together in the way that my ancestors lived with your ancestors? They replied: Art thou the one that they call the cleverest of animals? Thou art not clever but foolish. If we are afraid in the element in which we live, how much more in the element in which we would die! So it is with us. If such is our condition when we sit and study the Torah, of which it is written, 'For that is thy life and

the length of thy days,' if we go and neglect it how much worse off we shall be!

The Talmud relates that soon both R. Akiva and Pappus b. Judah were arrested and imprisoned. Nevertheless one can see how R. Akiva utilized a parable in order to answer the critical comments of his colleague. Since R. Akiva used fox parables in his instruction, it seems only natural that R. Meir's parabolic teaching was one of the ways that his teacher had influenced him. One must ask: Can the three hundred fox parables attributed to R. Meir—not to mention other parables—be accepted as an indication of how widely the parable was used in R. Meir's instruction in particular? To what extent may this have been representative of other sages as well? At least R. Meir seems to have followed R. Akiva in the use of parabolic instruction. Unfortunately only a comparative few parables have survived the process of transmission. Needless to say, the number three hundred does not have to be taken literally but signifies a great many and probably refers to variations of a basic pattern. At any rate these illustrations cited from Sifre Numbers and b. Berachot which were attributed to R. Akiva are depicted as having been told in the context of lively discussions. Apparently other parables were never transmitted from the oral stratum of the tradition into the literary stage.

Sifre Deuteronomy

Although the Talmud ascribes all anonymous statements in Sifre Deuteronomy to R. Simeon, most modern authorities have suggested that the present text has been influenced by the school of R. Akiva (cf. b. Sanhedrin 86a).[80] The work is connected to the biblical text of Deuteronomy and contains both agadah and halachah.[81] Here some of its parables will be examined in light of the context in which they appear.

SIFRE DEUTERONOMY PISKA 19 (P. 31)

As already noted, Sifre Deuteronomy contains a running commentary on the biblical book of the Torah for which it is named. The parable of "The Prince and his Inheritance" comes as an explanation of a specific narrative in Deuteronomy.[82] The parable is connected to the passage, "And I said to you, 'You have come to the hill country of the Amorites, which the LORD our God gives us. Behold, the LORD your God has set the land before you; go up, take possession, as the LORD, the God of your fathers, has told you; do not fear or be dismayed.'"[83] The parable is an illustration which describes the biblical text.

THE PRINCE AND HIS INHERITANCE

> "You have come to the hill country of the Amorites, which the LORD our God gives us" (Deuteronomy 1:20). A parable to a king who entrusted his son to a guardian. He took him and showed him around saying, 'All of these grapevines are yours. All of these olive trees[81] belong to you.' After [the guardian] had tired of showing him [his possessions,] he said, 'Everything that you see is yours!' Thus for the forty years that Israel was in the wilderness, Moses would say to them, "For the LORD your God is bringing you into a good land, a land of brooks of water, of fountains and springs flowing forth in valleys and hills" (Deut. 8:7). Because they came to the land, he said to them, "You have come to the hill country of the Amorites, which the LORD our God gives us" (Deut. 1:20). If you will say, 'The time has not yet arrived,' [you are mistaken]—the time has arrived! "Behold the LORD your God gives the land before you" (Deut. 1:21). I am not repeating a conjecture or hearsay—but what your eyes see, "Go up, take possession immediately, as the LORD, the God of your fathers, has told you" (Deut. 1:21).

The motifs used in this illustration are those which are common in other rabbinic parables. G. Kittel has referred to this parable as an allegory.[85] This terminology is entirely inadequate when one tries to describe this parable as a literary phenomenon in the context of the midrash.[86] True the son is representative of Israel, the guardian stands for Moses and the inheritance is connected to the promised land. But these motifs and their points of comparison are not unusual in parabolic instruction and should not be defined as pure allegory. Perhaps the more important aspect of this illustration is its relationship to the verse which it serves to explain. Here the parable is linked directly to the illustrand which is known from the biblical passage. This connection is clear from the explanation of the parable where the words of the verses themselves are interpreted on the basis of the story. The Israelites are permitted to view their future inheritance when they come to the mount of the Amorites. The parable emerges almost like a three dimensional picture of the biblical text. The emphasis is that the land is already theirs. The parable appears in the same context of Deuteronomy 1:20–21 in the Midrash Hagadol on Deuteronomy (cf. Midrash Tannaim).[87] Like here, the parable is anonymous in these parallels and the earliest reference seems to be this text from Sifre Deuteronomy.

Interestingly enough, the more or less same parable appears later on in Sifre Deuteronomy—but with a different application. Again it is related to a biblical verse from Deuteronomy. As in the first instance of this parable, it has parallels in the Midrash Hagadol (and cf. Midrash Tannaim) but with some slight variations.[88] In these parallels one discovers that like the second context in Sifre Deuteronomy, the illustration is employed to communicate a new theme. The parable also appears in the Yalkut Machiri on Psalms, where it is closer to the wording of the text in Sifre Deuteronomy than the other parallels.[89] In this second context, the parable is connected to the verse: "Blessed are you, O Israel! Who is like you, a people saved by the LORD" (Deuteronomy 33:29).

THE MAN'S SON AND HIS INHERITANCE

> "Blessed are you, O Israel!" (Deuteronomy 33:29)—Israel answers, "Who is like you, among the gods?" (Exodus 15:11). And the Holy Spirit says: "Blessed are you, O Israel!" (Deut. 33:29) "Blessed are you, O Israel . . ." All of Israel gathered before Moses. They said to him, 'Moses our teacher, tell us what good will the Holy One Blessed be He bestow upon us in the future.' He

> replied, 'I do not know what to tell you. Blessed are you because of what has been prepared for you.' A parable to a man who entrusted his son to a guardian. He took him and showed him around saying, 'All of these trees are yours. All of these grapevines belong to you and all of these olive trees are yours.' After [the guardian] had tired of showing him [his inheritance], he said, 'I do not know what to tell you—blessed are you because of what has been prepared for you.' "O how abundant is thy goodness which thou hast laid up for those who fear thee" (Psalm 31:19, Heb. vs. 20). "Blessed are you, O Israel! Who is like you, a people saved by the LORD" (Deut. 33:29), for there is no salvation but that obtained in His Presence. Israel is saved in the LORD—an everlasting salvation.

In the first case, the parable is employed in Sifre Deuteronomy to illustrate Israel's future inheritance in the land of Canaan. In the second case this illustration has been used to describe Israel's future salvation and blessedness in the world to come. Hence the same parable has been given two different applications in the very same midrash! In the first parable, the illustration speaks about a king and his son. Here the same story is told about "a man," who replaces the king character. Obviously it would seem that adaptation of a man to a king is the later development. Most probably a number of king parables originated as illustrations about "a man."[90] Some parables require a king figure. Here a man who owned property was sufficient. The fact that only one (possibly two) of Jesus' parables originally spoke about a king is another indication that this may well be a later adaptation (Luke 14:31–33; Matthew 18:23–35?). The motifs of "a householder" or simply "a man" are probably earlier than the wide proliferation of "the king" character in parables that do not require royalty. Nevertheless some early story parables require a king and it would be a mistake to suggest that all these illustrations are late. The natural tendency to aggrandize a parable can be further observed by some of the elements in the parallel from the Midrash Hagadol to this second illustration in Sifre Deuteronomy:

THE PRINCE SEES HIS INHERITANCE AT HIS WEDDING

> "Blessed are you, O Israel! Who is like you?" (Deuteronomy 33:29). Because Moses saw what was prepared for the righteous in the future, he said to them, 'I do not know what to tell you, but blessed are you because of what has been prepared for you.' They tell a parable. To what may the matter be compared? To a king who was giving his son in marriage. As the son stood under his marriage canopy *(chupato),* [the king] showed him and explained to him, 'My son, all these fields are yours, all of these vineyards are yours, all of these olive trees belong to you, and all of these palaces are yours.' Finally when the king had tired of showing his son [his inheritance], he said to him, 'My son, I do not know what to tell you, but everything that your eyes see in the world—belongs to you!' Thus because Moses saw what was prepared for the righteous in the future, he said, 'I do not know what to tell you, but blessed are you because of what has been prepared for you.'

The obvious element that has been added to this version of the parable is the marriage motif.[91] This theme is reminiscent of other traditions which speak of the joy of the world to come in terms of a wedding. Hence the king is showing his son all his inheritance while he stands under his wedding canopy. It is a colorful picture of God and the people of Israel. The fact that this is a later aggrandisement can be demonstrated because the parallel in the Yalkut Machiri does not contain any reference to a wedding celebration. However one notes immediately that the guardian (the Moses figure) has been eliminated possibly to emphasize the intimacy between God and Israel. Hence in the first instance of this parable in Sifre Deuteronomy (Piska 19)[92] the role of Moses is stressed. In addition, in the first appearance of this parable the text emphasizes that the people may enter the promised land "immediately" (מיד)—because it has already been given to them. However in the second case, the present reality is completely dispensed with, as the parable functions to describe Israel's future blessedness.

This illustration demonstrates how the same parable can be used for different purposes. One famous example of this phenomenon is the argument between the House of Shammai and the House of Hillel over the creation of the world. Both use a parable to support their positions, and both their illustrations are very similar one to the other.[93] Here the case is somewhat different. The same parable is employed to illustrate two different points in divergent contexts. This simply illustrates the flexibility and adaptability of parabolic instruction which is probably one of the causes that contributed to its wide usage in the literature. Here the parable has been utilized as an exegetical tool that elucidates the text in two diverse contexts. Hence in the darshan's treatment of the first chapter of Deuteronomy, a parable is employed to illustrate the relationship between God, Moses and the promised land which is offered as a present reality and also near the conclusion of Deuteronomy, the same illustration is used to describe Israel's future salvation in the world to come.

Pesikta Derav Kahana

The next section of this treatment of selected rabbinic parables will discuss a number of examples from Pesikta Derav Kahana and Seder Eliyahu. Sometimes these texts have been referred to as "homiletical midrashim." This term is more appropriate for the Pesikta than it is for Seder Eliyahu.[94] Among other materials, the Pesikta is a collection of *derashot* and homiletic pieces. The original context of all these materials is unknown but many of the *derashot* from the Pesikta are probably derived from homilies that were delivered on special occasions, on Sabbaths and on the Jewish festivals. Seder Eliyahu has a wealth of *derashot,* but is more thematic and concentrates more on ethical aspects of the Jewish faith.

Pesikta Derav Kahana 3:1

This parasha in the midrash Pesikta Derav Kahana deals with the episode of the battle between Israel and Amalek.[95] It takes Deuteronomy 25:17 as its point of departure, "Remember what Amalek did to you on the way as you came out of Egypt." After the proem from Proverbs 19:25 and some brief introductory comments, the parasha preserves a parable attributed to R. Levi (the two other parables in Piska 3 are also attributed to R. Levi). Why was Amalek permitted to attack Israel? According to the rabbis, it was because Israel had failed to remain true to the Torah. In fact in the following verse in Deuteronomy where it says, "He did not fear God" (25:18), most commentators have interpreted the passage as referring to Amalek. Not so in the mind of Israel's sages. According to their interpretation, this verse which speaks about the one who did not fear God refers to Israel and *not* to Amalek. Even the place where the event took place, Rephidim (from Exodus 17:7), is interpreted to mean "weak hands" (רפיון ידים).[96] In other words, Israel's hands had been weakened in obeying the law. Here is the context of the parable in the midrash.

> In a comment on "Remember what Amalek did unto thee" (Deut. 25:17) is cited the verse "When thou smitest a scorner, the simple will become prudent" (Prov. 19:25). By "scorner" in the words "When thou smitest a scorner" is meant Amalek; and by "simple" in the words "the simple will become prudent" is meant Jethro. When Amalek came to fight against Israel, what does Scripture say? "Then came Amalek, and fought with Israel on account of Rephidim" (Exod. 17:8) for before Amalek's attack Israel's hands had let go both Torah and commandments.[97] The actual name of the place was Massah-and-Meribah (Trying-and-strife), as revealed by the verse just preceding: "The Omnipresent called the name thereof Massah-and-Meribah (Trying-and-strife)" (Exod. 17:7). The Blessed One had so named it in His anguished crying out "At the striving of the children of Israel [against Him], and because they tried Him (ibid)." At that time Moses likewise had cried out in anguish saying, "Why strive ye with me? Wherefore do ye try the Lord?" (Exodus 17:2).

The proem mentions Jethro which becomes a proleptic reference to his future conversion. Thus the proem connects the episode of Israel's battle against Amalek with Jethro's reaction to the miracles that God had performed for Israel against Egypt and Amalek because in the continuation of the passage Jethro converts.[98] The parable that follows has a number of parallels in other midrashim.[99] In Exodus Rabbah one finds an abbreviated form of the parable which is preserved anonymously. Like midrash Tanchuma (not Buber's edition) and the Yalkut Shimeoni, Pesikta Derav Kahana attributes the illustration to R. Levi.[100] Here is the parable as it appears in the text of the Pesikta:

THE SPOILED SON

> R. Levi said: To what may Israel be compared? To one who had a son whom he placed on his shoulder and took to the market. There, when the son saw a desirable object, he said to his father, "Buy it for me," and his father bought for him what he wanted the first time he asked, the second time, and the third. But then, when the son saw someone whom he asked, "Have you seen my father?" He said to his son: "You fool, you are astride my shoulder, whatever you wish I buy for you, and yet you ask that man, 'Have you seen my father?'" What did the father do then? He threw his son from his shoulder, and a dog came and bit the son. Thus, after Israel went out of Egypt, the Holy One, encompassed them with seven clouds of glory, as is said "He compassed him about, He cared for him" (Deut. 32:10). They asked for manna: He gave it. For quail: He gave them. After He gave all that they asked, they proceeded to ruminate "Is the Lord among us, or not?" (Exod. 17:7). The Holy One said to them: You ruminate as to My presence in your midst? As you live, I shall make you aware of it. Here is a dog to bite you. And who was the dog? Amalek, for the very next verse in Exodus says, "Then came Amalek" (Exodus 17:8). Thus it was said, "Remember" (Deuteronomy 25:17).

R. Levi was a third generation Palestinian Amora who has often been noted as a master of the agadah.[101] He even served twenty-two years as the salaried darshan at R. Johanan's academy in Tiberias where he taught on the Sabbaths and delivered sermons.[102] His success as an agadist can be seen by the fact that although R. Zeira objected to agadic teaching, he instructed his disciples to go and listen to R. Levi because he always made original contributions.[103] One aspect of early rabbinic exposition involved "stringing pearls"—or connecting verses together from the Torah, the Prophets and the Writings.[104] Concerning this procedure, R. Levi commented, "Some are able to link together but not to penetrate, and some are able to penetrate but not to link together. But I am an expert both at linking and penetrating."[105] This demonstrates R. Levi's confidence in his own ability. As Bacher pointed out, R. Levi passes on traditions from early Amoraim and even from a number of Tannaim.[106] In addition, numerous parables have been attributed to R. Levi and this seems to be one of the essential elements of his teachings.

The parable cited here is a colorful illustration which describes the relationship between God and Israel. One may even discern some apologetic motives both in the realm of theodicy and perhaps in regards to Israel's misbehavior as described in the biblical text. God was justified in allowing Amalek to do battle with Israel because the people had forgotten their Father. The points of comaprison between the motifs of the father and son and between God and Israel is not that widespread. Probably some of the parables concerning king and prince were originally about father and son. A rabbinic parable which is similar to this illustration is that from the Mechilta where the father saves his son from successive dangers. This parable has been discussed above.[107] Also Jesus told the parable of the son who makes requests to his father (Matthew 7:7–11 and Luke 11:9–13). In the double tradition of the gospels, the application makes use of the *argumentum a minori ad maius* (קל וחמר, compare the Greek words πόσῳ μᾶλλου), if a father will provide his son with his needs how much more will God answer the petitions of his children who approach him in prayer.

The son is placed upon the shoulders of the father and has his every desire fulfilled. This describes a spoiled child. The interpretation that follows the important connecting word "thus" (כך) shows the relationship between the illustration and the illustrand and how it is a picture of the experiences of the children of Israel in the wilderness. Hence the *Bild* and the *Sache* are interrelated. The crisis of the story appears when the child forgets his father in spite of the fact that he is riding on his shoulders and receives everything he wants. The father throws the spoiled child down and the dog comes and bites him. The dog is obviously connected to Amalek.[108] However, in the parallels the dog does not always appear.[109] It may be a later addition as the main point of the parable is that Israel had forgotten their Father in heaven. The crisis aspect of the illustration could be adequately accentuated by the action of the father when he throws the child down from his shoulders. Compare how the dog is used in the parable concerning the king's son who breaks into his father's vineyard. After he enters the vineyard, the prince is bitten by the guard dog.[110] All in all the parable of "The Spoiled Son" emphasizes the intimacy between the people of Israel and their Father in heaven by picturing this relationship in terms of the closeness of family ties. Thus this parable is much more than an illustration of a biblical text and may very well exemplify early rabbinic preaching which by no means should be characterized as dry, legalistic or pedantic.

Pesikta Derav Kahana 12:24

The ten commandments are the subject of great interest for the sages and it is no surprise that the initial words of the decalogue from Exodus 20:2 became a matter of discussion. This is the context of the next parable. In Pesikta Derav Kahana it is attributed to the fourth generation Palestinian Amora, R. Nehemiah. In some of the parallels to the parable, both R. Yudah and R. Nehemiah are mentioned in the context but the parable itself is preserved in the name of R. Yudah.[111] The following is the text according to Pesikta Derav Kahana:

THE PRINCE WHO WAS CAPTURED

> R. Nehemiah said: What is *anochi?* It is from the Egyptian language. To what may the matter be compared? To a mortal king whose son had been captured. The son

spent a great many days among his captors, until the king, cloaked in vengeance, went to free his son. He brought him back, and then found that he had to talk with him in the captors' speech. Thus it was with the Blessed One. Israel had spent all the years of their servitude in Egypt where they learned the Egyptian speech. Finally, when the Holy One redeemed them and came to give them the Torah, they could not understand it. So the Holy One Blessed be He said: I will speak to them in the Egyptian language. Thereupon the Holy One used the word *anochi* which is a form of the Egyptian *anoch.* Thus the Holy One began to speak with them in their acquired way of speaking: "I *(anochi)* am the Lord thy God" (Exodus 20:2).

In Pesikta Rabbati, this same parable is paralleled within the midrashic section that treats the giving of the Torah and especially the decalogue. Buber pointed out that in the Yalkut Shimeoni this parable is cited as if it was actually taken from the Mechilta.[112] However it does not appear in the Mechilta which is extant today. Buber felt that this was a mistake for the Pesikta, but it is possible that the original source for this parable was another midrashic treatment closely connected to the ten commandments like a different version of the Mechilta or its sources which have not been preserved. At this juncture, it is worthwhile to cite the parable as it appears in Pesikta Rabbati.

THE PRINCE WHO WAS SENT TO A DISTANT COUNTRY

R. Judah and R. Nehemiah differed. According to R. Judah, in this particular context the term *anochi* is a way of expressing love, a way of expressing affection. To a king who sent his son away to a far country by the sea where he learned the language of the people by the sea, and when he returned from the far country by the sea, the king began to talk to his son in the language the son had learned. Thus since Israel were in the land of Egypt, they learned the Egyptian speech; and when they came

> before Mount Sinai, the Holy One, blessed be He, began His speaking to them with the word *anochi,* which is *anoch* in Egyptian. R. Nehemiah said: In this particular context *anochi* is a term intended to inspire fear, a term intended to inspire awe . . .

In comparison to the parable in Pesikta Derav Kahana, this version is different in several respects. For one thing R. Judah is not even mentioned in Pesikta Derav Kahana, much less a difference of approach between him and R. Nehemiah. In Pesikta Derav Kahana the idea of rescue is emphasized which is more appropriate for the nimshal, because Israel was being delivered from bondage to the Egyptians. However the common motif of someone being sent to a far away land by the sea may preserve the original storyline of the parable somewhat more accurately. At least it is difficult to imagine the picture of the king outfitting himself for war and sweeping into enemy territory in order to rescue his son from his captors as having being altered to the less colorful story of the son in a far away land.

This parable is another example of the relationship between God and his people Israel. At least in Pesikta Derav Kahana, the theme of God's redemptive act of delivering Israel from their captors and giving the Torah to them is primary while the question concerning the Egyptian origin of the word אנכי is secondary. Out of love, God speaks to his people in the language which they have learned during their captivity.[113] The parable functions to illustrate God's compassion for Israel.

Seder Eliyahu

Like Pesikta Derav Kahana, Seder Eliyahu is sometimes referred to as a homiletical midrash. The text treats many of the basic doctrines of ancient Judaism. It is an ethical treatise par excellence. In this respect, it is closely related to the *Derech Eretz* literature from the minor tractates of the Talmud.[114] Much debate has been aroused by the text's unique style, and approaches to the dating of the midrash vary considerably.[115] In some ways it defies categorization as can be seen by the specialists who have dealt with the text and arrived at quite diverse opinions. It is beyond the scope of the present work to resolve all of the critical problems raised by the unusual style and unique language in the midrash. The text is a thematic treatment of ethical instruction. Nevertheless Seder Eliyahu is not a collection of platitudes but rather it should be described as a creative and an artistic work that is alive and imaginatively deals with well-known themes.[116] The midrash seems to be close to early rabbinic discourse and is rich in parables and agadah.

Seder Eliyahu Rabbah Chap. 1 (p. 4)

The first parable to be treated here is connected to the theme of repentance on the day of atonement.[117] It describes the joy that forgiving Israel brings to God. The parable is unparalleled as far as the present author has been able to determine. The illustration is anonymous which is not at all unusual in so much of the text of Seder Eliyahu.

THE REFUSE ON THE KING'S DOORSTEP

> In another interpretation, the verse "Among the days that were to be fashioned, one of those days was to be wholly His" (Ps. 139:16) is taken to mean that God provided Israel with the Day of Atonement, a day of great joy for Him at whose word the world came into being, for He gave the day to Israel with abounding love. They tell a parable. To what may the matter be compared? To a mortal king whose servants and members of his household used to take the refuse and throw it out before the king's private doorway. When the king left the place and saw the refuse, great was his rejoicing [for he knew that the palace was clean]. Thus we are to understand the Day of Atonement which the Holy One bestowed with abounding love (and joy). Nay more! As God pardons the iniquities of Israel, great is His rejoicing: He has no misgivings. To the mountains and to the hills, to the streams and to the valleys, He says, Come and join Me in My great rejoicing, for I am about to pardon Israel's iniquities.

The Day of Atonement which is ordinarily observed as a solemn day of fasting and soul searching is described in this parable as a great day of rejoicing for God. The parabolist has employed the element of shock in order to surprise and to stimulate. What will the king do to the servants and household members who would dare to throw refuse on his doorway? Instead of becoming angry he rejoices. Again a few points of comparison between the illustration and the illustrand become evident. The king is representative of God and Israel is related to those who empty the garbage upon the king's doorway.

Seder Eliyahu Rabbah Chap. 1 (p. 6)

The following two parables appear as the climax of an argument between the disciple of the wise (סופר)[118] and a fire-worshiping priest (חבר).[119] The scholar has been drafted into the custody of the king. He is told by the priest that he will be released unharmed—if he answers some questions satisfactorily. Here is the context of these parabolic examples:

> One day as I was walking through the greatest city of the world, there was a roundup and I was roughly seized and brought into the king's house where I saw divans lavishly spread and silver vessels and gold vessels set out [in great number]. So, I said, "O LORD, thou God of vengeance, thou God of vengeance, shine forth!" (Ps. 94:1). Presently a [Parsee] priest came to me and asked me, "Are you a scholar?" I replied, "A bit of a one." He said, "If you can answer the particular question I am about to ask, you may go in peace." I replied, "Ask."

The historical setting of this section of Seder Eliyahu Rabbah has been viewed by a number of scholars as providing some important clues regarding the date of the midrash. While no one would cite one section of a midrashic text as sufficient evidence to prove its date, some of the observations made by J. Mann and J. Epstein are important contributions that elucidate the passage at hand. Mann convincingly argues that the event described in the text would be appropriate for the persecutions of Jews by Yezdejerd II (438–457) and Peroz (458–492) in Babylon and in Persia.[120]

The first question of the (Magian) priest regarded the purpose of reptiles and creeping things in the creation. According to Zoroastrian thought, the god of darkness Ahriman was responsible for the creation of these loathsome creatures.[121] The second question regarded the refusal of Jews to recognize that god is fire. The Parsee priest asserts that this is the teaching of the Torah because it is written, "eternal fire" (אש תמיד, Leviticus 6:6). As Mann further pointed out, this question would of course be related to the Zoroastrian belief in Ohrmazd who was identified as the god of fire and light.[122] Hence it seems that Mann's initial observations concerning the historical background of this passage are basically sound. In short the disputation between the sage and the priest described in the context of these two parables reflects the historical situation of the Jews when they were persecuted in Persia under the Sasanids when the Magian priests had powerful influence upon the government.[123] In response to the claim that the Torah teaches that god is fire, the disciple of the wise answers his interrogator by using parables.

THE LASH AND THE ANGEL OF DEATH

> . . . Then the Parsee priest brought up another matter saying, "You assert that fire is not God. Yet is it not written in your Torah 'fire eternal' (Lev. 6:6)?" I replied: "My son, when our forebears stood at Mount Sinai to accept the Torah for themselves, they saw no form resembling a human being, nor resembling the form of any creature, nor resembling the form of anything that has breath which the the Holy One created on the face of the earth, as is said, "Take ye therefore good heed unto yourselves—for ye saw no manner of form on the day that the Lord spoke unto you in Horeb" (Deut. 4:15); they saw only God, the one God—"He is God of gods and Lord of lords" (Deut. 11:17)—whose kingdom stands in heaven and on earth as well as in the highest heaven of heavens. And yet you say that God is fire! It

> is no more than a rod to be used upon men on earth. They tell a parable. To what may the matter be compared? To a king who took a lash and hung it up in his house and then said to his children, to his servants, and to the members of his household, 'With this lash I may strike you, may smite, may even kill you'—threatening them, in order that they would turn away from [sin] and repent. If they do not repent, do not turn back, then God says, 'I will have to strike them with the lash, will have to smite them, will even have to kill them.' Hence "fire eternal" is to be read in the light of the verse "For by fire will the Lord threaten judgment" (Isa. 66:16). Of course you might attempt to refute me by quoting the words "The Lord thy God is a devouring fire" (Deut. 4:24). But they tell a parable. To what may the matter be compared? To a mortal king whose children, servants, and members of his household did not behave properly. So he said to his children, to his servants, and to the members of his household, "Because of your ways I will growl at you like a bear, roar at you like a lion, seem to be coming at you like the angel of death." Such is the intent of "The Lord thy God is a devouring fire."

The two twin parables in this passage not only answer the inquiry of the Parsee priest but also exploit the situation to teach a further truth. One form of idolatry or false worship of which the author of the text is keenly aware is that which viewed god as fire. Thus Nimrod claims that he serves the god of fire.[124] Here God's reign is described as a present reality which is seen to counter any speculation that God would assume the form of fire. This fact concerning the kingdom of God is repeated in the episode concerning fire-worshiping Nimrod.[125] God is not fire as this priest contended, but fire will be used by God in the judgment. Fire as a means of divine punishment is well known from a wide range of sources. In the Midrash on Psalms, the future judgment of the wicked is described in terminology that recalls the fate of generations of wicked men in the scriptures which is closely connected to the verse in Psalm 11:5–6.

> "Upon the wicked He shall rain *pachim*" (Ps. 11:6)—that is, 'quick burning coals,' as in the phrase "As quick burning coals *(pecham)* are to live coals, and wood to fire" (Prov. 26:21). The Holy One, blessed be He, said: Whoever exalts himself in pride will finally be punished in fire as were the people of the generation of the flood . . . so, too, the people of the Tower of Babel . . . so, too, were the people of Sodom. . . . "Fire and brimstone . . . this shall be the portion of their cup" (Ps. 11:6). R. Yudan said: Whenever a man smells brimstone, his soul is distraught, for the soul knows that it will be punished in brimstone . . . [126]

The context of these parables from Seder Eliyahu Rabbah emphasizes that God's reign is a present reality and that he does not appear in any modalistic forms. The parables themselves teach a further truth. God is not revealed through the form of fire, but fire is a cautionary reminder to man that he must repent. Hence the lash in the first illustration, and the animals of prey as well as the angel of death in the second, represent fire and ultimately the future divine judgment. The impetus of these parables' message abandons the question of the Magian priest and addresses the theme of repentance, "'With this lash I may strike you, may smite you, may even kill you'—threatening them in order that they would turn from [sin] and repent. If they do not repent, do not turn back, then God says, 'I will have to strike them with the lash. . . .'" The strong ethical and moral approach of Seder Eliyahu is evident in this potent illustration which addresses man's need of repentance in order to escape God's judgment by fire.

Seder Eliyahu Rabbah Chap. 14 (pp. 62–63)

One of the themes which is treated in Seder Eliyahu deals with the study of the Torah and its relationship to the "way of the world" (*derech eretz* דרך ארץ). In many ways, the present examples from Seder Eliyahu are closer to similes than to story parables. Nevertheless they are parabolic sayings which may have contributed to the development of the story parable. The proper understanding of these parabolic sayings which are connected to the theme of Torah study hinges on the meaning of the term *derech eretz.* In this context, W. Braude has translated the expression by the words "worldly affairs."[127] This is one meaning of the expression the "way of the world" which is reflected in some early texts (e.g. Pirke Avot 3:6).[128] M. Kadushin has also interpreted the term in this context as referring to "business affairs."[129] However in this context it seems that the expression has a different sense and one that is more widely used in Seder Eliyahu as well as in the Masechtot Derech Eretz. Although this passage presents some difficulties (among others—textual) which cannot all be resolved in this treatment, here it would be suggested that the main theme of this text deals with the question: What is the relationship between study and action (or proper conduct)?

This controversy is reflected in a cluster of parabolic similes that contrasts the practice of good works (דרך ארץ = מעשים טובים) or proper conduct to the diligent study of the Torah (תורה = דברי תורה). The context of the parables asks the question, "Since you were thirteen, what Torah have you studied? What good works have you performed?" Thus the meaning of the parables must be understood in light of these questions.[130] The activities of God himself that are described in this passage also reflect the tension over the controversy of proper conduct and study. For one third of the day God recites Mishnah and reads scripture, the second third he pronounces judgment and during the final third he takes care of his creations by feeding them and by supplying their needs.[131] Both study and action are combined in this portrayal of God's activities. Thus a man should learn from the example of his Father in heaven. What is the difference between a man who studies Torah and one who attends only to the accomplishment of good works?

SIMILES CONCERNING THE TWO KINDS OF TOIL

There are two kinds of toil—toil in matters of Torah and toil in proper conduct *(derech eretz).* He who chooses to toil [only] in proper conduct finds that

> proper conduct takes its toll on him. Of this sort of man, Scripture says, "Man is born for toil" (Job 5:7). With what may he be compared? With a leather bag filled with water: once the water is poured out and gone, nothing is left in the leather bag. On the other hand, to him who chooses to toil in matters of Torah applies the verse "For the soul that labors [in Torah, Torah] labors for him" (Prov. 16:26). With what may this sort of man be compared? With a threshold upon which all step; with a plank over which all pass; with a tree into whose shade all come; with a lamp which provides light for the eyes of many.

Parabolic language is employed here to illustrate the differences between one who labors in proper conduct דרך ארץ and one who toils in the matters of the Torah דברי תורה. The passage has an important parallel which understood the tradition differently. In b. Sanhedrin one discovers this tradition:

> R. Eleazar said: Every man is born for toil, as it is written, 'Yet man is born for toil' (Job 5:7). Now, I do not know whether for toil by mouth or by hand, but when it is said, 'for his mouth craveth it of him.' I may deduce that toil by mouth is meant. Yet I still do not know whether for toil in the Torah or in [secular] coversation, but when it is said, 'This book of the Torah shall not depart out of thy mouth,' I conclude that one was created to labour in the Torah.[132]

This tradition in the name of R. Eleazar, makes the contrast between the toils of "labor" (מלאכה) and of the "mouth" (פה) or study. R. Eleazar's dictum is very similar to the passage from Seder Eliyahu. However there are significant differences. For one thing no similes appear in the text of the Talmud. Yet it would appear that the tradition as it is reflected in Seder Eliyahu would be considerably weakened without these examples and that they were most certainly originally connected with the passage. Moreover, it would seem that both the text of the Talmud and that of

Seder Eliyahu are derived from common source(s) and are not directly dependent one on the other. On the one hand the talmudic reference relates the teaching to the early tannaitic teacher R. Eleazar and on the other hand Seder Eliyahu preserves parabolic sayings that very probably were originally connected to the tradition.[133] According to the Talmud, the saying addresses the relationship between work and study. But is this the original meaning in Seder Eliyahu?

The Jewish source of the Two Ways which is preserved as the basis of the first six chapters of the Didache provides the *Sitz im Leben* of Seder Eliyahu's employment of the term *derech eretz.*[134] This source begins with the words, "There are two ways in the world: one of life and one of death, one of light and one of darkness; in them two angels are appointed, one of righteousness and one of wickedness, and a great difference is between the two ways."[135] Flusser has discussed the meaning of this text and also pointed to the Qumran Manual of Discipline where one discovers another reference to the ways of the earth, "These are their ways in the world for the enlightenment of the heart of man, and that all the paths of true righteousness may be made straight before him, and that fear of the laws of God may be instilled in his heart . . ." (ואלה דרכיהן בתבל). Thus the term *derech eretz* can have the sense of the way of life on earth that a man chooses. Hence it becomes clear that *derech eretz* has even a deeper significance than proper conduct. It is the way of life a person chooses for himself in this world. He may choose the way of life or the way of death. Here in Seder Eliyahu Rabbah it is contrasted to the study of the Torah. The motif employed in the simile concerning the leather bag is reminiscent of Jesus' parables about the new wine in old wineskins (Matthew 9:16–17; Mark 2:21–22; Luke 5:36–39). While the application of the parables of Jesus is different, at least the leather bag (נוד) is parallel to the synoptic gospel's wineskins (ἀσκοί). Both lose their contents. Seder Eliyahu compares a bag full of water which becomes useless to the one who only occupies himself with good works but does not learn as well. It will be difficult for the man who only toils to perform good works to maintain his motivation or have a basis for his activities.

However Seder Eliyahu also teaches that when God created the world that *derech eretz* preceded everything including the Torah.[137] But as Kadushin has suggested, the Torah sometimes takes precedence over *derech eretz.*[138] The Holy One himself watches over the one who has diligently learned Torah whereas only one angel guards him who has only occupied himself with *derech eretz* and *mitzvot* or keeping the commandments. Seder Eliyahu emphasizes the importance of studying Torah in order to learn proper conduct or *derech eretz.* When dealing with the civil war during the period of the judges (Judges 19–20), the men of Benjamin are condemned because their learning did not lead to proper behavior. The Holy One says, "I did not give my Torah except that they should read and study it in order to learn from it proper conduct *(derech eretz).*"[139] Later a mishnaic passage is cited in Seder Eliyahu, "The sages taught in the mishnah, 'If there is no Torah then there is no proper conduct *(derech eretz).* If there is no proper conduct there is no Torah' (Avot 3:17)."[140] One can discern a certain tension between the study of Torah and proper conduct.

The one who endeavors to study the Torah is compared to a threshold, a plank, a tree and a lamp. The verse from Proverbs 16:26 is important, "For the soul that labors [in Torah], Torah labors for him (נפש עמל עלמה לו)." The darshan interprets the passage as meaning that the study of Torah actually becomes an active force in one's life. Thus the Torah will motivate the student to behave according to proper conduct and also to accomplish good works. Proper conduct and good works result when one prepares himself through diligent study. A cluster of parabolic sayings are used to strengthen and reinforce this theme. This saying is partially paralleled in the minor tractates of the Talmud, "Be submissive to all, beloved by all, and humble before all. Be like a wineskin that needs not to be opened to let in air, and like a lower threshold over which all pass."[141] In many ways these texts which describe proper behavior on earth are similar to the Essene Manual of Discipline, "These are their ways in the world . . . that the fear of the laws of God may be instilled in his heart: a spirit of humility, patience, abundant charity, unending goodness . . ."[142] In Derech Eretz Zuta one finds this passage, "Do not be like an upper threshold, against which the feet strike, and which is bound to be torn down; nor be like a middle threshold, on which only the troubled rest; but rather be like a lower threshold, over which many people pass, and which remains in its place for ever, though the whole house be torn down."[143]

Learning must be related to humility and proper conduct. It provides a passageway for others. This approach can also be seen in the saying of the early Chasid, R. Chanina ben Dosa, "R. Chanina ben Dosa said: Everyone whose fear of sin precedes his wisdom—his wisdom endures. But everyone whose wisdom precedes his fear of sin—his wisdom will not endure, as it was said, 'The fear of the LORD is the beginning of wisdom' (Psalm 111:10). He used to say: Everyone whose works exceed his wisdom, his wisdom shall endure; but everyone whose wisdom exceeds his works, his wisdom shall not endure, as it was said, 'We will do and we will study [be obedient, hear]' (נעשה ונשמע, Exodus 24:7)."[144] Thus this passage from Seder Eliyahu seems to be closely related to the milieu of the stream within ancient Judaism represented by the early Chasidim like Chanina ben Dosa who struggled with the question: What takes precedence, the fear of sin or the study of Torah?[145] Seder Eliyahu seems to be emphasizing the fact that the one who toils in Torah will have the Torah to motivate him to proper conduct and good works.

The simile of light, "with a lamp which provides light for the eyes of many" employed here in the text of Seder Eliyahu, is also found in a different form in the gospels.[146] Jesus speaks about his disciples by using very similar language, "You are the light of the world. A city set upon a hill cannot be hid. Nor do men light a lamp and put it under a bushel, but on a stand, and it gives light to all in the house. Let your light so shine before men, that they might see your good works and give glory to your Father who is in heaven" (Matthew 5:14–16).[147] Here one discovers the language of comparison employing the simile of "light" as well as the theme of "good works." A similar illustration is employed in Sifre Numbers concerning Moses, "To what may Moses be compared at that time? To a light (נר) which is set upon a lampstand from which many lights are ignited. Nothing is lacking from this light in the same way as nothing was lacking in the wisdom of Moses."[148] Thus the same simile has been used to speak about wisdom and good works in early Christianity and Judaism from late antiquity. At any rate, these parabolic illustrations from Seder Eliyahu teach that a man who toils in the words of Torah will be humble and motivated to assist others by performing good works. The parable functions to illustrate and to communicate the theme of Seder Eliyahu's *derashah.*

SEDER ELIYAHU RABBAH CHAP. 12 (P. 55)

The parable concerning the king's ungrateful and rebellious servants introduces Seder Eliyahu's discussion of various events in the biblical book of Judges.[149] The main theme of the parable involves God's treatment of the children of Israel. In many ways the text betrays a tendency toward theodicy as it deals with the harshness of Israel's punishment as a consequence of Israel's sins. The parable is followed by an interpretation which is certainly necessary to explain the meaning of the illustration. An explanation of parables is not at all uncommon in rabbinic literature. Here is the parable (a blank space in the manuscript is indicated by . . .):

THE KING'S UNGRATEFUL SERVANTS

> To what may Israel be compared during the days when the judges ruled? To a mortal king who procured houses and servants. Some of the servants were six years old, some were five, some were four, some were three, some were two, some were one. He brought them up at his own table. All of them ate what he ate, all of them drank what he drank. After he had brought them up, he built houses for them, planted vines, trees and shrubs for them, and instructed them: Take care of these shrubs, take care of these trees, take care of these vines. But after they had eaten and drunk, they proceeded to root up the vines, cut down the trees and destroy the houses and the shrubs. Nevertheless, when the king came he was dis-

> posed to be indulgent, saying: They are still behaving like school children. What can be done about them? . . . [Go, he then said to his servants], fetch them, and spank them, not once, but twice, even thrice. Thus in the days when the judges ruled, were Israel regarded in the eyes of their Father in heaven. After they befouled themselves with their deeds, He turned them over to [an alien] kingdom [to be punished]. When they turned about and repented, He forgave them right away. You are thus to understand that Israel are not required to pay even the smallest fine without first having been brought to judgment, and that all that is then done to them is based on such judgment.

The parable opens a *derashah,* and introduces the theme of God's relationship to Israel in the context of his chastisement. Israel are represented here as the servants and are even referred to as "school children" (כתינוקות בית רבן). God is again represented by the king figure. The land of Israel is probably connected to the king's houses, vines, trees and shrubs that he procured for his servants. This parable has several vivid details that illustrate the inherent dangers of searching for special significance in each element of the illustration. The different ages of the servants do not have any special meaning. They are probably employed to generate the interest of the hearers. While one might be tempted to relate the motif of being spanked two or three times as possibly recalling the destructions of the Temples and the cruel exiles that followed, this kind of symbolism or allegorization for each detail of the parable is probably going too far. The parable echoes the events from the days of the judges when Israel were punished by successive foreign powers. Hence the idea of punishment by a foreign power as divine chastisement seems patent. The main theme of the parable is clear. God had done all for Israel but they had failed him. Thus he was justified in the punishment that he brought upon them. Nevertheless, when they repented God forgives them immediately. The parable and its interpretation focus on theodicy and God's great mercy despite Israel's severe chastisements.[150]

ALLEGORY—SIGN AND SYMBOL

After examining a number of rabbinic parables in their individual contexts, it is possible to ask some controversial questions. Are parables allegory? All parables, including the parables of Jesus, contain points of comparison between the image and the object being depicted. But defining parable as allegory is inaccurate and misleading. Points of comparison between the mashal and the nimshal are not necessarily making use of symbols or allegory. In a parable a king may be representative of God, or the king's wife may be connected to Israel. A good example of this kind of parabolic language is found in the well-known illustration of R. Johanan ben Zakai:[151]

THE KING'S BANQUET

> R. Johanan b. Zakai said: This may be compared to a king who summoned his servants to a banquet without appointing a time. The wise ones adorned themselves and sat at the door of the palace, ['for,'] said they, 'is anything lacking in a royal palace?' The fools went about their work, saying, 'can there be a banquet without preparations?' Suddenly the king desired [the presence of] servants: the wise entered adorned, while the fools entered soiled. The king rejoiced at the wise but was angry with the fools. 'Those who adorned themselves for the banquet,' ordered he, 'let them sit, eat and drink. But those who did not adorn themselves for the banquet, let them stand and watch.'

Here the crisis of the parable is related to the king's servants. This parable can be easily viewed as the acts of a play. R. Johanan b. Zakai tells the story of the king and his servants (introducing the cast). The king invites his servants to a banquet (act 1, the setting). The wise servants prepare themselves and the others who are foolish do not (act 2, the drama begins). Then the king comes to begin the feast and to inspect the actions of his servants in order to determine if they have prepared themselves (act 3, the crisis). Finally the crisis is resolved in a dramatic scene that contrasts the wise servants with the foolish ones. This is what might be described as the classic form of the story parable.[152] Although the king represents God and the servants' obligations are compared to man's responsibilities to their Creator, this illustration should not be described as an allegory. Perhaps a preferable term would be imaging. In some ways the parable is designed to be an agadic hologram. Yet the parable's intense mini-drama distinguishes it from a lifeless picture. The parable produces an image—however imprecise—which communicates or accentuates a specific relationship between the mashal and nimshal. The parable functions to illustrate this relationship or theme. Thus it functions to communicate a message.

In an attempt to explain the difference between allegory and parable, it is helpful to adopt some working definitions. These definitions are heuristic devices which may not hold true in every case.[153] An allegory uses symbolization. A symbol may have a number of meanings. A cross is a symbol. To one person it may symbolize salvation but to another it may have an entirely different meaning. The cross of the crusader symbolized one thing to the crusader and something quite different to his foe. Thus the meaning of the symbol is actually determined by the person. A sign is something quite different from a symbol because a sign has one meaning. A red traffic signal has only one interpretation. The *tertia comparationis* of a parable are more like signs whose meaning is determined by the storyteller himself. These signs are the link between the image and the object being depicted in the comparison. They can be understood by the context and the application. In fact this is the main difference between symbols and signs. In contrast to signs whose meaning is encoded by the parabolist himself, the interpretation of symbols is more or less left up to one's imagination. Hence the meaning is in the people[154] and the parable interpreter must allow the parabolist to supply the key to his code.

Points of comparison between the mashal and nimshal should be considered signs and not symbols. While signs may still resemble allegory to some interpreters, this definition is far removed from the allegorical method employed by the church fathers. Tertullian tried to determine whether the house in Jesus' parable of the lost coin symbolized the world or the church.[155] The house is a neutral element which is neither a sign nor a symbol but rather a part of the stage. Dodd called attention to Augustine's celebrated allegorical interpretation of the Parable of the Good Samaritan where every detail is given deep symbolic significance.[156] Tertullian and Augustine interpreted these elements of the parables as symbols. Their interpretation of these symbols was not even alluded to either in the context or in the application of the parables. The search for symbols in parables and their allegorical interpretation by the church fathers cast a dark shadow over the original message of Jesus. Signs of a parable are neither allegory nor symbols. They are code words which have a meaning assigned to them by the storyteller. The interpreter must allow the context and the application to impose the meaning of the signs upon the points of comparison within the framework of the parable.

The Function of the Parable

The application of the parable and the points of comparison between the mashal and the nimshal are essential for a proper understanding of the parable's function. Ultimately the function of the parable is dependent upon the storyteller himself. Hence the context of the parable often determines the message being conveyed. The application is the link between the parable and its context. Thus the same midrash, Sifre Deuteronomy, was able to use a single story parable to illustrate two different themes in divergent contexts—the rewards in the world to come and the people's inheritance in the land of promise.[157] Parables also seem to have been an important tool of argumentation where an illustration is used to prove a point.[158] Interestingly enough, not infrequently another story parable is adduced to present an opposing view and to neutralize the first illustration. A literary use of parables can be seen in the interpretation of the biblical text where parables often function to illustrate the meaning of a verse.[159] The text cited above from the Mechilta described a Sabbath homily which made use of parables.[160] Parables often function to describe the relationship between God and Israel. The rhetorical themes of theodicy and complaint can be observed. What is man's relationship to God and his fellow man? The dramas artistically created in these mini-productions deal with these complex issues and teach relevant truths. Inasmuch as parables are an integral part of agadah, the words of the *dorshe reshumot* are pertinent to this discussion: "If it is your desire to know Him who spoke and the world came into being—then study the agadah. From this endeavor you will come to know the Holy One Blessed be He and cling to His ways."[161]

The Literary Parable

J. Heinemann has discussed the problems of the transmission of public sermons which were originally delivered orally and then recorded in writing.[162] What changes and adaptations occurred as oral teachings were compiled as literature? This problem raises many questions which cannot be answered fully. Nevertheless, any treatment of parables should at least make an effort to outline some of the difficulties related to the literary parable. As will be seen in the continuation of this work, the process of transferring the teaching of Jesus and most certainly his parables from oral tradition into writing created many problems that are paralleled in talmudic literature. Heinemann believed that the midrashic proems were originally one of the oral forms employed to arouse the listeners' attention which was later incorporated into written traditions.[163] Parables were first employed in spontaneous oral teachings and discourses which were later transmitted in written form.

Is it possible to come nearer to the earlier form of the parables? Flusser has treated this entire question and spoken about the classic form of parables.[164] This type of parable retains the fresh and vivid atmosphere of spontaneous teaching. The more or less exegetical parables which are so directly dependent on the biblical text may actually be derived from the literary stage. Often the freer style of parabolic teaching such as appears in some of the homiletical midrashic traditions may be more representative of the spontaneous animated preaching of the early rabbis than that which is of a more purely exegetical nature. Most of the parables attributed to Jesus like so many rabbinic parables preserve this quality of spontaneity in spite of the fact that in both cases they have been transferred from oral to written traditions. Because the gospel parables have been preserved somewhat differently (in Greek translation derived from an early Semitic *Vorlage*) than those in rabbinic literature (from a long period of oral tradition), comparative research promises to greatly enhance one's knowledge of early parabolic teachings.

Thus one of the goals of the work at hand is to elucidate the homiletical parable. While the interpretation of holy writ retained a great urgency, animated preaching and homiletical discourse was a means of actualizing the word. Agadah in general and parabolic instruction in particular must not be viewed as a still photograph but rather as a dramatic moving picture. The listener was required to encounter the force of the parable's message. The parabolist was able to draw from a rich repository of known motifs.[165] He would employ them to accentuate his theme whether it be praise, complaint, theodicy, the need for sincere repentance or an aspect of man's relationship to his neighbor or to his Creator. According to Matthew and Luke, Jesus concluded one important section of his teaching known today as the so-called Sermon on the Mount with the Parable of the Two House Builders.[166] As noted above, in the Mechilta parables are said to have been employed to illustrate a Sabbath message at Yavneh.[167] In Sifre Numbers R. Akiva used the parable as a means of argumentation.[168]

The complexities of the historical questions cannot be overlooked. Although few if any rabbinic story parables can be attributed to the time of Hillel and Shammai, one would expect more of the classic form of parables from this period. Nevertheless one must observe that the materials preserved from this period are fragmentary. Even though this is true as noted above, already R. Johanan ben Zakai who lived before the national disaster in 70 C.E., and who pioneered the difficult transition from the days of the Second Temple to Yavneh, employed the parable as a teaching device. In the Tosefta one finds the story concerning the disciples of R. Tarfon gathering before him and saying, "Teach us, our master."[169] No parables appear in that text. However one could easily surmise that an occasion such as this would have provided the context for parabolic instruction. Much evidence has survived for the homiletical parable from the time of Jesus well into the periods of the Tannaim and the Amoraim. Considering the history of the formation of rabbinic literature, it should be no surprise that one finds more parables among the Amoraim.[170] Some researchers speak about the differences between Tannaitic and Amoraic parables as if there was a great revolutionary transformation of the parable at the beginning of the period of the Amoraim.[171] While many changes did occur during the transition from the Tannaim to the Amoraim as in the case of the proem or the structure of homilies, the truth is that this distinction as regards parables is somewhat misleading. The differences between a parable by R. Meir and one by R. Zeira are more related to differences in each sage's individual style than to the fact that one is a Tanna and the other is an Amora. When it comes to parables, rather than forming a sharp demarcation line between the Tannaim and the Amoraim, I would venture that the distinctions in parabolic teaching are primarily due to (1) the personality and unique style of the parabolist on the one hand and (2) the redaction of the parables in talmudic literature on the other. The parabolist adapts known motifs and creates a story designed to illustrate his theme. This whole question is much more complex than can be treated here in brief and is certainly worthy of further research.

While additional research is needed in this area, at this point it seems possible to observe that the later homiletical parables were to a large extent adaptations of earlier ones and that the basic form and structure of the Amoraic parable is quite similar to that of the Tannaim. The parables of Jesus have to be carefully considered in the study of rabbinic parables. Did Jesus invent the story parable? As has been noted, it seems more likely that Jesus employed a didactic device that was already in use and had been reflected in the biblical text (e.g. 2 Samuel 12:1–4). The rich legacy of rabbinic parables that have been preserved in talmudic literature testifies to the fact that parabolic teachings became a popular and an effective method of communication. The colorful illustrations of Jesus are similar to many rabbinic parables from a later period. Because of the early date of the synoptics, it appears that this classic form was indeed representative of the early parables. Perhaps the synoptic gospels more than other texts provide the opportunity for studying how the homiletical parable which was taken from the spontaneous animated teaching of Jesus was turned into the literary parable.

Notes

1) On the definition of agadah much has been written; cf. Z.H. Chajes, *The Student's Guide Through the Talmud,* translated, edited and annotated by J. Shachter (New York: Feldheim, 1960), pp. 139–147, and see his discussion of parables in the agadah, pp. 214–223; A. Heschel, *Between God and Man* (New York: The Free Press, 1959), pp. 175–180; W. Bacher, *Die exegetische Terminologie der jüdischen Traditionsliteratur* (Darmstadt: Wissenschaftliche Buchgesellschaft, 1965, reprint from Leipzig, vol. 1 1899, vol. 2, 1905), vol. 1, pp. 33ff, vol. 2, p. 44; idem, *Erche Midrash* (Jerusalem: Carmiel, 1970), vol. 1, p. 24ff, vol. 2, p. 175; J. Heinemann, *Agadot Vetoldotehen* (Jerusalem: Keter, 1974), pp. 7–15; I. Heinemann, *Darche Haagadah* (Jerusalem: Masada, 1970), pp. 1–14 and pp. 163–195; cf. with the more recent contribution which deals with the stories within agadic literature, by J. Fraenkel, *Eyunim Baolam Haruchani Shel Sipor Haagadah* (Tel Aviv: Hakibbutz Hameuchad, 1981); see the section concerning a man and his Maker, pp. 13ff and also the chapter entitled, "Inside the Bet Hamidrash," pp. 65–82; and see also the bibliographies in these works. See also L. Finkelstein, "Midrash, Halachot, Vehagadot," *Yitzhak F. Baer Jubilee Volume,* eds., S. Baron, B. Dinur, S. Ettinger, and I. Halpern (Jerusalem: Historical Society, 1960), pp. 28–47, English summary, pp. viii–ix.

2) The Manual of Discipline 6:6 (see Licht's edition, p. 140 and note on 6:6).

3) Josephus, *Contra Apion* 2.18 (175), *Ant.* 16:2.4 (43); Philo, *Vita Mosis* 2.39 (216), *Spec. Leg.* 2. 15 (62); Acts 15:21; Luke 4:16; and cf. Mechilta Derabbi Ishmael, on Exodus 13:2, (Horovitz, pp. 58–59); j. Megilah 75a, chap. 4, hal. 1; b. Baba Kama 82a.

4) S. Safrai, "Hebrew and Aramaic Sources," from S. Safrai and M. Stern, in cooperation with D. Flusser and W.C. van Unnik, *The Jewish People in the First Century* (Van Gorcum: Assen, 1974), vol. 1, p. 9.

5) Few studies on agadic teaching have devoted sufficient attention to parabolic instruction.

6) One can point to a number of examples where one parable is

used in different contexts to illustrate quite diverse themes; see the discussion below on "The Prince and His Inheritance," Sifre Deuteronomy 19 (Finkelstein, p. 31) and "The Man's Son and His Inheritance," Sifre Deuteronomy 356 (Finkelstein, p. 422). Cf. R.M. Johnston, "Parabolic Interpretations Attributed to Tannaim" (Unpublished doctoral dissertation, the Hartford Seminary Foundation, 1977), pp. 283–284, pp. 314–315 and pp. 620–624.

7) See S. Sandmel, "Parallelomania," *Journal of Biblical Literature,* 81 (March 1962), pp. 1–13. While Sandmel's cautionary remarks have great value especially when considering the misuse of important tools like Billerbeck's commentary, certainly the other extreme also retains inherent dangers.

8) See K. Bailey, *Through Peasant Eyes* (Grand Rapids: Eerdmanns, 1980), pp. xiiff.

9) For the parables concerning ordinary people, cf. Guttmann, *Hamashal,* pp. 37–52.

10) Jülicher, *Die Gleichnisreden Jesu,* vol. 1, pp. 164–173. Here R. Stein's observation bears repeating, "Jülicher's work, despite its great contribution to the interpretation of the parables, was not, however, without its own limitations. The first major limitation of Jülicher was that he overreacted against the former emphasis on the allegorical interpretation of the parables and denied the presence of any allegorical element in the parables of Jesus. Whenever such allegorical details or interpretations were present in the Gospels, their authenticity was denied, and they were attributed to the reworking of the parable by the early church. The reaction against the presence of allegory in the parables of Jesus is explained primarily by the fact that Jülicher depended on Aristotle and Greek theories of rhetoric for defining what a parable is rather than upon the Old Testament. Through the work of such men as Christian August Bugge and especially Paul Fiebig, however, it became clear that Jülicher had not only turned Jesus into an educated nineteenth-century German liberal theologian, but that he also had him educated according to classical Greek learning rather than in the environment of first-century Judaism"—idem, *An Introduction to the Parables of Jesus* (Philadelphia: Westminster, 1981), pp. 54-55. Stein's critique of Jülicher's overreaction against all allegorical elements in the parables is correct. However the study of the Old Testament for a definition of parable is bound to produce only fragmentary results. The careful research of rabbinic literature promises to be more fruitful. Moreover as will be seen in the continuation of this work, it is doubtful that one can eliminate the influence of the redaction of the gospel texts in the preservation of the

materials. See also the section at the end of this chapter, "Allegory—Sign and Symbol."

11) This text appears in Codex Assemeni 66 of *Torat Kohanim*. Fascinatingly enough, in this manuscript of Sifra, three more parables are augmented to this section of *Torat Kohanim* which further strengthen this same point. The importance of this manuscript has been discussed by Finkelstein, Codex Assemani 66, "Introduction," p. 18. However whether these parables formed an original part of Sifra is doubtful. Here only the last of these three illustrations will be cited.

12) Actually it would probably be more natural for the Canaanites to be connected to harlotry and the Egyptians to be associated with sorcery. Though they are very closely related, it is possible that the names or their roles have been reversed. Cf. also the Parable of the Prince's Stomach (Sifra on Lev. 20:21, Weiss, 93b) discussed below and see notes 58 and 59. That generation had learned the wicked ways of the nations and this is what led to their exile. The theme of this illustration augments that of the parable concerning the land vomiting up its inhabitants. However this parable is independent of the verse from Leviticus and highlights another aspect of the historical situation, namely the influence of the nations upon Israel.

13) See A. Wright, *The Literary Genre Midrash* (New York: Pauline Fathers, 1967); S. Safrai, "Hebrew and Aramaic Sources," *The History of the Jewish People,* vol. 1, pp. 16–17; G. Porton, "Defining Midrash," and L. Haas, "Bibliography on Midrash," in J. Neusner, *The Study of Ancient Judaism* (New York: KTAV, 1981), vol. 1, pp. 55–106; Bacher, *Die exegetische Terminologie der jüdischen Traditionsliteratur,* vol. 1, pp. 25ff, vol. 2, pp. 41ff and pp. 107f; idem, *Erche Midrash,* vol. 1, pp. 19–21 and pp. 71–72; vol. 2, pp. 173–174 and p. 221; cf. also J. Heinemann, *Derashot Betzibur Betekufat Hatalmud* (Jerusalem: Bialik, 1982), pp. 7–12; J. Heinemann, *Agadot Vetoldotehen* (Jerusalem: Keter, 1974), pp. 7–15. The word *midrash* appears twice in the Old Testament where it means exposition, interpretation or examination: 2 Chronicles 13:22; 24:27. The term also appears in the Dead Sea Scrolls, 1 QS 8:15; 4 Q Flor. 1:14. In Ben Sira 51:23 the word *midrash* is used in the sense of a house of study which is already very similar if not identical with the meaning in many rabbinic texts (cf. the inscription discovered upon the lintel from the house of study of R. Eliezar Hakapar, Joseph Naveh, *Al Psefas Veeven,* Tel Aviv: Carta, 1978, pp. 25f).

14) See J. Lauterbach, trans., "Introduction," *Mekilta de-Rabbi Ishmael* (Philadelphia: The Jewish Publication Society of America, 1976), p. xix. Concerning Lauterbach's work, see L. Finkelstein, "The Mekilta

and Its Text," *The Proceedings of the American Academy for Jewish Research,* vol. 5, 1933–1934, pp. 4–5 and note the claims made by Ben Zion Wacholder, "The Date of the Mekhilta de Rabbi Ishmael," *Hebrew Union College Annual* 39 (1968), pp. 117–144.

15) Lauterbach, "Introduction," pp. xixf and J. Epstein, *Mevoot Lasifrut Hatannaim,* pp. 545–548.

16) See the discussion by J. Heinemann, *Agadot Vetoldotehen* (Jerusalem: Keter, 1974), pp. 7ff.

17) The text appears in Horovitz's edition of the Mechilta on p. 59 for Exodus 13:2; Lauterbach, vol. 1, pp. 132ff. The main parallels to the parable are found in Tosefta Berachot 1:11 (Lieberman, *Zera'im,* pp. 4–5 and see especially his comments in his *Tosefta Kefshutah Zera'im,* pp. 13–14); b. Berachot 13a (and see Lieberman, *Tosefta Kefshutah Zera'im,* p. 14, were the variants from Dikduke Sofrim have been discussed and compare Amos 5:19); j. Berachot 4a, chap. 1 hal. 9. See also the different version of the parable "The Traveler and His Perils" cited from the Mechilta by R. Israel Ibn Al-Nakawa, *Menorat Ha-Maor,* H.G. Enelow, ed. (New York: The Bloch Publishing Co., 1931), vol. 2, p. 573. And compare also the Mechilta Derabbi Ishmael on Exodus 19:4 (Horovitz, p. 208); Seder Eliyahu Rabbah, p. 100 (see Friedmann's note 67) and Pesikta Derav Kahana 3:1, Mandelbaum, p. 36; cf. Tosefta Sotah 15:7 (Lieberman, *Sotah,* p. 241, and Lieberman, *Tosefta Kefshutah Sotah,* p. 756f). See Johnston, "Parabolic Interpretations Attributed to Tannaim," pp. 220–221. The context of these illustrations from the Mechilta has been treated by Bacher, *Die Agada der Tannaiten,* vol. 1, pp. 213f; idem, *Agadot Hatannaim,* vol. 1, part 1, pp. 161–162.

18) Here the meaning of the verb דרש seems to be related to the discourse delivered, but for the different meanings attached to this term, see Bacher, *Die exegetische Terminologie der jüdischen Traditionsliteratur,* vol. 1, pp. 25–27; idem, *Erche Midrash,* vol. 1, pp. 19–20, the entry for *darash.*

19) See also notes 2–4 above. Relatively recent discoveries, such as the Theodosius inscription or the lintel of R. Eliezar Hakapar's academy as well as talmudic tradition, suggest that among other uses the ancient synagogue functioned as a place of study; I. Levine *Ancient Synagogues Revealed* (Jerusalem: Israel Exploration Society, 1981), p. 3, p. 137 and pp. 155–156; *Ketovot Mesaprot* (Jerusalem: Israel Museum, 1972), pp. 182–185; Joseph Naveh, *Al Psefas Veeven,* pp. 1–2 and 25–26, and see S. Safrai, "The Synagogue," *The Jewish People in the First Century,* S. Safrai and M. Stern, eds. in cooperation with D. Flusser and W.C. Van Unnik (Assen: Van Gorcum, 1976), vol. 2, pp. 911–912. Safrai noted,

"The primary and seminal element in the synagogue was not prayer but Scripture reading" (ibid, p. 912). See j. Megilah 73d, chap. 1, hal. 1.

20) Double parables are also deeply embedded into the gospel tradition; see O. Linton, "Coordinated Sayings and Parables in the Synoptic Gospels: Analysis versus Theories," *New Testament Studies* 26 (1980), pp. 139–163.

21) See note 17 above.

22) The text appears in Horovitz's edition of the Mechilta on p. 125 for Exodus 15:1; Lauterbach's edition, vol. 2, p. 21f; see the parallels in the Mechilta Derabbi Simeon bar Yochai, on Exodus 15:1 (Melamed and Epstein, pp. 76–77, attributed to Rabbi), Leviticus Rabbah 4:5 (Margulies, vol. 1, pp. 87–89, R. Ishmael); b. Sanhedrin 91a–b (Judah the Prince); Midrash Tanchuma, Veyikra 6, Buber's edition, Veyikra 12; Yalkut Shimeoni, vol. 1, Remez 464. See the important article, L. Wallach, "The Parable of the Blind and the Lame," *Journal of Biblical Literature* 65 (1943), pp. 333–339. See also J. Heinemann, *Agadot Vetoldotehen,* p. 27.

23) See L. Wallach, "The Colloquy of Marcus Aurelius with the Patriarch Judah I," *Jewish Quarterly Review* 31 (1940–1941), pp. 259–286, where Wallach suggests that Antoninus should be identified with Marcus Aurelius. Cf. Bacher, *Die Agada der Tannaiten,* vol. 1, pp. 76ff; idem, *Agadot Hatannaim,* vol. 1, part 1, pp. 56ff where Bacher has discussed some of the disputations between Rabban Gamaliel and the Philosopher. See also the more recent article by M. Herr, "The Historical Significance of the Dialogues between Jewish Sages and Roman Dignitaries," J. Heinemann and D. Noy, eds., *Scripta Hierosolymitana Studies in Aggadah and Folk-Literature* (Jerusalem: Magnes, 1971), vol. 22, pp. 123–150. Herr mentions the discussions between Judah the Prince and Antoninus (p. 149), but does not attempt to identify Antoninus. The present discussion seems to be an inner Jewish one concerning the resurrection of the body; cf. Leviticus Rabbah 4:2 and the parable of R. Chiya, treated below.

24) Mechilta Derabbi Ishmael on Exodus 15:1 (Horovitz, p. 125) and see note 17 above.

25) B. Sanhedrin 91a–b.

26) G.F. Moore, *Judaism in the First Centuries of the Christian Era,* vol. 1, p. 487, note 1 and vol. 3, p. 148, note 206. See Wallach, "The Parable of the Blind and the Lame," pp. 333–334.

27) K. Holl, ed., Epiphanius, *Ancoratus und Panarion* (Leipzig: J.C. Hinrichs'sche Buchhandlung, 1915), vol. 2, pp. 515–517, on *Panarion haer.* 64, 70, 4ff; and see A. Denis, "Apocryphon Ezechiel," *Fragmenta*

Pseudepigraphorum Quae Supersunt Graeca (Leiden: Brill, 1970), pp. 121–122. The text was translated by M.R. James, *The Lost Apocrypha of the Old Testament* (London: SPCK, 1920), pp. 64–66; and see the new translation and introduction by J. Mueller and S. Robinson, "Apocryphon of Ezekiel," in J. Charlesworth, ed., *The Old Testament Pseudepigrapha* (New York: Doubleday, 1983), vol. 1, pp. 487–495. The parable has partial parallels in the Greek Anthology, see W.R. Paton, *The Greek Anthology* (London: William Heinemann, MCMXVII), vol. 3, pp. 8–9, "The Declamatory Epigrams," IX: 11, Phillippus or Isidorus, 12, Leonidas of Alexandria, 13, Plato the Younger, and 13b, Antiphilus of Byzantium. See Wallach, "The Parable of the Blind and the Lame," p. 334.

28) Josephus, *Ant.* 10.79–80. This is the opinion of Mueller and Robinson, "Apocryphon of Ezekiel," p. 488. However, see note by Marcus in the Loeb series on *Ant.* 10.79–80, p. 201. Marcus suggests that Josephus viewed the canonical version of Ezekiel as being divided into two sections of twenty-four chapters—one section dealt with desolation and the other with consolation.

29) Ibid. See also Mueller and Robinson's remarks concerning the original language of the Apocryphon of Ezekiel. Epiphanius' text seems to have been written in Greek. Without more evidence it would be difficult to know with certainty whether the Hebrew version was derived from the Greek or vice versa. Flusser suggested that the story may have actually originated in Persian sources (private communication). Indeed this illustration could have lent itself to a number of themes. The Zoroastrians had a dualistic approach to man's body and soul; see J. Hinnells, "The Cosmic Battle: Zoroastrianism," *The World's Religions* (England: Lion Publishing, 1982), pp. 86–87. Also in Persian Zoroastrian thought there is the conflict between fate and action. The seeming contradiction between a man's fate and his action has been explained by the similar metaphor of "the two bales on the back of a mule," cited by S. Shaked, *The Wisdom of the Sasanian Sages* (Boulder: Westview Press, 1979), pp. xliii–xliv. Needless to say this is pure speculation, but a parable could have been adapted to a number of different contexts. Wallach agreed with Moore that the original story of the Parable of the Blind and the Lame was derived from Indian sources, i.e. Wallach, "The Parable of the Blind and Lame," pp. 333–334. Epiphanius could be retelling the parable from his memory which makes it hazardous to use his text as the basis for determining the original language of the text. Nevertheless the motif also appears in the Greek Anthology; see note 27 above.

30) Bhadantacariya Buddhaghosa, *Visuddhimagga,* XVIII:35. The Pali text has been printed in the Harvard Oriental Series, H. Warren, ed.

and revised by D. Kosambi, *Visuddhimagga of Buddhaghosacariya* (Cambridge: Harvard University Press, 1950). An English translation was prepared by Pe Maung Tin, *The Path of Purity* (London: The Pali Text Society, 1971, first published 1923). A more recent translation has been made by B. Nyanamoli, *The Path of Purification (Visuddhimagga)* (Berkeley: Shambhala Publications, 1976).

31) See note 27 above.

32) See note 22 above.

33) Margulies, Leviticus Rabbah, vol. 1, p. 88, notes on line 1.

34) It should also be noted that the entire parable appears in the Mechilta Derabbi Simeon bar Yochai (on Exodus 15:1, Melamed and Epstein, pp. 76f), as well as manuscripts of the Mechilta Derabbi Ishmael. Later scribes who were acquainted with the illustration would have felt that it would be superfluous to repeat such a well-known parable and thus permitted themselves the liberty of abbreviating it.

35) The wide range of texts from various provenances and different themes demonstrates the adaptability of this vivid motif. The illustration has had a considerable amount of mileage. Unfortunately, it is very difficult at this point to trace its path from one source to another and thereby map out its development exhaustively.

36) I.e. see the context and discussion in Leviticus Rabbah 4:2.

37) The most well-known source for this fact is found in Acts 23:6–7, and see F. Jackson and K. Lake, *The Beginnings of Christianity the Acts of the Apostles* (Grand Rapids: Baker Book House, 1979, reprint from London, 1920–1933), vol. 4, p. 289, note 8. It should also be noted that the Essenes rejected the idea of a bodily resurrection and believed in the immortality of souls; see Josephus, *War* 2, 154–155; cf. *Ant.* 18, 18.

38) Here is Buddhagosha's text according to the more recent translation by Nyanamoli, *The Path of Purification,* vol. 2, pp. 690–691, "Furthermore, mentality has no efficient power, it cannot occur by its own efficient power. . . . It does not eat, it does not drink, it does not speak, it does not adopt postures. And materiality is without efficient power; it cannot occur by its own efficient power. . . . But for the purpose of explaining this meaning they gave this simile as an example: a man born blind and a stool-crawling cripple wanted to go somewhere. The blind man said to the cripple 'Look, I can do what should be done by legs, but I have no eyes with which to see what is rough and smooth'. The cripple said 'Look, I can do what should be done by eyes, but I have no legs with which to go and come'. The blind man was delighted, and he made the cripple climb up on his shoulder. Sitting on the blind man's shoulder the

cripple spoke thus 'Leave the left, take the right; leave the right, take the left.' Herein, the blind man has no efficient power; he is impotent; he cannot travel by his own efficient power, by his own strength. And the cripple has no efficient power; he is impotent; he cannot travel by his own efficient power, by his own strength. But there is nothing to prevent their going when they support each other. So too, mentality has no functions by its own efficient power; it does not arise or occur in such and such functions by its own efficient power. And materiality has no efficient power, it does not arise or occur in such and such functions by its own efficient power. But there is nothing to prevent their occurrence when they support each other."

39) The parable as it appears in Buddhaghosa's *Visuddhimagga* is most probably derived from earlier sources. In 1917 M. Nagai pointed out that the *Visuddhimagga* of Buddhaghosa is a revision of the *Vimuttimagga* written by Upatissa a thera from Ceylon (M. Nagai, "The Vimutti-magga: the 'Way to Deliverance,'" *The Journal of the Pali Text Society* 1917–1919, pp. 69–80). Upatissa lived about the time of King Vasabha of Ceylon (66–109 A.D.). While this work has not survived, the Cambodian priest Sanghapala translated it into Chinese (505 A.D.). These aspects of Buddhagosha's work have also been discussed by Bimala Charan Law, *The Life and Works of Buddhaghosa* (Delhi: Nag Publishers, 1976), pp. 70–71, note 1. See also K. Norman, who observes, " . . . there seems no doubt that Buddhaghosa made use of this earlier text when writing his own work, although it is going too far to say that the Visuddhimagga and Vimuttimagga are one and the same work appearing in different attires," in K. Norman, *A History of Indian Literature* (Wiesbaden: Otto Harrassowitz, 1983), pp. 120–121. See also Wallach, "The Parable of the Blind and the Lame," p. 333, who counters J. Scheftelowitz's contention that the Indian parable is much later than its rabbinic parallel, "Da dieses Gleichnis im Judentum etwa 300 Jahre früher auftritt als in Indien, ist Entlehnung dieses Motives aus Indien von vornherein sehr unwahrscheinlich" in, J. Scheftelowitz, "Ein Beitrag zur Methode der vergleichenden Religionsforschung," *Monatsschrift für Geschichte und Wissenschaft des Judentums* 65 (1921), p. 125.

40) See note 27 above.

41) See note 22 above.

42) For a different view see Wallach, "The Parable of the Blind and the Lame," p. 337.

43) R. Israel Ibn Al-Nakawa, *Menorat Hamaor,* ed. H.G. Enelow, part 3, pp. 99–100.

44) Midrash Hagadol on Deut. 32:2 (Fisch, p. 693); cf. Midrash Tannaim on Deut. 32:2 (Hoffmann, p. 185), and see Sifre Deut. 306 (Fin-

kelstein, pp. 340–341). The text from Midrash Tannaim was noted by Wallach, "The Parable of the Blind and the Lame," p. 337.

45) Genesis Rabbah 12:11 and parallels (Albeck, pp. 109f). See also Bacher, *Die Agada der Tannaiten,* vol. 1, pp. 129ff; idem, *Agadot Hatannaim,* vol. 1, part 1, p. 95.

46) Leviticus Rabbah 4:2 (Margulies, vol. 1, p. 90).

47) Midrash Hagadol on Leviticus 5:1 (Steinsaltz, pp. 108–109). The Parable of the Blind and the Lame does not appear in this text.

48) See the critical apparatus in Margulies, Leviticus Rabbah, vol. 1, p. 90.

49) See note 22 above.

50) Midrash Hagadol on Leviticus 5:1 (Steinsaltz, pp. 108–109).

51) See H.L. Strack and G. Stemberger, reviser, *Einleitung in Talmud und Midrasch* (Munich: Beck, 1982), pp. 244ff. Stemberger writes, "Dem Charackter von Lev entsprechend ist sein Inhalt fast ausschliesslich Halakha" (p. 245). However M. Herr has pointed out that the text also contains some beautiful agadic passages, *Encyclopaedia Judaica,* vol. 14, col. 1518. Perhaps the most complete introduction is that of L. Finkelstein, *Sifra or Torat Kohanim according to Codex Assemani LXVI* (New York: The Jewish Theological Seminary, 1956), pp. 1–77, which does treat many matters beyond the discussion of Codex Assemani LXVI. All anxiously await Finkelstein's new edition of Sifra, of which only two volumes have appeared at the time of this writing.

52) Cf. Leviticus Rabbah 7:3 (Margulies, p. 156) and Avot Derabbi Natan, Version A, Chapter 6. See also Safrai, "Education and the Study of the Torah," S. Safrai, and M. Stern, eds., *The Jewish People in the First Century* (Assen: Van Gorcum, 1976), p. 951. The origin and antiquity of this custom is difficult to ascertain. Safrai notes, "Information relating to this custom only goes back as far as the time of R. Akiba and even if it could be presumed to go back to several generations preceding him, we are still not justified in attributing this custom to such an early period in Jewish history as when instruction centred around the Temple service and its priests" (ibid).

53) Sifra on Leviticus 1:2 (Weiss, 4d); see the new edition of L. Finkelstein, *Sifra on Leviticus* (New York: The Jewish Tehological Seminary, 1983), vol. 2, p. 22; Finkelstein, Codex Assemani 66, pp. 11–12; cf. Friedmann, pp. 42–43.

54) See Z. Rapoport's commentary "Ezrat Kohanim," on Sifra, vol. 1, p. 14a, note 64; idem, *Sifra* (Vilna, 1845); and Finkelstein, *Sifra on Leviticus,* vol. 2, p. 22, note 41.

55 See Johnston, "Parabolic Interpretations Attributed to Tannaim," pp. 255–256.

56 Sifra on Leviticus 20:21 (Weiss, 93b), Finkelstein, Codex Assemani 66, p. 387.

57 Compare the slight difference between Codex Assemani 66 and Weiss. Codex Assemani 66 turns the negative statement into a positive one (. . . כשאר כל הארצות שמקבלות עוברי עבירות).

58) Sifra on Leviticus 18:25 (Weiss, 86a); cf. Also Midrash Lekach Tov on Leviticus 18:25 and Midrash Hagadol on Leviticus 18:25 (Steinsaltz, p. 528). Compare also the similar interpretation from Ecclesiastes Rabbah (1:4) which is attributed to the Amora, Resh Lakish, "R. Berekiah said in the name of R. Simeon b. Lakish: To whatever the Holy One, Blessed be He, created in man He created a parallel in the earth. . . . Man vomits and so does the earth, as it is said, 'That the land vomit not you out also' (Lev. XVIII, 28)."

59) Sifra on Leviticus 25:31 (Weiss, 109c). Of course many halachic requirements could not be observed outside the land of Israel. The importance of these commandments in early Jewish thought has been demonstrated once again recently by the beautiful mosaic discovered in the Rechov synagogue inscription which deals with these halachic questions; see J. Sussmann, "The Inscription in the Synagogue at Rehob," L. Levine, ed., *Ancient Synagogues Revealed,* pp. 146–153. J. Sussmann has treated the contents of this mosaic more extensively in two Hebrew articles, *Tarbiz* 43 (1974), pp. 88–158 and 45 (1976), pp. 213–257 and see also Naveh, *Al Psefas Veeven,* pp. 79–85.

60) See the Parable of the Prince and His Nursemaids referred to above in the beginning of this chapter which deals with a similar theme.

61) J.N. Epstein, *Mevoot Lesifrut Hatannaim* (Jerusalem: Magnes, 1957), p. 501.

62) On the hermeneutical principles see H.L. Strack and G. Stemberger, *Einleitung in Talmud und Midrasch* (Munich: Beck, 1982), pp. 25–40; and compare the important work, J. Doeve, *Jewish Hermeneutics in the Synoptic Gospels and Acts* (Assen: Van Gorcum, 1954), pp. 52–118.

63) Sifre Numbers 131 (Horovitz, p. 169, Friedmann, p. 47a); Yalkut Shimeoni vol. 1, remez 631; cf. P. Levertoff, *Midrash Sifre on Numbers* (New York: SPCK, 1926), pp. 133–134; this translation is incomplete and far from adequate to be as kind as possible. It has been consulted and used with many modifications. See also S. Safrai, *R. Akiva Ben-Yosef Chaiyav Umishnato* (Jerusalem: Bialik, 1970), pp. 250–251. See Paul's exegesis of this verse in 1 Corinthians 10:7.

64) The reading R. Meir was accepted by Friedmann, and see the critical edition by Horovitz (ibid).

65) Safrai has accepted the reading למודה; idem, *R. Akiva,* p. 250 and see Friedmann p. 47a, note 3 and Horovitz, p. 169.

66) Bacher, *Die Agada der Tannaiten,* vol. 1, p. 302, note 2; cf. p. 219, pp. 227–228, note 1; idem, *Agadot Hatannaim,* vol. 1, part 2, p. 52, note 1, and vol. 1, part 1, p. 171, note 1 and cf. pp. 164–165.

67) Concerning the differences between R. Akiva and R. Ishmael, see Safrai, *R. Akiva,* p. 51.

68) See m. Sanhedrin 4.5 (Albeck, p. 182).

69) Compare Horovitz, Sifre Numbers, op. cit., p. 169, note 8; cf. Jastrow, "a corruption of primipilum," *Dictionary of the Targumim, the Talmud Babli and Yerushalmi, and the Midrashic Literature,* vol. 2, p. 1177, and also *Aruch Hashalem,* vol. 6, p. 350; see especially note 5.

70) Friedmann, op. cit., emended the text to read, "like me."

71) See also Johnston, "Parabolic Interpretations," p. 273.

72) See note 63 above.

73) Cf. b. Sanhedrin 106b and Midrash Hagadol on Numbers 25:1 (Rabinowitz, p. 434).

74) Safrai, *R. Akiva,* p. 52.

75) Tos. Shebuot 1:7 (Zuckermandel, p. 446); b. Shebuot 26a and see b. Chagigah 12a (bottom), Gen. Rabbah 22:2 (Albeck, p. 206) and 53:15 (Albeck, p. 574). For the system of R. Ishmael see Sifre Numbers 112 (Horovitz, p. 121), b. Sanhedrin 90b, b. Sanhedrin 64b and cf. with Bacher *Die Agada der Tannaiten,* vol. 1, pp. 231–232; idem, *Agadot Hatannaim,* vol. 1, part 1, p. 174.

76) See Safrai, *R. Akiva,* pp. 50ff.

77) Ibid, p. 63.

78) B. Sanhedrin 38b (see Rashi's commentary) and see also H. Schwarzbaum, *The Mishle Shu'alim (Fox Fables) of Rabbi Berechiah Ha-Nakdan a Study in Comparative Folklore and Fable Lore* (Kiron: Institute for Jewish and Arab Folklore Research, 1979), pp. XXIII–XXIV and see p. 467, note 12.

79) See Schwarzbaum, *The Mishle Shu'alim,* pp. I–II and pp. 25ff. Schwarbaum refers to several fables which are similar to R. Akiva's illustration and remarks, "In my view, Rabbi Akiba's fable had been current in *oral tradition* long before Rabbi Akiba employed it as an illustration of his notion regarding the basic importance of Torah studies" (ibid, p. 26).

80) Epstein, *Mevoot Lesifrut Hatannaim,* p. 703; D. Hoffmann, *Mesilot Letorat Hatannaim* (Tel Aviv: Dvir, 1948), p. 77, and cf. M. Herr, "Sifrei," *Encyclopaedia Judaica,* vol. 14, cols. 1519–1520.

81) Strack and Stemberger, *Einleitung,* pp. 254–255.

82) Sifre Deuteronomy Piska 19 (Finkelstein, p. 31) and see parallel in Sifre Deuteronomy Piska 356 (Finkelstein, p. 424 and parallels); Midrash Tannaim on Deut. 1:21 (Hoffmann, p. 11); Midrash Hagadol on Deut. 1:21 (Fisch, p. 34); and cf. Midrash Lekach Tov on Deut. 1:21. Cf. Johnston, "Parabolic Interpretations Attributed to Tannaim," pp. 283ff. See also Flusser, *Die rabbinischen Gleichnisse,* pp. 271–272.

83) In Midrash Hagadol, op. cit., these two verses are cited at the beginning of the parable instead of at the end as in Sifre Deuteronomy; see also Finkelstein, p. 31, critical apparatus.

84) The Midrash Hagadol reads "all of these vineyards" instead of, "all of this grapevines." The more common number of elements in a list such as this is three instead of two (and compare Sifre Deuteronomy 356, Finkelstein, p. 424).

85) G. Kittel *Sifre zu Deuteronomium* (Stuttgart: W. Kohlhammer, 1922), p. 29f, note.

86) See Johnston "Parabolic Interpretations Attributed to Tannaim," pp. 283–284. Johnston criticizes Kittel's terminology. A distinction must be made between allegory and parabolic language. This distinction is discussed more fully below where the difference between a sign and a symbol is treated. The points of comparison between the mashal and nimshal do not turn a parable into a full-fledged allegory.

87) See notes 82, 83 and 84 above.

88) Sifre Deuteronomy Piska 356 (Finkelstein, p. 424 and see note 79 above); Midrash Hagadol on Deuteronomy 33:29 (Fish, p. 778); Midrash Tannaim on Deut. 33:29 (Hoffman, p. 222) and Yalkut Machiri on Psalm 31:28 (Buber, p. 101a). See Johnston, "Parabolic Interpretations Attributed to Tannaim," pp. 314–315.

89) Unlike Sifre Deuteronomy Piska 356, in the Yalkut Machiri on Psalm 31:28, the parable is a king parable. The differences between these two texts are slight, i.e. the Yalkut Machiri adds "all of these lands are yours" to the list of three elements mentioned already in Sifre Deuteronomy.

90) This of course is one of the weaknesses of I. Ziegler's work, *Die Königsgleichnisse des Midrasch beleuchtet durch die römische Kaiserzeit* (Breslau: Schlesische Verlags-Anstalt v. s. Schottlaender, 1903). The collection known as "king parables" is a somewhat artificial category and it is doubtful if one can learn very much about the life of royalty from these illustrations. See also, T. Guttmann, *Hamashal Betekufat Hatannaim* (Jerusalem: Abir Yaakov, 1949), pp. 78–79.

91) Midrash Hagadol on Deuteronomy 33:29 (Fisch, p. 778) and see notes 79 and 85 above.

92) See note 82 above.

93) Genesis Rabbah 1:15 (Albeck, p. 13 and parallels) and see also Guttmann, pp. 23f.

94) See Strack and Stemberger, *Einleitung,* pp. 270–273 and pp. 305–307. Stemberger refers to Seder Eliyahu as an ethical midrash which is more accurate. For Pesikta Derav Kahana, see also the introduction by W. Braude and I. Kapstein, trans. *Pesikta de-Rab Kahana* (Philadelphia: Jewish Publication Society, 1975), pp. ix–lvii.

95) Pesikta Derav Kahana 3:1 (Mandelbaum, p. 36). The English translation of W. Braude and I. Kapstein (p. 42) has been consulted and used with some modifications. The translation of the word *letz* as scorner has been retained which was a meaning of the word during the time of the Pesikta; however at an earlier period it had the connotation of "bad company" or even villain; cf. Jastrow, *A Dictionary of the Targumim, the Talmud Babli and Yerushalmi, and the Midrashic Literature,* vol. 2, p. 716.

96) See the Mechilta Derabbi Ishmael on Exodus 17:8 (Horovitz, p. 176; Lauterbach, vol. 2, p. 135) and the Mechilta Derabbi Simeon bar Yochai on Exodus 17:8 (Epstein and Melamed, p. 119). See the article by D. Flusser, "It is not a Serpent that Kills," *Judaism and the Origins of Christianity* (Jerusalem: Magnes, at the press), note 9. Flusser noted that this interpretation is unique to Israel's sages. The Greek, Latin and Aramaic translations all understood that Amalek was the one who did not fear God in Deuteronomy 25:18 (Flusser, ibid).

97) Ibid. The term "Rephidim" is not interpreted as a place name but rather as describing Israel's moral failure. It is understood as meaning "weak hands" from the words רפה and ידים.

98) Pesikta Derav Kahana 3:1 (Mandelbaum, p. 36). See the English translation by W. Braude and I. Kapstein, *Pesikta de-Rab Kahana,* p. 40.

99) For the parallels see Exodus Rabbah 26:2 where the parable has been abbreviated; Pesikta Rabbati 13 (Friedmann, p. 55a–b) where it is attributed to R. Berachiah Hakohen Berabbi; the dog does not appear in this version and see the English translation by W. Braude, *Pesikta Rabbati* vol. 1, pp. 252–253 and especially p. 253, note 34 concerning the Parma manuscript's version of the parable which is nearer to Pesikta Derav Kahana; Yalkut Shimeoni, vol. 1, remez 261, where the parable is attributed to R. Levi (from Pesikta Derav Kahana); Tanchuma, Yitro 3, the parable is attributed to R. Levi; Tanchuma, Buber's edition, Yitro, 4; cf. M. Kasher, *Torah Shelemah,* Beshalach, vol. 14, pp. 250f; and compare also the parable attributed to R. Simeon b. Yochai in the Mechilta on Exodus 13:1 (Horovitz, p. 59) its parallels; see note 17 above.

100) Ibid.

101) See Bacher, *Die Agada der palästinensischen Amoräer* (Strassburg: Trübner, 1896), pp. 296f; idem, *Agadat Amore Eretz Yisrael,* vol. 2, part 2, pp. 5ff.

102) Ibid. See j. Sucah chap. 55a, chap. 5 hal. 1; Gen. Rabbah 98:11 (Albeck, p. 1261) and see also A. Hyman, *Toldot Tannaim Veamoraim* (Jerusalem: Boys Town, 1964), vol. 3, p. 852.

103) J. Rosh Hashanah 59b, chap. 4, hal. 1 and cf. M. Margalioth, *Entzaiklopediyah Lechachame Hatalmud Vehageonim* (Tel Aviv: Yavneh, 1976), vol. 2, p. 618.

104) See the story about R. Eleazar b. Hyrcanos and R. Joshua from Song of Songs Rabbah 1:10, cf. Bacher, *Die Agada der Tannaiten* vol. 1, p. 124; idem, *Agadot Hatannaim,* vol. 1, part 1, p. 92.

105) Song of Songs Rabbah 1:10, cf. Bacher, *Die Agada der palästinensischen Amoräer,* vol. 2, pp. 299–300 and especially note 1 on p. 300 and also pp. 92–93 and note 6 on p. 92; idem, *Agadat Amore Eretz Yisrael,* vol. 2, part 2, pp. 7–8 and note 3 on p. 8; see also idem, vol. 2, part 1, p. 88, note 4 and Bacher, *Die Agada der Tannaiten,* vol. 1, p. 421, note 6; idem, *Agadot Hatannaim,* vol. 1, part 2, p. 134, note 4.

106) Bacher, *Die Agada der palästinensischen Amoräer,* vol. 2, pp. 300–303; idem, *Agadat Amore Eretz Yisrael,* vol. 2, part 2, pp. 8–10 and see his references there.

107) The Mechilta Derabbi Ishmael on Exodus 19:4 (Horovitz, p. 208) and see note 17 above.

108) See the interesting tradition in Pesikta Derav Kahana 3:8 (Mandelbaum, pp. 46–47) which is paralleled in the Midrash Hagadol on Exodus 17:8. The word Amalek is interpreted as meaning "with lapping" *(im lak).* Thus Amalek is understood as, " . . . the nation which comes to lap up the blood of Israel like a dog." Hence Amalek is again connected to a dog.

109) Pesikta Rabbati 13 and Exodus Rabbah 26:2 both delete the mention of the dog though Exodus Rabbah already does mention the "enemy." See also the preceding note.

110) Pesikta Derav Kahana 3:9 (Mandelbaum, p. 47).

111) Pesikta Derav Kahana 12:24 (Mandelbaum, p. 223 and compare Buber's edition, p. 109b, and see especially Buber's note 182). See the English translation of W. Braude and I. Kapstein, *Pesikta de-Rab Kahana,* p. 248. The colorful parable concerning the Exodus would certainly have been appropriate for a homily from the Mechilta, its sources or an early exposition concerning the redemption of Israel from Egypt. This parable does have a number of parallels; see Pesikta Rabbati 21,

attributed to R. Judah and R. Nehemiah. It may be of significance that the parable appears in Pesikta Rabbati in the section which deals with the decalogue. This section is an entity in itself and seems to have been derived from early sources. Parallels are also found in Midrash Hagadol on Exodus 20:2, in the name of R. Yudah and R. Nehemiah; Tanchuma (Buber's edition), Yitro, 16 (R. Nehemiah); Yalkut Shimeoni, vol. 1, remez 286 (R. Nehemiah) and cf. Kasher, *Torah Shelemah,* on Exodus 20:2, vol. 15, p. 9. Compare also the parable about the man exiled from country to country who heard his neighbor speak his own language, Seder Eliyahu Rabbah, p. 158. Interestingly enough, in another context the Pesikta actually states that Israel did not learn the language of the Egyptians; Pesikta Derav Kahana 11:6 (Mandelbaum, p. 182; Braude and Kapstein, pp. 205–206).

112) Pesikta Derav Kahana 12:24, Buber's edition, p. 109b, note 182.

113) A different view is expressed in Pesikta Derav Kahana 11:6 and see note 78 above. On the etymology of *anoch,* see Ben Yehudah, *Milon Halashon Haevrit,* vol. 1, p. 318, note 3.

114) Stemberger has correctly treated it under the category of "Ethische Midraschim," Strack and Stemberger, *Einleitung,* pp. 305ff.

115) A discussion of the various approaches to the text has been summarized by M. Kadushin, *The Theology of Seder Eliahu* (New York: Bloch Publishing Company, 1932), pp. 3–16 and more recently by W. Braude and I. Kapstein, *Tanna Debe Eliyyahu* (Philadelphia: The Jewish Publication Society of America, 1981), pp. 3–12. To date, Friedmann's long introduction to Seder Eliyahu in his edition of the text remains the most comprehensive treatment of the entire question. Shmuel Safrai has discussed the compilation of Seder Eliyahu, idem, "Chasidim Veanshe Maaseh," *Tzion* (1985), pp. 150f. See also Mann and Epstein in note 120 and Margulies in note 123 below.

116) As Braude and Kapstein have pointed out, "What animates and gives life to these concepts is the artistry with which they are fleshed out" (op. cit., note 79, p. 20). Seder Eliyahu is an "animated" midrash. E.E. Urbach has written an important contribution concerning Seder Eliyahu's unique language, idem, "Lesheelat Leshono Umekorotav Shel Sefer 'Seder Eliyahu,'" *Leshonenu* 21 (1957), pp. 183–197. Urbach suggests a later date for Seder Eliyahu because of its language. While his linguistic analysis is instructive, other authorities have not agreed with his conclusions with respect to the time of the text's composition (see preceding note and especially Safrai's article). As already noted, here it is impossible to treat the whole question concerning the date of Seder Elijah adequately; however whether Seder Eliyahu's lively, colorful language and

its unique style can be taken as the absolute proof of a late date for the text is questionable. The discovery of the Dead Sea Scrolls has revolutionized the study of the Hebrew language from the Second Temple Period. More philological research is needed to better understand the linguistic developments and characteristics of Hebrew during the various periods in which it was written and/or spoken.

117) Seder Eliyahu Rabbah, Chapter 1, (Friedmann, p. 4; Braude and Kapstein, *Tanna Debe Eliyyahu,* p. 46). Compare the use of the lash in Seder Eliyahu Rabbah, Chapter 5 (Friedmann, p. 25).

118) See Friedmann, "Introduction," Seder Eliyahu, p. 120.

119) For the word *chaver,* see the *Aruch Hashalem,* vol. 3, pp. 339–40 and J. Mann, "Date and Place of Redaction of Seder Eliyahu Rabba and Zutta," *Hebrew Union College Annual* 4 (1927), p. 306, note 137.

120) Mann, "Date and Place of Redaction of Seder Eliyahu Rabba and Zutta," p. 306 and cf. J. Epstein, *Mevo Lenusach Hamishnah* (Tel Aviv: Dvir, 1974), vol. 2, p. 762.

121) See Friedmann, "Introduction," Seder Eliyahu Rabbah, p. 33.

122) Mann, "Date and Place of Redaction of Seder Eliyahu Rabba and Zutta," p. 306 and see Friedmann, "Introduction," Seder Eliyahu Rabbah, p. 6, note 21 and cf. also b. Sanhedrin 39a. The dualism of Zoroastrianism can be seen in a passage from the Denkart (VI:31) discussed by Shaked, "Knowledge is a prerequisite of religion. It constitutes an essential distinction between the two powers: it is the desire of Ohrmazd to be known, while it is Ahreman's wish not to be known": S. Shaked, *The Wisdom of the Sasanian Sages,* p. xxv. Whether the Zoroastrian actually thought that Ohrmazd was fire as might be inferred from Seder Eliyahu is unlikely but fire was an important aspect of prayer and worship. Thus one reads, "It is necessary to direct a man's soul mostly to these three places: to the houses of sages, to the houses of good people, and to the houses of fire . . . to the houses of fire, so that the spiritual demon may turn away from him" (Denkart VI:323, Shaked, p. 129 and see his comments, idem, *The Wisdom of the Sasanian Sages,* p. xxix). Interestingly enough, the custom prevails that a Zoroastrian prays before some form of fire in order to concentrate on righteousness; see M. Boyce, *A Persian Stronghold of Zoroastrianism* (Oxford: The Clarendon Press, 1977), p. 29.

123) See also Friedmann, "Introduction," Seder Eliyahu Rabbah, pp. 82f, who preceded Mann. See also Epstein, *Mevo Lenusach Hamishnah,* vol. 2, p. 762 and compare M. Margulies, "Lebaiyat Kadmuto Shel Sefer Seder Eliyahu," *Sefer Asaf,* D. Cassuto, J. Klausner, and J. Guttmann, eds. (Jerusalem: Mossad Derav Kook, 1954), pp. 385f. Cf. J. Hinnells,

"The Cosmic Battle: Zoroastrianism," *The World's Religions* (England: Lion Publishing, 1982), p. 84.

124) See Seder Eliyahu Rabbah, p. 27 and cf. Kadushin, *The Theology of Seder Eliahu,* p. 73; and also Seder Eliyahu Rabbah, p. 27 in connection to the Kingship of God and cf. Kadushin, op. cit., p. 58.

125) Ibid.

126) Midrash Psalms 11:5, W. Braude, *The Midrash on Psalms* (New Haven: Yale University Press, 1959), vol. 1, pp. 161–163 and cf. Genesis Rabbah 51:3 (Albeck, pp. 534ff).

127) W. Braude and I. Kapstein, *Tanna Debe Eliyyahu,* p. 183. On the meaning of *derech eretz* see Safrai, "Chasidim Veanshe Maaseh," p. 146.

128) The saying is attributed to R. Nechunya b. Hakanah the disciple of R. Akiva and R. Joshua, "He that takes upon himself the yoke of the Law, from him shall be taken away the yoke of the kingdom and the yoke of worldly care" (Danby's translation, p. 450). This saying is tannaitic and seems to reflect a time of persecution. See now D. Flusser, "A Rabbinic Parallel to the Sermon on the Mount," *Judaism and the Origins of Christianity* (Jerusalem: Magnes, at the press), notes 22, 23 and 25.

129) M. Kadushin, *Organic Thinking a Study in Rabbinic Thought* (New York: The Jewish Theological Seminary of America, 1938), pp. 118–119 and p. 299, notes 133–134.

130) Seder Eliyahu Rabbah, p. 62. The author is greatly indebted to S. Safrai for his valuable insights into this text (private communication). See also Safrai, "Chasidim Veanshe Maaseh," pp. 144–147.

131) See parallel in Seder Eliyahu Rabbah, p. 90.

132) B. Sanhedrin 99b and paralleled in Yalkut Shimeoni, vol. 2, remez 6. Of course toil by mouth refers to learning by recital and by repetition.

133) One often noted characteristic of Seder Eliyahu is that the text seldom refers to the tradent of the materials it preserves.

134) See G. Alon, *Mechkarim Betoldot Yisrael* (Israel: Hakibbutz Hameuchad, 1978), vol. 1, pp. 274–275, and especially D. Flusser, *Yehadut Umekorot Hanatzrut,* pp. 235ff. See the contribution of Safrai, "Chasidim Veanshe Maaseh," pp. 133–144 and especially pp. 150–152. Compare also J. Licht, "An Analysis of the Treatise on the Two Spirits in DSD," *Scripta Hierosolymitana* (Jerusalem: Magnes, 1965), vol. 4, pp. 94–95 and see D. Flusser, "A New Sensitivity in Judaism and the Christian Message," *Harvard Theological Review* 61 (1968), pp. 113–114.

135) The more original version has been preserved in the Latin text;

see H. Lietzmann, *Die Didache mit kritischem Apparat* (Bonn: A. Marcus und E. Weber's Verlag, 1912), p. 3. See now Flusser, "A Rabbinic Parallel to the Sermon on the Mount," note 23.

136) Ibid and see Flusser, op. cit., note 101 above. This text appears in 1QS 4:2–3 and see G. Vermes, *The Dead Sea Scrolls in English* (Baltimore: Penguin, 1965), p. 76 and the fine critical edition with commentary by J. Licht, *Megilat Haserachim* (Jerusalem: Bialik, 1975), p. 95. The Qumran Sect interpreted the motif of the two ways within their belief of divine election. The two ways became the two spirits and the idea of man's free choice was minimized or eliminated completely.

137) Seder Eliyahu Rabbah, p. 1. See Safrai, "Chasidim Veanshe Maaseh," p. 151.

138) Kadushin, *Organic Thinking,* p. 300, note 160.

139) Seder Eliyahu Rabbah, p. 56.

140) Seder Eliyahu Rabbah, p. 112.

141) M. Higger, *Masechtot Derech Eretz* (Jerusalem: Makor, 1970), vol. 1, pp. 77–78, English translation, vol. 2, p. 38. Here Higger's translation has been modified from leather bottle to wineskin.

142) 1QS 4:2ff; see Licht, *Megilat Haserachim,* p. 95 and Vermes, *The Dead Sea Scrolls in English,* p. 76 and compare the Didache 3:7–8 and Galatians 5:22–23. See David Flusser, "The Dead Sea Sect and Pre-Pauline Christianity," p. 249 and especially notes 116 and 117.

143) Higger, *Masechtot Derech Eretz,* vol. 1, pp. 95–96, English translation, vol. 2, p. 42, Derech Eretz Zuta 2:9 and compare also Midrash Tannaim on Deuteronomy 15:7 (p. 81) where the expression "like a lower threshold" is related to poverty.

144) Avot Derabbi Natan Version A, chapter 22, English translation by J. Goldin, *The Fathers According to Rabbi Nathan* (New York: Schocken, 1974), p. 99. See also Avot 3:9 and cf. T. Hereford, *The Ethics of the Talmud the Sayings of the Fathers* (New York: Schocken, 1975), pp. 76–77 and C. Taylor, *Sayings of the Jewish Fathers* (London: Cambridge University Press, 1877), pp. 63ff. Compare also James 2:17.

145) Compare b. Niddah 70b and see Flusser, "A Rabbinic Parallel to the Sermon on the Mount," notes 25–26. See also S. Safrai, "Teaching of Pietists in Mishnaic Literature," *Journal of Jewish Studies* 16 (1965), pp. 15–33 and idem, "Mishnat Hachasidim Besifrut Hatannaim," *Eretz Yisrael Vechachameha Betekufat Hamishnah Vehatalmud* (Israel: Hakibbutz Hameuchad, 1983), pp. 145–160 (Hebrew translation of English article). See especially Safrai, "Chasidim Veanshe Maaseh," pp. 144–154. The classic work on the Chasidim is A. Büchler, *Types of Jewish Palestinian Piety from 70 B.C.E. to 70 C.E.* (London: Jews' College Pub-

lications, 1922); see especially pp. 83f. Cf. the discussion of the deeds of R. Chanina b. Dosa, G. Vermes, "Hanina ben Dosa," *Post-Biblical Jewish Studies* (Leiden: Brill, 1975), pp. 178–214.

146) Matthew 5:14–16; Mark 4:21; Luke 8:16, 11:33; John 8:12.

147) Cf. also the saying of R. Simeon b. Eleazar, "When Israel does the will of the Omnipresent, then is His name magnified in the world, as it was said 'When all the kings of the Amorites heard . . .' (Josh. 5:1)" (The Mechilta Derabbi Ishmael on Exodus 15:3, Horovitz, p. 128; The Mechilta Derabbi Simeon bar Yochai on Exodus 15:3, Melamed and Epstein, p. 80 and parallels). See P. Billerbeck, vol. 1, pp. 239–240.

148) Sifre Numbers Piska 93 (Horovitz, p. 94) and Sifre Numbers Zuta on Numbers 11:17 (Horovitz, p. 271).

149) Seder Eliyahu Chapter Rabbah (11) 12 (Friedmann, p. 55) and see Braude and Kapstein, *Tanna Debe Eliyyahu,* p. 166.

150) Compare the parables in b. Shabbat 153a (R. Johanan b. Zakai) and b. Shabbat 152b. The element of theodicy is missing in these parables. See the important discussion, Flusser, *Yehadut Umekorot Hanatzrut,* pp. 162ff.

151) B. Shabbat 153a and cf. Semachot Derabbi Chiyah 2:1 (Higger, pp. 216f) and Ecclesiastes Rabbah 9:7.

153) See Flusser, *Yehadut Umekorot Hanatzrut,* pp. 174ff and idem, *Die rabbinischen Gleichnisse,* pp. 22–28.

153) This point must be emphasized. The distinction made here between symbol and allegory is by no means to be considered a technical definition.

154) See S.I. Hayakawa, *Language in Thought and Action* (New York: Harcourt Brace Jovanovich, Inc., 1978), pp. 22–25.

155) Tertullian, "On Modesty," VII, A. Roberts and J. Donaldson, *The Ante-Nicene Fathers* (Grand Rapids: Eerdmans, 1965), vol. 4, p. 80.

156) Augustine, *Quaestiones Evangeliorum* II, 19, cited by C.H. Dodd, *The Parables of the Kingdom* (Great Britain: Collins, 1961), pp. 13–14.

157) See notes 82 and 88 above.

158) See note 63 above.

159) I.e. Sifra, op. cit., notes 53 and 58 above.

160) See note 17 above.

161) Sifre Deuteronomy Piska 49 (Finkelstein, p. 115) and see Bacher, *Die Agada der Tannaiten,* vol. 1, pp. 31–32; idem, *Agadot Hatannaim,* vol. 1, part 1, p. 24. See also J. Lauterbach, "The Ancient Jewish Allegorists in Talmud and Midrash," *Jewish Quarterly Review* 1 (1910–1911), pp. 304ff. One may question whether this passage actually sup-

ports Lauterbach's theory concerning the *dorshe reshumot* as being allegorists who tried to explain away portions of scripture which described God in a way they found objectionable.

162) J. Heinemann, *Derashot Betzibur Betekufat Hatalmud,* pp. 11ff.

163) J. Heinemann, "The Proem in the Aggadic Midrashim—A Form Critical Study," *Scripta Hierosolymitana,* (1971), vol. 22, pp. 100f. Heinemann observed, "The editors of the classical Midrashim, especially of the so-called homiletical Midrashim, which have come down to us, undoubtedly drew upon material used, in the first place, in public sermons delivered on Sabbaths and festivals. This is not to say, however, that the midrashic homilies are identical with the sermons as they were actually preached in public. It appears that the compilers of the Midrashim used for each of their homilies a variety of actual sermons, fully or in part, and combined them into a new entity, which we may perhaps call 'the literary homily'" (ibid, p. 100).

164) Cf. Flusser, *Die rabbinischen Gleichnisse,* pp. 21, 26f, 33ff, and see also C. Thoma, "Prolegomena zu einer Übersetzung und Kommentierung der rabbinischen Gleichnisse," *Theologische Zeitschrift* (1982), pp. 518–531 and also idem and S. Lauer, *Die Gleichnisse der Rabbinen Erster Teil Pesiqta deRav Kahana (PesK)* (Bern: Peter Lang, 1986).

165) See Flusser, *Yehadut Umekorot Hanatzrut,* p. 157.

166) Matthew 7:21–27; Luke 6:46–49 and compare the different context in Luke's text. See also the parallel in Avot Derabbi Natan, version A, chapter 24. The Sermon on the Mount material is more properly understood as a collection or compilation of sayings and teachings of Jesus. Nonetheless Jesus may very well have concluded his teachings with parable(s) as the evangelists here indicate.

167) See note 17 above.

168) See note 63 above.

169) Tos. Berachot 4:16 (Lieberman's edition, pp. 22f) and see the parallels cited by Liebermann, *Tosefta Kefshutah,* Order Zeraim, pp. 68–69.

170) Cf. Feldman, *The Parables and Similes of the Rabbis,* pp. 5–6, and compare J. Klausner, *Jesus of Nazareth* (London: Macmillan, 1925), pp. 264f.

171) E.g. Guttmann, *Hamashal,* p. 76.

THE PARABLES AND THE GOSPELS: THE SYNOPTIC PROBLEM

The parables of Jesus are recorded in the synoptic gospels and must be studied in their individual contexts and in light of their parallels in the other gospels. The textual analysis of Matthew, Mark and Luke is determined to a certain extent by a researcher's fundamental understanding of the mutual dependence of these three documents. This, of course, makes the procedure adopted in interpreting synoptic relationships of primary importance in the study of the three earliest gospels. Hence, any adequate examination of the gospel narratives cannot afford to ignore the challenge of elucidating synoptic interrelationships.[1] While this is true, one must beware of the danger of determining the text of the gospels solely upon the basis of an approach to the synoptics. Here, the purpose of the discussion is not to present a comprehensive analysis to the synoptic problem, but rather to explain the method and approach which is presupposed throughout the treatment of the texts in this work.

The Synoptic Problem

The brief analysis devoted to this issue in the following pages cannot aspire to solve the synoptic problem—once and for all—especially in light of so many highly talented scholars who have presented more comprehensive treatises dealing with the major elements of synoptic disputes. Yet, in spite of all the benefits to be derived from the evidence accumulated by treatments of the synoptic problem, sometimes this evidence can be used to support specious theories that somewhat compromise the facts. The facts are always to be considered more important than the theories. One ubiquitous question must always be asked and asked again: How can this accumulated data be evaluated and integrated into a comprehensive working hypothesis that yields an overall effectual approach to the analysis of the texts themselves? Nonetheless scholars evaluate the evidence differently and there are probably as many approaches to the synoptic problem as there are New Testament scholars. At least though one group of researchers can arrive at a general consensus concerning a particular theory, one often discovers significant differences among them when they evaluate a text and apply their methodology.

In an effort to interpret the accumulated evidence of synoptic interrelationships, twentieth century New Testament scholarship has arrived at a general consensus that accepts the theory of Marcan priority as a working hypothesis. Briefly stated, this hypothesis theorizes that Mark was written prior to Matthew and Luke. Moreover, Matthew and Luke use Mark as one of their sources, and independently rework his text. In addition, Matthew and Luke had another hypothetical source often referred to as the document Q, which they edited along with other materials into their Marcan source. This basic two document hypothesis (or variations of it) forms the foundation of most recent exegesis of the synoptic gospels.

Today this theory of Marcan priority has gained such wide acceptance that it is seldom challenged. Those who question this hypothesis are sometimes thought to have refused to recognize the veracities of modern scholarship. W.R. Farmer's observation often holds true in regard to how Marcan priorists view researchers who find their theory difficult to implement.

> . . . after Streeter they were proliferated and transmuted into evidence that Matthew and Luke had altered the more primitive text of Mark. The argument is in fact very allusive and in the minds of many in the post-Streeter period who were convinced of Markan priority on the basis of a received scholarly consensus, it constituted a seemingly impregnable fortress into which one could retreat, and from which one could look down with condescension if not disdain upon efforts to determine the established position in Synoptic studies.[2]

Nevertheless, some researchers have remained unconvinced by the arguments that support Marcan priority. Are Matthew's and Luke's texts in the triple tradition always best understood as a secondary corruption of the more original Mark? Is Luke's version of Jesus' Preaching at Nazareth, for instance, best viewed as a free reworking of the more primitive version of Mark (Luke 4:16–30; Mark 6:1–6; Matthew 13:53–58)? Perhaps E.P. Sanders has articulated one of the fundamental difficulties with the conventional approach to the synoptic problem, and it is not that the theory has met with wide approval which it has, " . . . but that the dominant hypothesis is frequently held too rigidly." Sanders continues, " . . . it [Marcan Priority] is accorded a degree of certainty which it does not merit."[3] Furthermore, Sanders provides a list of passages in Mark which are considered secondary to Matthew or Luke by various prominent New Testament scholars who all accept the two document theory as a working hypothesis.[4] Hans-Herbert Stoldt's important work, *History and Criticism of the Marcan Hypothesis,* not only questions the evidence amassed to prove Marcan priority but also studies the intellectual situation of German New Testament scholarship that gave rise to the two document hypothesis.[5] A careful reading of Stoldt's scholarship underscores the need to re-examine the whole question of synoptic relationships. General scholarly consensus should never be translated too rapidly into fact. Marcan priority is at best a theory, and as a theory it must stand upon its own merits and must be evaluated according to the evidence. Is the evidence for the priority of Mark conclusive? Not all students of the gospels feel comfortable with the strict application of the two document hypothesis.

The Argument of Order

One of the arguments considered to strongly favor the theory of Marcan priority is based on the phenomenon of sequential agreement of pericopes in the triple tradition. In the first half of the nineteenth century, Karl Lachmann[6] noted that Matthew and Luke almost always agree with Mark's arrangement of the pericopes. Moreover, Matthew and Luke do not correspond to each other's placing of materials which are not parallel to Mark. Matthew agrees with Mark against Luke in his placing of the story units and Luke agrees with Mark against Matthew in his arrangement of his material. Hence the suggestion has been forwarded that Matthew and Luke depended on Mark's gospel for their basic outline. They changed his structural order independently.

The argument for Marcan priority on the basis of the synoptist's outline is somewhat misleading. In order for the argument to succeed, one must first accept the fundamental assumption of Marcan originality. Otherwise the observations concerning the synoptic arrangement do not necessarily support the theory of Marcan priority in the formation of their basic outline.[7] Is it possible to accumulate evidence to support a theory based on the theory itself? It is just as logical and possible to theorize either that Mark based his outline on Matthew's gospel and that Luke was influenced by Mark, or that Mark derived his basic outline from Luke and that Matthew's outline was influenced by Mark. Nevertheless, any argument for the priority of one of the synoptics formulated entirely on observations made concerning the sequential arrangement of the pericopes must be deemed inconclusive and wholly inadequate. A datum must be interpreted and all the possibilities must be considered before it is admitted as evidence. It is impossible to survey the arrangement of all the pericopes in the triple tradition and to conclude confidently who influenced whom.

So while Marcan priorists have theorized that Matthew and Luke independently changed Mark's arrangement, they have too hastily precluded other possible explanations. Because Matthew and Luke do not agree in their dislocations from Mark, one could ask another question: Is Mark responsible for either Matthew's non-concurrence in arrangement with Luke or for Luke's non-concurrence in arrangement with Matthew? In other words, could Mark be the *mediator* that causes Matthew to follow Marcan order in the contexts when Luke's order is different than Mark's arrangement? Of course, the converse could be asked concerning Luke's agreement with Mark's order in relation to Matthew's gospel.

Matthew diverges from Marcan sequence in eight different contexts (cf. figure I).[8] Only one of these pericopes is found in the passages of Lucan divergence from Marcan order. Both Matthew and Luke position the "Appointment of the Twelve" (Mark 3:13f and parallels) in a different context than Mark. Nevertheless, Matthew and Luke do not support each other in dislocating this unit by placing it in the same position in their respective gospels. Matthew positions two or three of his dislocations from Mark around his Sermon on the Mount material (Matthew 4:23 par. Mark 1:39; Matthew 4:25 par. Mark 3:10, 7, 8; Matthew 8:1–4 par. Mark 1:40–45). Matthew places the healing of a leper after the discourse as Jesus descends from the mountain.[9] The people have already marveled at the authority of Jesus' teaching (Matthew 7:28). This effect of the discourse seems to have been transferred from the Marcan parallel describing Jesus in the Capernaum synagogue (Mark 1:22; Luke 4:32). Then Matthew transfers some material concerning miracles that occurred in the Capernaum area, the "Stilling of the Tempest" and the "Exorcism of the Demoniacs"[10] from a later Marcan context (Mark 4:35–5:20), to follow the teaching of the sermon and the healing of Peter's mother-in-law. One cannot help but suspect that perhaps some editorial forethought went into the rearrangement of this material.[11]

W.D. Davies has suggested that Matthew desired to present Jesus as the second Moses presenting a new Torah from Mount Sinai number two.[12] Too much should not be read into Matthew's arrangement; however it is possible that some of these divergences from the Marcan outline are due to Matthew's own editorial interests. Certainly it is remarkable that seven out of eight of Matthew's non-concurrences with Marcan order appear in his first ten chapters. The one remaining divergence occurs in chapter twenty-one where both Matthew and Luke correspond in non-concurrences with Mark's arrangement by positioning the "Cleansing of the Temple," after the "Entry into Jerusalem" (Matthew 21:1–17; Luke 19:31–38, 45–46).[13] Matthew combines the narrative of the "Cursing of the Fig Tree" and the "Withering of the Fig Tree" instead of dividing it into two sections like Mark (Mark 11:12–14, 20–25), while Luke does not contain the "Cursing and the Withering of the Fig Tree."

Nine differences of order occur between Luke and Mark (cf.

figure 2). In at least six of these differences in arrangement, Luke's version of the pericope shows a distinguishable independence from the Marcan form of the tradition (Luke 4:16–30, 5:1–11, 7:36–50, 10:25–28, 11:14–23, 12:10, and 22:24–30). Joachim Jeremias would attribute most of these divergences in order and in wording to what he has called "Luke's special source."[14] Jeremias regards this special source very highly and suggests that this source, as it is reflected in Luke, sometimes more originally preserves the tradition than the parallel passage in Mark.[15] David Flusser has gone one step further: "My experience, chiefly based on the research of R.L. Lindsey, has shown me that Luke mostly preserves, in comparison to Mark (and to Matthew, when depending on Mark), the original tradition, and that Mark has rewritten his source (or sources) and so unfavorably influenced Matthew."[16] At least Jeremias found it difficult to explain some superior texts of Luke as secondary corruptions of Mark. In many ways Jeremias' "special source" approach is attractive and it illustrates that a Marcan priorist like Jeremias, who showed an unique acumen for elucidating the textual foundation essential for comprehending the historical Jesus, found it necessary at times to explain the phenomenon of Lucan originality in the preservation of gospel materials. Thus also H. Schürmann suggested that Luke's version of Jesus' preaching at Nazareth which is so different from Mark's was derived from a another saying source employed by Luke (Luke 4:16–30; Mark 6:1–6; Matthew 13:53–58).[17] Has the importance of Luke been minimized? The Lucan form of the tradition merits serious consideration, and one should avoid the danger of always treating Luke as a freehanded reworked version of Mark's gospel.

The divergences of order in the narratives between Luke and Mark are fairly scattered equally throughout their narratives with perhaps somewhat more divergence after the third passion prediction (Mark 10:35f). At least no major concentration of disagreements in order may be discerned in one specific area of the narrative as is seen in Matthew. Four non-concurrences of arrangement occur in the first third of Mark's gospel;[18] then follows the so called "great omission,"[19] and finally five divergences of order appear in Mark's last six chapters.[20] This should be contrasted with the situation that exists between Matthew and Mark, where seven out of eight non-agreements in order appear in Mark's first six chapters (about one third of his gospel) and in five chapters of Matthew (chapters four, seven, eight, nine and ten).

The changes in order between Luke and Mark are sometimes more radical[21] than are the changes of sequence that occur between Mark and Matthew. Thus the "Preaching at Nazareth" that Luke records at the outset of Jesus' ministry (4:16f) does not appear until almost one third of the way through Mark's gospel (6:1f), and Luke's "Anointing in the House of a Pharisee" (7:36f), which occurs relatively early in Luke's narrative, does not appear in Mark's gospel until late in the passion week (Mark 14:3f). Moreover, it should be borne in mind that Luke's gospel only contains 320 verses of Mark's 661 verses. In contrast to Luke, Matthew retains approximately 606 verses (equivalent to about 500 verses in their Matthean form) of Mark's 661 verses.[22] Thus Matthew had more opportunity to depart from Marcan order and yet follows Mark rather faithfully. One might assume that Luke would contain more divergences from Marcan order, if more of the material was paralleled in Luke. But this final observation is made from silence and therefore can neither be substantiated nor denied. Mark's shorter length can also have the effect of an optical illusion that leads the researcher to the conclusion that the longer gospels are following the shorter. This illusion must be verified or refuted by other facts.

The statistics concerning the relationships of the arrangement of the gospels exist. However, they may be interpreted and analyzed differently. It is conceivable that Matthew and Luke independently changed Mark's order. However, it is also quite possible to suggest that Mark is the mediator between Matthew and Luke, and that Mark altered the arrangement of the earliest gospel and then influenced the sequence of pericopes in the remaining gospel. The entire question is somewhat more complex than what has been presented in this short discussion (cf. figures I and II).[23] In any case, the data from the study of the sequential order of the three synoptics can be comprehensibly accounted for by explaining that Mark omitted much of Luke's gospel and somewhat rearranged Luke's material. Then Matthew followed Mark's order. He was influenced by Marcan reordering of Lucan sequence and also performed some editorial work of his own on Mark's edited arrangement. But this is by no means the only possible explanation. Since the statistics concerning the synoptic order in the triple tradition can be interpreted in various ways, other considerations must be examined in order to understand the relationship between the three earliest gospels.

The suggestion that Mark would have abbreviated or omitted so much material from Luke, Matthew or "Q" is inconceivable to many Marcan priorists. The shortest gospel is most likely to be the earliest gospel according to their view. However, this perspective engages the theory that the gospel writers were averse to deleting any known material and were essentially copiers, who faithfully reproduced their sources in a "scissors and paste"[24] fashion. On the contrary, the evangelists were authors and editors in their own right[25] and no one should doubt that they were capable of omitting sections of their sources.

Ironically, Marcan priorists who have claimed that Mark would not be able to pass over sections of a longer gospel source have been forced to explain the long Lucan omissions of Mark. Nearly half of Mark's gospel fails to appear in Luke. B.H. Streeter suggested that Luke replaces much of this Marcan material with substitutions from another source.[26] Nevertheless, this still leaves a long section (Mark 6:18–29; 6:45–8:26) that does not appear in Luke's narrative. How strange it would seem that Luke would have deleted the story unit concerning the Syrophoenician woman (Mark 7:24–30; Matthew 15:21–28), because he is often noted for his emphasis on the role of women (cf. Luke 8:1f) and for his interest in non-Jewish characters (cf. Luke 10:29f). Did Luke knowingly omit this incident?[27] To avoid ascribing an omission to the evangelist, the theory of an Urmarkan text was formulated.[28] Hence, it was postulated that Luke's copy of Mark did not contain these verses and that they were added later.

However, John Hawkins showed that the "great omission" is derived from the same hand which penned Mark's gospel.[29] Streeter affirmingly added, "In fact, the style and vocabulary of this section (Mark 6:45–8:26) are, if anything, more Markan than Mark."[30] In spite of the evidence which showed that this section was an original part of the gospel of Mark, Streeter still could not imagine that such material would be omitted by one of the evangelists. To overcome his difficulty, he speculated that Luke's version of Mark had been partly damaged in this section.[31] Therefore, Luke was unable to read this section of Mark's gospel because of a faulty manuscript. Should one presume that an evangelist could *not* knowingly omit a section or sections of his source in the compilation of his gospel? Is this assumption justified to the extent that one is permitted to formulate a theory to support the assumption?

At this point, it should be observed that Mark was capable of omitting portions of his source(s). For instance, Mark appears to abbreviate John the Baptist's remarks (Mark 1:8) and does not include the saying concerning the baptism of fire (Luke 3:16–17; Matthew 3:11–12). Flusser noted that the Baptist's reference, which speaks of fire and judgment, was most certainly in the original source.[32] Matthew and Luke agree against Mark by preserving the statement. After all, it is difficult to imagine why a somewhat unclear statement would have been added on to the second part of the sentence. Mark apparently stops in the middle of the sentence and therefore omits some of the few words known from John's prophetic preaching.[33] Most of the gospel materials from Matthew and Luke which are unparalleled in Mark are comprised of Jesus' teaching. Mark seems to be acquainted with Jesus' teaching.[34] Nevertheless, by comparison to Matthew and Luke, Mark considerably abbreviates his gospel by discarding a great deal of teaching material. Either he omitted it, or he did not know it at all. The didactic material that Mark does preserve[35] indicates that he very well may have been acquainted with more traditions of Jesus' teaching than he elected to incorporate into his gospel. Perhaps this teaching material, which bears the marks of a Semitic background and Jewish milieu, would not have been suitable for Mark's intended readership. Is it possible that Mark tried to limit his gospel more to the acts of Jesus and therefore omitted much of Jesus' instruction?

Mark was interested in compiling a gospel of activity. Indeed his narrative is a story of action par excellence. This may be illustrated by Mark's use of the word *euthus*. As has often been noted,

Mark employs this term over forty times in his short gospel. By comparison, Luke uses this expression once.[36] In Mark's gospel, Jesus is depicted as performing one task and immediately *(euthus)* proceeding on to the next in continuous motion. Jesus is not even able to eat (Mark 3:20–21). Thus Mark seems to emphasize the idea of Jesus' constant movement and that sizable crowds were following Jesus. What role would the instruction of Jesus play in Mark's somewhat dramatic presentation? If the teaching of Jesus was already known in Mark's source, then why would he be required to recopy it and insert it into his story? Moreover, a shortened edition of the gospel could have performed some important functions. For one thing, it certainly could have provided an effective tool for communicating the gospel to Hellenistic society. The instruction of Jesus would probably be less important to a non-Jewish, pagan audience. Conversely, the miracles and activities of Jesus would be considered a better vehicle of communication. While it is impossible to know exactly why Mark omitted sections of Jesus' instruction, if he was attempting to present a gospel story of action unobstructed by teaching narration, he succeeded superbly. Nevertheless, extreme caution must be taken in ascribing motive to one of the evangelists. Be that as it may, Mark was capable of editorially deleting portions of his source(s), for his own reasons, as he compiled his gospel.

Mark also seems to be aware of outside sources. These materials may have influenced the shaping of his narrative. For instance, in the temptation narrative Mark's text is decisively different from that of Luke and Matthew. Not only is it much shorter but Mark adds the colorful element, " . . . and he was with the wild beasts." Where did this motif originate? It is paralleled in the Testament of Naphtali (8:4), " . . . the devil will flee from you, and the wild beasts will be afraid of you . . . and the angels will keep close to you."[37] Not only do the wild beasts appear in this passage, but also the angels. Angels find a place both in Mark's text and in Matthew's version which may have been influenced by Mark.[38] Only Mark records that Jesus recites the "Shema Yisrael" and in Luke's version of the parallel passage, the lawyer answers the question instead of Jesus (Mark 12:29;

Luke 10:27; Matthew 22:36). The passage has been treated by Flusser who discussed the problems of Mark's version in comparison to Luke's text.[39] Did Luke delete the 'Hear, O Israel . . . ' and then transfer a saying attributed to Jesus in Mark into the mouth of the lawyer who was depicted as one of his opponents? Matthew does not cite the "Shema" but he attributes the answer to the question concerning the greatest commandment in the law to Jesus and not to the lawyer. Could early Jewish liturgy or tradition have influenced Mark to add the reference to the "Shema Yisrael"?[40] Moreover, Mark's often observed use of thaumaturgic healing techniques which do not appear in Matthew and Luke have their parallels in Hellenistic miracle stories where spittle was employed by the miracle worker and one finds another story where the blind man first sees trees after being healed (Mark 7:32–37; 8:22–26).[41] At least it is possible that Mark was familiar with healing practices of other miracle workers during the period. His knowledge and acquaintance with Jewish sources needs further investigation. Interestingly, many of these features of Mark's text can often be recognized in the Marcan material unparalleled in Luke. Was Luke purposely omitting these sections of Mark and adapting his material?[42] Did he use an Urmarkus source which significantly differed from the extant Mark? Another possibility, namely that often Luke preserves the tradition concerning the life of Jesus more faithfully and that Mark reworked his sources, must also be considered. Marcan methodology is an area of synoptic studies which needs further research.

Mark was not averse to deleting sections of his source(s) and it seems that he revised his texts on the basis of his knowledge of other texts and traditions. At times he also seems to have been ready to expand his sources. Thus, one can observe Mark's longer version of the "Epileptic Child Healed" (Matthew 17:14–21; Mark 9:14–29; Luke 9:37–43). The miracle occurred after Jesus and those disciples who had accompanied him descended from the mount of transfiguration. Matthew mentions that the crowd came to meet Jesus, and in Luke one discovers the description of the large crowd ὄχλος πολύς. Mark also mentions the large crowd but he is the only evangelist who offers the colorful detail which describes the scribes who were arguing with the disciples (Mark

9:14). The scribes were already mentioned in Mark 9:11 (and Matthew 17:10). While Luke records that the crowds were astonished after Jesus performed the miracle (Luke 9:43 ἐξεπλήσσοντο δὲ πάντες), Mark depicts the crowds as being amazed at the very sight of Jesus καὶ εὐθὺς πᾶς ὁ ὄχλος ἰδόντες αὐτὸν ἐξεθαυμβήθησαν καὶ προστρέχοντες ἠσπάζοντο αὐτόν (Mark 9:15). In Mark, the large crowd runs to greet Jesus (Mark 9:15). Moreover, it seems that Mark has expanded the narrative to include graphic details of the child's malady and his exorcism (Mark 9:21, 22b–25a, 25c–27).[43] Here, Matthew agrees with Luke (more probably Luke's source) against Mark and omits this stylistically Marcan aggrandizement. Similar Marcan technique can be observed in Mark's treatment of the "Gadarene Demoniac" (Mark 5:1–20; cf. especially vs. 3–5). Other interpreters may suggest that Mark is more original in these details and that Matthew and Luke have abbreviated Mark. But would the two evangelists have conspired to delete these colorful details from Mark unless they had employed what they considered to be (a) better source(s)?

As has often been noted, in the passion narrative Luke's gospel is considerably different than the synoptic parallels. Flusser pointed out that in Luke's text ἤγγιζεν δὲ ἡ ἑορτὴ τῶν ἀζύμων ἡ λεγομένη πάσχα was not precise and that in Mark the timing has been clarified, as being two days before the feast, μετὰ δύο ἡμέρας (Luke 22:1; Mark 14:1).[44] Would Luke have deleted this fact from his source or would he have desired to retain this significant detail as did Matthew in the parallel (Matthew 26:2)? Lindsey and Flusser have claimed that Luke was actually one of Mark's sources. Lindsey suggested that Mark somewhat embellished Luke's version of "Herod's Opinion of Christ" (Mark 6:14–16; Matthew 14:1–2; Luke 9:7–9).[45] Luke records that Herod wondered whether or not Jesus might possibly be either John the Baptist or one of the other prophets who had returned to life. Herod wanted to see Jesus, apparently to examine his features in order to compare him with John's appearance. However, the element of doubt is missing in Mark. He states categorically that Herod was convinced that John the Baptist had risen from the dead, ὃν ἐγὼ ἀπεκεφάλισα Ἰωάννην οὗτος ἠγέρθη. One should also compare Luke's somewhat ambiguous statement concerning the "Day of the Son of Man," καὶ ἐροῦσιν ὑμῖν ἰδοὺ ἐκεῖ ἤ ἰδοὺ ὧδε (Luke 17:23). Mark's version seems more specific. Instead of speaking of the Son of man (Luke 17:22), Mark employs the designation ὁ Χριστός, and introduces false christs and false prophets into the section (Mark 13:21–22). Mark feels obliged to explain Jewish customs (Mark 7:3–4), and yet this text is unparalleled in Luke. While interpreters account for these textual matters by different explanations, others may not feel entirely comfortable with an approach that presupposes that Luke and Matthew have always secondarily changed, adapted and embellished their Marcan source.

The "Minor" Agreements

Another important textual phenomenon that appears in the synoptic gospels has been called the minor agreements. These are agreements between the texts of Matthew and Luke against Mark. Streeter helped to apply the term "minor" to these verbal agreements, which could serve to undermine their importance.[46] T. Stephenson more accurately described these verbal concurrences by the terms "minor agreements" and "major agreements."[47] Indeed, while some of these agreements may only consist of a single word or of an agreement to delete some of Mark's narrative, others may comprise several words. W. Lockton counted over seven hundred such concurrences between Luke's and Matthew's texts against Mark.[48] E.A. Abbott put the figure at about two hundred and thirty.[49] Perhaps the exact number of these agreements is not as important as the simple observation that with the exception of the Parable of Fig Tree (Mark 13:28–29 and parallels), they occur in every pericope of the triple tradition. The textual data has been carefully compiled by Frans Neirynck.[50]

To explain the appearance of the minor agreements on the basis of Marcan originality has always been a near impossible feat. Indeed, to maintain that two authors independently altered the wording of a third writer's text with the exact same words would seem to be an example of *reductio ad absurdum*. Nevertheless, gifted scholars with a great acumen have been able to accept the theory of Marcan priority in spite of the evidence adduced from these agreements. Caution is always desirable in analyzing textual phenomena. However, mere coincidence,[51] oral tradition or some sort of evolution in the textual transmission does not, in the opinion of the present author, constitute viable explanations to the existence of the concurrences in wording between Matthew and Luke against Mark. The alternative explanations are simpler and more likely to have occurred. Either Matthew or Luke was acquainted with the other's text or they both used (a) common source(s). The mutual source hypothesis appears to be a reasonable explanation of the evidence presented by these verbal connections between Matthew and Luke.

The Marcan Cross Factor

The question may then be asked: Why is the verbal agreement of Matthew and Luke against Mark sometimes meager and not more substantial? This question seems even more puzzling in light of the observation that Matthew and Luke often show remarkable verbal agreement between their texts in the double tradition.[52] For the most part, Lindsey has provided a viable answer to this question. His discovery, which he called the Marcan Cross Factor, is the corollary which naturally follows these observations. The result, which Lindsey discusses at some length,[53] is based on two fundamental observations: (1) the triple tradition often lacks uniformity in wording between Matthew and Luke; (2) the double tradition often contains uniformity in wording between Matthew and Luke. Does this indicate that Mark was known to one of the other evangelists but not to the third? In short, Mark is the difference between the double and the triple tradition. Therefore, it seems that Mark is somehow responsible both for the presence of verbal agreement between Matthew and Luke in the double tradition and for the absence of this agreement in the triple tradition. Can Mark again be viewed as the mediator between Luke and Matthew? If so, it means that Mark's text in comparison to Matthew and Luke is less reliable than is often maintained. The Marcan Cross Factor also indicates that Mark influenced the formation of either Matthew's or Luke's tradition. Because Matthew reproduces Mark's text more faithfully, it is more likely that Matthew was being influenced by Marcan wording and arrangement. Matthew seems to have considered Mark's gospel as authoritative[54] and thus often accepts Mark's wording in preference to his other source(s).

The Synoptic's Sources

Any explanation of the formation of the gospel tradition or of the sources employed by the evangelists in the compilation of their gospels is necessarily based to a greater or lesser degree upon conjecture. Conjecture can be very helpful when it is based on evidence and when it allows the researcher to conceptualize and to understand the creative processes involved in the compilation of the gospel texts. However, the danger always exists that speculation will become too solidly crystallized, sometimes to the extent that a theory has to be justified in spite of the evidence. Hopefully, the suggestions forwarded here will justify themselves by accounting for some of the textual phenomena that the student of the synoptics encounters. Nevertheless, speculation is speculation and evidence may be construed differently by researchers.

Inevitably, any treatment of the sources of the synoptics must assume that the evangelists used some hypothetical sources which are no longer extant. Hence, Streeter discerned four basic hypothetical sources in his proposal of the Proto-Luke theory.[55] The standard two document hypothesis has theorized the existence of the source Q. W. Bussmann recognized two different sources in the Q material and suggested that the evangelists used two logia sources.[56] He understood that in one group of passages Matthew and Luke retain almost complete verbal uniformity and in the second group of texts from the double tradition much less agreement is found between them. Among others, Theodore Rosche has questioned whether the document Q ever existed.[57] As noted above, Jeremias postulated at least two non-existent written sources for the evangelists' texts in addition to Matthew and Luke's employment of Mark's gospel.[58] The differences between scholars when speculating on the nature of the sources which formed the synoptics demonstrate the somewhat equivocal state of the evidence. Indeed, G.D. Kilpatrick admits that after a certain point of textual analysis, further " . . . conjectures must rest on most uncertain ground."[59] However, one thing seems clear and that is that the evangelists did use sources. Moreover, in spite of the fine suggestions of H. Riesenfeld[60] and B. Gerhardsson,[61] the evangelists who compiled the extant gospels seem to have employed written sources.[62]

The approach to the synoptics' sources utilized in this thesis is based primarily on the combined efforts of Lindsey and Flusser in what may be loosely designated as the Jerusalem school.[63] It has been considerably modified from their earlier theory of a narrative source and a logia source.[64] At this point, the various stages of development in the formation of the synoptics' tradition which characterizes the approach used in the analysis of Jesus' parables that follow are succinctly presented (also refer to figure III).

(1) The first stage involved the composition of the gospel in a Semitic language. This stage could be described by what E.G. Lessing would have called the *Urevangelium.* Patristic evidence supports this hypothesis. Eusebius records Papias' testimony, Ματθαῖος μὲν οὖν Ἑβραΐδι διαλέκτῳ τὰ λόγια συνετάξατο ἡρμήνευσεν δ' αὐτὰ ὡς ἦν δυνατὸς ἕκαστος ("Matthew collected the oracles in the Hebrew language, and each interpreted [translated] them as best he could").[65] The church fathers thought that Papias was referring to the extant Matthew and modern scholars have identified it with the sayings source Q. However Jeremias is probably correct in surmising that Papias' terminology *ta logia* here probably refers to a gospel story [events, happenings] and not exclusively to the sayings of Jesus.[66] It seems that the Semitic language of this *Urevangelium* was Hebrew and not Aramaic as is often maintained.[67] However, the theory of a Hebrew *Vorlage* is not based on the patristic witness alone, which is not always reliable.[68] This conjecture can also be substantiated from the gospel texts themselves which often bear the marks of (a) translated Semitic source(s). For example, after Luke's prologue which has often been noted for its Hellenistic or even semi-

classical Greek style, the reader is arrested by Luke's sudden change in style. This change is due to Luke's translation Greek source.

(2) Next, this Hebrew *Urevangelium* was literally translated into Greek. It does not appear that the extant synoptics were acquainted with this early Hebrew source. Their work can best be understood as having occurred in the Greek stage of the texts after it had already been translated.

(3) Third, the story units, discourses, parables and narratives of this translated document were somehow detached and removed from their original context. They were reorganized and rearranged so that their original sequence was lost. At least the outline of all three of the evangelists indicates that they were acquainted with the problem of the original order of events. Of course they were not compiling a biography in the modern sense, but it seems that a reorganization of an earlier life of Jesus had already been done before they received their sources and that they made an effort to recover the sequence of events. How this reorganization occurred is a complex and enigmatic question. Could it have happened during the translation stage? The translator may not have translated each story unit in its original order. The work of M.D. Goulder, though based on a great deal of speculation in regard to his reconstruction of the lectionary biblical readings of the synagogue in the first century and its relationship to the gospel texts, may offer some clues.[69] Could the rearrangement of the evangelist's narratives be related to lectionary readings of the gospels in the early church? Was the arrangement of the gospels based upon collections of teaching materials selected and placed together at random with miracle stories in the framework of the story of Jesus' career, death and resurrection? The problem is indeed complex as one can recognize a basic outline and an artificial groupings of materials within the structural frame of the synoptics. A great deal more research has to be done in order to establish all the facts, and it appears that the evidence is too fragmentary to be conclusive. In practice this third stage underscores the previous observations of K. Schmidt who stated that the framework of the present gospels is largely artificial.[70] The result means that while the individual pericopes preserve

trustworthy tradition, their arrangement by the evangelists is not always reliable.

(4) Fourth, this reorganized source underwent redaction and abridgement. This resulted in a shortened form of the reorganized source which became the first reconstruction of the life of Jesus and probably provided Luke with his basic outline. This is not an Urmarkus text as this document contained redacted teaching materials which do not appear in Mark. Luke used both the reorganized source and the abbreviated reconstruction. These two sources also may provide some clues concerning the doublets in the synoptics. This first reconstruction that was based upon the reorganized source contained much of the materials in Luke 3–9; 18–24, and also much of the double tradition material of Luke which shows significant divergence in wording from its parallel in Matthew.[71]

Thus Luke's gospel is understood as being comprised of two primary sources, the reorganized source text and the first reconstruction. These two sources are hypothetical. However, their probable existence is strongly reflected in the extant gospel texts. They account for the Lucan doublets (Luke 8:16 and 11:33; 8:17 and 12:2; 8:18 and 19:26; 9:3–5 and 10:3–12; 9:23 and 14:27; 9:24 and 17;33; 9:26 and 12:9; 9:46 and 22:24; 20:46 and 11:43; 21:14–15 and 12:11–12; 14:11 and 18:14). In addition, they explain why Matthew and Luke sometimes closely agree verbally in the double tradition and at other times fail to demonstrate uniformity in wording which was a phenomenon already noted by Bussmann.[72] Luke is following the reorganized source text when his version agrees with Matthew's tradition. Luke is utilizing the first reconstruction when his account shows significant dissimilarities with Matthew's narrative in the double tradition. The minor and major agreements of Matthew and Luke against Mark indicate that both Matthew and Luke employed a common source, the reorganized source text.

According to Lindsey, Mark was less careful in the preservation of the wording of his sources and was acquainted with Luke and the reorganized source text in the composition of his gospel.[73] Flusser has suggested that this reorganized source text probably predates Paul's epistles and that Mark's acquaintance with Pauline idiom is another indication of secondary influence in his text.[74] Matthew seemed to employ both Mark and the reorganized source text. Matthew's narrative is less reliable when his text betrays dependence upon Mark. This reorganized source text as reflected in the synoptic gospels is probably the most reliable tradition for Jesus' life and teachings. Sometimes Matthew follows this source more faithfully than Luke. Generally speaking, a gospel text that displays signs of a Semitic undertext is one of the better indications that the tradition may have been derived from the Greek translation of the Hebrew *Urevangelium.* Additionally, all three of the evangelists interject their own style and their own distinctive characteristics into their compilations. These editorial emendations are easily recognized by carefully studying each evangelist's unique vocabulary and special literary techniques.

THE SYNOPTIC PROBLEM AND MARK

The gospel of Mark cannot and should not be minimized in any consideration of the synoptic problem. The close literary interrelationships between the three earliest gospels is not disputed. However at times a tendency can be observed to emphasize the importance of the originality of Mark to the extent that the possibility that either Matthew or Luke might preserve a more reliable part of a tradition is excluded. Each text must be carefully considered and the danger of establishing the more original tradition only upon the basis of one's theory of synoptic dependence should be avoided and will lead to fragmentary results. Many scholars who accept Marcan priority as a working hypothesis have at times accepted the originality of Matthew or Luke relative to the text of Mark.[75] Are Matthew and Luke best understood as secondary deviations of their Marcan source? Many adaptations of the basic two document theory have been advanced to better understand the relationship of Matthew and Luke to Mark. Was there an overlapping of tradition between Mark and Q? Did Luke at times employ a special source as Schürmann and Jeremias among others have claimed (cf. figure IV)? Did Matthew and Luke use an earlier version of Mark?

Many scholars feel comfortable with an Urmarkus theory and the Proto-Luke hypothesis won adherents.

The aim of this brief discussion of the synoptic problem is not to prove beyond doubt that one approach is superior to all others. Rather it is needed to recognize that Matthew and Luke can sometimes preserve texts that are more original than Mark. Interpreters—many of whom accept Marcan priority—explain these phenomena in different ways. The approach presupposed or adopted as a working hypothesis in the work at hand is based to a large degree on the method developed by Lindsey and Flusser in Jerusalem. The Jerusalem school's approach accounts for the accumulated evidence that has resulted from the careful research of synoptic interrelationships and has proven its utility in practice. All three of the synoptic gospels must be carefully studied in order to discover their sources. The attempt to rediscover what precious little can be known about the earthly Jesus involves the return to and the recovery of the early Greek sources for the life and teachings of Jesus and when possible to reconstruct them into Hebrew.

FIGURE I

Variations of Arrangement Between Matthew and Mark

Eight variations according to Barr's Diagram:

Matthew	*Mark*	*Luke*
4:23	1:39	4:44
8:1–4	1:40–45	5:12–16
4:25	3:7–8	6:17
10:2–5	3:16–19a	6:12–16
8:28–34	5:1–20	8:26–39
9:18–26	5:21–43	8:40–56
10:1	6:7	9:1
21:18–22	11:12–14, 20–24	

Other variations in arrangement:

Matthew	*Mark*	*Luke*
11:10	1:2	7:27
5:15	4:21	8:16
10:26	4:22	8:17
7:2	4:24	6:38b
13:12	4:25	8:18b
8:23–27	4:35–41	8:22–25
9:35–36	6:6b; 6:34	8:1
10:42	9:41	(6:23, 35)
5:13	9:50	14:34–35
18:3	10:15	18:17
21:18–22	11:12–14, 20–24	
6:14–15	11:25–26	(11:4; 6:37)
10:17–22	13:9–13	21:12–19
24:42	13:35	12:40

FIGURE II

Variations of Arrangement Betwen Luke and Mark

Nine variations according to Barr's Diagram:

Luke	*Mark*	*Matthew*
5:1–11	1:16–20	
6:12–16	3:13–19	10:1–4
11:14–23; 12:10	3:20–30	12:22–27
4:16–30	6:1–6	13:53–58
22:24–27	10:42–45	20:24–28
10:25–28	12:28–34	22:34–40
7:36–50	14:3–9	26:6–13
22:21–23	14:17–21	26:20–25
22:56–62	14:66–72	26:69–75

Other variations in arrangement:

Luke	*Mark*	*Matthew*
6:38	4:24	7:2
13:18–19	4:30–32	13:31–32
12:1	8:15	16:6
14:34	9:50	5:13
17:2	9:42	18:6
16:18	10:11–12	5:32
13:30	10:31	19:30
17:6	11:23	17:20
11:4	11:25	6:9–13
17:31	13:15–16	
17:23	13:21–23	24:26

FIGURE III

The Stemma Proposed by the Jerusalem School:

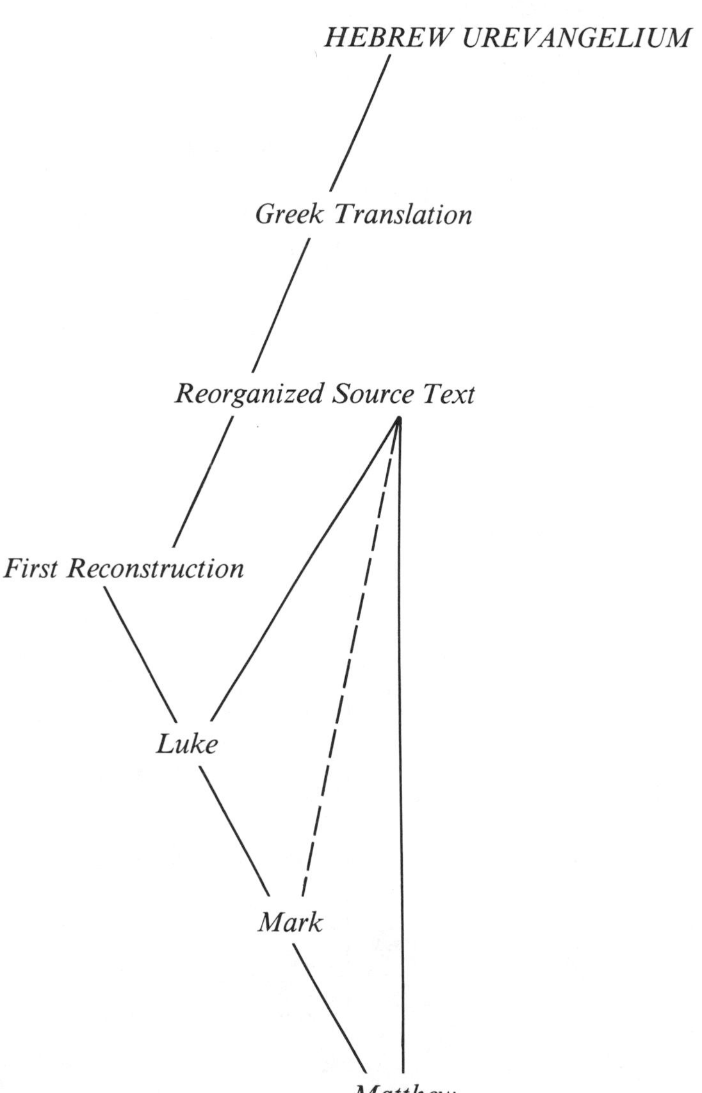

FIGURE IV

The Stemma Proposed by Jeremias:

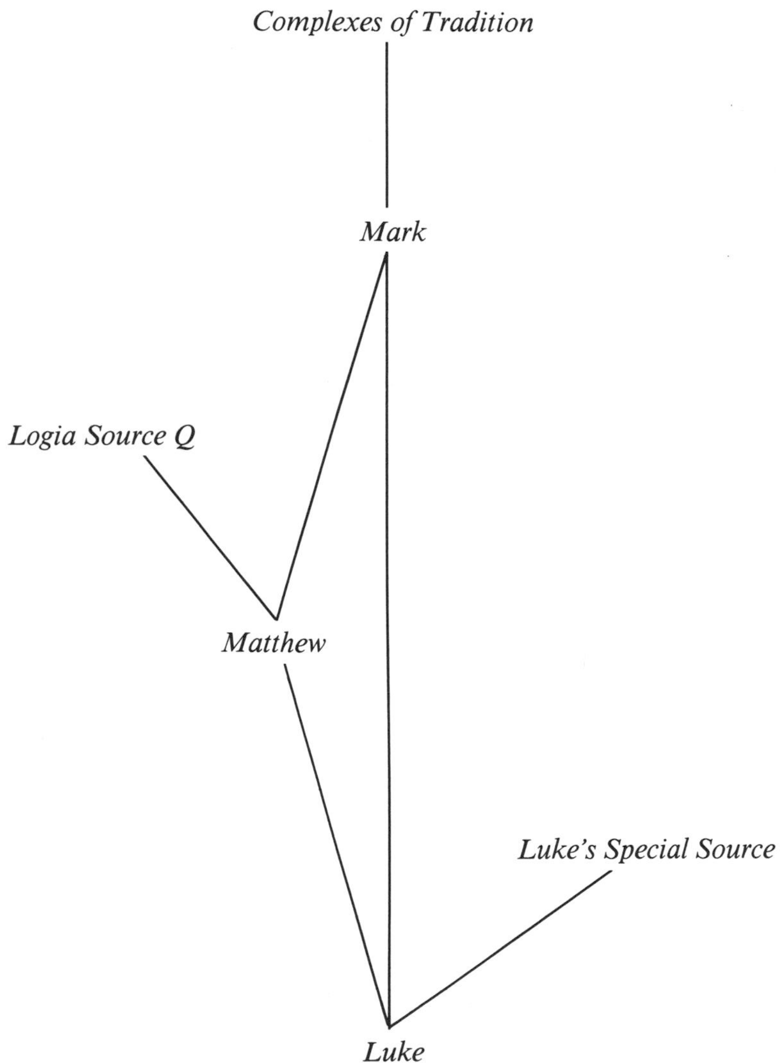

Notes

1) A discussion of the synoptic problem is preparation for any examination of the parables. Norman Perrin observed, "The first step in the hermeneutical process is that of *textual criticism:* We begin by establishing the text to be interpreted." See Perrin, *Jesus and the Language of the Kingdom* (London: SCM Press, 1979), p. 2. Along with evaluating the evidence for determining the best reading of any gospel text, inevitably one must also endeavor to determine the words of Jesus—so far as this is possible—from the traditions preserved by the evangelists. This of course entails a careful analysis of the interrelationships between the synoptics.

2) W.R. Farmer, *The Synoptic Problem* (New York: Macmillan, 1964), p. 161. Farmer ascribes to the view of Matthean priority.

3) E.P. Sanders, *The Tendencies of the Synoptic Tradition* (Cambridge: Cambridge University Press, 1969), p. 279.

4) Ibid, pp. 290–293.

5) Hans-Herbert Stoldt, *Geschichte und Kritik der Markushypothese* (Göttingen: Vendenhoeck und Ruprecht, 1977); the work has been translated into English by D. Niewyk, *History and Criticism of the Marcan Hypothesis* (Edinburgh: T. and T. Clark, 1980).

6) Karl Lachman, *De Ordine Narrationum in Evangeliis Synopticis* (Theologische Studien und Kritiken, 1835), pp. 570ff; cited by Joachim Jeremias, *New Testament Theology* (London: SCM Press, 1978), p. 37.

7) See R.L. Lindsey who has pointed out that such a claim maintains that Luke agrees with Mark against Matthew and that Matthew agrees with Mark against Luke. Lindsey writes " . . . Matthew and Luke, who are described as independent of each other, could hardly have supported Mark *against* each other if both derived from Mark!" Idem, *A Hebrew Translation of the Gospel of Mark* (Jerusalem: Dugith Publishers, 1973), p. XIV.

8) Allan Barr, *Diagram of Synoptic Relationships* (Edinburgh: T. and T. Clark, 1976); Lindsey, *A Hebrew Translation,* pp. IX-XVI. These are the more substantial disagreements of order. A more complete list may be seen in figure I. Cf. also note 23 below and especially E.P. Sanders' important article concerning the differences of order in the synoptics discussed there.

9) Cf. J. Jeremias, *Jerusalem in the Time of Jesus* (Philadelphia: Fortress, 1981), p. 206, note 191. Matthew seems to place the healing of the leper in the Capernaum area. The cleansed leper would first show him-

self to local priests (Jeremias, ibid, t. Neg. 8:2, j. Sot. 18a, chap. 2, hal. 2, Sifra on Lev. 14:3, Weiss, p. 70b). The healed leper must present the offering that Moses prescribed which would be done in the Temple in Jerusalem (cf. Sifra on Lev. 14:13, Weiss, p. 71df). Lepers were purified at the Nicanor Gate (m. Sotah 5:6).

10) Matthew 8:23–34.

11) W.C. Allen, *The International Critical Commentary Gospel According to St. Matthew* (Edinburgh: T. and T. Clark, 1977), pp. XIV–XV.

12) W.D. Davies, *The Setting for the Sermon on the Mount* (London: Cambridge University Press, 1977), pp. 25ff, pp. 187ff. Luke places the sermon in a different location on the plain (Luke 6:20f). One also finds Jesus sitting and teaching from a boat in Luke's gospel (5:3). Only Matthew describes Jesus as going to the mountain to teach from the Torah. Did the detail have significance for Matthew? It seems that Matthew's Jesus is a new Moses, but since he does not explicitly state that this is his purpose, one must be content with what appears to be an implicit analogy. At least the setting of Jesus' sermon in Matthew appears to be a Matthean formulation.

13) Because Luke does not contain the "Cursing of the Fig Tree," this cannot be considered a total agreement between Matthew and Luke against Marcan order. It has been suggested that the episode of the fig tree may be a Marcan adaptation of Luke's parable of the fig tree (Luke 13:6–9), with possible influences from other Jewish sources (see note 40). Matthew is very similar to Mark's version.

14) Joachim Jeremias, *The Eucharistic Words of Jesus* (Philadelphia: Fortress Press, 1977), pp. 97ff, idem, *New Testament Theology,* pp. 39ff.

15) Jeremias, *The Eucharistic Words of Jesus,* pp. 98ff., pp. 161ff. Jeremias notes that "Luke's special source" contains many fine Semitisms. Moreover, he observes that in Luke, in contrast to Mark, Jesus speaks of his betrayer after the institution of the supper. Judas leaves before partaking of the paschal meal in Mark's gospel. This element is more original in Luke. *"Nevertheless,"* Jeremias writes, *"Luke is linguistically more strongly reworked than Mark"*—ibid, p. 162. But Jeremias is favorably impressed with the Semitic nature of Luke's narrative.

16) David Flusser, "The Last Supper and the Essenes," *Immanuel* 2 (1973), p. 25.

17) H. Schürmann, "Zur Traditionsgeschichte der Nazareth-Perikope Lk 4, 16–30," eds. A. Descamps et A. de Halleux, *Mélanges bibliques en hommage au R.P. Béda Rigauz* (Gembloux: Duculot, 1970), pp. 191–205. Fitzmyer rejects Schürmann's suggestion, idem, *Luke,* vol. 1, p.

527. He prefers to view the Lucan version of the preaching at Nazareth as an adaptation and expansion of Mark (ibid). See also H. Schürmann, *Das Lukasevangelium* (Basel: Herder, 1969), vol. 1, pp. 223f.

18) Luke 5:1–11 and Mark 1:16–20; Luke 6:12–16 and Mark 3:13–19; Luke 11:14–23; 12:10 and Mark 3:20–30; Luke 4:16–30 and Mark 6:1–6.

19) Mark 6:18–29; 6:45–8:26. Most of these narratives have absolutely no parallel in Luke. This Marcan material comprises nearly one third of his gospel.

20) Luke 22:24–25 and Mark 10:42–45; Luke 10:25–37 and Mark 12:28–34; Luke 7:36–50 and Mark 14:3–9; Luke 22:21–23 and Mark 14:17–21; Luke 22:56–62 and Mark 14:66–72.

21) Luke and Mark usually show low verbal identity in these sections.

22) W. Barclay, *The Gospels and Acts the First Three Gospels* (London: SCM Press, 1977), vol. 1, p. 86. Scholars do not always agree on the tally of these verses. Compare also Theodore R. Rosche, "The Words of Jesus and the Future of the 'Q' Hypothesis," *Journal of Biblical Literature,* 89 (1960), pp. 210–220, Jeremias, *New Testament Theology,* p. 39 and Allan Barr, *op. cit.* Barclay's statistics are adopted for convenience and not necessarily because they are more accurate. The differences between these statistics are generally not that great.

23) It is impossible to consider all of the evidence in a brief discussion of the phenomenon of synoptic order. Figures I and II should help to develop a more complete picture of other minor disagreements from Marcan order in Matthew and Luke which comprise less than two verses and do not form a complete pericope. Cf. E.P. Sanders, "The Argument from Order and the Relationship between Matthew and Luke," *New Testament Studies* 15 (1968–69), pp. 249–261 and Frans Neirynck, *The Minor Agreements of Matthew and Luke Against Mark* (Leuven, Belgium: Leuven University Press, 1974), pp. 291–322. Neirynck discusses Sanders position at length.

24) B.H. Streeter, *The Four Gospels a Study of Origins* (London: Macmillan, 1924), p. 156. Streeter conceived of the evangelists as copiers. However, with the rise of redaction criticism his view becomes questionable.

25) This does not mean that they were not always faithful in the preservation of the tradition. Care must be taken to elucidate the redaction of the texts and the unique style of each evangelist. The special problems related to the redaction of Matthew's gospel are discussed here in the treatment of the "Parable of the Wicked Husbandmen."

26) Streeter, pp. 172–173.

27) Apparently the answer should be affirmative. Matthew's account differs from Mark in several places and some of these indicate a Semitic source (γυνὴ Χαναναία = אשה כנענית.) This shows that Matthew knew another source (probably what has been termed here as the reorganized source text) besides Mark.

28) John Hawkins, "Three Limitations of St. Luke's Use of Mark's Gospel," W. Sanday, ed., *Studies in the Synoptic Problem* (Oxford: Clarendon Press, 1911), p. 63 and see also note 1 where Hawkins rejects A. Wright's (*Gospel of Luke,* p. 83) suggestion that an Urmarkus gospel ever existed.

29) Ibid, p. 67.

30) Streeter, p. 74.

31) Ibid, p. 175.

32) Cf. Flusser, "Die synoptische Frage und die Gleichnisse Jesu," in *Die rabbinschen Gleichnisse,* pp. 193–233 and also idem, *Yahadut Umekorot Hanatzrut,* pp. 28–49.

33) Mark may even have been acquainted with the tradition in Matthew 3:7–10; Luke 3:1–14 from his source. At least it seems that Mark omitted the tradition represented in Luke 3:16c–18 and Matthew 3:11c–12. It would be difficult to imagine that the saying concerning the baptism with fire and the burning of the chaff in unquenchable fire could be the invention of Matthew or/and Luke. It is an integral part of the entire passage that would not have been added later. Other interpreters have tried to explain that this is an overlapping between Q and Mark and that here Mark abbreviates. In any case it can be seen that at times Mark abridged his source(s). Lindsey suggested that Mark was acquainted with Acts 1:5 and 11:16 where a baptism with the Holy Spirit is mentioned without fire and that this led Mark to delete the reference to the baptism of fire.

34) Mark 2:15–22,27; 3:28–30,35; 4:1–33; 7:6–23; 8:34–38; 9:35–50; 10:2–12; 23–31; 43–45; 11:22–25; 12:1–44; (13:1–37 Mark's eschatological discourse).

35) Ibid.

36) Luke 6:49. However, Luke does use the Greek word *eutheos* six times (Luke 5:13; 12:36,54; 14:5; 17:7; 21:9).

37) M. de Jonge, trans. "The Testaments of the Twelve Patriarchs," H.F.D. Sparks, ed., *The Apocryphal Old Testament* (Oxford: Clarendon, 1984) p. 571; H.C. Kee, trans., "The Testaments of the Twelve Patriarchs," J.H. Charlesworth, ed., *The Old Testament Pseudepigrapha* (Garden City: Doubleday, 1983), vol. 1, p. 813; M. de Jonge, *The Testaments of the Twelve Patriarchs* (Leiden: Brill, 1978), p. 122 and cf. vs.

5 about angels. Cf. also Test. Issachar 7:7, Test. Dan. 5:1, and Hodayot Fragment 4:6 (Licht, p. 228). Concerning the account of Jesus' temptation and the Testament of Naphtali 8:4 see also, C.G. Montefiore, *The Synoptic Gospels* (New York: KTAV, 1968, reprint from 1927), vol. 1, p. 9 and V. Taylor, *The Gospel according to Mark* (Grand Rapids: Baker Book House, 1981, reprint from 1966), p. 164. Cf. David Flusser and Shmuel Safrai, "Who Sanctified the Beloved in the Womb?" *Immanual* 11 (1980), p. 49 and especially note 10.

38) Cf. Exodus 19:14; 24:20; 23:23, 32:34, 33:2; I Kings 19:5–7.

39) Flusser pointed out how that the recital of the 'Shema' in Mark should be considered the addition of the evangelist, idem, *Yahadut Umekorot Hanatzrut,* pp. 30–31. On the question of the lawyer, cf. Flusser, *Die rabbinischem Gleichnissse,* p. 110, note 14.

40) Another example of outside influence might be seen in Mark's treatment of "The Cursing of the Fig Tree" and "The Fig Tree Withered" (Matthew 21:18–20; Mark 11:12–14, 20–21). This episode is reminiscent of "The Parable of the Barren Fig Tree" (Luke 13:6–9) and is remarkably similar to a Jewish parallel. Montefiore advances this question: "Has a parable, such as that of Luke xiii. 6–9, been turned first into an allegory, and then externalized into a miracle?" (C.G. Montefiore, *The Synoptic Gospels,* New York: KTAV, 1968, vol. 1, p. 265). The entire passage of the cursing and withering of the fig tree is lacking in Luke's text. Matthew is acquainted with the tradition from Mark, but does not retain Mark's detail, " . . . it was not the season for figs." This detail seems to recall the story in the Talmud which tells how R. Jose sought figs for his father's workers (b. Taanit 24a, see Billerbeck, vol. 2, pp. 26–27, cf. vol. 1, pp. 858f.; also discussed by C.G. Montefiore, *Rabbinic Literature and Gospel Teachings,* New York: KTAV, 1970, pp. 309–310). This tradition is certainly considerably later than the gospel and it is impossible to know to what extent it could reflect an earlier legend, but the similarity to Mark is intriguing. R. Jose said to the tree, "Fig tree, fig tree, bring forth thy fruit. . . . " It is then reported that the fig tree provided food for the workers. R. Jose's father reprimanded his son by saying, "My son, you have troubled your Creator to cause the fig tree to bring forth its fruit before its time. . . . " Mark 11:12–14, 20–21 is written in a Greek style and may very well be based on Luke's parable where the owner of the fig tree seeks fruit and is disappointed (Luke 13:6–9). Could an earlier version of this or a similar Jewish legend and/or Luke's parable (or its source) have been known to Mark? Is it possible that Mark has been secondarily influenced by additional sources and his knowledge of Luke's source or gospel as Montefiore suggested? Here

Luke's "Parable of the Barren Fig Tree" (Luke 13:6–9) shows signs of being translated from a Hebrew *Vorlage,* but Mark's "Cursing of the Fig Tree" and "The Withered Fig Tree" display evidence of Mark's rewriting and reworking of the episode in Greek.

41) These techniques are unique to Mark and John. V. Taylor noted, "A striking Hellenistic parallel is cited by Klostermann, 88, and Rawlinson, 108, with reference to a blind man, Alcetas of Halice, who saw a vision in which the god Asclepios appeared to go over his eyes with his fingers, with the result that 'the first things he saw were the trees in the temple precincts' (Dittenberger, *Sylloge Inscr. Graec.* iii. 1168; *v. VGT,* 30)." Taylor, *The Gospel According to St. Mark* (Grand Rapids: Baker Book House, 1981), p. 371. See E. Klostermann, *Das Markus Evangelium* (Tübingen: J.C.B. Mohr, 1950), pp. 77–78; Klostermann rightly points out that these details were designed to demonstrate not the suddenness of the miracle but its difficulty. Cf. A Rawlinson, *St. Mark* (London: Methuen and Co., 1960), p. 108, also note 1. Cf. Campbell Bonner, "Traces of Thaumaturgic Technique in the Miracles," *Harvard Theological Review* 20 (1927), pp. 171–181; M. Dibelius, *From Tradition to Gospel* (New York: Charles Scribner's Sons, p. 86); J. Hull, *Hellenistic Magic and the Synoptic Tradition* (London: SCM Press, 1974), pp. 76ff. See W. Barclay, *The Mind of Jesus,* p. 69; he cites accounts that tell how Vespasian opened a blind man's eyes with his spittle (Tacitus, *Histories* 4.81; Suetonius, *Vesp.* 7). Spittle was noted as a cure for eye problems in rabbinic literature; see b. Baba Kama 126b; cf. A. Cohen, *Everyman's Talmud* (New York: E.P. Dutton, 1949), pp. 205 and 253; Billerbeck, vol. 2, pp. 15f. Although Hogan does not try to explain why thaumaturgic technique is unique to Mark and John, his study is helpful; cf. L. Hogan, "Healing in the Second Temple Period" (Unpublished dissertation, presented to the Senate of the Hebrew University in March 1986).

42) Jeremias suggested that Luke was using blocks of material from his sources and employed five sections from Mark. He also used blocks of new material, in Luke 1:1–4:30; 5:1–11; 6:20–8:3; 9:51–18:14; 19:1–28; 19:39–44; 22:14–24:53 (idem, *New Testament Theology,* pp. 39–41). But in the triple tradition Luke's version is often significantly different in content and wording from Mark. Lindsey's translation work has suggested that Luke's gospel preserves many Semitisms which were changed in Mark (Robert L. Lindsey, *A Hebrew Translation of the Gospel of Mark,* pp. 9–84 and cf. Flusser, *op. cit.,* note 32).

43) It is doubtful that these colorful details appeared in Mark's source(s). At times, such details have been ascribed to eye-witness accounts that might have originated from Mark's experience as a trans-

lator for Peter. This suggestion is based on the well-known testimony of Papias that Mark was Peter's interpreter (Eusebius, *Ecclesiastical History* III, 39). However, this tradition must be seriously questioned if it is to be applied to the present gospel which bears Mark's name. At least one must maintain reservations about accepting Papias' evidence in regard to the canonical Mark, if for no other reason, because Mark omits the account of Peter walking on the water with Jesus (Matthew 14:28–31; parallel Mark 6:45–52). Were the present Mark Peter's translator, the omission of this detail would be unfathomable.

44) Compare David Flusser, *Die letzten Tage Jesu in Jerusalem* (Stuttgart: Calwer Verlag, 1982), pp. 69f.

45) Robert L. Lindsey, *A Hebrew Translation of the Gospel of Mark,* pp. 30–31.

46) Ibid, p. 27. In an earlier article, Lindsey noted, "The tendency of Markan priorists to hide or explain away these agreements is really inexcusable"; idem, "A Modified Two-Document Theory of the Synoptic Dependence and Interdependence," *Novum Testamentum* 6 (1963), p. 244.

47) T. Stephenson, "The Overlapping of Sources in Matthew and Luke," *The Journal of Theological Studies* 21 (1920), p. 128 and p. 132. Stephenson believed that the distinctions between the lesser and more substantial agreements of Matthew and Luke against Mark was caused by an overlapping of the sources. The major agreements are due to the hypothetical document Q.

48) T.W. Lockton, *Certain Alleged Gospel Sources* (New York: Longmans, Green and Co. Ltd., 1927), p. 50.

49) E.A. Abbott, *The Corrections of St. Mark* (London: Adam and Clark Black, 1901), pp. 307–324. Cf. W. Sanday, *Studies in the Synoptic Problem,* p. 10. Sanday wrote, "But in any case the instances (of the minor agreements) are too numerous to be entirely the result of accident."

50) The parable of the fig tree (Huck number 220, Mark 13:28–29 and parallels) does not contain any minor agreements. This appears to be the only pericope which fails to show some agreement of Matthew and Luke against Mark. Cf. Frans Neirynck, *The Minor Agreements of Matthew and Luke Against Mark.*

51) Neirynck has performed a monumental task in collecting and analyzing the minor agreements. Nevertheless, he is somehow able to attribute these "coincidences" to "the phenomena of literary style" (ibid, p. 199). However, he seems to have missed the significance of these verbal agreements. *Of course* they agree stylistically and grammatically. That is

the point. The fact that they agree *together,* and often, suggests the high probability that Matthew and Luke had a mutual source. At any rate, Neirynck's work cannot rule out this possibility. Cf. W.G. Kümmel, *Introduction to the New Testament* (London: SCM Press, 1975), pp. 65ff.

52) Lindsey, *A Hebrew Translation of Mark,* p. 22; cf. T.W. Manson, *The Sayings of Jesus* (London: SCM Press, 1977), pp. 15–21. See also Kümmel, *Introduction,* p. 65, note 55a where he notes, "Thus de Solages, 1047; similarly Morgenthaler, 165. Carlston and Norlin, 71, 77, estimate a verbal agreement in the material common to Mt and Lk at 71 percent—27 percent higher than in the Markan material they have in common." See also the following note.

53) Lindsey, *A Hebrew Translation of Mark,* pp. 19–22. See also the preface and introduction in Elmar Camillo dos Santos, collator and compiler, and Robert L. Lindsey, ed., *A Comparative Greek Concordance of the Synoptic Gospels* (Jerusalem: Dugith, 1985). Halvor Ronning is presently preparing his doctoral dissertation at the Hebrew University which deals with the analysis of the Marcan Cross Factor and the precise statistical evidence. The preliminary results of the statistic based to a certain extent upon the works of B. de Solages (*A Greek Synopsis of the Gospels,* Leiden: Brill, 1959), A. Honoré ("A Statistical Study of the Synoptic Problem," *Novum Testamentum* 10, 1968, pp. 95–147), R. Morgenthaler (*Statistische Synopse,* Stuttgart: Gotthelf-Verlag, 1971), and also J. Tyson and T. Longstaff (*Synoptic Abstract,* Wooster: Biblical Research Associates, 1978) strongly support the original observations of Lindsey concerning the verbal uniformity between Matthew and Luke in the double tradition in contrast to a lack of agreement between them in the triple tradition though other researchers may interpret the results of these facts differently (private communication with Halvor Ronning). Nonetheless the picture is more complex because Matthew and Luke either show *very* close verbal agreement between each other in the pericopes of the double tradition or quite different wording, and see also the preceding note.

54) Perhaps Mark's details might have influenced Matthew to think that the tradition in Mark was derived from an eyewitness account; see note 43.

55) Streeter, pp. 150f; cf. Vincent Taylor, *Behind the Third Gospel, a Study of the Proto-Luke Hypothesis* (Oxford: Clarendon Press, 1926), pp. 4ff.

56) D. Wilhelm Bussmann, *Synoptische Studien* (Halle: Buchhandlung des Waisenhauses, 1925) in three volumes; see volume 2, pp. 124–126. Compare also Manson, p. 20.

57) Theodore Rosche, pp. 219–220; cf. Austin Farrer, "On Dispensing with Q," D.E. Nineham, ed., *Studies in the Gospels* (Oxford: Clarendon Press, 1957), pp. 55–88. Nonetheless, Q remains a widely accepted theory as can be seen in the recent work by J. Kloppenborg, *Q Parallels* (California: Polebridge Press, 1988).

58) Jeremias, *New Testament Theology,* pp. 37–41.

59) G.D. Kilpatrick, *The Origins of the Gospel According to St. Matthew* (Oxford: Clarendon Press, 1946), p. 36.

60) Harald Riesenfeld, *The Gospel Tradition* (Philadelphia: Fortress Press, 1970), pp. 1–29.

61) Birger Gerhardsson, *Memory and Manuscript: Oral Tradition and Written Transmission in Rabbinic Judaism and Early Christianity* (Lund: G.W.K. Gleerup, 1964); idem, *Tradition and Transmission in Early Christianity* (Lund: G.W.K. Gleerup, 1964); idem, *The Origins of the Gospel Traditions* (London: SCM Press, 1979).

62) See Kilpatrick, p. 35. Kilpatrick gives good reasons for assuming written sources: " . . . evidence of structures. There is also evidence of conflation and of other forms of editing. The presence of stereotyped explanations of several parables and the fact that the material has often been handed down in a relatively unchanged form are in favor of a written tradition." The nature of the synoptic gospels is primarily a result of editorial work with written sources. Cf. Morton Smith, "A Comparison of Early Christian and Early Rabbinic Tradition," *Journal of Biblical Literature,* 82 (1963), pp. 169–176. Smith criticizes Gerhardsson for, among other difficulties, supposing that the early gospel materials were transmitted in the same way as later rabbinic literature.

63) The designation "Jerusalem school" is somewhat inadequate. At least, this method of synoptic study has been developed for the most part by David Flusser and Robert L. Lindsey during the numerous years which these scholars have labored together in Jerusalem. But, as was once stated by S. Safrai, the Jerusalem school may be described as whatever someone teaches today in Jerusalem. This does not limit the "Jerusalem school" to just the study of the synoptic gospels nor does it suggest that someone could not teach a different approach tomorrow. So the term Jerusalem school is applied to the painstaking labors of Lindsey and Flusser in this work. This designation is used for lack of a more appropriate title. In addition, though Flusser and Lindsey have worked together in the development of this approach, no one should have any illusion that Lindsey and Flusser share total agreement on matters regarding the formation of the gospel tradition; cf. note 32 above.

64) Lindsey, *A Hebrew Translation of Mark,* pp. XVIIIf. Lindsey ear-

lier conceived of a narrative and a teaching source. Cf. David Flusser, *Yahadut Umekorot Hanatzrut,* pp. 29–30. A document that contained the sayings of Jesus might have existed separately, and could have been similar to the tractate *Pirke Avot* according to a suggestion made earlier by David Bivin. At least Flusser remains open-minded concerning the possible existence of another logia source.

65) Eusebius, *Ecclesiastical History* III, 39 (Loeb, vol. 1, p. 296). Quoted also by A. Huck, *Synopsis of the First Three Gospels* (Oxford: Basil Blackwell, 1968), p. VII, and see revised edition, A. Huck and H. Greeven, *Synopse der drei ersten Evangelien* (Tübingen: J.C.B. Mohr, 1981), p. VIII and K. Aland, *Synopsis Quattuor Evangeliorum* (Stuttgart: United Bible Societies, 1964), p. 531.

66) See Jeremias, *New Testament Theology,* p. 38. Lessing also discussed the patristic evidence; cf. Henry Chadwick, *Lessing's Theological Writings* (California: Stanford University Press, 1972), pp. 65–81.

67) The debate concerning the original language of Jesus must continue. The prevalent view in regard to the language of Palestine in the first century has been that the Jewish people spoke Aramaic. Cf. Emil Schürer, *The History of the Jewish People in the Age of Jesus Christ,* revised and edited by Geza Vermes, Fergus Miller and Matthew Black (Edinburgh: T. and T. Clark, 1979), vol. 2, pp. 20–28. The Aramaic argument has been presented. However, the importance of Hebrew is considerably ignored. No one should doubt that Hebrew was spoken and written during this period. Cf. Jehoshua Grinz, "Hebrew as the Spoken and Written Language of the Second Temple," *Journal of Biblical Literature* 79 (1960), pp. 32–47, and idem, *Perakim Betoldot Bayit Sheni* (Jerusalem: Marcus, 1969), pp. 79–101; cf. Chaim Rabin, "Hebrew and Aramaic in the First Century," S. Safrai, M. Stern, D. Flusser, and W.C. van Unnik, eds., *The Jewish People in the First Century Volume* (Van Gorcum: Amsterdam, 1976), vol. 2, pp. 1007–1039; cf. M.H. Segal, *A Grammar of Mishnaic Hebrew* (Oxford: Clarendon Press, 1978), pp. 1–20. Segal comments, ". . . what was the language of ordinary life of educated native Jews in Jerusalem and Judea in the period from 400 B.C.E. to 150 C.E.? The evidence presented by MH [Mishnaic Hebrew] and its literature leaves no doubt that that language was MH" (ibid, p. 13). The Greek text of the gospels show every indication of being based upon a Hebrew undertext. Cf. Lindsey, *A Hebrew Translation of Mark,* pp. XIX–XXVI. For a more detailed discussion of the original language of the *Urevangelium* and the parables, see the section in the chapter above on "The Parables and Their Interpreters: Modern Parable Research," entitled, "The Original Language of the Parables," and also the additional biblio-

graphical materials cited there. As Flusser once noted, it is highly doubtful that the words of Jesus, considered sacred to his disciples, would have been preserved in Aramaic rather than Hebrew.

68) See also Lessing, op. cit., note 66 above.

69) M.D. Goulder, *Midrash and Lection in Matthew* (London: SPCK, 1974) and idem, *The Evangelists' Calendar* (London: SPCK, 1972).

70) K. Schmidt, *Der Rahmen der Geschichte Jesu* (Darmstadt: Wissenschaftliche Buchgesellschaft, 1964) p. 317. Schmidt concludes "Nur ab und zu mal werden wir aus Erwägungen über den inneren Charakter einer Geschichte diese zeitlich und örtlich etwas genauer Fixieren können. Aber im ganzen gibt es kein Leben Jesu im Sinne einer sich entwickelnden Lebengeschichte, keinen chronologischen Aufriss der Geschichte Jesu, sondern nur Einzelgeschichten, Perikopen, die in ein Rahmenwerk gestellt sind."

71) This proposal may appear to resemble another version of an Urmarkus theory. However, the first reconstruction is by no means an Urmarkus document. It contained teaching and narrative material which are not paralleled in Mark. Therefore it would be incorrect to merely view this source as an earlier version of Mark. Neither should it be considered strictly as a logia source, though it did contain teaching material. In short, it is a redaction of the reorganized source text.

72) See note 56 above.

73) Lindsey, *A Hebrew Translation,* p. 51, and idem, "Synoptic Dependence and Interdependence," pp. 243f.

74) Flusser, *Yahadut Umekorot Hanatzrut,* pp. 29–30.

75) See notes 3 through 5 above.

THE PARABLES AND THEIR CONTEXT: REAPPLICATION AND INTERPRETATION IN THE PARABLES

Since the work of Jeremias it has become a fixed principle of exegesis that the parables of Jesus have undergone revision during the process of transmission.[1] This process has sometimes modified significantly the applications and the main themes of the parables. Fortunately the interdependence of the synoptic gospels provides the opportunity of comparative study. Ironically, often the revisions of the parables are betrayed because the redactors seem to have endeavored to conceal their work. Here some parables from the double tradition will be studied in order to clear away some of the secondary elements that changed the original meaning of the illustration. The synoptic parallels often provide the key to penetrate behind the revisor's work and rediscover the message of the parable as it appeared in the mutual sources of the gospels. Moreover, because the work of the redactors seems to have been accomplished after the Semitic *Vorlage* had been translated into Greek, the task of research has been considerably simplified by philology.[2]

The Parable of the Talents and the Parable of the Pounds Matthew 25:14–30 and Luke 19:11–27 (Mark 13:34)

The first question to be entertained when treating the Parable of the Talents (Matthew 25:14–30) and the Parable of the Pounds (Luke 19:11–27) is whether these parables were originally two illustrations used on different occasions or whether they represent two versions of the same story. As J. Fitzmyer has pointed out, A. Feuillet, L. Fonck, N. Geldenhuys, P. Joüon, J. Knabenbauer, A. Plummer, P. Schanz, J. M. Vosté, and T. Zahn regarded the parables to be independent of each other.[3] However the close linguistic ties between the two texts make this position very difficult to maintain. As Fitzmyer further observed,

> Today, this solution is generally abandoned because of the obvious parallelism of the bulk of the two forms (Luke 19:13,15b–23,24b,26 = Matt 25:15,19–27,28,29), and especially because of such common (or nearly common) phrases as 'Excellent . . . good servant' (19:17); 'I was afraid' (19:21); 'because you are a stern man' (19:21); 'you reap what you have not sown!' (19:21); 'wicked servant!' (19:22); 'You knew, did you' (19:22); 'reaping what I have not sown?' (19:22); 'my money in a bank account' (19:23); 'with interest on my return' (19:23); 'Take the pound away from him' (19:24); 'give it to the one with ten' (19:24); 'from the one who has nothing even what he has will be taken away' (19:26). This parallelism seems to suggest that one parable is at the root of the two forms.[4]

Indeed the texts share too much common material to be independent. It could also be added that often the parallelisms of these texts can be reconstructed into good Hebrew and may well betray the Semitic *Vorlage* of the synoptics. However, the additional elements—especially in Luke's version—are much more problematic. The prehistory of these texts is very difficult to unravel and interpreters will no doubt have different opinions all of which are by necessity somewhat speculative. While Fitzmyer suggests that "one parable is the root of the two forms," the present writer would feel more comfortable with a solution that postulates a common source behind the texts of Matthew and Luke. Most probably Luke's parable is a "grandson" and Matthew's text is a "son" of this common source.[5]

Regardless of the number of parallelisms already noted, the differences between the two versions of the parable are no less remarkable.[6] In Matthew's gospel the Parable of the Talents appears after the Parable of the Ten Virgins and before the description of the Last Judgment—a context which seems to keep in focus the theme of preparedness for the coming of the Son of Man. However in Luke's gospel the passage is situated at the end of the Lucan Travel Account and follows the story of Zacchaeus the tax collector. Luke or the pre-Lucan redactor does all to make the parable fit this context. First he adds the genitive absolute, "As they heard these things" in order to tie the parable to the story of Zacchaeus (vs. 11) and make it sound as if Jesus related this illustration on that occasion. Next he emphasizes that they are on their way to Jerusalem which again is an effort to provide continuity for the *Reise Bericht.*[7] Finally he adds the theological statement, "because they supposed that the kingdom of God was to appear immediately," which has far-reaching implications for Jesus' message concerning the kingdom and the coming of the Son of Man. This entire verse from the phrase, "As they heard these things," to the δοκεῖν αὐτοὺς ὅτι παραχρῆμα κλτ, is stylized in Greek and would be difficult to translate literally into idiomatic Hebrew. While the expression מלכות תתגלה is known, the Greek text μέλλει ἡ βασιλεία τοῦ θεοῦ ἀναφαίνεσθαι is better understood as being formed in Matthew or Mark. The passage connects the parousia with the kingdom of heaven theme and seems to address the question of delay. The verse is absent from Matthew and certainly is secondary. In Luke's text the parable has been adapted to his context and employed to introduce a new theme.

The new theme of the king who goes away to receive a kingdom, as has often been noted, resembles Archelaus who traveled to Rome in order to obtain his reign.[8] The resemblance hardly seems accidental.[9] Matthew's version of the parable does not even allude to the king or the kingdom but focuses on the relationship between the man and his servants. But the revisor of the parable in Luke's version was able to weave another message into the fabric of the illustration. As a delegation of prominent Jews and Samaritans went to Rome in order to object to Archelaus' reign, likewise the πολῖται of this parable hate the would-be king and reject his kingship. Therefore the nobleman who becomes king does not merely deal with his servants, but has to contend with his citizens who reject him as well. The whole passage has been adapted to this theme. The words king, kingdom or rule appear five times (vs. 11, 12, 14, 15, and 27). In contrast to Matthew's text, in Luke the servants are rewarded with authority over cities, which again highlights the idea of kingship.

At the conclusion of the Lucan parable, the citizens have been transformed into enemies and are slaughtered before the king. Though anything goes in the surrealistic world of parabolic language where shock elements may be employed as a teaching technique, these final words hardly seem appropriate for the same one who taught his followers to love their enemies (Mt 5:44ff).[10] Can these harsh words possibly allude to the actions of Archelaus?[11] If not, and these elements are a later Christian reference to the Jewish enemies of Jesus who objected to his reign, then Luke's version of the parable seems to contain an inherent anti-Jewish polemic that would be quite far removed from Jesus. While Luke does not make a direct identification between these enemies and the Jewish people, it seems that such an interpretation could have arisen by later commentators of the revised parable. However Origen interprets the parable to refer to *both* Jews and Gentiles who did not believe, "And His citizens who did not wish Him to reign over them when He was a citizen in the world in respect of His incarnation, and perhaps Israel who disbelieved Him, and perhaps also the Gentiles who disbelieved Him."[12] One must keep in mind that parabolic teaching can lend itself to the dramatic, and the shock effect of slaughtering the enemies before the king could have had a didactic purpose.[13] The threat is general enough to be a prophetic warning of the impending doom awaiting all those who reject the prophet's message. Such warnings are not so uncharacteristic of prophetic discourse.[14] The reference to the citizens does not necessarily relate directly to the Jewish people as a whole, many of whom in Luke's account responded to Jesus' call. A case in point is Zacchaeus who is referred to as a "son of Abraham" because he has returned to the way of life according to Jewish piety after encountering the person of Jesus. The redacted text of Luke's version of the parable does not necessarily make an implicit reference to the so called Jewish rejection of Jesus as Luke's narrative often presents the mixed picture—some respond and others do not.

However Matthew's version of the same parable is more Semitic and more accurately reflects the better sources for the text. Even so Matthew's introduction to the parable is very similar in wording to Mark's condensed version (Mark 13:34) which has become an enigmatic parable of the servants in charge of an empty house without the owner. In Matthew, the ending of the parable employs Matthew's favorite punishment, "And cast the worthless servant into the outer darkness; there men will weep and gnash their teeth" (Matthew 25:30). Nevertheless, the redaction of the parable in Luke's text deals with the problem of the delayed parousia.[15] The catalyst for the revision seems to have been connected somehow to the historical events surrounding the reign of Archelaus.

Luke's adaptation and reapplication of the story impaired the moral implications of the parable. Matthew's text more correctly preserves the original thrust of the illustration. The master is coming and will settle accounts with his servants. The introduction of the wicked citizens who reject the reign of the nobleman who traveled to a distant land to receive his kingship only detracted from the primary theme of the parable. The effectiveness of the story had been undermined by crowding too many details into one illustration. In Matthew one encounters only master and servants. The servant who has been faithful and trustworthy to be productive will be rewarded while the slothful one will be punished. The illustration draws upon the everyday agricultural life from the land of Israel in the first century which would have been familar to sharecroppers and farm workers as well as to landowners. The words from Luke 19:13 πραγματεύσασθε ἐν ᾧ ἔρχομαι were probably an original part of the parable and are reflected in Matthew 25:19. They are to continue in the master's work until he returns. The dramatic element of the story is the coming of the master which goes beyond the threat of the eschatological judgment and accentuates the necessity of preparedness by responding to Jesus' challenge. After the master comes, he will then settle accounts with his servants who have been entrusted with his possessions. Preparedness for the day of reckoning becomes the main thrust of the parable, but Luke's revised version has weakened the force of the illustration by creating two scenes for settling accounts—the first with the king's servants and the second with the citizens who rejected the king's reign (Luke 19:20–24 and 27).[16]

The Parable of the Great Supper Matthew 22:1–14 and Luke 14:15–24

A comparison of the two versions of the Parable of the Great Supper from the synoptics will again reveal the activities of (a) revisor(s). The illustration is also paralleled in the Gospel of Thomas and a remarkably similar story is related in the Jerusalem Talmud which has been made well known by the work of Jeremias.[17] A study of the synoptic versions of the parable bring to light the problems of redaction and interpretations within parabolic teaching. Unlike in the preceding example, the text of Luke seems to have been preserved far better in comparison to its parallel in Matthew. The observation of T.W. Manson will stand up to the careful scrutiny of the texts, "The superiority of the Lucan version of the parable is obvious. It is clear, consistent, and straightforward."[18] Matthew's version has introduced several allegorizing features to the illustration and augmented it with another story at the conclusion of the parable. Luke's version of the parable is situated in the Travel Account and an editorial interest to link the parable to the preceding context can be seen in verse 15. Luke 14:1 tells the readers that Jesus had been invited to eat at a Pharisee's home (cf. Luke 7:36), where after performing a miracle of healing he is said to have "marked how they chose the places of honor" (vs. 7). This created the setting for his teaching on humility (vs. 7–14). Now someone at the table makes a comment concerning the blessedness of him who will eat bread in the kingdom of God (vs. 15). Then comes the Parable of the Great Supper. Hence Luke—and it seems that this is probably the work of Luke rather than a redactor(?)—has made an effort to provide the proper atmosphere for the telling of this parable. Matthew places the Parable of the Wedding Feast as the third of a trilogy of parables which occur after the triumphal entry into Jerusalem and the cleansing of the Temple and therefore it would have been told during Jesus' last days before his passion (Matthew 26:1–2). Matthew's text ties all three of these parables to the inquiry of the chief priests and the elders of the people concerning the authority by which Jesus accomplished these acts (Matthew 21:23–27 and see the connecting verses, 28, 33 and 22:1). Both evangelists have created fresh and artificial settings for the parable—Matthew within the Temple complex and Luke at a Sabbath meal in the home of a Pharisee.

The parable in Luke begins with a certain man who prepared a great dinner for many (Luke 14:16).[19] Matthew on the other hand has turned this great supper into a wedding feast (Matthew 22:2 and cf. Luke 14:8).[20] In parallel to the certain man Matthew has ἀνθρώπῳ βασιλεῖ. Perhaps the most startling innovation is Matthew's reference to the son of the king who is not even alluded to in the Lucan version of the parable. Here one must compare the mention of the son with the context of Matthew and see the preceding Parable of the Wicked Husbandmen where the son of the householder plays a prominent role and is murdered (Matthew 21:37–39). One cannot help but speculate as to whether in the mind of Matthew an allegorical interpretation of his source was taking place as the evangelist (or the final Matthean redactor) preserved this illustration. The king is God, the marriage banquet is the eschaton and the son is Christ. The two sets of messengers would not be of insignificance. The first set of servants met with the refusal of the invited guests to come to the feast. The second set of servants first encounter a similar reaction (compare Matthew 22:5 with Luke 14:18–20), but then a major shift in the parable occurs when they fall into the hands of violent opposition (vs. 6). The text employs the words οἱ δὲ λοιποὶ which seems to be a rather unseemly way of verbally pointing a finger. After having attracted the audience's attention toward this group, Matthew (or more probably the gospel's final revisor) then recounts their wickedness, "while the rest seized his servants, treated them shamefully, and killed them" (Matthew 22:6).

The motif of the killing of the prophets has many parallels but the word picture formed here recalls also the treatment of the servants and the son in the preceding parable (Matthew 21:35–

39). Manson suggested, "If the detail may be pressed the first invitation will correspond to the mission of the great prophets, the second to that of Jesus and the Apostles. The invited guests are then the recalcitrant Jews. They reject both invitations."[21] How far all the allegorizing elements of the Matthean version of the parable may be taken to their extreme interpretation will depend upon the extent to which the theology of replacement permeated the thought of the final redactor of Matthew or of the evangelist himself. The intensity of the idea contained in this revision of the parable comes to the surface in verse 7, "The king was angry, and he sent his troops and destroyed those murderers and burned their city." The anger of the man is mentioned also in Luke 14:21, but the graphic details of dispatching the murderers and burning their city do not appear, and if these words were contained in Luke's source, he surely would have recorded them.

One discovers a rather striking parallel concept to that found in Matthew 22:7 expressed in the unique Matthean statement from the Parable of the Wicked Husbandmen, "Therefore I tell you the kingdom of God will be taken away from you and given to a nation producing the fruits of it" (compare also Matthew 8:12 and 13:38). In the Parable of the Marriage Feast, the ones who have rejected the king's invitation and murdered his messengers will be punished. Here the king's son is not killed as in the Parable of the Wicked Husbandmen and perhaps the revisor of the parable felt that would be going too far or just did not think to complete his interpretation. Nevertheless the king will send his troops to avenge the deaths of his servants and to burn the city of the murderers. Does this saying from Matthew 22:6 which has no parallel in Luke speak of the national tragedy of the Jewish people at the hands of the Romans?[22] One thing seems clear enough—this verse must be derived from a secondary revision of the parable. As John A.T. Robinson aptly noted, "The introduction of a military expedition while the supper is getting cold is particularly inappropriate."[23] Before the wedding celebration can continue, the king sends his troops to *destroy and to burn the city of those murderers* which certainly stretches to the limits the meaning of men who declined an invitation to a marriage feast. Of course according to Matthew's version they did kill the servants. Nonetheless the fact that this implicit reference to Jerusalem's fate is missing in Luke and appears in Matthew's version may well have significance for determining the time of the final compilation of Matthew and of Luke.

After these wicked ones have been properly disposed of, it is possible for the servants to go into the streets to gather all they could find. Interestingly much of the parallelisms contained in Luke and to a certain extent in the Gospel of Thomas, which make for a good story and very likely come from the Semitic background of the parable, do not appear in Matthew. The readers miss the complete list of excuses (Luke 14:18–20)[24] and the parallel expressions, "Go quickly to *the streets and lanes* of the city and bring in *the poor and maimed and blind and lame*" (Luke 14:21) as well as the "*highways and hedges*" (vs. 23, underlining is the author's emphasis). Hence the unwanted and rejected members of society are called to replace the invited guests.[25] Instead of the poor, maimed, blind and lame, Matthew speaks rather of "both bad and good" (vs. 10). Moreover at the conclusion of the illustration, Matthew's version attaches another mini-parable which takes the theme of the marriage banquet and addresses the need for the proper wedding garment. The king comes to examine his guests and finds one without a wedding garment. Jeremias has concluded that what is meant here is a garment which is soiled.[26] But this mini-parable does not mention the condition of the man's attire and evidently refers to one of the bad (Matthew 22:10) who was admitted to the wedding festivities. According to Matthew, he does not even have a wedding garment.[27] The king asks this man a question, "Friend, how did you get in here without a wedding garment?" The direct address ἑταῖρε is a word found only in Matthew (11:16, 20:13, 22:12 and 26:50). The man is overwhelmed by his fear for the king and is left speechless. The king has him bound hand and foot and cast into outer darkness. Of course the phrase "outer darkness; there men will weep and gnash their teeth" is a saying which Matthew found well suited for his taste, and the conclusion, "For many are called, but few are chosen" also has its parallels as a floating logion.[28] The question must be asked whether Matthew invented this mini-parable. One can see a number of Mattheanisms in these few short verses and the story could be somehow related to Luke's teaching on humility which mentions a marriage feast (Luke 14:7–14;[14:20]). However Linnemann has made an effort to reconstruct an earlier version of the parable by deleting the secondary concluding verses and by providing it with an introduction.[29] While her introduction could compete with any redactor for secondariness, she may be correct in looking for a more original parable which was derived from Matthew's source and adapted to form the basis for this illustration. But because this text has been so extensively revised, any proposed reconstruction would have to be highly conjectural.

By adding this mini-parable as the climax of the three preceding illustrations, Matthew or more probably the final revisor of the gospel has shifted his theme from the murderers of the prophets to the evil hypocrites within his own circle. Interestingly enough, already Irenaeus connects the wedding garment with works of righteousness and the receiving of the Holy Spirit. He applies Matthew's message of this mini-parable to the church:

> But those who have indeed been called to God's supper, yet have not received the Holy Spirit, because of their wicked conduct "shall be," He declares, "cast into outer darkness." He thus clearly shows that the very same King who gathered from all quarters the faithful to the marriage of His Son, and who grants them the incorruptible banquet, [also] orders that man to be cast into outer darkness who has not on a wedding garment, that is one who despises it. For as in the former convenant, "with many of them was He not well pleased," so also is it the case here, that "many are called, but few are chosen."[30]

Thus it seems that Irenaeus' allegorical application of the illustration was already conceived in the mind of the Matthean revisor who spoke about the gathering together of "both bad and good." But this approach to the Parable of the Great Supper, which can already be detected in the final stages of the compilation of the canonical gospels, has caused an estrangement between Jesus and his people by adapting the parable for a new audience. Harnack correctly observed, "The main distinction between the two versions is that St. Matthew has transformed a genuine parable into an allegory with an historical motive."[31]

Is it possible to come closer to a more original version of this parable or even to approach the very *ipsissima verba* of Jesus? The Lucan version is strikingly different from that of Matthew's and many of the secondary features discussed above do not appear. A linguistic analysis of the two versions will reveal that Luke's text is closer to the Semitic *Vorlage* of the sources of the synoptics than that of Matthew. Moreover the additional allegorical features of Matthew do not appear in Luke. As already noted above, in Luke there is no king, no marriage feast and no son. Luke has only one servant to do the bidding of the man who has prepared a banquet and invited many. While the man becomes angry at the negative response of the invited guests, he does not burn their city.

In addition, one should not miss the humor and the colorful elements within the Lucan version of the illustration. The audience learns three of the excuses of the many invited guests. Three examples is a common feature in storytelling, as Fitzmyer has pointed out, "The storytelling technique in the parable should not be missed: The threesome, the three sendings of the servant, the three excuses . . . "[32] The threesome could be compared to more modern stories that tell about the Frenchman, the Englishman and the Irishman or Jesus' parable of the Good Samaritan which contains the priest, the Levite and the Samaritan.[33] Hence to search for logical and reasonable excuses from this threesome is the wrong approach.[34] In fact, it is quite probable that the absurdity of the replies were intended to be humorous. Would someone buy a field without first going to see it (vs. 18)? Would a farmer pay for five yoke of oxen before having an opportunity to test them (vs. 19)? Is the man who takes a wife so occupied that he refuses all dinner invitations (vs. 20)? While it may be pressing the point to claim that everyone laughed when they heard this menagerie of excuses, it is fair to say that the people would have at least grinned. The Gospel of Thomas contains four expanded excuses which seem to contain some embellishments. The natural tendency in the preservation of a story parable like the Great Supper is to make an effort to improve it. To enlarge upon the excuses merely detracts from the story. The artful storyteller knows how to introduce humor and colorful elements without deviating from the main theme. The illustration is destined to tell how none of the invited guests came to the dinner and not to elaborate on their good reasons for refusal. Apparently the Gospel of Thomas felt that the married man had a good excuse. At least in his version of the parable, the man is not married but making preparations for his friend's wedding banquet, "He said to him: 'My friend is to be married and I am to arrange a dinner (δεῖπνον); I shall not be able to come. I pray to be excused (παραιτεῖσθαι) from the dinner' (δεῖπνον)."[35] Certainly since he is not the one being married he could have made arrangements to attend the dinner prepared for him. Has the originality of the Gospel of Thomas in respect to this parable been exaggerated?

However both Matthew and the Gospel of Thomas have only one call to the outcasts to come and take the place of the invited guests. In Luke the man sends his servant to gather the outcasts twice:

> Then the householder in anger said to his servant, 'Go out quickly to the streets and lanes of the city, and bring in the poor and maimed and blind and lame.' And the servant said, 'Sir, what you commanded has been done, and still there is room.' And the master said to the servant, 'Go out to the highways and hedges, and compel people to come in, that my house may be filled.' (vs. 21b–23)

Commentators have suggested that originally the servant was sent out only one time. Certainly the story would be complete enough without the servant being commanded the second time to go and compel the people to come to the dinner in order that the house would be filled to capacity. Robinson suggested that in the mind of Luke the first mission was that to the Jewish people and the second that to the Gentiles.[36] On this point care must be taken not to invest too much credibility in the parallels. Matthew was interested in adding his additional mini-parable to the illustration. He could easily have overlooked this detail, and as has already noted been above, here the Gospel of Thomas betrays some independent tendencies. It is quite difficult to imagine that here Jesus could have alluded to a mission to the Gentiles no matter what thinking one attributes to Luke.

Could the second command to compel the people to come to the feast until the place was filled be an original part of the parable? It certainly forms a good parallelism and emphasizes the imperative of the evangelization of the outcasts. At least in a rabbinic parable attributed to R. Eleazar one discovers an emphasis on the size of the banquet. The king prepares a *great* banquet and tells his stewards to invite the merchants but not the artisans. But the servants return and tell the king that the provisions for the banquet are so plentiful that the merchants will not be able to consume all the food and therefore an invitation is extended also to the artisans as well.[37] It seems doubtful that the motif in Jesus' Parable of the Great Supper where the master sends out his servant twice to call the common people to the dinner has deep significance or an allegorical interpretation.[38] The man had prepared a great banquet! The invitation is extended to the common people which nobody cared about and to outcasts of society. Even after they have been invited, the banquet is so large that there is additional room. The householder sends his servant a second time to call the common people for the dinner in order that the servant may *compel* them to come to his banquet that his "house may be filled." The proclamation of the kingdom was destined to reach over and beyond the rich and powerful or even the pure intellectual stratums of society. It was designed to speak to the "poor in spirit" and the people who might be mistakenly considered insignificant. In any case, the two sendings in Luke form a parallelism which may have been an original part of the parable and stressed the urgency of the message of Jesus.

Context and Parable

One of the first rules of hermeneutics is to study the context. Perhaps this principle of interpretation is nowhere more important than with parables. However it can also be very misleading. What is the context? The analysis above has demonstrated again the problem that all students of the parables encounter. The same parable has a context in Luke and an entirely different context in Matthew or Mark. Too often commentators simply try to chose between one of three options. The truth is that a parable may have several contexts. Luke has adapted the parable to his narrative, Matthew has applied it to his context and Mark has done the same. None of the evangelists may preserve the "original" context of the parable and yet all have placed the illustration within the framework of their individual texts.

In reality a parable has an independent quality that transcends the confines of its strict literary context. This is no more evident than in the introduction and conclusion of the parables in the synoptics. The introduction often ties the parable with the preceding pericope and the conclusion generally attempts to summarize the enigmatic message of the parable and/or tries to link it with the next passage. Nevertheless the simple story parable is usually well preserved and the secondary details can be recognized. This approach to the parables requires extreme care because it can be destructive as well as creative and the exegete must pay close attention to the text. Sometimes the creative aspect can be as dangerous as the destructive. In essence the approach advanced here is similar to the methodology employed by Adolf Harnack, Karl Schmidt, T.W. Manson and many others.[39] The interrelationship between the synoptic parallels points to common sources that have been revised and adapted by both the evangelists and the gospel redactors who worked to compile their own novel and distinctive texts. A careful analysis of the parallels can often shed light upon the common sources. Though scholars may disagree on a basic approach to the synoptic problem, they often can find more agreement concerning what text is secondary and which passage preserves the saying more originally. From the comments above concerning the Parables of the Talents and the Great Supper it would be possible to reconstruct a hypothetical Greek source text for both parables. A number of scholars have pursued experimental research in this fascinating area of source text retrieval.[40] After the source text has been reconstructed into Greek it is then possible to recover the Semitic *Vorlage* by careful retranslation.

It has not been the aim of the above brief analysis of the

Parables of the Talents and the Great Supper to seek out all the connections between these illustrations and early Jewish thought and literature. The motifs of workmen being responsible to their masters appears in a number of rabbinic parables. While the Parable of the Talents does not have a complete parallel in rabbinic literature, Flusser discovered a very similar parable. In Semachot Derabbi Chiya, a parable attributed to R. Nathan (circa 125) is very similar to the Parable of the Talents. A king builds a palace and places his men servants and maid servants in charge of the estate. He provides them with gold and silver to carry on business and warns them not to steal from each other. After the stage has been set, in the next scene the king travels to a distant land and the drama begins. The servants are not faithful and steal from one another. After a long delay the king returns and discovers that his servants have stolen from each other and are standing outside naked. The point of the parable is to say that likewise the wicked steal from each other in this world and will appear naked—without good works—before God.[41] R. Nathan's illustration has many similarities with the gospel parable but it has a different theme and application. Flusser also noted the play on words of Bar Kapara which presents a message that is analogous to the gospel parable. The tanna Bar Kapara interpreted the verse, "Honor the LORD with your substance [מהונך]" (Proverbs 3:9), by saying that it referred to what God had graciously given to you [ממה שחננך].[42] Thus the idea is very similar—God must be honored with what he has entrusted to each individual. The concept of the one who is faithful with what he has been entrusted, receiving more responsibility as a reward, appears elsewhere both in the gospels and in rabbinic literature.

As Jeremias noted, the parabolic example of the Great Supper echoes the story about Bar Mayan in the Jerusalem Talmud.[43] Bar Mayan, the tax gatherer, performs a good deed by inviting the poor to partake of a banquet prepared for the more prestigious members of the community who refuse to fraternize with a man of his questionable character.[44] Also the words in Luke's gospel (14:17), ἔρχεσθε ὅτι ἤδη ἕτοιμα ἐστιν [πάντα], are partially paralleled in a passage full of parabolic imagery in Pirke Avot and attributed to R. Akiva who says, והכל מתקן לסעודה (3:16). The structure of R. Johanan b. Zakai's parable of the king's banquet is similar to the successive scenes in Jesus' Parable of the Great Supper. These texts from Jewish literature that contain similar ideas, motifs and structural similarities may have a bearing upon how one understands the parables of Jesus concerning the Talents and the Great Supper. However here it can be seen that these two parables from the synoptic gospels have been edited and redacted in the literary stage of their transmission in much the same way as other parables preserved in rabbinic literature.[45]

In the preceding section of this book it has been seen how the same rabbinic parable may be attributed to different authorities in parallel versions. Like the gospel parables, the same rabbinic parable may appear in different contexts far removed from one another. The primary characters in the parables may be altered to emphasize a specific point or to adapt an illustration to a new context. Thus the Parable of the Spoiled Son in Pesikta Derav Kahana contains a dog who comes and bites the son who did not recognize his father. The dog can be identified with Amalek from the context of the parable in the midrash—but the dog figure is deleted in a number of the parallels.[46] Sifre Deuteronomy employs the same parable to illustrate two different themes and makes minor adaptations in the story in order to accentuate special aspects of the divergent messages it seeks to communicate in each context.[47] Sometimes the differences have no great significance. A man or a householder may be transformed into a king of flesh and blood merely because the transmitter of the parable wishes to improve the story in his own way. The tendency to embellish or aggrandize a story is a natural part of the preservation of folklore. Many of these same tendencies found in rabbinic parabolic teaching can be paralleled in the synoptic gospels. Luke's certain man becomes a king in Matthew. Instead of Luke's banquet, Matthew has a wedding feast and introduces what could be understood as a messianic figure—the king's son. The fact that the gospel parables and rabbinic parables have both been redacted in similar ways is another indication that both are derived from a common *Gattung*. They have many stylistic characteristics in common.[48] One of the differences between them seems to be the process by which they were preserved.[49] The gospels have been translated from Hebrew and transmitted in Greek. Most of these secondary elements seem to have been introduced into the texts at the Greek stage. Of course it is also possible that translators of the early sayings of Jesus could have changed some of the motifs. However this possibility is unlikely because translators of antiquity generally prepared literal word for word translations using equivalents rather than editing their source as they worked. On the other hand, each one of the evangelists seem to have employed his own creative genius as he compiled his text. Moreover sometimes the work of later scribes and editors can surface from the text. A case in point is the anti-Jewish tension which occurs in select edited passages from the Gospel of Matthew which seem to be derived from the work of the text's final revisor.[50]

To a certain extent, the storyteller's parable is independent of the literature in which it appears. The parable is an entity in itself though it becomes the slave of many masters. Both rabbinic texts and the gospels have commandeered the parables to serve their own purposes. One fact has become clear: though these intriguing illustrations are related to other literary forms like the fable or proverb, the story parable *Gattung* is an outstanding achievement of Jewish thought which has its roots in the faith and piety of the Jewish people during the days of the Second Temple period. The parables are deeply embedded into the earliest traditions of the synoptic gospels and indicate that Jesus was one of the outstanding parabolists of his time. Because this genre is unparalleled in other early sources and is so well documented in later Jewish literature, it seems quite reasonable to assume that Jesus' parabolic teaching is representative of other contemporary Jewish didactic techniques.

At the conclusion of this section it is necessary to return again to the problem of the literary parable. It is not enough to read the parables; one must endeavor to listen to the storyteller. A single parable may have many contexts, and the setting of the illustration and the audience for whom it was designed are always essential features for the proper hermeneutic. The number three hundred in regards to R. Meir's fox parables is certainly not meant to be taken literally.[51] It simply means a great many. One hundred would not be a large enough number and five hundred would probably overdo it. But these numerous illustrations probably refer to variations of a smaller number of basic scenarios applied to different situations. It does not require a great deal of imagination to think of all the predicaments and situations that a fertile mind like R. Meir could have invented for the fox of the animal kingdom. The possibilities are unlimited. Like R. Meir, the tanna Bar Kapara was also known to have a series of fox parables. Bar Kapara's three hundred fox fables were so interesting that the guests at the banquet did not eat their food in order to listen to his fascinating stories.[52] Akiva's parables cited above seem to be derived from intense discussions and arguments with his colleagues. But as these vivid illustrations passed from the spontaneous storytelling stage into the literary stage, several adaptations were possible. As parables were committed to writing, they received a new narrative form. Standardized introductory formulas were added and a change of audience occurred when the parable was given a new context. The rabbinic parables not infrequently contain scripture verses which were added at the conclusion of the story. The evangelists sometimes added logia or secondary conclusions in order to intepret the parable or apply it to a new situation.

At the literary stage of the parables a certain amount of adaptation and reapplication of the parables was inevitable both in rabbinic literature and in the gospels. To what extent is it possible to recreate and recapture the original setting of the parables? One must see over and beyond the superficial framework and view the individual blocks which form the entire edifice. The parables of Jesus must be interpreted in the context of his total message, and care must be taken to discover the work of the individual evangelists and their collaborators.

Notes

1) Jeremias, *Parables,* pp. 23–114; E. Linnemann, *Parables of Jesus,* pp. 16–18 and Flusser, *Die rabbinischen Gleichnisse,* pp. 36–38 and pp. 63ff.

2) The original language of the parables of Jesus has been discussed at the end of the chapter on "Parables and Their Interpreters." The Sem-

itic background of the synoptics is widely accepted even if most scholars persist in maintaining that the gospels were originally written in Aramaic; see Jeremias, *New Testament Theology,* pp. 3–8 and even B. Metzger, *A Textual Commentary on the Greek New Testament* (New York: United Bible Societies, 1975), p. xxviii.

3) J.A. Fitzmyer, *The Gospel according to Luke* (New York: Doubleday, 1985), vol. 2, p. 1230. Another abbreviated version of the parable appears in the Gospel of the Nazaraeans, "But since the Gospel [*written*] in Hebrew characters which has come into our hands enters the threat not against the man who had hid [*the talent*], but against him who had lived dissolutely—for he [*the master*] had three servants: one who squandered his master's substance with harlots and flute-girls, one who multiplied the gain, and one who hid the talent; and accordingly one was accepted (with joy), another merely rebuked, and another cast into prison—I wonder whether in Matthew the threat which is uttered after the word against the man who did nothing may refer not to him, but by epanalepsis to the first who had feasted and drunk with the drunken." P. Vielhauer, "The Gospel of the Nazaraeans," E. Hennecke, ed. *New Testament Aprocrypha,* vol. 1, p. 149. Jeremias discusses this parallel, *Parables,* pp. 58f. It is fragmentary and in some ways recalls the Parable of the Prodigal Son (Luke 15:11–32). In any case it is doubtful if it could represent an earlier version of the parable than that contained in Matthew and Luke.

4) Ibid.

5) See the discussion of the synoptic problem above. Matthew's text on the whole is more reliable on this text. The question remains as to what extent Luke permitted himself to edit his source. The changes in this parable are so radical as to suggest that he was employing a redacted source. See Manson, *The Sayings of Jesus* (New York: SCM Press, 1977), p. 245, who assigns the Lucan version of the parable to L.

6) See A. Harnack, *The Sayings of Jesus* (New York: Williams and Norgate, 1908), pp. 122–126. Harnack comments on the relationship between the texts of Matthew and Luke and then exclaims, "A very perplexing case!" See also Manson, *The Sayings of Jesus,* pp. 245–248 and 312–317.

7) Compare Luke 9:51,53; 17:11 and 18:31.

8) The resemblance has long been noted; see H.W.A. Meyer, *Luke,* p. 512 and Jülicher, *Gleichnisreden,* vol. 2, p. 486. The matter was also discussed by Rayner Winterbotham, "Christ, or Archelaus?" *Expositor,* 8th Series, 4 (1912), pp. 338-347. Winterbotham accepted the Lucan version of the parable at face value and tried to explain why Christ would compare himself to Archelaus. See also J.T. Sanders, "The Para-

ble of the Pounds and Lucan Anti-Semitism," *Theological Studies* 42 (1981), pp. 660–668, who has minimized the relationship between Archelaus and the Lucan form of the parable without sufficient evidence. Compare Jeremias, *Parables,* p. 59, who theorizes that an independent parable of a throne claimant had been combined to the Parable of the Pounds (Luke 19:12–27). His suggestion is ingenious but it is difficult to retreat from the secondary nature of the parable as it has been revised in Luke.

9) Compare Josephus, *Ant.* 17:299–318, 339ff and *War,* 2:80–100 and 111ff. See also Emil Schürer, *The History of the Jewish People in the Age of Jesus Christ,* revised and edited by G. Vermes and F. Millar, (Edinburgh: T. and T. Clark, 1973), vol. 1, pp. 355–356.

10) The motif of killing unworthly workmen could have been an effective shock element in the parable. Compare the parable attributed to R. Jose Hagalili in Midrash Proverbs, where the workers are executed by the order of the king (chapter 16, Buber, p. 41b; Semachot Derabbi Chiyah 3:6, Higger, pp. 222–223). However because this element is missing in the parallel in Matthew, it may well be secondary in Luke's version of the parable.

11) Some scholars may desire to see a reference to the destruction of the Temple in the words of the verse but this interpretation seems unlikely, and see the important article, C.H. Dodd, "The Fall of Jerusalem and the 'Abomination of the Desolation,'" *The Journal of Roman Studies* 37 (1947), pp. 47–54. Rayner Winterbotham suggested that Archelaus may well have taken revenge against those who objected to his rule, "It was probably quite in keeping with the character of Archelaus that on his return from Rome, triumphant over Antipas, he should have the Jews who had petitioned against him collected together and slaughtered before his eyes. Whether he actually did this is immaterial. Everybody knew that nothing would have better pleased the tiger-cub who had inherited his father's lust for blood." Idem, "Christ, or Archelaus?" *Expositor* 8th series, 4 (1912), p. 338. Flusser (private communication) pointed out that the accusation made against Archelaus by Antipater the son of Salome may be connected to the parable though the event is said to have occurred before the envoy went to Rome in order to oppose Archelaus' reign. Josephus described Antipater's claims: "Proceeding to the main contention of his speech, he laid great stress on the multitude of Jews who had been massacred around the sanctuary, poor people who had come for a festival and, while offering their sacrifices, had themselves been brutally immolated. There had been, he said, such a pile of corpses in the temple as would have been raised even by the ruthless inroad of a foreign foe" (Josephus, *War,* 2:30; *Ant.* 17:218 and

237). In his notes to Josephus, Thackeray observed the resemblance of the story to Luke 13:1 (Loeb, vol. 2, p. 335). In any case the slaughter of the enemies who oppose the king in the parable would be consistent with what Archelaus was capable of doing—if not a reference to an actual event which could have occurred.

12) See Origen, Commentary on Matthew XIV:12, *The Ante-Nicene Fathers,* vol. 10, p. 503.

13) See note 10 above.

14) Compare also Dodd, "The Fall of Jerusalem," pp. 49–53.

15) Thus also Jeremias, *Parables,* p. 63, "The merchant becomes a king, and the whole parable an announcement and confirmation of the delay of the *Parousia.*"

16) See Dodd, *The Parables,* p. 111, who correctly observed, "It is surely evident that the central interest lies in the reckoning, and in particular in the position of the cautious servant, whose hopeful complacency receives so rude a rebuff."

17) Jeremias, *Parables,* p. 178. The parallel appears in the Gospel of Thomas 64 (A. Guillaumont, *et al,* pp. 34–37). See the story of Bar Mayan, j. Sanh. 23c, chap. 6, hal. 8; j. Chagigah 77d, chap. 2, hal. 2.

18) Manson, *Sayings,* p. 129.

19) The Greek word *mega* does not appear in Marcion and a ninth century uncial. While one might be tempted to suggest that this detail was added later at an early stage of the textual tradition, the point of the parable is that it was a great supper and the word *mega* is well attested. See also the rabbinic parable attributed to R. Eleazer in Midrash Psalms 25:9 (Buber, p. 106b) where the size of the banquet is a decisive part of the story (see note 37 below).

20) In Luke 14:8, the words *eis gamous* are missing in codex Bezae and some other versions. No wedding is mentioned in the version of this passage which was augmented to Matthew 20:28 in codex Bezae. Neither do the rabbinic parallels to this passage mention a marriage feast (see notes 31–41 below). However it is unlikely that the words *eis gamous* were added to Luke 14:8. A scribe probably deleted them in order to harmonize the text to Luke 14:1.

21) Manson, *Sayings,* p. 225.

22) Again one should remember the observations made by Dodd, "The Fall of Jerusalem and the 'Abomination of Desolation,'" pp. 49ff. However it is quite possible that either Matthew or his redactor was alluding to the burning of Jerusalem and it must be remembered that this verse is missing in Luke. Interestingly, the first clear archaeological evidence for the burning of Jerusalem has recently been uncovered; see

N. Avigad, *Discovering Jerusalem* (Israel Exploration Society: Jerusalem, 1980), pp. 120–123.

23) John A.T. Robinson, *Redating the New Testament* (London: SCM Press, 1978), p. 19. The motif would emphasize the king's anger.

24) Compare the excuses mentioned in Sifre Deuteronomy 192 (Finkelstein, p. 233) for those who are not permitted to retreat in time of war, " . . . lest they should say, he has built a house, or has planted a vineyard or has betrothed a wife . . . " (concerning the context in Sifre Deuteronomy, see also b. Sotah 44b, m. Sotah 8:5 and j. Sotah 23a, chap. 8 hal. 10).

25) See the ones forbidden from the assembly, "No man smitten in his flesh, or paralysed in his feet or hands, or lame or blind, or deaf, or dumb, or smitten in his flesh with a visible blemish . . . " (1Qsa 2:6ff, Vermes, *The Dead Sea Scrolls,* p. 120; see J. Licht, *Megilat Haserachim,* pp. 264–265; see Licht's note on lines 5–6; and also Fitzmyer, *Luke,* vol. 2, p. 1057). The attitude of the Qumran sect probably was based upon the requirements for the priesthood. At any rate, Jesus enumerates members of society which were unable to provide for themselves in the economic conditions of the first century. By necessity, the handicapped had to rely on their families and upon the generosity of almsgivers. As is well known, almsgiving was stressed greatly in much of the literature from the period. However it seems that in some circles, these unfortunate individuals were viewed as outcasts as 1Qsa illustrates (compare the question in John 9:2 and cf. 5:12).

26) Jeremias, *Parables,* p. 187. The same idea was taken over by Linnemann, p. 96 and see also R.H. Gundry, *Matthew a Commentary on his Literary and Theological Art* (Grand Rapids: Eerdmanns, 1982), p. 439. Jeremias' suggestion presents an attractive theory which he supports from Revelation 22:14; 19:8 and Leviticus Rabbah 29:2 (Margulies, pp. 250f). It could also be observed that Johanan ben Zakai's parable concerning the king's banquet also speaks of garments which had been properly cleaned (b. Shabbat 153a and see also Ecclesiastes Rabbah 9:7 and Semachot Derabbi Chiyah 2:1, Higger, pp. 216f). Also m. Taanit 4:8 speaks about the white garments which have to be immersed. However the passage from the Mishnah states, " . . . and these were borrowed, that none should be abashed which had them not . . . " So on some occasions the proper garment was important as well as its state of cleanliness.

27) See preceding note.

28) It appears also in some manuscripts of Matthew 20:16 and compare Matthew 7:14 and Luke 13:24. See also Gundry, *Matthew,* pp. 440–441.

29) Linnemann, *Parables,* p. 96.

30) Irenaeus, *Against Heresies* 36:6, *The Anti-Nicene Fathers,* vol. 1, p. 517.

31) Harnack, *Sayings,* p. 121.

32) See Fitzmyer, *Luke,* vol. 2, p. 1056. See also note 24 above.

33) The comments made by Fitzmyer on the Parable of the Good Samaritan are well taken and are also applicable to the present example; *Luke,* vol. 2, p. 883.

34) See Fitzmyer, *Luke,* vol. 2, p. 1056.

35) Gospel of Thomas 64 (A. Guillaumont, *et al,* pp. 34–37). The excuse, which employs the words friend, wedding and dinner, seems to be closely related to the cannonical gospels.

36) Robinson, *Redating the New Testament,* pp. 19–20. Marshall also suggests that the second call was intended for the Gentiles. However he contests the approach which claims that the second sending out of the servant is an embellishment: "It is far from certain that Luke has expanded the original parable here"; idem, *The Gospel of Luke* (Grand Rapids: Eerdmanns), vol. 1, p. 590.

37) Midrash on Psalms 25:9 (Buber, p. 107a) and Yalkut Shimeoni, vol. 2, remez 702. Flusser first called the author's attention to this parable. See also Buber's note 32. Some scribes desired to emphasize the difference between the more honorable merchants and the less important workers or artisans. In the Midrash on Psalms, the parable of R. Eleazar is followed by another parable attributed to R. Jose bar Chanina in which the guests are invited to the banquet and do not respond to the invitation—until late in the evening. Thus one discovers some instructive parallels to the motifs employed in the gospels. Cf. Bacher, *Die Agada der palästinensischen Amoräer,* vol. 2, p. 74, on R. Eleazar b. Pedat.

38) See Robinson's suggestion discussed in note 36. More recently M. Lowe suggested that the two sendings could be connected to the ministries of John the Baptist and Jesus respectively; idem, "From the Parable of the Vineyard to a Pre-Synoptic Source," *New Testament Studies* 28 (1982), pp. 258–259. However the problem with this solution is twofold. First it may be trying to attribute significance to each detail of the parable when the primary theme could have been simply an intensive mission aimed at proclaiming the kingdom of heaven to the common people. Secondly the original context of the parable has not been preserved. It is doubtful that the original audience would have connected the first mission to the work of John the Baptist unless he had been mentioned in the preceding discussion.

39) One discovers many lasting merits in Adolf Harnack's work, *The Sayings of Jesus,* and it remains one of the more significant textual studies of gospel sources (English translation, 1908 of idem, *Sprüche und Reden Jesu; Beiträge in das Neuen Testament* 1906). W. Bussmann worked diligently on a Greek reconstruction of the sources in his work which appeared in three parts, *Synoptische Studien* (Halle: Buchhandlung des Waisenhauses, 1925–1929). See also the contribution of T.W. Manson, *The Sayings of Jesus* (first published in 1937). Karl Schmidt's work, *Der Rahmen der Geschichte Jesu* (Darmstadt: Wissenschaftliche Buchgesellschaft, 1964) also deals with the problem of the redaction of the gospel text. M. Dibelius wrote in the preface to his celebrated work on *Formgeschichte,* "In the first place, by reconstruction and analysis, it seeks to explain the origin of the tradition about Jesus, and thus to penetrate into a period previous to that in which our Gospels and their written sources were recorded" (*From Tradition to Gospel,* New York: Charles Scribner's Sons, 1934, which was the English translation of his book, idem, *Die Formgeschichte des Evangeliums,* 1919). Though the methodology may differ, it has become recognized that a careful critical analysis of the texts of the synoptics can "penetrate" behind the gospels' redaction and come nearer to their sources.

40) See the preceding note and especially the works of Harnack and Bussmann.

41) Semachot Derabbi Chiyah 3:3 (Higger, pp. 221–222). See also the important treatment of this parallel by Flusser, *Die rabbinischen Gleichnisse,* pp. 24f, 123, 154–155 and also idem, *Yahadut Umekorot Hanatzrut,* pp. 154–155.

42) Pesikta Derav Kahana 10:3 (Mandelbaum, p. 164); Pesikta Rabbati 25 (Friedmann, p. 127a): Tanchuma, Reah 12 (Buber's edition, 9); Yalkut Shimeoni vol. 1, remez 892, vol. 2, remez 932. See also Bacher, *Die Agada der Tannaiten,* vol. 2, p. 513, note 9, idem, *Agadot Hatannaim,* vol. 2, part 2, p. 175, note 64.

43) See Luke 16:10–12; cf. Exodus Rabbah 2:3 (Shenan's edition, vol. 1, pp. 106–107); Tanchuma, Shemot, 7; L. Ginzberg, *Genizah Studies* (New York: Hermon Press, 1969), vol. 1, pp. 46–47, and compare J. Mann, *The Bible as Preached in the Old Synagogue* (New York: KTAV, 1971), vol. 1, p. 205 (Hebrew) and cf. m. Demai 2:2. See Billerbeck, vol. 1, p. 972, vol. 2, p. 222.

44) See note 17 above.

45) See the section above on "Parable Agadah and Tradition."

46) Pesikta Derav Kahana 3:1; compare the parallels, Pesikta Rabbati 13 (Friedmann, p. 55a–b); Exodus Rabbah 26:2; Yalkut Shimeoni vol.

1, remez 261; Tanchuma, Yitro 3, (Buber's edition, Yitro 4); and see also M. Kasher, *Torah Shelemah,* vol. 14, pp. 250f. This parable was treated in the preceding chapter.

47) See the Parable of the Prince and His Inheritance and its parallels which was discussed in the preceding chapter, Sifre Deuteronomy Piska 19 (Finkelstein, p. 31) and Piska 356 (Finkelstein, p. 424); Midrash Tannaim on Deut. 1:21 (Hoffmann, p. 11); Midrash Hagadol on Deut. 1:21 (Fisch, p. 34).

48) On this point see also N. Perrin, *Jesus and the Language of the Kingdom* (Philadelphia: Fortress, 1973), p. 95. He notes also the close "cultural proximity" between the parables of Jesus and those of the rabbis.

49) Further research is needed to deal with this question. See the critical comments made by M. Smith, "A Comparison of Early Christian and Early Rabbinic Tradition," *Journal of Biblical Literature* 82 (1963), pp. 169–176.

50) Flusser observed, "If one knows Hebrew and Greek, and is able to apply method of literary criticism to the analysis of the synoptic Gospels, one finds that probably all the passages expressing an anti-Jewish tension came into being only in the Greek stage of those Gospels, and one notices that in most cases these changes in the original Hebrew narratives and sayings appear in only *one* of the three Gospels or are the work of one Evangelist"; idem, "Two Anti-Jewish Montages in Matthew" *Immanuel* 5 (1975), p. 37. See also the important article by L. Gaston, "The Messiah of Israel as Teacher of the Gentiles," *Interpretation* 29 (1975), pp. 24–40. Compare Flusser, "Matthew's Versus Israel,“ *Judaism and the Origins of Christianity* (Jerusalem: Magnes Press, at the press).

51) B. Sanhedrin 38b (also cf. Rashi's commentary), and see Bacher, *Die Agada der Tannaiten,* vol. 2, p. 7, notes 2–3; idem, *Agadot Hatannaim,* vol. 2, part 1, p. 3 and p. 5 notes 26–27; see Schwarzbaum, *The Mishle Shu'alim (Fox Fables) of Rabbi Berechiah Ha-Nakdan a Study on Comparative Folklore and Fable Lore,* p. 467, note 12. Schwarzbaum suggested that the number three hundred might be connected to the story about Samson and the three hundred foxes in Judges 15:4. Compare also the three hundred fox fables which Bar Kapara told at a banquet in order to exasperate the host (Leviticus Rabbah 28:2, Margulies, pp. 653ff; Ecclesiastes Rabbah 1:3; Midrash Hagadol Genesis 3:23, Margulies, p. 111).

52) See preceding note.

THE PARABLES OF THE KINGDOM OF HEAVEN

Needless to say, Jesus' teaching concerning the kingdom of heaven is a primary theme in the synoptic gospels.[1] Matthew uses the expression of heaven (God) thirty-eight times, Luke employs it thirty-two times and Mark fourteen times.[2] Matthew uses the term somewhat more frequently than the other evangelists and connects it with a number of parables. It has already been suggested that Luke secondarily introduced the kingdom concept to the Parable of the Talents. Likewise Matthew seems to have proliferated the introductory phrase concerning the kingdom of heaven and added it to a number of parables that may or may not have originally dealt with the theme of God's kingship.[3] For instance, in order to cite a parable concerning forgiveness, Matthew starts out by saying that his story illustrates the kingdom of heaven (Matthew 18:23; cf. 13:24, 31, 33, 44, 45, 47, 52; 20:1; 22:2; 25:1). Only once is a parable introduced as illustrating the kingdom of heaven by all three of the synoptic gospels. The Parable of the Mustard Seed is a part of the triple tradition and only here can one find that all three evangelists refer to the text as a kingdom parable.[4] Significantly in the continuation of the pericope, both Matthew and Luke relate the Parable of the Leaven to the kingdom of heaven—a passage which does not appear in Mark.

Both the Parable of the Mustard Seed and the Parable of the Leaven could be described as parables of growth and seem to have been originally connected to the idea of the expansion of God's kingship. Could this introduction (Matthew 13:31; Mark 4:30; Luke 13:18) have been derived from the better sources of the synoptics and then somehow have become a contributing cause for the secondary proliferation of the standardized kingdom preamble which was attached to other parables? Here one encounters the core problem when beginning to analyze the kingdom parables. What parables actually deal with the kingdom theme? Norman Perrin once noted that after Dodd and Jeremias, anyone desiring to treat the parables must by necessity first discuss the kingdom in the teachings of Jesus.[5] However both Dodd and Jeremias have assumed that a large number of parables illustrate the kingdom and they have treated them as forewarning of the great eschatological crisis which would be consummated with the appearance of the kingdom of heaven.

Some of the problems associated with the strict application of this approach have already been discussed. Nevertheless it should be noted that perhaps one of the more weighty pieces of evidence which call this approach to the kingdom into question appears here in the Parables of the Mustard Seed and the Leaven. These parables, which seem to have been connected to the kingdom of God at the earliest stages of the gospel tradition, delineate a gradual process of growth instead of the sudden manifestation of a new dispensation. Can the kingdom be both present and future?[6] Attempts have been made to alleviate the tension between two contradictary views of the kingdom of heaven—the first in which the kingdom is conceived as an eschatological event and the second position which teaches that the kingdom in the proclamation of Jesus is a present reality. Some have preferred to address these differences in terms of the spatial and temporal aspects of the kingdom motif. Both Dodd and Jeremias have treated the question in depth.[7]

Johannes Weiss attacked many of the current views concerning the kingdom of God in his day for minimizing the eschatological implications of Jesus' proclamation of the kingdom. The kingdom was directly connected to the eschatological overthrow of the rule of Satan.[8] However if a dominical saying would point to the kingdom of God as already present, Weiss tried to explain it as a preview of God's strength in the miracles performed by Jesus. He writes, "Also nicht etwa, weil eine Jüngergemeinde da ist, in welcher der Wille Gottes geschieht, also die 'Herrschaft Gottes' von Seiten der Menschen verwirklicht wird, sondern weil durch das Wirken Jesu die Macht des Satan, der vor allem der

Bringer der Uebel ist, gebrochen wird, darum redet Jesus bereits von einem gegenwärtigen Reiche Gottes: Aber dies sind Augenblicke erhabener prophetischer Begeisterung, wo ihn ein Siegesbewußtsein überkommt."[9] In this illuminating passage one can already discern the beginnings of the idea of a realized eschatology. He does not say it in so many words, but Weiss seems to view the miracles of Jesus and his proclamation concerning the kingdom as the eschatological kingdom operating in advance. It was the defeat of the Satanic realm in the present work of Jesus which transferred the future kingdom into the present for a brief interlude that Weiss attributes to the "prophetische Begeisterung" of Jesus. Nevertheless Weiss cannot be credited with the idea of "realized eschatology" but rather attacked his contemporaries for not grasping the eschatological message contained in Jesus' proclamation of the kingdom.

The physician, organist, theologian and original religious thinker Albert Schweitzer also became involved in the discussion of Jesus' eschatology. He observed in the introduction to the third edition of his most well-known work, *The Quest of the Historical Jesus (Von Reimarus zu Wrede. Eine Geschichte der Leben-Jesu-Forschung,* 1906, English translation, 1910), "While some critics were thus denying all eschatology to Jesus, towards the end of the nineteenth century others were moving in exactly the opposite direction."[10] Certainly Schweitzer, like Weiss, was among the latter group of critics. He developed the idea of *consequente Eschatologie* and treated the question of the failed parousia. In the midst of these studies Schweitzer tried to interpret the kingdom of heaven as being the same as the coming of the Son of Man. He writes, "The Parousia of the Son of Man, which is logically and temporally identical with the dawn of the Kingdom. . . . "[11] But is it so simple to equate two different themes as being "identical"? Can the parables of growth be adapted to this scenario?

Dodd correctly pointed out that a pan-eschatologization of the gospels was not consistent with a number of texts that speak about Jesus overcoming the power of Satan in the present (cf. Luke 11:20; Matthew 11:2–6; Luke 7:18–23).[12] He observed, "This declaration that the Kingdom of God has already come necessarily dislocates the whole eschatological scheme in which its expected coming closes the long vista of the future. The *eschaton* has moved from the future to the present, from the sphere of expectation into that of realized experience."[13] Thus Dodd was able to speak concerning the eschatological kingdom being realized in the present. The "realized eschatology" position developed by Dodd was also adopted by Jeremias who developed the idea further. Jeremias was not entirely comfortable with the idea that the kingdom had actually been realized at a point in time during the ministry of Jesus. He preferred to describe the kingdom in the teaching of Jesus' parables as representing "an eschatology that is in the process of realization." Hence Jeremias emphasizes the *process.* He adopted the terminology from correspondence with Ernst Haenchen who used the descriptive words, *"sich realisierende Eschatologie."* So Jeremias pushed the realized eschatology of Dodd further into the future. It was an eschatology which was realizing itself. In the concluding footnote to his book on the parables, Jeremias noted that to his "joy," Dodd had accepted this position.[14]

Here it is by no means the purpose of this review to deny that Jesus had a highly developed eschatology. A number of the dominical sayings concerning the Son of Man, his warnings concerning the eschatological judgment and parables like the ten virgins (Matthew 25:1–13) all are permeated with a keen awareness of the future time of recompense. However it must be seriously questioned whether the kingdom of heaven and the parousia of the Son of Man can be treated as identical themes in the framework of Jesus' teaching as Schweitzer claimed. A basic contradiction remains. The kingdom cannot be depicted both as a gradual process and as the sudden advent of a new age. These two diverse conceptions of the kingdom are mutually exclusive. One of the more tempting solutions to this problem has been advanced by P. Vielhauer who has suggested that two distinct themes of the gospels have become fused together.[15] The eschatological teaching concerning the coming of the Son of Man who will execute judgment and the theme concerning God's reign became confused. Thus sometimes the evangelists connected parables concerning the eschatological judgment with the kingdom of heaven theme (cf. Matthew 13).

Too often discussions of the kingdom of heaven have presented the evidence as an "either or" proposition. Either the kingdom is a future consummation or it is a present reality. Flusser pointed out that Jesus, like the rabbis, taught that God's reign was *both* present *and* future.[16] He also quoted the important observation of Leonhard Ragaz which is well worth repeating here.

> Ganz unmöglich ist die Vorstellung, dass Jesus sozusagen auf seine Erwartung der Nähe des Gottesreiches eine Art Ethik und Theologie aufgebaut habe, die dann natürlich wegfielen, wenn diese Erwartung sich nicht erfüllt hätte. So etwas geschieht wohl in theologischen und philosophischen Studierstuben . . . Das Verhältnis ist genau umgekehrt, als die eschatologischen Systematiker es auffassen. Nicht die eschatologische Erwartung ist es, die Jesu Verständnis Gottes und des Menschen . . . bestimmt, sondern umgekehrt bestimmt sein Verständnis Gottes und des Menschen . . . seine eschatologische Erwartung . . . Man muss schon eine Professorenbille vor den Augen haben, um das nicht zu sehen.[17]

Jesus' understanding of the eschaton was surely based upon his perception of the relationship between man and his neighbor, on the one hand, and between man and his Maker on the other. Certainly it is a mistake to view eschatology as the primary motivating factor in Jesus' ethical and moral theology.[18] It was Jesus' understanding of man and God which determined his approach to the eschatological future. The tension between God's reign in the present less than perfect world and the future consummation was summarized by the distinguished Sefardic rabbi, David de Sola Pool, "For the Jewish view, God's Kingship over Israel and the world is and always has been established, but only after the Messianic kingdom will it be for the first time fully revealed."[19] Just because Jesus felt the dynamic force of God's reign as a present reality in his ministry and in the progression of his movement does not mean that the kingdom would cease in the eschatological future. On the contrary God's reign would be further extended and revealed. When one speaks only of the future consummation, the present force of God's reign is minimized. Jesus was keenly aware of this dynamic force. The kingdom would not begin in the future but was already in operation. The idea of a "process of realization" pushes the kingdom too far into the distant eschatological future. However the force of God's power revealed in the work of Jesus and his movement did not negate or minimize the awareness that at the judgment God's reign would be expanded and more fully consummated.

Weiss and Schweitzer desired to interpret Jesus' employment of the expression kingdom of heaven as an eschatological concept which was linked to Jewish apocalyptic expectations.[20] The attempt to understand Jesus' usage of the term *solely* on the basis of Jewish apocalyptic is beset with a number of difficulties. For one thing, it seems doubtful if the expression the kingdom of God or kingdom of heaven ever became a technical term in apocalyptic literature. R.H. Charles, the great authority on pseudepigraphic and apocalyptic literature from the previous generation of scholarship noted, "I shall not delay further here on this subject, but merely add that the expression [kingdom of heaven] hardly ever occurs in apocalyptic, though the thing itself is presupposed."[21] Nor has the discovery of the Dead Sea Scrolls provided direct parallels to Jesus' use of the expression kingdom of heaven.[22] Nevertheless in the pseudepigrapha, the idea of God's eternal reign which confronts and battles the work of Satan finds expression in a few select texts.[23] The term kingdom of heaven is analogous to the expressions "the kingdom of the Lord" *(hē basileia kuriou)* in the Testament of Benjamin (8:1), the "kingdom of the immortal king" in the Sibylline Oracles (3:47), and the "kingdom of our God" *(hē basileia tou theou hēmōn)* in the Psalms of Solomon (17:4). While the sources from the pseudepigrapha and early Jewish apocalyptic do not present a fully developed or unified understanding of the concept of the kingdom of God, at least in the Testament of Moses and in the Testaments of the Twelve Patriarchs one discovers a close correlation between God's reign and the defeat of Satanic activity in the world.

In the Testament of Moses, the appearance of God's reign is understood as the defeat of Satan's power, "Then his kingdom will appear throughout his whole creation. Then the devil will have an end. . . . For the Heavenly One will arise from his kingly throne."[24] However the fact that God arises from his kingly throne suggests that all along God was in control. However his dominion has to be *revealed* and Satan's influence destroyed. In the Testament of Benjamin, moral and ethical precepts are to be meticulously observed—otherwise the kingdom of the Lord will be removed: "But you, my children, run from evil, corruption, and hatred of brothers; cling to goodness and love. . . . From the words of Enoch the Righteous I tell you that you will be promiscuous like the promiscuity of the Sodomites and will perish, with few exceptions. You shall resume your actions with loose women, and the Kingdom of the Lord will not be among you, for he will take it away forthwith."[25] Immoral conduct will cause the kingdom of the Lord to be removed, and it seems that the righteous way of life is the result of men who accept God's reign.

In the Testament of Dan, God's presence among the people and his rule in their lives provides protection against the dominion of the enemy, "And Jerusalem shall no longer undergo desolation, nor shall Israel be led into captivity, because the Lord will be in her midst [living among human beings]. The Holy One of Israel will rule over them in humility and poverty, and he who trusts in him shall reign in truth in the heavens. And now fear the Lord, my children, be on guard against Satan and his spirits. Draw near to God and to the angel who intercedes for you, because he is the mediator between God and men for the peace of Israel. He shall stand in opposition to the kingdom of the enemy. Therefore the enemy is eager to trip up all who call on the Lord, because he knows on the day in which Israel trusts the enemy's kingdom will be brought to an end" (Testament of Dan 5:13–6:5). The conflict between the enemy and God's rule is clear. In 2 Enoch one discovers the use of the word yoke which is similar to the rabbinic idiom of the yoke of the kingdom (cf. Matthew 11:28). The generation of the flood is denounced, "I know the wickedness of mankind, how they will not carry the yoke which I have placed on them . . . they have renounced my yoke, and they will take on another yoke . . . and do obeisance to vain gods. And they will reject my sole rule" (2 Enoch 34:1; in

Greek sole rule was μοναρχία).[26] In the Wisdom of Solomon, the righteous receive the glorious kingdom as God takes vengeance on his enemies.[27] The Sibylline Oracles connect the revealing of the "kingdom of the immortal King" with God's judgment.[28] Ultimately God is in control, but the full power and glory of his dominion in a corrupt world is yet to be manifested. So Charles' initial observation holds true (note 21), but it should be taken one step further. The expression itself, "the kingdom of heaven," in early Jewish apocalyptic literature is unknown and variations of the term are quite rare even if the concept does surface from the background in a number of texts.

In contrast to Jewish apocalyptic, the term kingdom of heaven occurs quite frequently in the synoptic gospels and expresses a well defined concept. One could even call it a technical term in the mouth of Jesus. The closest parallels to Jesus' employment of the term appear in rabbinic literature. The expression "kingdom of heaven" represents a distinct idea in the minds of Israel's sages. This concept, as it is expressed in rabbinic literature, should not be considered the *equivalent* of Jesus' usage of the term. Nevertheless, the meaning is analogous enough to suggest that the expression developed within the atmosphere of a similar religious environment, both in the teaching of the sages and in the teaching of Jesus. They seem to share a common milieu.

A comparison of Jesus' employment of this term with the rabbinic understanding of the concept can help to elucidate the fundamental significance of the kingdom of heaven not only in the teachings of Jesus but also in the minds of the rabbis. First, it should be recalled that there is no difference between the Lucan (Mark never uses kingdom of heaven) terminology, kingdom of God, and the Matthean preference, kingdom of heaven. Heaven became a circumlocution for God at least as early as the Maccabean period, or as early as the composition of the book of Daniel, and perhaps popularly speaking even earlier.[29] Second it should be remembered that the Hebrew word מלכות is a verbal noun derived from the verb מלך which means to reign. Dalman therefore is quite correct when he interprets the designation of the kingdom of heaven as expressing the idea of God's reign.[30] Perhaps it is even somewhat precarious to approach the concept too much like systematic theologians and attempt to define it in purely temporal or spatial terms. The kingdom of God simply delineates that God is in control or that he rules in a given situation.

The often quoted passage from the Mishnah certainly is relevant to this discussion (m. Berachot 2:2, j. Berachot 4b, chap. 2, hal. 3).[30a] R. Joshua b. Korcha, a fourth generation tanna and student of R. Johanan b. Nuri, explains that whoever recites the Shema has accepted the "yoke of the kingdom of heaven" and that this is the first step to receiving the "yoke of the commandments." As Ephraim Urbach has pointed out, "The acceptance of the yoke of the kingdom of heaven means to acknowledge the God who is One and Unique, and to bear witness that there is no other god."[31] For R. Joshua b. Korcha, this signifies a surrender to the divine will and a move that will lead the individual to a more complete observance of the commandments. A very similar idea is already reflected in the book of Jubilees in the prayer of Abraham, "My God, the Most High God, you alone are God to me. And you created everything, and everything which is was the work of your hands, and you and your kingdom I have chosen" (Jubilees 12:19). Abraham had come to recognize that God is one and that there is no other god beside him. Therefore he chooses God's kingdom. Thus like the dictum of R. Joshua b. Korcha, the book of Jubilees speaks of Abraham's realization of the one God and also of his kingdom.

In another rabbinic text, R. Simeon bar Yochai makes the connection between God's reign and obedience to the commandments, "He who said, 'I am the LORD thy God who brought you out of Egypt' (Exodus 20:2)—I am He! As you received my kingdom upon yourselves in Egypt, where they responded, 'Yes, yes,' thus you received my kingdom. They received my decrees, as it was said, 'You shall have no other gods before me' (Exodus 20:3). It is He who said, 'I am the LORD thy God' (Exodus 20:2), I am He! As you received my kingdom at Sinai where they said to him, 'Yes, yes,'—thus you received my kingdom. They received my decrees."[32] R. Simeon bar Yochai's colorful interpretation of Exodus 20:2 sees a direct relationship between Israel's distant past and the present demand of God's reign. Jesus also taught his followers to seek first the kingdom of God and his righteousness which requires an individual to acknowledge the sovereignty of the one God and accept his lordship (Matthew 6:33; Luke 12:31). When Jesus teaches his disciples to pray "Thy kingdom come . . . " is he envisioning the future inauguration of the consummation of the ages? It seems more probable that Jesus is expressing the desire that all men will accept the yoke of the kingdom and come under the jurisdiction of God's reign. This is certainly compatible with Jesus' call to repentance (cf. Luke 13:1–5). Each individual must receive God's kingdom and inaugurate God's authority in his own life.[33]

The recital of the Shema is the acceptance of God's rule and is the liberation from the tyranny of lawlessness. The yoke of the kingdom of heaven should also be understood in contrast to its alternative. R. Ishmael's mentor, the second generation tanna, R. Nechunya b. Hakanah, taught, "He that takes upon himself the yoke of the Law, from him shall be taken away the yoke of the kingdom . . . " (Avot 3:5). R. Nechunya is referring to the yoke of political oppression. Thus the yoke of God's sovereignty can be contrasted to the yoke of an earthly regime. An interpretation of the verse, "If they were wise, they would understand this *(zot)*" (Deuteronomy 32:29) appears in the midrash Sifre Deuteronomy. The anonymous midrash understands the word "this" *(zot)* as referring to the Torah and also the words of Jacob. It connects the kingdom of heaven to man's relationship to his neighbor and the fear of God. The text states, "If Israel had shown regard for what Jacob their father had said, no nation or kingdom could have ruled them. What did he say to them? 'Receive upon yourselves the [yoke] of the kingdom of heaven and reconcile yourselves one with the other in the fear of heaven and conduct yourselves toward one another in loving kindness.'"[34] No other authority can rule over Israel when they repent and accept fully the yoke of God's reign. The one who accepts the Torah, though outwardly oppressed, is inwardly free because he has submitted to the higher authority. In some ways the Torah in the thinking of the sages could be described as the Magna Charta of freedom, especially in comparison to many despotic regimes of history.

Although the term kingdom of God never appears in the

Hebrew scriptures of the Old Testament, the idea of God's kingdom is alluded to many times. The first reference to the kingdom is found in the Song of the Sea when God liberates the children of Israel from the bondage of Egypt. In the Septuagint the Hebrew verb in the text from Exodus 15:18 is translated into Greek as a present participle, κύριος βασιλεύων τὸν αἰῶνα κλτ. This Greek translation seems to represent an early understanding of the verse and should not be viewed strictly as a mere literal transcription of the text in Greek. This interpretation of the Hebrew verse stresses the present aspect of God's reign—God is reigning now in this age.[35] In a text from the Mechilta, R. Jose Hagalili connected the verse from the Song at the Sea which celebrated the deliverance of the people from Pharaoh's army with the need for Israel to recognize the kingship of God and to obey his commands. He midrashically applys the verse to Israel's reluctance to accept the rule of God, "Had the Israelites at the sea said: 'The Lord is king for ever and ever, no nation or kingdom would ever have ruled over them. But they said: 'The Lord shall reign for ever and ever'—in the future . . . "[36] Hence he interprets the imperfect of the Hebrew verb "to reign" as meaning that the people were not yet willing to accept the rule of God. The children of Israel should have proclaimed God king מלך for by so doing they would have avoided foreign oppression in the future. Thus one discovers an imaginative play on the words king and the verb "to reign." R. Jose Hagalili desired to emphasize the response of the people and in many ways his remarks reflect the idea that when Israel accepts God's reign they receive his liberation. At least the Septuagint translators seem to see God's deliverance of Israel from Egypt as the manifestation of his rule as a present reality. An anonymous parable from the Mechilta illustrates how the conception of the kingdom was linked to the deliverance of the people in the minds of Israel's sages.

THE KING AND HIS RELUCTANT SUBJECTS

(Mechilita Derabbi Ishmael on Exodus 20:2)

They give a parable. To what may this be compared? To the following: A king who entered a province said to the people: May I be your king? But the people said to him:

> Have you done anything good for us that you should rule over us? What did he do then? He built the city wall for them, he brought in the water supply for them, and he fought their battles. Thus God. He brought the Israelites out of Egypt, divided the sea for them, sent down the manna for them, brought up the well for them, brought the quails for them. He fought for them the battle of Amalek. Then He said to them: I am to be your king. They said to Him: Yes, yes. Rabbi says: This proclaims the excellence [חן] of Israel. For when they all stood before Mt. Sinai to receive the Torah, they all made up their minds to act alike to accept the reign of God joyfully.[37]

This vivid illustration and the words of Rabbi in the context of the Mechilta's treatment of the decalogue connect three powerful themes of Jewish thought. Deliverance, Torah and the people's obedience to the challenge of the Torah are inseparably bound together. The parable draws a colorful picture of a king and his reluctant subjects. The parable employs a number of points of comparison as it allegorizes the mighty acts of God which liberated and protected the people of Israel. It comes as no surprise that in the turning point of the parable (see the word *kach,* translated as "thus") the king figure is identified as God who came to redeem Israel. When they receive the law as they stand before Mount Sinai, they accept the rule of the king who had delivered them. Hence the Mechilta integrates the themes of liberation, Torah and the kingdom of heaven.

Likewise, Jesus' conception of the kingdom of heaven is closely related to the theme of deliverance. When Jesus casts out a demon, he proclaims the rule of God in this liberating act. Satan's rule had been overthrown by the power of God's authority. In Luke, Jesus explains to unsympathetic critics, "But if I cast out demons by the finger of God then the kingdom of God has come upon you" (Luke 11:20 and see parallel Matthew 12:28). Jesus' use of the expression "by the finger of God" must be associated with the exclamation of Pharaoh's magicians when they were incapable of coping with the signs performed by God through Moses and Aaron. When the magicians stood powerless before the Pharaoh, they declared, "This is the finger of God" (Exodus 8:19). Hence the metaphor "finger of God" signified God's liberating power. The finger of God is also said to have inscribed the decalogue upon the tablets of stone (Exodus 31:18; Deuteronomy 9:10). Could Jesus be alluding to God's previous acts of deliverance when he verbalizes the well-known biblical phrase "the finger of God"? The demon has been exorcised, God's creation is liberated and therefore God's sovereign reign has been inaugurated in an act of redemption. The synoptic gospels accentuate the conflict of Jesus with Satan. Jesus overcomes Satan in the temptation, he exorcises demons, he sends his disciples on a healing mission and they confront the enemy, and Satan also appears in the passion narrative. The gospels portray Jesus as overcoming the realm of Satan and establishing God's reign.

Moreover in the synoptic gospels, Jesus' disciples are active participants in this drama of redemption. The disciples are commissioned to fulfill a special task. Jesus sends them on an embassy to Jewish villages as an extension of his own activities (Matthew 10:1, 5–16; Mark 6:7–13, Luke 9:1–6; and Luke 10:1–12). Their purpose is to continue the work of their master and also as Matthew adds, κηρύσσετε λέγοντες ὅτι ἤγγικεν ἡ βασιλεία τῶν οὐρανῶν (Matthew 10:7; parallel Luke 9:2). Can one aspect of the kingdom theme be connected to the movement itself?[38] Jesus honors John the Baptist and John's movement seems to have provided a basis from which sprang Jesus' own following. Nevertheless a dominical saying elevates all members of the kingdom of heaven above John. One thus encounters a paradox. How can John's work be deemed so important and yet he himself is actually excluded from the kingdom? John is viewed as the last prophet of the biblical period (Matthew 11:11–14 and Luke 7:28; 16:16). John never became an active follower of Jesus. Not only is he imprisoned and put to death without becoming a follower of Jesus, but in one passage he even sends his disciples to question Jesus (Matthew 11:1–6; Luke 7:18–23). Nevertheless the revivalist movement of John was viewed as preparing the way for Jesus' preaching. While other authorities may disagree, it seems that John's message was a call to repentance while Jesus proclaimed the kingdom. Only Matthew attributes the preaching of the kingdom of heaven to John the Baptist; it seems that this is a secondary development. Here the text of Luke is preferable where Jesus preaches the kingdom and John calls the people to a baptism of repentance.[39] John never became a part of Jesus' kingdom movement even though according to the synoptics he was Jesus' precursor. Thus even the least important participant in the kingdom of heaven movement gains prominence over John the Baptist.

The Qumran manuscripts throw light on some aspects of the kingdom of heaven issue and its relationship to Jesus' movement. The Qumran convenanters were intensely interested in the exegesis of biblical texts. They believed that the scriptures were related directly to their own community and ascribed special meaning to biblical terminology. For example, when interpreting certain passages, the sectarians found references to their community in words like the humble or the poor.[40] These self-appellations are derived from the rich heritage of various biblical texts. Apparently Jesus, like the Qumran sectarians, linked the language of the Hebrew scriptures with his group of followers. At least this is a likely interpretation of Jesus' phraseology in the text of the beatitudes.[41] When Jesus declares, "Blessed are the poor in spirit . . . " he addresses none other than his disciples. Jesus extends the expression beyond the ideology of the sectarian thought of the Essenes. He united the motif of the kingdom of heaven with the movement of his disciples who are referred to as the "poor in spirit." Jesus concludes the blessing for the poor in spirit by introducing the theme of God's sovereignty and by saying, " . . . for theirs [from these] is the kingdom of heaven." Both Matthew and Luke relate these sayings to the disciples (Luke 6:20; Matthew 5:1). In light of the Qumran passages, Matthew and Luke have a solid historical basis for ascribing such terminology to Jesus' disciples.[42] Like the Qumran sectarians, Jesus referred to his disciples with the appellation עניי רוח derived from the imagery of biblical idiom. This was a descriptive term which characterizes his disciples and refers to the numerous texts from the Hebrew scriptures which mention the poor and the humble. Jesus' idea of the kingdom of heaven is interrelated to the appellation "poor in spirit." The kingdom concept distinguishes Jesus' use of this Hebrew phrase from the world of the Qumran sectarians. The convenanters did not use the term the kingdom of heaven. But for Jesus and the rabbis, this expression represented a well-defined idea. Hence Jesus' use of the expression connects the disciples directly with the kingdom theme.

The context of another saying connected with this idea is found on the occasion when the disciples were preventing children from approaching Jesus (Matthew 19:13–15). The children were brought to Jesus for his touch and blessing. The Jewish custom of blessing children is probably ancient as Israel Abrahams has attested, even if it is not always well documented.[43] The reason for the disciples' discourteous actions is unknown. Regardless of their intentions, Jesus sternly rebukes them for forbidding the children's access and then declares, ἄφετε τὰ παιδία καὶ μὴ κωλύετε αὐτὰ ἐλθεῖν πρός με, τῶν γὰρ τοιούτων ἐστὶν ἡ βασιλεία τῶν οὐρανῶν (Matthew 19:14; Mark 10:14; Luke 18:16).[44] The genitive form τοιούτων is often construed as a possessive genitive, meaning that the kingdom belongs to the childlike. Though this is possible, it seems to be unlikely that this was the original meaning of Jesus' saying. Is God's kingdom an object which can be possessed? The form would be better understood as a partitive genitive which signifies members of a group. The grammarians, H.E. Dana and J.R. Mantey simply put it, "A noun may be defined by indicating in the genitive the whole of which it is a part."[45] Apparently Jesus is comparing the disciples to children. The comparison is a familiar one. Then the statement is made, τῶν γὰρ τοιούτων ἐστὶν ἡ βασιλεία τῶν οὐρανῶν. In Hebrew the text would have read, כי מכאלה מלכות שמים. The force of the text would entail the idea of the partitive genitive and could be rendered into English, " . . . for such as these comprise the kingdom of heaven." It is not therefore a matter of possession; rather it is the childlike who make up the kingdom. The suggestion is forwarded that the "such as these" childlike ones designate Jesus' disciples. This of course, makes their rebuke all that more severe, because they valued their access to their master. The statement also helps to delineate the realm of the kingdom by describing its members.

In addition the blessing pronounced in the beatitude text (Matthew 5:3–12) carries a similar if not identical meaning. The Greek phrase, ὅτι αὐτῶν ἐστιν ἡ βασιλεία τῶν οὐρανῶν (Matthew 5:3 and parallel Luke 6:20) has often been understood as conveying the idea of a possessive genitive. The Revised Standard translation renders the passage, " . . . for theirs is the kingdom of heaven" (Matthew 5:3). The parallel beatitude in Luke has been changed from the third person to the more intimate second person and betrays the work of Luke.[46] The unusual phrase "poor in spirit" which would be difficult to understand in Greek has been changed into simply the "poor." Certainly Jesus had a high evaluation of poverty but the expression should not be limited to economic status. Some have maintained that Matthew was spiritualizing, but this seems unlikely as the phrase has been paralleled in Hebrew from the Dead Sea Scrolls. Luke's change to the second person ὑμέτερος seems to be the work of Luke or his redactor. This Greek word never appears in Matthew or Mark and seems to be best understood as the work of Luke.[47] But is the meaning of the phrase ὅτι αὐτῶν ἐστιν ἡ βασιλεία τῶν οὐρανῶν (Matthew 5:3) to be understood as a possessive genitive as it is regularly translated? If one examines the linguistic evidence and searches for the wording of the Semitic *Vorlage* of the gospel text, two possibilities suggest themselves. The Greek words ὅτι αὐτῶν could have been translated from either the Hebrew words להם or מהם. Frans Delitsch translated the Greek wording of Matthew by להם which is similar in meaning to most translations that have been made into modern European languages. Delitsch's translation reflects the possessive genitive in Greek. However a translation which contains the notion that the poor in spirit can obtain ownership or possession of God's kingdom is meaningless. If the possessive idea was already contained in the Semitic undertext, it probably would have been rendered into the Greek dative of advantage, αὐτοῖς.[48] The Septuagint translators often translated the Hebrew expression להם by the Greek dative, αὐτοîs.[49] The translators generally but not always employed a preposition like an ἐκ or ἀπό to indicate a partitive genitive. The translator of the *Urevangelium* did not supply the preposition which would have made the partitive genitive idea clear. Had the undertext contained the idea that the poor in spirit would somehow possess the kingdom, the translators would probably have employed the dative of advantage. Hence the Greek phrase ὅτι αὐτῶν can best be understood as a partitive genitive. The poor in spirit are those who as disciples of Jesus possess these characteristics and thus they make up the kingdom of heaven. W.F. Albright and C.S. Mann have interpreted the passage in this way in their commentary from the Anchor Bible series. They discuss Matthew 5:3 and write, "The best sense here is 'the Kingdom will consist of such as these'. . . ."[50] The poor in spirit are the followers of Jesus who form the kingdom movement as they have come under the jurisdicition of God's reign. Jesus' disciples play an active role in the redemptive actions of their master and thereby assist in bringing God's reign upon the people who respond to the message and participate in the movement inaugurated by the activities of Jesus. Those individuals who have sumbitted to God's authority in repentance have become a part of the kingdom.

THE PARABLES OF THE MUSTARD SEED AND LEAVEN (MATTHEW 13:31–33; MARK 4:30–32; LUKE 13:18–21)

The Parables of the Mustard Seed and the Leaven are partner illustrations. Both of the parables appear in the Gospel of Thomas but in different contexts (logia 20 and 96). However these parables were probably originally connected with one another and employed to illustrate the same theme.[51] Mark only contains one of the dual illustrations—the Parable of the Mustard Seed. Nevertheless both Matthew and Luke agree with each other in placing the two parables together. Matthew's text is more closely connected to Mark's version of the parable than to Luke's, and Vincent Taylor even referred to Matthew as being viewed correctly as "a conflation of Mark and Q."[52] Whether Matthew should be understood as being based upon a Q document may be questioned, but he seems to have a source that closely resembles Luke and also betrays the influence of Mark.[53] However except for the introductions, the Parable of the Leaven in Matthew and Luke shows an almost total verbal identity. It would seem that Matthew and Luke are both derived from a common source, and that though Mark probably was acquainted with the other parable, he elected to delete it. The fact that the Gospel of Thomas preserves both parables in different contexts should not be taken to prove that the parables were not originally twin illustrations. While one should not over-simplify the question, there is little evidence that the Gospel of Thomas tried to preserve an original sequence from its sources and it is possible that he has taken the parables and adapted them for the context of his own gospel with clusters of new sayings.[54]

Both parables work together to illustrate the common theme of the gradual growth of the kingdom.[55] Jeremias has perceived a reference to the eschaton and the ingathering of the Gentiles as the primary message of the Parable of the Mustard Seed. He claims, "The eschatological character of the metaphor of the tree or shrub is established by the fact that κατασκηνοῦν (Mark 4:32; Matthew 13:32; Luke 13:19) is actually an eschatological technical term for the incorporation of the Gentiles into the people of God. . . . "[56] To support this position he cites both Joseph and Aseneth 15 and also Enoch 90:30, 33, 37.[57] However one might ask why the word κατασκηνόω must be considered "an eschatological technical term" when it is used in many contexts without eschatological implications.[58] The imagery of the parable recalls a number of biblical passages, Daniel 4:11,12,21 and Ezekiel 17:5, 23; 31:6.[59] Moreover only Theodotion's version of Daniel 4:12 employs the verb κατασκηνόω and the gospel text reflects the so called "Theodotionic" translation of Daniel 4:12, " . . . and the birds of the air dwelt in its branches."[60] In the Septuagint's version of the same verse, the Aramaic text of Daniel is translated by the word ἐνόσσευον. This is also the case in verse 21. In Ezekiel 17:23 the Septuagint translators rendered the Hebrew phrase ושכנו תחתיו כל צפור by the Greek καὶ πᾶν πετεινὸν ὑπὸ τὴν σκιὰν αὐτοῦ ἀναπαύσεται. Matthew 25:31 also speaks of the gathering together of the nations for the eschatological judgment but uses a different verb.[61] While the same Greek word does appear in Joseph and Aseneth, it hardly seems to be "an eschatological technical term" as Jeremias claimed. Moreover while the idea of the ingathering of the Gentiles is reflected in Jewish thought (e.g., Zechariah 14:16),[62] it seems unlikely that suddenly one would find a reference to the incorporation of the Gentiles into Israel in the Parable of the Mustard Seed. One should avoid the ever present danger of ascribing too much meaning to each detail of the parable.

Although a large number of minor agreements between Matthew and Luke against Mark appear in the Parable of the Mustard Seed, the text of Matthew is much closer to Mark.[63] Both Matthew and Luke retain the phrase ὃν λαβὼν ἄνθρωπος, but Matthew reads ἔσπειρεν instead of Luke's ἔβαλεν. Matthew's text reflects Mark's wording, σπαρῇ. Matthew speaks of the seed being sown "in his field," Mark's text contains the wording, "upon the ground" and Luke uses the phrase "in his garden." Some commentators have tried to view these differences in wording between the synoptics as betraying a halachic significance. Robert Gundry notes, "In Palestine, sowing mustard in fields was allowed (so Matthew), but not in gardens (see *m. Kil.* 3:2; *b. Kil.* 2:8)."[64] Fitzmyer says exactly the opposite, "According to *m. Kil.* 2:9, mustard was not to be grown in a 'field,' but in 3:2 'in a garden bed.'"[65] The mishnaic tractate, Kilaim, deals with the commandments from the Pentateuch which prohibit the planting together of diverse kinds.[66] Rabban Simeon b. Gamaliel said that it was permitted to cultivate mustard and saffron on the perimeters of a vegetable garden. It was also taught that one may plant a row of mustard in the middle of a field as long as there was sufficient distance between the mustard and other crops.[67] The idea behind these laws was of course the observance of the commandments concerning diverse kinds. Jesus has taken the mustard seed as an example in this parable because of its proverbial smallness which could be contrasted to the size of the shrub that it produces. Whether these halachic discussions concerning the cultivation of mustard and saffron either on the border of a vegetable garden or in an isolated row of a field are related to Jesus' parable seems improbable. Thus it seems futile to search for some great halachic significance in the differences between the synoptics, as the mishnaic passages and the Jerusalem Talmud permit sowing mustard seed in both a garden (at least on the perimeters) and in a field—under prescribed circumstances.

Thus it is highly improbable that in this case the distinctions of the halachah are reflected by the different wording in the texts of Matthew, Mark and Luke. These differences are best understood as the work of the evangelists or the redactors of the gospels. While one cannot be certain, here it seems that Matthew's text is preferable. In the New Testament, the word for garden, *kēpos,* appears only here in Luke and three times in the gospel of John.[68] Luke sometimes stylizes his text in Greek and he may have tried to improve his source by adding a more exact term like garden instead of field. Perhaps for some reason he felt that cultivation of mustard was more suitable in a garden than in a field. Matthew would probably not have changed Mark's version unless he had another source, and in this case, as the minor agreements suggest, his source seems to be very close in wording to the text of Luke. As will be seen, this source appears to be one of the better sources for the life and teachings of Jesus.

In Mark's version of the parable one discovers the phrase μικρότερον ὂν πάντων τῶν σπερμάτων which reflects a similar Greek expression from the third centruy B.C. that appears in Antigonus of Carystus.[69] Matthew also contains this saying which is missing in Luke. Mark also emphasizes, " . . . and puts forth *large* branches . . . " (compare the Septuagint of Ezekiel 17:23 κέδρον μεγάλην).[70] Neither Matthew nor Luke describes the branches as being large but rather simply affirms that the birds of the air made their nests in its branches. Moreover Matthew and Luke do not contain a reference to the shade of the branches. Thus the Marcan phrase δύνασθαι ὑπὸ τὴν σκιὰν αὐτοῦ which appears neither in Matthew nor in Luke seems to be a colorful embellishment. Mark may have adopted this detail from the Septuagint (cf. Ezekiel 17:23 and 31:6; compare also Theodotion's version of Daniel 4:9 where the word *skiazō* appears). All in all Mark's text contains a number of innovations which seem to be editorial details like the phrase "the smallest of all the seeds," which were probably added in the Greek stage of the development of the gospel tradition. A number of these innovations also appear in Matthew. In this respect the gospel of Luke seems to be closer to the sources of the synoptics. After all, why would Luke delete these colorful embellishments if they appeared in his source? His version preserves several characteristics which could be described as Semitisms. At least this simple illustration, beginning from verse 19 after the introduction, contains parallelism, tautology, parataxis and preserves a syntax that permits a reconstruction into Hebrew without changing the word order of the Greek. The Greek words, τίνι ὁμοιώσω αὐτήν, were probably added by Luke (13:18). The parable may be reconstructed into Hebrew as follows. This is an experimental translation and it should be noted that much more linguistic study is needed. Here an effort has been made to capture the idiom between later biblical and mishnaic Hebrew.[71]

The Mustard Seed

למה דומה מלכות שמים? דומה לגרגר של חרדל. נטלו אדם ושם
אותו בשדהו וצמח והיה לעץ ועוף השמים שכנו בענפיו

The picture is one of a man who almost inadvertently plants a mustard seed. The parallelisms emphasize the process of growth. First he planted it, then it grew. The tiny seed finally becomes a tree and in the end even the birds of the air are able to make their home in its branches. In every stage of the development of the short illustration the idea of progressive action is depicted. The seed grows into a tree. The concept of growth is further emphasized in the partner parable. As already noted, the Parable of the Leaven is parallel to the Parable of the Mustard Seed and they both complement each other to illustrate the same theme.

Again one discovers that Matthew and Luke cannot agree on an introduction to the parable. Matthew states, "He told them another parable, 'The kingdom of heaven is like . . . " Luke records, "And again he said, 'To what shall I compare the kingdom of God? It is like . . . " Luke's wording recalls of course the familiar rabbinic introduction to parables, למה הדבר דומה. However Luke has employed the word *homoiōsō* "to what shall I compare . . . " which would not be idiomatic in Mishnaic Hebrew. So it seems that both Matthew and Luke tried in their own ways to tie the two parables together in the context of their gospels. Probably the parables originally followed one another in a rapid sequence without connecting phrases to introduce the twin parable. After the introductions, Matthew and Luke preserve the parable with total word for word verbal identity! The primary difference between them in the former parable is Mark. Like the Parable of the Mustard Seed, one discovers an emphasis on a series of actions that illustrates a progression. First the woman takes the leaven, then she hides it in the three measures of flour and finally—what must have seemed miraculous—the leaven had permeated all the flour. The growth aspect of both parables is the dominant theme. In some ways the illustrations seem almost banal. Everyone was familiar with the growth of a seed in cultivation or the use of leaven in baking. The parables point to the miraculous within nature and also one can sense an element of wonder, surprise and even suddenness when the seed has become a nesting place for birds and the leaven has permeated the flour. It should also be remembered that Jesus referred to his disciples as the salt of the earth and the light of the world. These similes refer to something common and yet points to the special qualities of salt and light which people often take for granted. The reign of God is being realized in the work and ministry of Jesus and his followers. The process is one that grows and permeates. It may appear deceptively commonplace but after the growth period, it will culminate suddenly in its full grandeur.

The leaven in Jewish thought often conveys negative connotations.[72] Hence a paradox appears. Why would the kingdom be compared to leaven? One could also point to the biblical images associated with the mustard seed illustration. In Daniel (4:11–12:20ff) the tree is related to Nebuchadnezzar and his great empire. The prophet Ezekiel uses the similar metaphor which likens the Pharaoh of Egypt to a great cedar (Ezekiel 31:5ff). Neither of these metaphors was meant to be complimentary. Rather they were intended to illustrate the pride of the kings. However in Ezekiel 17:22–24, a passage considered to be an addition by some Old Testament critics,[73] the text speaks of the restoration of God's kingdom in similar imagery, " . . . on the mountain of Israel will I plant it, that it may bring forth boughs and bear fruit, and become a noble cedar; and under it will dwell all kinds of beasts; in the shade of its branches birds of every sort will nest. And all the trees of the field shall know that I the LORD bring low the high tree, and make high the low tree ... " (Ezekiel 17:23–24).[74] So the tree was used also in a positive sense as well and it was also seen as a metaphor of a righteous man (Psalm 1:3; cf. Avot 3:17). But whether these passages from the Old Testament should be directly connected to the Parable of the Mustard Seed is a matter of conjecture. The allusion to Daniel is clear (Matthew 13:32; Mark 4:32; Luke 13:19); however while the parable makes use of similar imagery it may not be teaching the same message. Of course it is tempting to see an association between the affirmation of God's sovereignty in Daniel (4:34–35) and Ezekiel (17:22–24) and also Jesus' kingdom parable which portrays a tree growing forth from a tiny mustard seed which provides a nesting place for all the birds of heaven.

The sages associated the leaven with the evil inclination of man.[75] When the leaven was removed from the household at Passover, the people related the action with the removal of something symbolic of the impure. An early reference to this thought is preserved by the apostle Paul when he writes against incest at the church in Corinth. He writes, " ... Do you not know that a little leaven leavens the whole lump? Cleanse out the old leaven that you may be a new lump, as you really are unleavened. For Christ, our paschal lamb has been sacrificed" (1 Corinthians 5:6–7; cf. Galatians 5:9). Paul affirms the celebration of Passover (vs. 7) and speaks about the leaven as representing sin. Comparing the kingdom to leaven may have seemed somewhat daring to some of Jesus' contemporaries. It also illustrates the flexibility of parabolic language. Even Jesus employed the leaven as a negative metaphor, when he referred to the "leaven of the Pharisees."[76]

Nevertheless in this kingdom parable Jesus makes use of the permeating action of the leaven to illustrate God's reign. Flusser has discussed the metaphor of the amora Chiya bar Abba (ca. 280 C.E.) which compares the influence that the study of the Torah exerts upon a man to the powerful action of the leaven.[77] The Torah is said to contain leaven. Even if the children of Israel abandon God and yet they continue to occupy themselves with the study of Torah, the leaven of the Torah will bring the people back to God.[78] Furthermore a later rabbinic parallel to Jesus' Parable of the Leaven provides another fascinating example of how the sometimes negative symbol of leaven could be used to illustrate a positive value. The elements of shock and surprise may have been original features of this parable which compares peace to leaven. At least one sees how parabolic language can be employed to illustrate quite different values. The illustration appears in the minor tractates of the Talmud and is attributed to R. Joshua b. Levi, an authority from the transition period between the Tannaim and the Amoraim. He teaches, "Great is peace for as peace is to the land so is leaven to the dough. Had the Holy One blessed be He not given peace to the land, the sword and the beast would have devastated it. What is the reason? It is written, 'And I will give peace in the land, and you shall lie down, and none shall make you afraid; and I will remove evil beasts from the land, and the sword shall not go through your land' (Lev. 26:6)."[79] Thus in this tractate, R. Joshua b. Levi makes the comparison between peace and leaven. He conceives peace as a powerful force in the world which prevails over man and beast in the same way that leaven permeates the dough. In the gospels Jesus has taken leaven to illustrate the permeating force of the kingdom of God and its gradual growth which cannot be abated. The parable is concerned with the *action* of the leaven which distinguishes it somewhat from R. Joshua b. Levi's parable which deals more with the pervading presence of the leaven that is a power—unseen but nevertheless at work. Like its partner the Parable of the Mustard Seed, also the Parable of the Leaven can be reconstructed into an experimental Hebrew translation.

The Leaven

לשאור שנטלה אשה וטמנה בשלש סאים של קמח עד שחמץ כלו.

The Parables of the Hidden Treasure and The Pearl of Great Price (Matthew 13:44–46)

The Parables of the Hidden Treasure and the Pearl of Great Price are found only in Matthew and the Gospel of Thomas.[80] Matthew introduces the parables as describing the kingdom.

These two companion illustrations are twins and they are correctly ascribed to the kingdom of heaven theme by Matthew. Dodd has rightly asked the question whether these parables are meant to teach the value of the kingdom or the cost of discipleship.[81] However both aspects of this question are complementary, for the cost of discipleship describes the value of the kingdom and the value of the kingdom is commensurate with the commitment required of a disciple. Nevertheless the parables appear in Matthew's great chapter of parables, and it is very difficult to ascertain the original occasion of these two illustrations. The disciple must be willing to risk everything for the kingdom of heaven.

The first parable speaks about a man who discovers a treasure hidden in a field. This discovery is accidental. As has often been pointed out, Josephus already noted that valuables were often hidden in order to prevent them from being taken during periods of political instability which characterized Jewish Palestine in the first century (cf. Matthew 25:25).[82] The Dead Sea Scrolls, the treasured holy writ of the Qumran sect, were stored away secretly in this way and the Copper Scroll provides a lucid example of the practice. In this kingdom parable, the man is willing to sell all that he has in order to purchase the field and thus obtain the treasure legally. The parable stresses that he entered the venture with "joy" and *risked* everything he owned in order to acquire the treasure which he had discovered. In contrast to the first parable, in the second illustration the merchant is a seeker. He has traveled in search of fine pearls. He is a connoisseur, and when he discovers the extraordinary pearl of great price he went and sold all in order to obtain it. In the second parable the man's joy is not mentioned but he also is willing to sacrifice everything to purchase the valuable pearl. One need not consider the joy mentioned in the first parable secondary. Unlike the merchant who was searching for pearls, the first man did not anticipate finding anything. Both men surrender all they possess for the prizes they have found.

Why were these parables connected to the kingdom? They do not allude to eschatological events leading up to the consummation of all time. A number of sources from rabbinic literature may provide some insights that elucidate a possible setting for these illustrations. It must be remembered that ordinarily a disciple who followed his master had made many sacrifices in order to study Torah.[83] Though similar, it is not the same as the early Greek peripatetic teachers who despised wealth and sought wisdom through an austere existence.[84] A very common term in talmudic literature is the תלמיד חכם who of course is not a wise disciple but rather a disciple of the wise. Lieberman has correctly pointed out that the term was originally in the plural and referred to a disciple of the sages תלמיד חכמים.[85] Büchler pointed out that often one discovers the sages teaching their disciples outside—in the fields, marketplaces, under trees or even in the shadow of the temple.[86] Pirke Avot says that a disciple should literally cover himself with the dust of his master's feet.[87] The description of Jesus and his band of followers seem to be an early reference to a teacher and his disciples. In Amoraic times one discovers a conversation between R. Johanan and Chiya b. Abba where R. Johanan discusses everything he had to give up in order to study the Torah. The agadic story is a beautiful piece where R. Johanan tells how he surrendered what was created in six days for what was given in forty days and nights—namely the Torah.[88] The critical scholar may not wish to accept all the details of the story but the fundamental message is clear—a student of Torah often had to make tremendous sacrifices to engage in study. From an earlier period one discovers the tradition concerning R. Jose b. Kisma who would not be tempted by wealth and riches to abandon a place that afforded him the opportunity to learn at the feet of the sages.[89]

Jesus makes the comparison between the kingdom and between the hidden treasure and the pearl of great price. In the context of Jesus' teaching concerning worry and man's desire for material goods he tells his disciples to seek first God's kingdom and God's righteousness (Matthew 6:33; Luke 12:31).[90] The question seems to have been a live issue with the disciples because Peter points out to Jesus, "Lo, we have left our homes and followed you" (Luke 18:29; Mark 10:28; Matthew 19:27). According to the gospels, Jesus did not make it easy for someone to become a disciple and the person was required to consider the costs and the disadvantages before making a decision that he might regret later.[91] One can only speculate if greater restrictions were placed upon the inner circle of disciples. These two companion parables preserved in Matthew portray Jesus' extremism in regard to the kingdom of heaven. They illustrate the inestimable value of God's reign and the fact that one must surrender everything in order to take the yoke of the kingdom.

The Parables of the Inheritance

Too often the study of rabbinic parables and their gospel counterparts have been confined to alleged parallels and the relationship between them or the basic issue of who influenced whom. Such an approach has neglected the creative and artistic aspects of parabolic instruction. Two partner parables from the Mechilta are derived from the same *Gattung* which is very similar to the substructure of Jesus' Parables of the Hidden Treasure and the Pearl of Great Price. In the Mechilta Derabbi Ishmael, the first parable is attributed to R. Jose Hagalili and the second to R. Simeon b. Yochai. It is paralleled in the Mechilta Derabbi Simeon bar Yochai where it is also transmitted by R. Jose and R. Simeon.[92]

THE INHERITANCE AND THE TREASURE
(Mechilta Derabbi Ishmael on Exodus 14:6)

> Another interpretation: "the mind of Pharaoh and his servants was changed" (Ex. 14:5). They said: Because of them good has come upon us. R. Jose Hagalili said: A parable, to what can this be compared? To a man to whom there has fallen as an inheritance a *bet-kor* of land which he sold for a trifle. The buyer, however, went and opened up wells in it, and planted gardens, trees and orchards in it. The seller, seeing this, began to choke because he had sold his inheritance for a trifle. Thus it happened to the Egyptians who let go without realizing what they let go. Of them it is stated in the traditional sacred writings: "Your shoots are an orchard of pomegranates," etc. (Song 4:13). Another interpretation: R. Simeon b. Yochai said: A parable, to what may this be

> compared? To a man to whom there had fallen as an inheritance a residence in a far off country which he sold for a trifle. The buyer, however, went and discovered in it hidden treasures and stores of silver and of gold, of precious stones and pearls. The seller, seeing this, began to choke—thus also did the Egyptians, who let go without realizing what they let go. For it is written: "And they said: 'What is this we have done that we have let Israel go,' etc." (Ex. 14:5).

The two illustrations are closely connected to their context in the Mechilta's treatment of Exodus 14:5, "When the king of Egypt was told that the people had fled, the mind of Pharaoh and his servants was changed toward the people, and they said, 'What is this we have done, that we have let Israel go from serving us?'" The parables in the Mechilta explain why Pharaoh changed his mind. The parallels to these parables in the Mechilta Derabbi Simeon bar Yochai and the Midrash Hagadol on Exodus omit the reference to the "inheritance" in the first illustration. However the inheritance was retained in the second parable which spoke about the palace in a far country which the man inherited and then sold for an insignificant sum. Most likely the first illustration did not originally contain a reference to the inheritance as the texts of the Mechilta Derabbi Simeon bar Yochai and the Midrash Hagadol indicate. It was probably added to the first parable on the basis of the second and tied both illustrations more closely together. The Yalkut Shimeoni seems to be acquainted with the parables from the text of the Mechilta Derabbi Ishmael.

The parables are also related in Pesikta Derav Kahana and Song of Songs Rabbah.[93] In these parallels one discovers some extensive innovations. Instead of two parables one discovers three—all of which speak of an inheritance. The first concerns a piece of land covered with dung, the second the field, and finally a thicket of cedars. All three of these parables are companions which work together to illustrate the same theme. Both Song of Songs Rabbah and Pesikta Derav Kahana relate the first parable to R. Simeon bar Yochai. However the parable of the field is attributed to R. Jonathan in Song of Songs Rabbah and to R.

Yosah in Pesikta Derav Kahana. In addition, Song of Songs Rabbah attributes the third parable of the thicket of cedar to R. Jose and the Pesikta preserves it in the name of R. Nathan—a sage who appears quite frequently in Pesikta Derav Kahana. Here it is worthwhile to cite the first of these three parables according to Song of Songs Rabbah.

THE DUNGHILL AND THE TREASURE
(Song of Songs Rabbah 4:12)

> R. Simeon b. Yochai taught: [The Egyptians were] like a man who inherited a piece of ground used as a dunghill. Being an indolent man, he went and sold it for a trifling sum. The purchaser went right to work. He began digging it up, and found a treasure, there, out of which he built for himself a fine palace, and he began going about in public followed by a retinue of servants—all out of the treasure he found in it. When the seller saw it he was ready to choke, and he exclaimed, 'Alas, what have I thrown away.' Thus when Israel were in Egypt they were set to work at bricks and mortar, and they were despised in the eyes of the Egyptians. But when the Egyptians saw them encamped under their standards by the sea in military array, they were deeply mortified and exclaimed, 'Alas, what have we sent forth from our land!' as it says, "When Pharaoh let the people go . . . " (Ex. 13:17).

The parallel from Song of Songs Rabbah illustrates the literary and artistic development of the parables. The darshan has added color to the story. The exact literary connection between the Mechilta and this parable is difficult to unravel with a great deal of certainty because the two versions are so different one from the other and it would seem that there was an intermediate stage about which one can know little. However it seems that the Parable of the Inheritance and the Treasure as well as the Parable of the Dunghill and the Treasure have undergone significant transformation. Instead of a field's potential being realized by an innovative developer, here one sees a dung heap with a lazy owner. He sells it to an industrious individual who starts digging. In the Mechilta the treasure was merely found in the palace. In Song of Songs Rabbah, the new owner first discovers the treasure in his dung heap and builds a palace with the money. In fact he becomes so wealthy that he has a retinue of servants who follow him around in the marketplace. Naturally his good fortune causes the former lazy owner who sold the dung heap for a trifle tremendous grief and anguish. The parabolist is quick to make the parable apply to the Israelites who were slave laborers in Egypt. The Egyptians are mortified when they view the glory of Israel after they themselves have sent the Israelites away. Then Song of Songs Rabbah continues with two other parables, the first of which is very similar to the Mechilta's parable of the *Bet Kor* of land. The texts of Song of Songs Rabbah and Pesikta Derav Kahana as well seem to preserve embellished and aggrandized parallels to the more simple illustrations in the Mechilta. Nevertheless in both contexts the parables are related to Israel's deliverance from the bondage of Egypt. In this respect they are closely related to the text of the Pentateuch but it should also be noted that these illustrations certainly could have developed in oral teachings and would have been appropriate for the celebration of the Passover.

Jesus' parables of the kingdom concerning the Hidden Treasure and the Pearl of Great Price are by no means direct parallels to the illustrations of R. Jose Hagalili and R. Simeon b. Yochai from the Mechilta and parallels.[94] Nevertheless they are distant cousins. They have been employed by parabolists from different times and used to elucidate diverse themes. In Matthew, Jesus speaks concerning the kingdom of heaven and the Mechilta illustrates an aspect of the biblical story of the exodus. However one discovers a startling number of key elements in common between these parabolic examples. All of these parables contain buyers, sellers, fields, and valuables (fields, palace, precious stones) whose true worth is not recognized by their first owner. The storyline constructs a mini-drama around the attention attracting theme of buying and selling. The listeners are interested to find out who benefits most from the business transactions described in the parables. The rabbinic parables emphasize the anguish of the seller who greatly undersold his merchandise not knowing its true value. These are identified with the Egyptians. Jesus' parables stress the other side of the business transaction—the joy of the man who discovers a treasure in a field and of the entrepreneur who finds the pearl for which he has been searching. All these parables are intended for a popular audience and successfully communicate. These rabbinic parables and the parables of Jesus are formulated on the basis of a common framework. However while the motifs and substructure of the parables are similar, their messages are quite different.

The Kingdom and Eschatology

The parables of the kingdom discussed above deal with the growth process and discipleship. Is the kingdom of heaven a future reign to be established? Even texts like the Assumption of Moses which speak of the appearance of the kingdom and the overthrow of Satan do not negate entirely the notion that God's kingdom was in some ways a present reality.[95] He reigns but his kingdom has yet to be fully revealed. However in these parables of the kingdom, God's reign is being more firmly established. The requirements of one who desires God's reign is immense—at least in the parables the men sell all they own to acquire the field and the pearl. This point illustrates both the value of the kingdom and the costs of discipleship.[96] However one discovers a third parable attached to the Parables of the Hidden Treasure and the Pearl of Great Price. In his great chapter of parables, Matthew has added the Parable of the Dragnet as a third example of kingdom parables:

THE NET AND THE FISH
(Matthew 13:47–50)

> Again, the kingdom of heaven is like a net which was thrown into the sea and gathered fish of every kind; when it was full, men drew it ashore and sat down and sorted the good into vessels but threw away the bad. So it will be at the close of the age. The angels will come out and separate the evil from the righteous, and throw

> them into the furnace of fire; there men will weep and gnash their teeth.

Unlike the two preceding kingdom parables, the story of the dragnet which brings in both good and bad fish deals with the eschatological judgment. In many ways it is a companion to the Parable of the Wheat and the Tares (Matthew 13:24–30) which speaks concerning the harvest.[97] At the time of harvest, the useless tares will be separated from the wheat. Certainly the message of the parable opposes an acute eschatologization of the present age because it describes the interim period before the judgment when the forces of evil are in conflict with good. In another unique Matthean passage, one reads concerning the Son of Man who "comes in his glory, and all the angels with him, then he will sit on his glorious throne. Before him will be gathered all the nations, and he will separate them one from another as a shepherd separates the sheep from the goats . . . " (Matthew 25:31ff). This passage describes a scene of judgment and uses the biblical metaphor of the shepherd who divides his flock (Ezekiel 34:22). The Parable of the Ten Virgins contrasts the wise who were prepared with the foolish who were shut outside at the coming of the bridegroom (Matthew 25:1–13). A passage from the double tradition compares the coming of the Son of Man to the days of Noah and Lot. The men of Sodom and Gomorrah were not prepared for the judgment of fire and likewise the eschatological day of reckoning will catch many people unawares (Matthew 24:37–44 and Luke 17:26–37). Hence it has not been the aim of the above consideration of the kingdom theme to minimize the eschatological thrust of the teachings of Jesus but rather to place it in its proper perspective.

Nevertheless the above analysis has left many questions unanswered. What is the relationship between the Son of Man sayings that predict Jesus' passion and those which refer to eschatological judgment?[98] Jesus speaks of the Son of Man in the third person. Does he refer to himself or to someone else? Is the Son of Man coming as a judge figure paralleled in pre-Christian apocalyptic? Flusser has recently written an article concerning Jesus, the Son of Man and the sign of Jonah which deals with a number of these questions.[99] Here it is important to note briefly that the eschatology of Jesus in the gospels seems to be directly linked to his teachings concerning the last judgment and dominical logia concerning the future coming of the Son of Man. However the above analysis of the kingdom parables suggests that the kingdom of heaven theme was deemed a present reality in the life and ministry of both Jesus and his followers. Like the rabbis, Jesus connected the yoke of the kingdom to repentance and obedience to God's commands. The proliferation of the secondary kingdom introductions to a number of parables contributed to a misconception of the kingdom of heaven as a future monarchy which would only be established by God at the end of time. Thus it seems that at an early stage in the synoptic tradition, the two distinct themes of the eschatological judgment and of the reign of God became firmly fused together. The combination of these two themes does not appear to have originated with Jesus but developed during the redaction of the gospel texts.

In conclusion, Jesus' message of the kingdom of heaven focused primarily upon the power of his ministry, obedience to the divine will and the people who became his disciples. The kingdom was not the *eschaton* being realized in an "unprecedented and unrepeatable" fashion as Dodd thought. Nor was it a future reign which was in the process of realization. The kingdom is bursting forth in the dynamic ministry of Jesus and his followers as men respond to the call of total obedience. The kingdom is present now. The risk to the disciple is great. The demands of the kingdom are complete surrender to the will of heaven. The people responding to the message of the kingdom release a dynamic power which is like leaven in the dough or like a tiny mustard seed that grows and grows. When men forgive those who have offended them, or when they love those who hate them, a dynamic force is released which will bring redemption to a hurting world.

Notes

1) One's understanding of the kingdom theme has great import on one's interpretation of Jesus' parables. See N. Perrin, *Jesus and the Language of the Kingdom* (Philadelphia: Fortress, 1980), p. 97. When dis-

cussing the work of Jeremias, Perrin observed, "It is obvious that a discussion of the parables of Jesus will be deeply affected by the understanding of the kingdom of God in the message of Jesus, since the *matter (Sache)* with which the parables are concerned is the Kingdom of God" (ibid).

2) See W.F. Moulton, A.S. Geden, and H.K. Moulton, *A Concordance to the Greek Testament* (Edinburgh: T. and T. Clark, fifth edition, 1978), pp. 141–142. The synoptic comparison has been considerably simplified with the appearance of the new work, E. dos Santos and R.L. Lindsey, *A Comparative Greek Concordance of the Synoptic Gospels* (Jerusalem: Dugith, 1985), pp. 146–149. In the triple tradition the term appears in one or more of the evangelist's texts twenty-four times and in the double tradition fifteen. It appears in unique Matthean material thirteen times which is significantly higher frequency in comparison to the unique Lucan texts—three times and only one time in material peculiar to Mark. Nine texts contain the term in all three of the synoptics in parallel to one another (Mt 12:25,Mk 3:24,Lk 11:17; Mt 13:11,Mk 4:11,Lk 8:10; Mt 13:31,Mk. 4:30, Lk 13:18; Mt. 16:28,Mk 9:1,Lk 9:27; Mt 18:3,Mk 10:15,Lk 18:17; Mt 19:14,Mk 10:14,Lk 18:16; Mt. 19:23,Mk 10:23,Lk 18:24; Mt 19:24,Mk 10:25,Lk 18:25; Mt 26:29,Mk 14:25,Lk22:18). The authenticity of the use of the term cannot be determined by the parallels. However it does appear that the term was secondarily proliferated as an introduction to some of the parables.

3) See the preceding note.

4) See Matthew 13:31; Mark 4:30; Luke 13:18 and compare also Matthew 13:33 and Luke 13:20.

5) N. Perrin, *Jesus and the Language of the Kingdom,* pp. 37–40 and pp. 97f. See also James C. Little, "Parable Research in the Twentieth Century I. The Predecessors of J. Jeremias," *The Expository Times,* 87 (1976), p. 360 and idem, "Parable Research in the Twentieth Century II. The Contribution of J. Jeremias," *The Expository Times* 88 (1977), pp. 40f.

6) George E. Ladd, "The Kingdom of God—Reign or Realm?" *Journal of Biblical Literature* 81 (1962), pp. 230–238 and idem, *Jesus and the Kingdom* (Waco: Word, 1969). Ladd endeavored to harmonize between the future and present ideas. Bultmann saw the kingdom in Jesus' teaching primarily as a future event which failed to materialize as Jesus had proclaimed it would. He writes, "On the contrary, Jesus clearly expected the irruption of God's Reign as a miraculous, world-transforming event—as Judaism, and later also his own Church, did," R. Bultmann, *Theology of the New Testament* (New York: Charles Scribner's Sons,

1951), vol. 1, p. 22. See also, idem, *History and Eschatology the Presence of Eternity* (New York: Harper, 1957), p. 38. Compare also W.G. Kümmel, *Promise and Fulfilment the Eschatological Message of Jesus* (London: SCM Press, 1981), pp. 19–43. Kümmel states that although Jesus refused to speculate concerning the actual time of the *eschaton,* he did consider that the kingdom was a "future reality" (ibid, pp. 42–43). A more recent discussion of the materials has been advanced by E.P. Sanders, *Jesus and Judaism* (London: SCM Press, 1985), 123–173. Sanders minimizes the importance of Luke 11:19–20 and Matthew 12:27–28. Sanders claims that Jesus could not have considered that God's reign had been established when anyone but Jesus exorcised demons (Matthew 12:28 and Luke 11:20). How then would Jesus view the overthrow of Satan in Jewish exorcism of the period (ibid, pp. 134 and 138)? Sanders' treatment is less than convincing (cf. Mark 9:38–39). Neither does his interpretation of Matthew 12:28 and Luke 11:20 explain away the preceding logion in Luke 11:19 and Matthew 12:27. Can one so easily dismiss the critical and philological analysis of the texts for the proper understanding of the sayings of Jesus as Sanders suggests (ibid, pp. 134ff)?

7) Dodd, *Parables of the Kingdom,* pp. 29–61, Jeremias, *Parables,* pp. 115–124 and p. 230 and idem, *New Testament Theology,* pp. 31–35.

8) Johannes Weiss, *Die Predigt Jesu vom Reiche Gottes* (Göttingen: Vandenhoeck & Ruprecht, 1892), pp. 18ff, and see the English translation by R. Hiers and D. Holland, idem, *Jesus' Proclamation of the Kingdom of God* (Philadelphia: Fortress, 1971), p. 76.

9) Ibid, p. 21, English translation, p. 78.

10) Albert Schweitzer, *The Quest for the Historical Jesus* (London: SCM Press, 1981), p. vii; first published as *Von Reimarus zu Wrede. Eine Geschichte der Leben-Jesu-Forschung* (Tübingen: J.C.B. Mohr, 1906).

11) Schweitzer, *The Quest for the Historical Jesus,* p. 357.

12) Dodd, *The Parables of the Kingdom,* p. 41.

13) Ibid, pp. 40–41.

14) Jeremias, *Parables,* p. 230 and see especially note 3.

15) Phillip Vielhauer, "Gottesreich und Menschensohn in der Verkündigung Jesu" *Aufsätze zum Neuen Testament* (Munich: Kaiser Verlag, 1965), pp. 55–91. Vielhauer has gone too far when he suggests that the sayings concerning the Son of Man originated with the church after the resurrection. See Seyoon Kim, *"The 'Son of Man'" as the Son of God* (Tübingen: J.C.B. Mohr, 1983), pp. 77–78. Nevertheless Vielhauer is certainly correct when he differentiates between the expectation of the com-

ing of the Messiah and the kingdom of God in Jewish thought (Vielhauer, p. 87). Can one justify tying the two themes together as synonyms without hard evidence?

16) David Flusser, *Jesus in Selbstzeugnissen und Bilddokumenten* (Hamburg: Rowohlt, 1968), pp. 86–87.

17) L. Ragaz, *Die Botschaft vom Reiche Gottes* (Bern: Verlag Herbert Lang, 1942), p. 280. Cited by Flusser, *Jesus in Selbstzeugnissen und Bilddokumenten,* p. 86 and see the English translation in Flusser, *Jesus* (Herder and Herder, 1969), pp. 88–89.

18) The idea that eschatology determines one's understanding of morals, ethics and the law has led a number of scholars to unsound conclusions. Compare W.D. Davies, *The Torah in the Messianic Age and/or the Age to Come* (Philadephia: Society of Biblical Literature, 1952) and more recently, Harmut Stegemann, "Some Aspects of Eschatology in the Texts from the Qumran Community and the Teachings of Jesus," *Biblical Archaeology Today* (Jerusalem: The Israel Exploration Society, 1985), pp. 408–426. It is impossible to deal with this entire question here. Stegemann sees a fundamental difference between Jesus and some Pharisees in that Jesus interpreted the law on the basis of a realized eschatology which had been formulated in the atmosphere of concepts derived from the Qumran community (p. 420). However it is difficult to see how the core of the composite teachings of Jesus such as one finds in the Sermon on the Mount would have contradicted the Pharisaic approach to the Torah. On the contrary, the Pharisees maintained and practiced a very similar approach in their oral interpretations of the law. Many of the materials from Jesus' teachings are closely paralleled in rabbinic thought and it is doubtful that his instruction was directly influenced by highly developed eschatological schemes but rather the interest in a proper understanding of the Torah as it relates to man's relationship with God.

19) David de Sola Pool, *The Old Jewish-Aramaic Prayer, the Kaddish* (Leipzig: Rudolf Haupt, 1909, reprinted, Jerusalem: Sivan Press, 1964), p. 28.

20) See notes 8 and 10 above.

21) R.H. Charles, *Religious Development between the Old and the New Testaments* (New York: Henry Holt and Company, 1914), p. 48. One must be very careful in analyzing the meaning of terms. For instance, it is hard to accept the suggestion that the kingdom and the convenant should be studied as synonymous concepts in rabbinic thought; see Sanders, *Jesus and Judaism,* pp. 141f.

22) The dualistic concept of the power of the dominion of light which is in battle with the dominion of darkness is a well-known feature of the

scrolls. However the technical term "kingdom of heaven" never appears. The words "Your kingdom" appear in the angelic liturgy and see now the published doctorate with revisions by Carol Ann Newsome, *Songs of the Sabbath Sacrifice: A Critical Edition* (Atlanta: Scholars Press, 1985), on 4Q 400 l ii, 1f, pp. 89–90, pp. 107–109, on 4Q 400 2, pp. 110–113 and pp. 136 on 4Q 401 14 i 6–8. These texts from the angelic liturgy must be carefully compared with the well-known blessing which was said in the Temple on Yom Kipur, "Blessed be the name of the glory of his kingdom for ever and ever!" which has been discussed by S. Safrai, "Avodat Yom Hakipurim Babet Hamikdash Beyame Bayit Sheni," *Machanayim* 49 (1961), p. 122. The blessing appears in m. Yoma 6:2, 3:8; Sotah 7:6; b. Yoma 35b; j. Yoma, 40b, chap. 3, hal. 3; Sifra on Leviticus 16:11 (Weiss, 80d and 81a); Genesis Rabbah 90:1 (Albeck, p. 1202 and also see p. 1252). Cf. also the blessing of Rebecca in Jubilees 25:12 which is similar to the blessing which was said in the Temple but does not refer to the kingdom (O.S. Wintermute, "Jubilees," *The Old Testament Pseudepigrapha,* Charlesworth, ed., vol. 2, p. 105).

23) Testament of Moses 10:1ff; Testament of Benjamin 9:1ff; Testament of Dan 5:13–6:1; The Sibylline Oracles 3:46–55; Wisdom of Solomon 1:14, 5:15–17; (3 Baruch 11:2). The idea of God's eternal reign over his people is expressed in the Psalms of Solomon 5:21 (Charles, vol. 2, p. 638; the Greek word *en* does not appear in the better manuscripts and thus Charles' translation has been changed here; also cf. Damascus Document 7:14–16), "They that fear the Lord rejoice in good (gifts), And Thy goodness is upon Israel, Thy kingdom. Blessed is the glory of the Lord, for He is our king." Compare also the similar idea concerning the kingdom, Psalms of Solomon 17:1 and 4–6 (Charles, vol. 2, pp. 647–648; the words "in judgment" are missing in a number of important manuscripts and thus here have been deleted from Charles' translation). "O Lord, Thou art our King for ever and ever, For in Three, O God, doth our soul glory. . . . And the kingdom of our God is for ever over the nations. Thou, O Lord, didst chose David (to be) king over Israel, And swaredst to him touching his seed that never should his kingdom fail before Thee. But for our sins, sinners rose up against us; They assailed us and thrust us out . . . " The text is an explanation of the Song of the Sea (in Exodus 15) and God's kingship is viewed as eternal. See also notes 34 and 35 below.

24) Testament of Moses 10:1f (Charlesworth, vol. 1, p. 931f, translated by J. Priest). On the date and historical background of the text see, J. Licht, "Taxo, or the Apocalyptic Doctrine of Vengeance," *The Journal of Jewish Studies* 12 (1961), pp. 95–103. Licht's approach to the text has been accepted and developed by G.W.E. Nickelsburg, *Studies in the Tes-*

tament of Moses (Cambridge, Mass.: Society of Biblical Literature, 1973) and see H.F.D. Sparks *The Apocryphal Old Testament* (Oxford: Clarendon, 1984), p. 603 and also J. Charlesworth, *The Pseudepigrapha and Modern Research* (Michigan: Society of Biblical Literature, 1961), pp. 163–167. Cf. my study, *The Jewish Background to the Lord's Prayer* (Austin: The Center for Judaic-Christian Studies, 1984), pp. 10–13 and p. 39 note 13. Compare the binding of Beliar which is mentioned in the Testament of Levi 18:12 (Charlesworth, vol. 1, p. 795, translated by H.C. Kee), "And Beliar shall be bound by him. And he shall grant to his children the authority to trample on wicked spirits" (see the critical edition by M. de Jonge, *The Testaments of the Twelve Patriarchs,* Leiden: Brill, 1978, p. 49). Compare also the prayer of Abraham where he recognizes the one God, chooses his kingdom and asks to be delivered from "evil spirits which rule over the thought of the heart of man" (Jubilees 12:19–20, O.S. Wintermute, "Jubilees,' *The Old Testament Pseudepigrapha,* Charlesworth, ed., vol. 2, p. 81).

25) Testament of Benjamin 8:1 and 9:1 (Charlesworth, vol. 1, p. 827, translated by H.C. Kee; See the critical edition of the Greek text prepared by de Jonge, *The Testaments of the Twelve Patriarchs,* pp. 174–175. De Jonge has made an English translation of the Testaments of the Twelve Patriarchs, in H.F.D. Sparks, *The Aprocryphal Old Testament,* pp. 515–600. See also the Testament of Dan 5:13–6:5 and the preceding note. It becomes clear in the Testaments of the Twelve Patriarchs that the power of Satan is at battle with God's reign. When the people obey, Satan's power is defeated and God rules in their midst. Nonetheless we should note that the Testament of Benjamin 9:1ff betrays signs of editorial work and one must ask whether the reference to the kingdom is original. I cannot accept the view *pace* de Jonge that the Testaments of the Twelve Patriarchs are a later Christian work. Charles' approach which views the Testaments as a Jewish work that was revised by later hands is much more accurate. On the Testament of Benjamin 9:1f, see, R.H. Charles, *The Greek Versions of the Testaments of the Twelve Patriarchs* (Oxford, 1908), p. 200, n.1.

26) The author expresses his gratitude to David Flusser who pointed out this reference (private communication). See F.I. Andersen, "2 Enoch," Charlesworth, vol. 1, p. 159; A. Vaillant, *Le livre des secrets d'Hénoch: Texte slave et traduction française* (Paris, 1952, reprint, Paris, 1976), pp. 34–35.

27) The Wisdom of Solomon 5:15–17 (Charles, vol. 1, p. 543), "But the righteous live for ever, And the Lord is their reward. . . . Therefore shall they receive a glorious kingdom. . . . And shall take his jealousy as

complete armour, And shall make the *whole* creation his weapons for vengeance on *his* enemies." The editor (Holmes) pointed also to Daniel 8:18 and 22 and cf. Wisdom of Solomon 1:14.

28) The Sibylline Oracles 3:46–55 (Charlesworth, vol. 1, p. 363), "But when Rome will also rule over Egypt guiding it toward a single goal then indeed the most great kingdom of the immortal king will become manifest over the scepters of the earth forever, as time presses on. Then also implacable wrath will fall upon Latin men. . . . Alas, wretched one, when will that day come, and the judgement of the great king immortal God?" See also note 23 above.

29) 1 Maccabees 3:18–19; 2 Maccabees 7:11, 8:20; Daniel 4:26.

30) G. Dalman, *The Words of Jesus* (Edinburgh: T. and T. Clark, 1902), pp. 92–94.

30a) After writing this chapter, my friend David Bivin has called my attention to the fact that the word "yoke" in the phrase "yoke of the kingdom of heaven" does not appear in the Kaufmann manuscript of the Mishnah. This manuscript is of great importance and Kutscher considered it to be the best manuscript of the Mishnah. In addition, the word "yoke" does not appear here in the parallel text in the Jerusalem Talmud. Interestingly, in the Kaufmann manuscript moreover, the word "yoke" is missing in the well-known story of Rabban Gamaliel who was unwilling to remove the "yoke of the kingdom" for one moment—even on his wedding night" (m. Berachot 2:5). According to the better reading of the Kaufmann manuscript, he does not wish to reject the "kingdom of heaven" for one moment. It seems that the word "yoke" from the phrase "yoke of the commandments" was added to the expression "kingdom of heaven" (see also the discussion of the Amoraim in the context of the Jerusalem Talmud, j. Berachot 4a, chap. 2, hal. 1).

31) Ephraim Urbach, *The Sages Their Concepts and Beliefs* (Jerusalem: Magnes Press, 1975), vol. 1, p. 400. Compare the words of R. Eleazar ben Azaryah in Sifra on Leviticus 20:26 (Weiss, 93d). The commandments are not to be observed on the basis of one's personal preference but because God has given the command and man must respond and separate himself from transgression in order to accept God's authority.

32) Sifra on Leviticus 18:2 (Weiss, 85d). See Weiss' comments. Finkelstein, Codex Assemani 66, p. 371. The translation is based on Codex Assemani. One immediately notices the sudden transitions from the second person, "you received my kingdom" to the third person, "they responded . . . " At first it is tempting to suggest an emendation to the text which would change the third person to the second person which

could easily have happened due to scribal abbreviation. However it seems that the midrash connects the audience with the generation in Israel's past who were redeemed from Egypt and accepted God's reign at Sinai. Thus the people who hear the exposition of R. Simeon b. Yochai are confronted with the redemption of ancient Israel from Egypt and the receiving of the law at Sinai. When they receive God's kingdom in the present, they are repeating the "yes, yes" of the ancient Israelites and are united together with them by agreeing to obey God's decrees. This kind of telescoping can also be seen in the words of Rabban Gamaliel who says that each person must regard himself as being redeemed from Egypt (m. Pesachim 10:5; E.D. Goldschmidt, *Hagadah Shel Pesach,* Jerusalem, Bialik Institute, 1977, p. 125). God's redemptive acts of history in the past must be viewed as a present reality.

33) See J. Duncan Derrett, *Jesus's Audience* (London: Darton, 1973), p. 187. Derrett correctly observes, "There have been so many notions of what [the kingdom of heaven] meant that it must be regarded as controversial; but I take it to be the concept of Yahweh as the real ruler, and Satan as the apparent ruler, and the 'coming' of Yahweh's kingdom means that his commands are actually obeyed in the area in question."

34) Sifre Deuteronomy 323 (Finkelstein, p. 372 and see the parallels Midrash Tannaim on Deuteronomy 32:29, Hoffmann, p. 199; Midrash Hagadol on Deuteronomy 32:29, Fisch, p. 721). The passage was discussed by Israel Abrahams, *Studies on Pharisaism and the Gospels* (New York: KTAV, 1967, reprint of volume 1, 1917 and volume 2, 1924 editions), vol. 2, pp. 8–9. See also Flusser who discussed this passage and noted that the foreign oppression of Israel was thought to be caused by the people's sins, idem, *Jesus,* p. 83. Compare the text of Jose Hagalili in note 36 below.

35) Compare also the Aramaic Targums on Exodus 15:18 which speak about the kingdom both in the present world and in the future (A. Sperber, *The Bible in Aramaic,* Leiden: Brill, 1959, on Onkelos vol. 1, p. 114); M. Ginsburger, *Pseudo-Jonathan* (Berlin: S. Calvary, 1903) p. 126 and now D. Rieder, *Targum Yontan Ben Uziel Al Hatorah* (Jerusalem, 1984), p. 105 (text), p. 126 (Hebrew translation); Targum Neophyti, Diez Macho, vol. 2, pp. 101, English translation, p. 452 and M. Klein, *The Fragment-Targums of the Pentateuch* (Rome: Biblical Institute Press, 1980), vol. 1, pp. 79–80 p. 172 and vol. 2, pp. 48 and p. 130. The Latin Vulgate retains the future sense, *Dominus regnabit in aeternum* (Exodus 15:18) and compare Psalm 146:10 where the Hebrew phrase from Exodus 15:18 is paralleled but is usually translated by the future tense perhaps because of the context.

36) The Mechilta Derabbi Ishmael on Exodus 15:18 (Horovitz, p. 150, Lauterbach, vol. 2, p. 80). See the parallels, the Mechilta Derabbi Simeon bar Yochai on Exodus 15:18 (Epstein, p. 100) and Midrash Hagadol on Exodus 15:18 (Margulies, p. 311). See Bacher, *Die Agada der Tannaiten* vol. 1, p. 360, idem, *Agadot Hatannaim,* vol. 1, part 2, pp. 92–93. Flusser suggested that the saying of R. Jose Hagalili was directed against the Zealots and the apocalyptists, "Das ist anscheinend nicht nur gegen die futuristischen Hoffnungen der Apokalyptiker, sondern auch gegen die zelotischen Himmelstürmer gerichtet . . . " (idem, *Jesus,* p. 83). Here the Mechilta Derabbi Simeon bar Yochai also adds an interesting parable before R. Jose Hagalili's saying. The parable speaks about a king whose palace was overtaken by thieves who kill his servants. The king comes and delivers his palace and pronounces judgment upon these wicked brigands. Thus the king's "kingdom was made known." Clearly the inference is to the redemption of the people of Israel from Egypt who were delivered from the Egyptians by God's sovereign power. His power and might were made manifest in their deliverance.

37) The Mechilta Derabbi Ishmael on Exodus 20:2 (Horovitz, p. 219, Lauterbach, vol. 2, p. 229). Cf. Brad Young, *The Jewish Background to the Lord's Prayer,* pp. 14–15.

38) See Flusser, *Jesus,* pp. 87–88 and Lindsey, *A Hebrew Translation of the Gospel of Mark,* p. XXIV. See note 50 below.

39) Compare Matthew 3:1–2 with the text of Mark 1:4 and Luke 3:3. In contrast to Luke and Mark who maintain that John preached a baptism of repentance for the forgiveness of sins, Matthew teaches that John proclaimed that the kingdom was at hand. Matthew seems to have transferred a dominical saying and attributed it to John (compare Matthew 4:17 and Mark 1:14–15 as well as Luke 3:3 and Mark 1:4). John's ministry is certainly best understood as a revivalist movement in which he called the people to baptism and repentance. This is a sound evaluation of the historical evidence (Jos. *Ant.* 18:117; Mt 3:6; Mk 1:5; Lk 3:10–14; Mt 14:4; Mk 6:18). No doubt this is one reason that he received the appellation "John the Baptizer." It is easy to understand how a saying of Jesus would have been attributed to John. For a different understanding of Luke 3:3, see H. Conzelmann, *The Theology of St. Luke* (Philadephia: Fortress, 1961), p. 23 and see note 1. Conzelmann tried to show that Luke had a motive in trying to say that Jesus was the first to proclaim the kingdom, "In Luke John is thought of as quite unconnected with the message of the Kingdom." But it seems that John preached repentance and Jesus proclaimed the kingdom. Dodd understood these texts, idem, *Parables,* p. 39, note 20.

40) See the Thanksgiving Scroll 18:14–15 and the War Scroll 14:7. See also the discussion of J. Licht, *Megilat Hahodayot* (Jerusalem: The Bialik Institute, 1957), p. 47. See especially Flusser, "Blessed are the Poor in Spirit . . . " *Israel Exploration Journal* 10 (1959), pp. 1–13 and idem, "Some Notes to the Beatitudes," *Immanuel* 8 (1978), pp. 37–47.

41) One should not hasten to associate Jesus directly with the Essene sect at Qumran, cf. W.D. Davies, *The Setting for the Sermon on the Mount* (London: Cambridge University Press, 1977), p. 251, "True, its [poor in spirit] equivalent in Hebrew has only appeared in the scrolls, but this merely proves its Palestinian origin."

42) See note 40.

43) Abrahams, *Studies,* vol. 1, pp. 118–120.

44) Matthew 19:14 and parallels Mark 10:14 and Luke 18:16.

45) H.E. Dana and J. Mantey, *A Manual Grammar of the Greek New Testament* (New York: Macmillan, 1951), p. 79.

46) Luke (pre-Lucan redactor) seems to have formulated an antithesis for the blessings which he knew from Matthew's source. For example, he contrasts the blessing for the hungry with a curse for the satisfied and thus he secondarily and antithetically builds his woe passages (Luke 6:24–26).

47) F. Blass and A. Debrunner, *A Greek Grammar of the New Testament* (Chicago: University of Chicago Press, 1961), p. 149, paragraph 285.

48) The author is grateful for Lindsey's suggestions on the translation of this text back into Hebrew.

49) See the discussion of Blass and Debrunner, *Grammar,* pp. 90–91, paragraph 164. Cf. N. Turner, ed., J.H. Moulton, *A Grammar of New Testament Greek* (Edinburgh: T. and T. Clark, 1963), vol. 3, pp. 208–212 and A.T. Robertson, *A Grammar of the Greek New Testament in the Light of Historical Research* (New York: Hodder and Stoughton, 1915), p. 502.

50) W.F. Albright and C.S. Mann, *The Anchor Bible Matthew* (New York: Doubleday, 1981), p. 46. Albright and Mann have employed the future tense but both the Greek *estin* and the hypothetical Hebrew reconstruction *ki mehem malchut shamayim* would retain the force of a present reality, "they make up the kingdom of heaven" or "they are the kingdom of heaven." David Flusser called my attention to the Damascus Document 7:16–17 where the king is understood as the assembly, המלך הוא הקהל! See Chaim Rabin, *The Zadokite Documents* (Oxford: Clarendon Press, 1954), pp. 28–29. Rabin proposes a different conjectural reconstruction of the text (ibid, p. 29, note 1). Flusser has rejected his

conjecture (private communication) and there is no sufficient reason to emend the text.

51) Jeremias is not convinced that the two parables belong to one another, idem, *Parables,* p. 146. See Flusser, *Die rabbinischen Gleichnisse,* pp. 65 and 203f.

52) Vincent Taylor, *The Gospel according to St. Mark* (Grand Rapids: Baker, 1981, reprint of 1966 edition), p. 269.

53) Flusser, *Die rabbinischen Gleichnisse,* pp. 198–202.

54) See the context in the Gospel of Thomas for logia 21 and 96 (Guillaumont, *et al,* pp. 12–15 and 46–51).

55) See Flusser, *Jesus,* pp. 87–88.

56) Jeremias, *Parables,* p. 147.

57) Ibid. See M. Philonenko, *Joseph et Asénath: Introduction, texte critque, traduction et notes* (Leiden: Brill, 1968), pp. 182–183; see the notes of C. Burchard "Joseph and Aseneth," Charlesworth, ed., *Old Testament Pseudepigrapha,* vol. 2, p. 226; D. Cook, "Joseph and Aseneth," Sparks, ed., *The Apocryphal Old Testament,* p. 488 and E.W. Brooks, *Joseph and Asenath* (London: SPCK, 1918), p. 58.

58) Cf. Josephus, *Ant.* 9:36 and Bauer, *A Greek-English Lexicon of the New Testament,* p. 418.

59) Dodd, *The Parables of the Kingdom,* p. 190.

60) See E. Würthwein, *The Text of the Old Testament* (London: SCM Press, 1979), pp. 54f, and H.B. Swete, *An Introduction to the Old Testament in Greek* (New York: KTAV, 1968, reprint of 1902 edition), pp. 46ff.

61) Of course this is not the exact same idea because the nations are not being incorporated into the people of Israel.

62) Thus Jeremias, *Parables,* p. 147 and see also Zechariah 14:6.

63) Cf. F. Neirynck, *The Minor Agreements of Matthew and Luke against Mark* (Leuven, Belgium: Leuven University Press, 1974), pp. 94–95.

64) Gundry, *Matthew,* p. 268. Gundry has made a mistake in the reference. B. Kil. 2.8 should be j. Kil. 28a, chap. 2, hal. 8.

65) Fitzmyer, *Luke* vol. 2, p. 1017.

66) Leviticus 19:19 and Deuteronomy 22:9–11, and see Albeck, *Shishah Sidre Mishnah,* vol. 1, pp. 95–100.

67) This is the opinion of Rabban Simeon b. Gamliel in the Jerusalem Talmud, Kilaim 28a, chap. 2, hal. 8, and cf. m. Kilaim 2:9 and 3:2 (see Albeck's notes, *Shishah Sidre Mishnah,* vol. 1, pp. 106–107 and 109).

68) See Bauer, *A Greek-English Lexicon of the New Testament,* p. 430 and cf. Jos. *Ant.* 9:227.

69) See Bauer, *A Greek-English Lexicon of the New Testament,* p. 751. Antigonus of Carystus 91 (O. Keller, p. 24) and Diodorus Siculus I, 25, 2 (L. Dindorf, p. 27).

70) See the critical apparatus for Luke 13:19, where the word *mega* has been added in a number of manuscripts and among them is the early P45.

71) Cf. Pinchas Lapide, *Hebrew in the Church* (Grand Rapids: Eerdmans, 1984), pp. 89–91.

72) See also 1 Corinthians 5:6–7, b. Berachot 17a, j. Berachot 7d, chap. 4, hal. 2, Midrash Hagadol on Genesis 6:6 (Margulies, p. 142) and cf. Wünsche, *Erläuterung,* pp. 165–166; Billerbeck, vol. 3, pp. 359f. and I. Abrahams, *Studies,* pp. 51–53.

73) G.A. Cooke, *The International Critical Commentary: The Book of Ezekiel* (Edinburgh: T. and T. Clark, 1970), p. 191.

74) L.F. Hartmann and A. di Lella, *The Anchor Bible the Book of Daniel* (New York: Doubleday, 1983), pp. 176–177. The imagery of the tree and its branches also appears in the Thanksgiving Scroll 6:15–16 (Licht, p. 114) and 8:4–14 (Licht, p. 133) and cf. Flusser, *Jesus,* pp. 87–88 (English trans., pp. 90–91.

75) See note 74 above.

76) Luke 12:1; Mark 8:15; Matthew 16:6, 11 and 12.

77) Flusser, *Die rabbinischen Gleichnisse,* pp. 206f.

78) Ibid. See j. Chagigah 76c, chap. 1, hal. 7; Pesikta Derav Kahana 15:5 (Mandelbaum, p. 254); Lamentations Rabbati, Petichta 2 (Buber, pp. 1a f); cf. b. Erubin 54a–b (see Flusser, *Die rabbinischen Gleichnisse,* p. 228, note 31). Cf. Bacher, *Die Agada der palästinesischen Amoräer,* vol. 2, p. 197.

79) M. Higger, *Masechtot Derech Eretz* (Jerusalem: Makor, 1970), vol. 2, p. 248 and compare his English translation, vol. 2, pp. 84–85. See especially I. Abrahams, *Studies,* vol. 1, p. 53 who discusses this text from the Chapter on Peace in the Minor Tractates of the Talmud and noted the connection of the tradition to Sifra on Leviticus 26:6 (Weiss, p. 111a) which speaks about the peace between beasts of prey which God will give in the land. See also Bacher, *Die Agada der palästinensischen Amoräer,* vol. 1, p. 136, idem, *Agadat Amore Eretz Yisrael* vol. 1, part 1, p. 135. See also note 72 above. According to R. Abahu in the name of R. Johanan (R. Simeon b. Lakish), the time required for fermentation is that required to walk four Roman miles (b. Pes. 46a where it says one mile, but see the parallel in j. Pes. 30a, chap. 3, hal. 2 where four miles is surely the proper reading).

80) The Gospel of Thomas splits up the two illustrations (logion 109 for Matthew 13:44 and logion 76 for Matthew 13:45). See also Jeremias,

Parables, pp. 32–33 and 198–201. Jeremias discusses the parallels in the Gospel of Thomas. Logion 76 is closer to Matthew's version. However in regards to logion 109, Jeremias observed, "The version of the parable of the Treasure hid in the Field as given in the Gospel of Thomas (109) is utterly degenerated. . . . This has hardly anything in common with the Matthaean version, which is certainly original" (ibid, p. 32). Logion 76 of the Gospel of Thomas emphasizes the prudence of the merchant and it seems that Matthew's version is again superior (see also ibid, p. 199).

81) Dodd, *Parables,* pp. 84–85. He writes, "For their interpretation the only real question that arises is whether the *tertium comparationis* is the immense value of the thing found, or the sacrifice by which it is acquired" (ibid). The heart of these twin parables' message was described by Linnemann with the contrast between the "unique opportunity" and "the deliberate risk" (Linnemann, *Parables,* pp. 101–103). Certainly the risk factor was one of the primary thrusts contained in the illustrations.

82) Thus Josephus describes the valuables and treasures that were hidden and buried in the ground when Titus destroyed Jerusalem, *War,* 7:112–114. See also Jeremias, *Parables,* pp. 198f.

83) See for instance the often referred to story where the Amora R. Johanan tells Aba bar Chiya that he sold his land in order to pursue a life of Torah study (Pesikta Derav Kahana 27:1, Mandelbaum, pp. 402–403; Song of Songs Rabbah 8:7; Leviticus Rabbah 30:1, Margulies, vol. 4, pp. 688–690; Exodus Rabbah 47:5; Tanchuma, Buber's edition, Ki Tisa, 29). See Bacher, *Die Agada der palästinensischen Amoräer,* vol. 1, pp. 221–222; idem, *Agadat Amore Eretz Yisrael* vol. 1, part 2, pp. 16–17. Compare also the remarks of R. Jose b. Kisma in Avot 6:9 who would not leave a center of learning though offered a great deal of wealth (Bacher, *Die Agada der Tannaiten,* vol. 1, pp. 399–400; idem, *Agadot Hatannaim,* vol. 1, part 2, pp. 119–120). Avot 6:5 also speaks of the ways in which Torah is acquired which include suffering. The gospels record that Jesus had made very strong statements concerning the requirements of discipleship (Matthew 10:37–39; Luke 14:25–27; 17:33; [Matthew 19:21; Mark 10:21; Luke 18:22] and cf. Matthew 19:23–30; Mark 10:23–31 and Luke 18:24–30). On the austere life of some of the sages see, L. Ginzberg, *Students, Scholars and Saints* (Philadelphia: Jewish Publication Society, 1958), pp. 55–57.

84) Compare Chaim Ryans, *Torah Umoser* (Jerusalem: Mosad Derav Kook, 1954), pp. 119–123 and see also G. Murray, *Five Stages of Greek Religion* (London: Watts, 1935), pp. 90–95.

85) S. Lieberman, *Hayerushalmi Kefshuto* (Jerusalem: Darom Publishing Co., 1934), "Introduction," pp. 22f.

86) A. Büchler, "Learning and Teaching in the Open Air in Pales-

tine," *Jewish Quarterly Review* 4 (1913–14), pp. 485–491. Many sources could be cited that show that it was common for the sages to teach outside. Cf. for example j. Avodah Zarah 43b chap. 3, hal. 13, Rabban Johanan ben Zakai sits and teaches in the shade of the Temple; tos. Berachot 4:16, Lieberman, p. 22, idem, *Tosefta Kefshuto,* p. 68 (R. Tarfon); m. Yebamot 12:6 (R. Horkanos); b. Erubin 54b (R. Eleazer b. Pedat).

87) Avot 1:4 and see the sources which refer to the sages discussing the Torah as they walk or travel, Avot 3:7; Sifre Deuteronomy 305 (Finkelstein, p. 325), Avot Derabbi Natan, ver. a, chap. 4; j. Chagigah 77a chap. 2, hal. 1; Mechilta Derabbi Ishmael on Exodus 31:12 (Horovitz, p. 340), b. Yoma 85a. See also Higger, *Masechtot Derech Eretz,* vol. 2, pp. 302–303, English translation, vol. 2, pp. 113–114, where discussion of the Torah in the bath house is a subject of inquiry.

88) See note 79 above.

89) Avot 6:9 and see note 79 above.

90) W.D. Davies has suggested that the expression "to follow Jesus" was a technical term which meant that a person had gone to a rabbi to become his servant, idem, *The Setting for the Sermon on the Mount* (Cambridge: Cambridge University Press, 1977), pp. 422–423. This is an attractive theory but little solid evidence exists to prove it. A number of texts show that a sage might be followed by his disciples as they go from place to place, but this is not exactly the same as approaching the sage to become his servant and in one description Rabban Gamliel's servant walks *before* him and R. Elai behind him (j. Avodah Zarah 40a, chap. 1, hal. 9; and see variations in Leviticus Rabbah 37:3, Margulies, p. 861). See also Billerbeck, vol. 1, pp. 187f, pp. 499f, and note 83 above.

91) Cf. Matthew 19:16–22; Mark 10:17–22 and Luke 18:18–23 and see the two parables in Luke 14:25–33 and Matthew 10:37–38.

92) Mechilta Derabbi Ishmael on Exodus 14:6 (Horovitz, p. 87–88, Lauterbach, vol. 1, pp. 197f); Mechilta Derabbi Simeon bar Yochai on Exodus 14:6 (Epstein, p. 50); Song of Songs Rabbah 4:12, Pesikta Derav Kahana 11:7 (Mandelbaum, p. 183); Midrash Hagadol on Exodus 14:6 (Margulies, p. 258); and Yalkut Shimeoni, vol. 1, remez 230, vol. 2, remez 988. Cf. Bacher, *Die Agada der Tannaiten,* vol. 1, pp. 363–364, idem, *Agadot Hatannaim,* vol. 1, part 2, pp. 95–96. Jeremias mentioned the parallel from Song of Songs Rabbah, idem, *Parables,* pp. 32–33. See also P. Fiebig, *Die Gleichnisreden Jesu* (Tübingen: J.C.B. Mohr, 1912), pp. 91–93. In his criticism of A. Drews, Fiebig discusses the difference between the rabbinic parable and the gospel text of Matthew by claiming that Jesus' parable speaks about the lost sinner and the Mechilta deals with the search for the wisdom of the law. As has been seen, it is very

unlikely that Jesus' parable of the kingdom is related to the search for the lost sinner. It is the inestimable value of the kingdom and the price one pays to become a disciple.

93) Song of Songs Rabbah 4:12 and Pesikta Derav Kahana 11:7 (Mandelbaum, p. 183) and see preceding note.

94) Cf. Flusser, *Die rabbinischen Gleichnisse,* p. 130.

95) See also notes 25–28 above.

96) Compare the observations of Linnemann, *Parables,* pp. 102–103.

97) Flusser pointed to the similarity between the Parable of the Net and the Fish and between the Parable of the Wheat and the Tares. He correctly saw them as parallels which describe the eschatological separation between the righteous and the wicked. See idem, *Die rabbinischen Gleichnisse,* pp. 63–65. These parables and Jesus' approach to the kingdom probably created tension between him and John the Baptist. At least the idea of the kingdom as a growth process and the concept of the wicked and the righteous living together until the final judgment is not compatible with the views of the Baptist expressed in Matthew 3:11–12, Mark 1:7–8 and Luke 3:15–18 where a speedy revival will save those who repent from the sudden judgment of fire.

98) In a work on the parables, it is impossible to open and fully treat the ever controversial subject of the meaning of the Son of Man in the teachings of Jesus. In the last twenty years a great deal has been written on the issue. Seyoon Kim's monograph, *"The 'Son of Man'" as the Son of God* (Tübingen: J.C.B. Mohr, 1983) contains a working bibliography of the more recent works and see now W. Horbury, "The Messianic Associations of 'the Son of Man,'" *Journal of Theological Studies* 36 (1985), pp. 34–55. Horbury's article is certainly an important contribution which demonstrates that the title "Son of Man" had messianic associations during the time of Jesus and earlier. I hope to deal with the Son of Man theme more fully in a subsequent study.

99) Flusser, "Jesus and the Sign of the Son of Man," *Judaism and the Origins of Christianity* (Jerusalem: Magnes Press, forthcoming). See also idem, "Hishtakfutan Shel Emunot Meshichiyot Yahudiyot Banatzrut Hakadumah," *Meshichiyut Vaescatologiyah* (Jerusalem: The Zalman Shazar Center, 1984), p. 103–134 and compare Horbury, op. cit., preceding note.

JESUS, THE JEWISH SAGES AND THEIR PARABLES

Many rabbinic parables are closely parallel to the parables of Jesus in the gospels. The question is often asked by scholars and laymen alike: Who has borrowed from whom? After all, every creation has an originator and can be copied by less innovative imitators. In the present study, we will examine a number of these parallel texts and try to understand how parabolic teaching evolved and developed into a unique genre both in rabbinic literature and in the gospels.

After building a foundation by studying rabbinic parables in the context of Jewish literature and the parables of Jesus in the context of the synoptic gospels, a number of facts emerge that present several perplexing questions.[1] First we see that the rabbinic parables are preserved in a literature that was compiled some time after the gospels. Second we discover in the gospel and rabbinic parables a unique literary type that is for the most part identical—with a few qualifications—especially when we analyze them and compare them to a mini-drama that has an attention attracting plot, concentrated action, colorful characters, a crisis turning point and a specific message all of which are combined to produce a response from the audience. Certainly some classic story parables are more successful than others, but more often than not they conform to this basic form and structure. Third we noted that story parables are unknown outside rabbinic literature and the synoptic gospels. How did this specialized genre evolve from oral illustration into a powerful tool of communication in diverse literary settings?

The Evolution of Parabolic Teachings

What processes were at work which gave birth to the story parable illustration? Is it proper to speak of stages of development? All proposed answers to these fascinating questions must remain conjectural. Moreover such questions must be distinguished from a purely historical analysis which only seeks to discover the earliest example of the story parable. The parables attributed to Jesus in the synoptic gospels provide early materials and may give clues concerning the characteristics of the parable in its earlier stages.[2] Noteworthy is the fact that while Jesus alludes to biblical passages, it is doubtful if he ever originally made a direct quotation of a verse in his parables. However biblical citations appear in numerous rabbinic parables from the expositional texts that are of a purely exegetical nature. Many other rabbinic parables on the other hand are characterized by their more popular themes and are not directly dependent on verse quotations. Is it proper to look for stages of development here or did both applications of the parable develop at the same time? It seems more likely that the pure exegetical use of the parable was a later development which certainly would have proliferated in the literary stages because of its versatility.

But what can be known of the earlier stages before the story parable passed from the oral teachings and became a literary genre? It is indeed daring to speak about the development of the parable as a literary genre because all analyses must remain hypothetical. Here three possibilities will be considered—all or none of which may have played a role in the development of the parable as a didactic technique: 1. fictitious tales and fables which were close precedents to the story parable; 2. actual happenings which could be adapted to illustrate a theme; 3. wisdom sayings or verses which could be developed into a story.[3] Consideration of these points can shed light on the ubiquitous problem of the relationship between the parable and its context, between the mashal and the nimshal, and also the main purpose of the parables. It has already been noted that the parable was originally designed to be told. Several scenarios are possible, but these three forerunners could have paved the way for the creative processes which produced and popularized the story parable. Nevertheless the story parable should always be viewed as an independent and natural achievement and not as an aberration of a wise saying or a fable.

The fable is an important forerunner of the parable. No fables appear in the gospels. It must be distinguished from the latter in that it employs animals and sometimes plants, attributing human characteristics to them. The antiquity of the fable is not disputed. Perry noted, "In the early period of Greek literature, and in the Alexandrian Age, fables might be the subject-matter of separate poems, but much more commonly they were used subordinately as illustrations in a larger context, whether of poetry as in Hesiod, Aeschylus, Sophocles, and Aristophanes, or in prose, as in Herodotus, Xenophon, Plato, and Aristotle."[4] Hence Greek literature preserves fables in both prose and poetry. Also Schwarzbaum has stressed the antiquity of the fable: "It should also be pointed out that some of the antecedents of the so-called Aesopic fables are to be found in a highly developed tradition from the Ancient Near East (Mesopotamian, Egyptian etc.) . . ."[5] Jacobs observed that many of the fables of rabbinic literature are paralleled in both Greek and Indian sources.[6] Thus the fable was a widely circulated didactic mode. The well-known fable of the Oak and the Reeds appears in the Indian Mahabharata xii.4198, Avian and Babrius 64 as well as in talmudic literature.[7] The oak is not pliable and breaks as it stands against the powerful wind. The flimsy reed however bends with the wind and thus survives the storm. Flusser noted that the fable is probably behind the words of Jesus in regard to John the Baptist, "What did you go out in the wilderness to behold? A reed shaken by the wind?" (Matthew 11:7; Luke 7:24). John's uncompromising nature put him on a collision course with Herod Antipas.[8]

In Exodus Rabbah a fable is used by the Amora R. Judah bar Shalom (ca. 350 A.D.) to elucidate the predicament of Israel who in spite of their deliverer Moses still had to worry about Pharaoh. The fable from the midrash expounds Exodus 5:21, "They [Israelites] said to Moses: 'To what are we compared? To a lamb which a wolf comes to devour, and after which the shepherd pursues, in order to save it from the wolf. Meanwhile, the lamb is torn by the wolf.'"[9] This is a variation of an earlier illustration which was revised for its new context. Another fable is told by Joshua b. Chananyah (ca. 80 A.D.) in Genesis Rabbah, "A wild lion killed [an animal], and a bone stuck in his throat.

Thereupon he proclaimed: 'I will reward anyone who removes it.' An Egyptian heron, which has a long beak, came and pulled it out and demanded his reward. 'Go,' he replied, 'you will be able to boast that you entered the lion's mouth in peace and came out in peace' [unscathed]. Even so, let us be satisfied that we entered into dealings with these people in peace and have emerged in peace."[10] The Egyptian heron did not receive the promised reward but he was not killed by the lion either. In the context R. Joshua b. Chananyah is saying that although Israel is oppressed and misled by the authorities, at least they had thus far been able to deal with them without physical harm. The fable is meant to be a comfort in the midst of adversity, but it has a realistic and perhaps even a pessimistic outlook.[11] The fable has many earlier predecessors.[12] Already in the Bible, the fable of Jotham presents an allegorical representation of the distrubing events in Shechem. He likens Abimelech to a bramble and creates a fable where the trees seek a king—first in an olive tree, then in a fig tree and in the vine—only to accept the wholly unsuitable bramble as their ruler (Judges 9:7–21).[13] Jotham's fable and similar ones were widely known, but it would have been meaningless for someone to transform a known fable into a parable. What point would have been served if a fox character from a fable was turned into a merchant and the story was further adapted to form a parable? Would a known fable be transformed into a parable? Nevertheless one can readily perceive the similarities between the early fables and later story parables. Fables may have played a role in the development of a more realistic story line and provided the pattern or model for rabbinic and gospel parables. Obviously fables are not parables and a parable has its own unique form, structure and purpose which is far removed from the world of fable lore.

The Parable of the Good Samaritan (Luke 10:29–36) is a story which could actually have occurred. This does not mean that the parable would be an accurate telling of something that happened but rather that the parable would take the basic outline of the event and adapt the details for its own purpose. Flusser has suggested that the Parable of the Good Samaritan is an adaptation of a somewhat shocking incident which is reported in rabbinic literature. Two priests were running side by side in the Temple and one was stabbed in his heart.[14] The father of the wounded priest rushed over to see his son who was dying and in convulsions. When the father saw that his son was not yet dead, he declared that the knife—the instrument of his son's death—was still ritually clean. At least this disturbing episode tells how ritual purity could take precedence over a father's concern for the life of his son and functioned to provide a solemn warning. A similar message emerges from the Parable of the Good Samaritan (Luke 10:29–37) where a dying man is not given assistance apparently because of the desire to preserve ritual purity.[15] Another passerby, in this case an enemy, provides the needed care for the wounded man.[15a] Of course the whole story seems to be based upon the Hebrew word *rea* (cf. Leviticus 19:18) which could be interpreted as meaning only one's friend or neighbor but certainly not an enemy. The priest and the Levite saw the dying man and refused to allow basic human compassion to motivate them to help him. They had more important obligations and apparently they were on their way to the Temple to perform their religious functions. According to Jewish law, they were required to help the man in agony who would probably die even if they did provide him with immediate medical attention by binding his wounds and taking him to a place where he had a better chance for survival. Israel's sages placed tremendous value on the preservation of life at all costs.[16] But a dying man must be treated the same way as anyone else even if death seems certain (Semachot 1:1, Higger, p. 97). The Samaritan, who most certainly would be outside the definition of the Hebrew word *rea* for some who listened to the parable, stopped to give life-saving assistance to the stranger in desperate need. Under similar laws of purity, the Samaritan did not consider the risk of ritual uncleanness but helped his neighbor who was in mortal danger. Who is the neighbor *(rea)* in this illustration? Is he the Samaritan or is he the injured man? Jesus is saying that there is a reciprocity in human relationships, and in order to grasp how to answer the question of who is one's neighbor *(rea),* one must take action and behave like a neighbor to all in need regardless of the consequences. Perhaps J. Mann was correct when he detected sharp friction between Jesus and the Temple priests who for the most part were Sadducees and rejected the Jewish oral law.[17] Jesus' carefully constructed illustration connects different aspects of Jewish faith, piety, and culture from the period into a unified storyline that has far-reaching moral implications.

In any case, the basic outline and idea of the Parable of the Good Samaritan could have been based upon a real incident such as the two priests in the Temple or a needy traveler who received help from a stranger. R. Eleazar ben Shamua (ca. 135 A.D.) is also said to have aided a shipwreck survivor.[18] So the basic storyline of the Parable of the Good Samaritan is not necessarily a fictitious invention but could be based upon a real incident and the intricate staging of the parable, its plot, characters and moral message form a cohesive unit that is designed to communicate and to fulfill a specific purpose. In some ways a parable of this kind could be compared to an historical novel, which though placed in a realistic setting does not attempt to be true to all the facts and may actually change some details in order to develop the plot. The Parable of the Prodigal Son is another example of an illustration which could be based on a true story.[19] The family tensions between the two sons and their father depicted in the parable could have been based upon a true life situation where a son abandoned his home. In the Old Testament, the prophet Nathan's tale of the wealthy man who took the poor man's only sheep was intended to portray David and Bathsheba (2 Samuel 12:1–4). Of course this example from the Old Testament is not referred to as a story parable, but it certainly has many characteristics of the parable and it is a case in point where the illustration was developed as a kind of dramatic replay drawn from King David's actions. A parable may be modeled upon an event. However the parabolist is not interested in relating a story or an accurate telling of something he has seen or heard. He desires to communicate a message, and the parable must be conformed to his purpose.

Sayings of the wise could have provided the theme or basic idea for a parable. Jesus says that if the blind leads the blind both the leader and the follower will fall into a ditch. While this saying is unparalleled in Jewish literature, it seems to have originated as a Greek saying because a version of it already appears in Plato.[20] While no parable was ever developed from this saying, one could ask whether a simple logion could have been developed into a more extensive illustration.[21] Of course sometimes the opposite is true, namely that logions were secondarily augmented to a parable. In a Jewish context, wise sayings that teach relevant truth with practical applications were often derived from the sacred writings which would have included works like Ben Sira as well as the corpus of literature that would be canonized later. The widely circulated theme of the two ways already is spoken of in almost proverbial terms in the scriptures, "Thus says the LORD: Behold, I set before you the way of life and the way of death" (Jeremiah 21:8). In Proverbs 16:25 one reads, "There is a way which seems right to a man but its end is the way to death" (also Proverbs 14:12). It is closely paralleled in Ben Sira 21:10, "The way of sinners is smoothly paved with stones, but at its end is the pit of Hades."[22] Inherent in these passages is the theme of the two ways which has many parallels and adaptations. For example in 2 Esdras 7:12–13 one reads, "And so the entrances of this world were made narrow and sorrowful and toilsome; they are few and evil, full of dangers and involved in great hardships. But the entrances of the greater world are broad and safe, and really yield the fruit of immortality." Also in recension A of the Testament of Abraham, Abraham is shown the "two ways: the one way was narrow and tortuous and the other was wide and spacious . . ."[23] One should compare recension B (chap. 8) where the two ways become the two gates, "Then Michael said to Abraham, 'Do you see these two gates, the small one and the large one? These are those which lead to life and destruction.'"[24] The Jewish source text of the Didache (1:1) begins with the theme of the two ways, "There are two Ways, one of Life and one of Death, one of Light and one of Darkness . . ."[25] The ways of light and darkness also appear in 2 Enoch 30:15, "I pointed out to him the two ways—light and darkness."[26]

Fascinatingly the theme has been adapted in the Essene Manual of Discipline to accommodate the doctrine of predestination, "He has created man to govern the world, and has appointed for him two spirits in which to walk until the time of

His visitation: the spirits of truth and falsehood. Those born of the truth spring from a fountain of light, but those born of falsehood spring from a source of darkness. All the children of righteousness are ruled by the Prince of Light and walk in the ways of light, but all the children of falsehood are ruled by the Angel of Darkness and walk in the ways of darkness."[27] Here a significant adaptation can be detected as it is not incumbent upon a man to choose which of the two ways he wants to go, but rather God has already chosen and rejected whom he wills. One should also examine the Testaments of the Twelve Patriarchs. The Testament of Asher speaks of the two ways, "God has granted two ways to the sons of men, two mind-sets, two lines of action, two models, and two goals. Accordingly, everything is in pairs, the one over against the other. The two ways are good and evil . . ."[28] In the Testament of Levi, Jacob instructs his sons, "Choose for yourselves light or darkness, the Law of the Lord or the works of Beliar" (Test. Levi 19:1). In the Testament of Judah, like the Essene Manual of Discipline, one discovers the two spirits—one of truth and one of falsehood, "So understand, my children, that two spirits await an opportunity with humanity: the spirit of truth and the spirit of error. In between is the conscience of the mind which inclines as it wills."[29] Though the two spirits are mentioned, unlike the Manual of Discipline the conscience of the mind *(tēs suneseōs tou noos)* is the determining factor in man's choice. Of course the analogy of the two ways appears in a mitigated form in the gospels where wide is the gate and easy is the way that leads to destruction (Matthew 7:13–14 and Luke 13:23–24). Although this is a text from the double tradition, one finds little agreement between Matthew and Luke and one should note that the language of the parallel in Tabula of Cebes (15:1ff) is close to the wording of Matthew.[30] Clearly the idea of the two ways was well known and widely circulated. It was used within the framework of the Essene doctrine of predestination and in the gospels as a challenge to choose the way of life and reject the path that leads to destruction. It is not the purpose of this brief overview of texts to deal with the question of influence and the possible interconnections between these sources. However, the seed of the idea of the two ways was contained in the imagery of a number of biblical passages like Jeremiah 21:8, Proverbs 16:25 or even Deuteronomy 11:26–28 where one finds the dualism between the blessing and the curse and the mention of the way in which God had commanded the people to live. Nevertheless none of these texts discussed so far preserve a parable that illustrates this concept.

An anonymous parable has been transmitted in Sifre Deuteronomy which developed the picture of a man standing at a fork in the road where two paths stretch out before him. Hence the tannaitic midrash, in its interpretation of the biblical text that discusses the dualism of the blessing and the curse, takes the theme of the two ways one step further. Here one discovers a parable that illustrates the motif of the two ways.

THE PARABLE OF THE TWO WAYS

> "Behold, I set before you this day a blessing and a curse" (Deut. 11:26). Why is this said? Because it says, "I have set before you life and death, blessing and curse" (Deut. 30:19)? Lest Israel should say: Since the Omnipresent has set before us two ways, a way of life and a way of death, we may walk in which ever we choose. The scripture says: "And you shall choose life" (Deut. 30:19). A parable. It may be compared to one who sat at the crossroads [where two paths parted]. Two paths were before him, one which was smooth at its beginning, but its end was thorny, and the other which was thorny at its beginning, but its end was smooth. He would tell those who were coming and going, "You see this path which is smooth at its beginning? For two or three steps you walk in its smoothness but it ends up in thorns. You see this other path which is thorny at its beginning? For two or three steps you walk in thorns, but it ends up in smoothness." Thus Moses spoke to Israel: You see the wicked who are prosperous in this world? For two or three days they prosper, but they end up being confounded afterwards, as it is said, "for the evil man has no future" (Proverbs 24:20). It says, "And, behold he tears of the oppressed" (Ecclesiastes 4:1) and "The fool folds his

> hands" (Ecclesiastes 4:5). Further it says, "The way of the wicked is deep darkness" (Proverbs 4:19). You see the righteous who are afflicted in this world? For two or three days they are afflicted, but they end up rejoicing afterwards. Thus it says: "[that he might humble you and test you,] to do good to you in the end" (Deut. 8:16). It says, "Better is the end of the thing than its beginning" (Ecclesiastes 7:8). It says, "For I know the plans I have for you, [says the LORD, plans for welfare and not for evil]" (Jeremiah 29:11). It says: "The path of the righteous is like the light of dawn" (Proverbs 4:18).[31]

Thus in Sifre Deuteronomy one finds a parable constructed upon the idea contained in the verses of scripture which speak about death and life, blessing and curse. As in the teachings of Jesus, the idea of choice is patent which is to be sharply differentiated from the Essene theology of dualism in the Manual of Discipline. In the explanation of the mashal, one discovers a further application. The darshan took up the question of why the righteous suffer while the wicked prosper. In reformulating one of the classic answers to the question, he also stresses the idea that each individual must decide which path to follow. The shift in content that makes the parable an explanation of the sufferings of the righteous may be an adaptation of the illustration made by the darshan. At least one should not rule out the possibility that the core parable was derived from an earlier source and expanded in a new context in the midrash. While one cannot be certain, originally the parabolist seems to have desired to stress man's choice. In any case, the parable illustrates how a basic theme of the two ways could be developed into a parable and therefore it is instructive in any discussion of the evolution of parabolic teaching.

The Teaching on Humility

One also discovers examples of teaching materials in rabbinic literature and the gospels which, although they do not appear with the outer trappings of a parable, are nevertheless already on the way to becoming a parabolic illustration. For instance in Luke 14:7–11, Jesus' teaching on humility has many elements that are contained in story parables. The passage appears in Codex Bezae as well as a number of other manuscripts after Matthew 20:28.[32] The version of Matthew is different from that of Luke in a number of points and one may ask if it is merely a scribal addition based on Luke 14:8–10 or whether it was derived from another parallel source.[33] At any rate the text contains mention of a feast, invited guests, the host, a conversation, action and an application. All these elements would make a fine parable, and Luke himself refers to the passage as a *parabolē;* nonetheless, it is not a story illustration.[34] The instruction concerning humility does not dramatize the characters and action to form a parable. However by making a few modifications one is able to develop a parable out of the teaching:

> "It may be compared to a man who was invited to a [marriage] feast and took the place of honor. A more eminent man was invited by the host. The eminent guest and the host came to the man and said, 'Give place to this man.' Then the man took the lowest place with shame. Thus when you are invited, go and sit in the lowest place, so that when your host comes he may say to you, 'Friend, go up higher'; then you will be honored in the presence of all who sit at table with you. For every one who exalts himself will be humbled, and he who humbles himself will be exalted."

Here one can see how easily the instruction concerning humility could be adapted to form a parable. By adding a minimal introduction, dramatizing the action and developing the plot of the illustration, and changing the second person into the third person, the passage has been transformed into a story parable.

The teaching on humility however is one example which is very closely related to the verse in Proverbs 25:6–7, "Do not put yourself forward in the king's presence or stand in the place of the great; for it is better to be told, 'Come up here,' than to be put lower in the presence of the prince" (cf. Ben Sira 3:17–20). The proverb is related to the proper behavior in the presence of royalty but Jesus' instruction as recorded in Luke makes a more general application of the passage. The verse from Proverbs is reflected in the passage from Luke and seems to have contributed to the evolution of the instruction. This teaching is very closely paralleled in rabbinic literature where the sages also employed the passage from Proverbs. Many commentators have discussed the relationship between the rabbinic parallels and gospel teachings.[35] Here it would be suggested that the rabbinic parallels provide clues that may elucidate the original setting of the gospel text.

In Leviticus Rabbah the verses from Proverbs 25:6–7 are expounded by the Amora Joshua of Siknin (ca. 320 A.D.) in the name of the well-known agadist, R. Levi (ca. 220 A.D.).[36] After the verse a saying attributed to R. Simeon ben Azzai (ca. 120 A.D.) follows which is transmitted by R. Akiva, "Go two or three seats lower and take your seat, until they say to you, 'Come up,' rather than that you should go up and they should say to you, 'Go down.' Better that people say to you 'come up, come up,' and not to say to you, 'go down, go down.'" The text continues and quotes Hillel's famous dictum, " . . . and so used Hillel to say: 'My self-abasement is my exaltation, my self-exaltation is my self-abasement' What is the proof? 'He that raiseth himself is to [be made to] sit down, he that abaseth himself is to be [raised so that he is] seen (Psalm 113:5–6)."[37] Hillel's saying is not only reflected in Luke 14:11, but in other gospel passages as well (Matthew 18:4; 23:12 and Luke 18:14). However what is fascinating about this parallel in Leviticus Rabbah is that Hillel's saying appears after Simeon ben Azzai's instruction in the same order as preserved in Luke 14:8–11. Does this indicate that the floating logion, "For every one who exalts himself will be humbled, and he who humbles himself will be exalted," was originally connected to Luke 14? However the verse from Proverbs is not quoted in Luke. Furthermore, in parallels to Leviticus Rabbah from Avot Derabbi Nathan, Ben Azzai gives the advice, "Go down from your place two or three places and sit in order that they will say to you, 'come up' . . ." and then cites the verse from Proverbs. There Hillel's saying does not appear.[38] The teaching on humility in Leviticus Rabbah has other important parallels in rabbinic literature.

A significant parallel is transmitted in the name of the early tannaitic teacher R. Jose Hagalili (ca. 110) in Avot Derabbi Nathan, "R. Jose said: Go down and you will be up, go up and you will be down. He who exalts himself by his knowledge of Torah will in the end be brought low; he who humbles himself by his knowledge of Torah will in the end be exalted."[39] One can study Torah for the wrong motives. What does it mean to hate the *rabanut?* The words *rav* and *rabanut* in the time of Jesus would have referred to lord and lordship respectively. In Avot Derabbi Nathan one reads this reply, "What does it mean? It teaches that no man should put a crown on his own head, but others should put it on him. . . . R. Akiba said: Whoever exalts himself by his knowledge of Torah, to what is he like? To a carcass which lies in the road, anybody passing by puts his hand to his nose and moves far away from it . . ."[40] In Sifre Deuteronomy an anonymous passage teaches that one should study from the motivation of love for God, "Lest I should say that I study Torah in order that I shall be called a Sage, or occupy [a prominent] seat [אשב בישיבה], or lengthen my days in the world to come . . ."[41] In the context of Sifre Deuteronomy the idea is conveyed in the name of R. Eleazar who spoke in the name of R. Tzadok that one must perform the teachings of the Torah for their own sake[42] and it recalls Johanan b. Zakai (ca. 60 A.D.) who taught that one must not congratulate himself for the study of the Torah because it is for this purpose that man was created.[43] These rabbinic passages indicate that within the milieu of Jewish learning the sages were aware that the danger existed that one might try to exalt himself through the study of Torah. In the teachings of Jesus, the disciples are not to seek lordship over one another, but the greater one becomes the servant of all (Luke 22:25–26).

Early commentators of the gospels have noted the rabbinic parallels to the saying of Jesus. A. Wünsche (1878) noted that Luke 14:11 was parallel to Hillel's (ca. 20 B.C.) dictum[44] and connected Matthew 23:12, "whoever exalts himself will be humbled and whoever humbles himself will be exalted" to the passage in the Babylonian Talmud: "This teaches you that him that humbles himself the Holy One, blessed be He, raises up, and him who exalts himself the Holy One, blessed be He, humbles; from him who seeks greatness, greatness flees but him who flees from greatness, greatness follows . . ." (b. Erubin 13b).[45] The context in the Talmud relates a argument between the school of Shamai and the school of Hillel concerning the proper requirements for the Sucah. R. Johanan Hacoranit, a tanna who flourished before the destruction, appears in the context. He observed the festival of Sucot in the manner of the school of Hillel although he was of the school of Shamai. However the final saying conerning humility does not appear in the parallels to the tradition.[46] The saying should be compared with the Minor Tractate of the Talmud, "If you humble yourself, the Holy One Blessed be He will exalt you, but if you have exalted yourself before your fellow, the Holy One Blessed be He will humble you."[47] H.A.W. Meyer noted the passage from the Babylonian Talmud and gave it an eschatological interpretation, "A *general* law of retribution, but with an intentional application to the *Messianic* retribution."[48] Meyer cites the rabbinic parallel to support his interpretation. More recent commentators have sought for great differences between Jesus and the rabbis.

Though Jeremias agrees with Meyer's stress on divine retribution, he contrasts the Jewish sources with Luke 14:11. Whereas the Jewish sources are concerned with "table-manners," "practical wisdom" and "social etiquette," the saying in the gospel "is speaking of God's eschatological activity, the humbling of the proud and the exaltation of the humble in the Last Day. Hence the direction in Luke 14:11 about the desirability of modest behaviour in a guest becomes the introduction to an 'eschatological warning', which looks forward to the heavenly banquet, and is a call to renounce self-righteous pretensions and to self-abasement before God."[49] Marshall writes, "But whereas for the rabbis the saying was merely a piece of worldly wisdom, for Jesus it is an expression of God's verdict upon men."[50] Fitzmyer asks the question, "Are these rabbinical traditions possibly influenced by the early Christian tradition?"[51] A positive answer to Fitzmyer's question seems unlikely. The multiple parallels and versions of these sayings indicate that one is dealing with materials that were deeply embedded into early Jewish thought. Furthermore there is little evidence that the rabbis borrowed from Christian tradition or that they had significant contact with early Christians.[52] The contacts between church and synagogue is a complex historical question and should not be oversimplified—but it seems doubtful that it would have been necessary for Jewish sages to adopt teachings on humility from the early Christians. The saying of Hillel is not a word for word parallel and it could well capture the unique individuality of the sage who lived some years before the rise of Christianity. It seems much more reasonable to suppose that both traditions are derived from a common stream of Jewish humanistic thought which blossomed in full bloom during the Second Temple period. This is especially the case when one examines the wording of the saying attributed to R. Jose Hagalili in Avot Derabbi Nathan and to Hillel in Midrash Hallel. A colorful word play becomes evident; literally the text says, "Descend upwards and ascend downwards."[53] It is unlikely that this word play was formed from the gospel text! However the influence of the verse in Proverbs 25:6–7 should not be minimized. One might even suppose that both Luke and the words of Ben Azzai could have been developed independently on the basis of the Proverb. However the combination of the saying with that of Hillel and Luke 14:11 indicates that more is involved than two independent treatments of Proverbs 25:6–7.

What was the original context of these sayings? When one carefully examines all the rabbinic parallels it becomes clear that much more than table manners is involved. Instead of being motivated to study for the sake of learning and in order to gain greater understanding of the Torah, one can apply himself for his own self-exaltation. At least this is the message inherent in the words of R. Jose.[54] Nevertheless the notion that God will humble the mighty and exalt the lowly as a part of the eschatological judgment was current.[55] Also the saying in *Masechet Derech Eretz* states that God himself humbles the one who exalts himself. Is this accomplished at the judgment or in the present life? While R. Jose says that the "Holy One Blessed be He" will exalt the one who humbles himself, the passage in the gospel uses the passive. Is this what Jeremias described as the "divine passive" or is this saying of Jesus more anthropocentric?[56] Hillel's saying stresses the idea that he humbles himself and this action of self-humiliation becomes his exaltation.[57] Hillel is saying that a man's arrogance humiliates him and that by humbling oneself a man actually bestows honor upon himself. Jesus' saying would probably be best understood in light of his remarks concerning one who serves, "let the greatest among you become as the youngest, and the leader as one who serves . . ." (Luke 22:26; Mark 10:43; Matthew 20:26).

This example from Luke 14:7–11 demonstrates the importance of the verses from Proverbs 25:6–7 in a teaching which is almost a story parable. Could this passage represent a stage in the development of parabolic teaching? It certainly was formulated at a time when parables were already in use as can be clearly shown from the gospels. Nevertheless the passage could illustrate the direction that was taken as teachers began to use parables to illustrate their instruction. While it is difficult to evaluate the processes which were at work in the development of the story parable, the teaching on humility introduces another question. How is it possible to evaluate the direct parallels between gospel teachings and rabbinic literature? To consider this problem in greater depth it is necessary to examine further texts.

The Solid Foundation

Both Matthew and Luke record the Parable of the Solid Foundation and relate the story to Jesus' teaching materials that could be loosely designated the Sermon on the Mount (Matthew 7:15–20 and Luke 6:43–45). A close rabbinic parallel to this parable is attributed to Elisha b. Avuyah (ca. 110 A.D.) and appears in Avot Derabbi Nathan.[58] Elisha b. Avuyah was designated by the name *Acher* because he became involved in some kind of theosophical speculation that led him away from the observance of the Torah. Here it is beyond the scope of this work to investigate the numerous possibilities concerning the exact nature of his heretic views and actions which have been advanced by numerous studies[59] but rather to examine the text of the parabolic illustrations attributed to him in this chapter of Avot Derabbi

Nathan which is devoted entirely to his teachings. It should be pointed out that he was a leading teacher of his time and taught no less an eminent authority than R. Meir.

The texts of Matthew and Luke in the double tradition contain numerous differences in wording (Matthew 7:21, 24–27 and Luke 6:46–49). Both evangelists connect the illustration to a preceding teaching by concluding the parable with the editorial suture, "And when Jesus finished these sayings" (Matthew 7:28; and compare Luke 7:1). Both Matthew and Luke cite the parable as the conclusion of the Sermon on the Mount and the Sermon on the Plain respectively, though Luke preserves much of the teaching materials paralleled here in Matthew elsewhere in another context. Moreover both evangelists introduce the parable by the passage on saying Lord, Lord. Matthew's text reads, "Not every one who says to me, 'Lord, Lord,' shall enter the kingdom of heaven, but he who does the will of my Father who is in heaven . . ." and Luke turns the text into a question, "Why do you call me 'Lord, Lord,' and not do what I tell you?" (Matthew 7:21; Luke 6:46). Most probably the address "Lord" had messianic associations.[60] Matthew has placed another "Lord, Lord" passage concerning the judgment on the last day here (Matthew 7:22) which appears in another context in Luke 13:25–27. While on the whole the wording of Matthew's version may be preferable to Luke 13:25–27, one can only doubt whether his placement of the passage here before the parable is more original. At least one can easily understand why Matthew would have connected these two passages together because both contain the address "Lord, Lord" and the evangelist was collecting and arranging the teaching materials for his Sermon on the Mount section. Moreover it is difficult to imagine that either Luke or his redactor would have torn the two texts apart if they were positioned next to one another in his source. While it is true that strong arguments could be advanced to support the unity of Matthew 7:21–23, when one separates verse 21 from verses 22–23 an antithetical parallelism emerges. It is connected to the word *pas* in Matthew's version which then contrasts the phrase οὐ πᾶς ὁ λέγων κλτ with the introduction to the parable, πᾶς οὖν ὅστις ἀκούει κλτ. Hence it seems that Matthew 7:22–23 has been inserted here into a new context.[61]

On the whole, it seems that Matthew's wording is to be preferred to Luke's version (Matthew 7:21, 24–27; Luke 6:46–49).[62] Nevertheless Matthew secondarily adds the word *toutous* (verses 24 and 26) apparently to connect the parable directly with the sermon. Neither Matthew's *omoiothesetai* nor Luke's *hupodeixo humin* makes good sense in Hebrew. However in this context, if Luke's text be punctuated as a question, τίνι ἐστὶν ὅμοιος, it could be an early example of the Hebrew phrase one encounters in many rabbinic parables, למה הוא דומה. Only Matthew contains the contrast between the wise man *fronimos* and the foolish man *mōros*. This is most probably an original element even though it is missing in Luke. The contrast between the wise and the foolish is a common theme of storytelling in parables and also appears in Matthew's Parable of the Ten Maidens (Matthew 25:1–12).[63] Excluding the Parable of the Ten Maidens and the present context, the word *fronimos* appears only two other times in Matthew (10:16 and 24:25) and twice in Luke (12:42 and 16:8). It never occurs in Mark. The word *mōros* never appears in Luke though he does employ the synonym *afrōn* two times (11:40; 12:20). Outside the Parable of the Ten Maidens and the Two Builders, Matthew uses the word *mōros* three more times (5:22; 23:17, 19) and the term also appears in Mark 7:13. Luke seems to have been keen on stressing the work necessary to lay the foundation and this may have led him to omit any reference to the theme of the wise and the foolish. Thus he emphasizes that the man ἔσκαψεν καὶ ἐβάθυνεν καὶ ἔθηκεν θεμέλιον. The word *skaptō* appears three times in the New Testament and all three occurrences are found in Luke (6:48, 13:8, and 16:3). In addition the word *bathunō* appears only here in the New Testament (Luke 6:48). The description of arduous labor in preparing the foundation seems to be a result of the redaction of Luke's text. At least the parallel in Matthew simply states, "who built his house upon the rock" and this has more claim to originality.

Luke's description of the flood also contains vocabulary unique to the third evangelist. Both *plēmmura* and *prosrēssō (prosrēgnumi)* are words unique to Luke. Also Luke's description that the house could not be shaken because it had been built well betrays signs of Greek stylizing.[64] Needless to say, the addition of the preformative *sun* to the verb *piptō* in verse 49 must also be attributed to an interest in style. The second house in Luke falls when it is inundated by the stream of water because it had been constructed upon "the ground without a foundation." Again one encounters an emphasis on the foundation. Matthew's description of a storm with wind and rain seems preferable. In Pirke Avot one discovers a strikingly similar description. According to R. Eleazar b. Azaryah a man whose works exceed his wisdom may be compared to a great tree with deep roots.[65] Even in a storm where strong winds assail him, he stands firm. Compare the wording in the Hebrew text, שאפילו כל הרוחות שבעולם באות ונושבות בו אין מזיזות אותו ממקומו (Avot 3:17).[66] Moreover the wording in Matthew preserves parallelism which is a characteristic of Semitic poetic style. The rain falls, the floods come and the winds blow but the house stands firm. Concerning the differences between Matthew and Luke, Harnack gives his opinion, "St. Matthew thinks of storms of rain and wind, but to St. Luke it seemed improbable that these could overturn a house, and he therefore supplies a flooded river."[67] It is difficult to say with certainty what was going on in the minds of Matthew and Luke; however, Matthew's text is much easier to reconstruct in Hebrew and seems to be closer to the original source. Harnack may be correct in surmising that Luke (redactor?) thought that winds could not knock over a house. Nonetheless in Job 1:19 one discovers the description of a great wind that literally blew the house to the ground, a tragedy that killed Job's children (cf. also Ezekiel 13:11–14; Ben Sira 22:17–18). But Matthew's texts makes a contrast between the wise and the foolish builders. The wise man constructs his house upon the rock in contrast to the fool who builds on the sand. These simple images are more original than Luke's version which stresses the idea of the labor required to prepare the foundation and betrays evidence of restylizing in Greek.

After these preliminary remarks concerning the more original Greek form of the parable, it is possible to offer a tentative

Hebrew reconstruction of the text. It is important to stress that this is an experimental reconstruction and that much more research in linguistics is needed to recover the exact language of the parables.

THE TWO BUILDERS

לא כל שקורא לי אדון אדון יבוא למלכות שמים אלא מי שעושה רצון אבי
שבשמים. כל ששומע [דברי] ועושה אותם למה הוא דומה? לפקח שבונה
ביתו על הסלע. וירד גשם ובאו נהרות ונשבו הרוחות ופגעו בבית
ולא נפל כי נוסד על הסלע.
כל ששומע ואינו עושה אותם דומה לטפש שבנה ביתו על החול.
וירד גשם ובאו נהרות ונשבו הרוחות ופגעו בבית ונפל ומפלתו גדולה.

After examining the editorial aspects of the parable in Matthew and Luke, one can propose a Hebrew reconstruction which more closely reflects the *ipsissima verba* of Jesus or at least the hypothetical Hebrew *Urevangelium* which underlies the texts of the synoptic gospels. More philological study is needed to determine to what extent one should look for a Hebrew closer to biblical or mishnaic. Was the vav consecutive employed? It seems that in a popular story parable that the vav consecutive would have been considered too literary. Here the passage, "Saying Lord, Lord" has been attached to the parable because it appears in both Matthew and Luke and could be an original part of the text. Though this is true, it is possible that it was derived from a different context.[68] Perhaps one of the more remarkable aspects of the parable is the phrase, "who hears my words and does them." The text stresses the teachings of Jesus.[69] The phrase which refers to hearing and doing may allude to the passages from the Pentateuch which speak about the giving of the law. The people of Israel responded with the affirmation, "we will do and we will hear [obey]."[70] Interestingly in Hebrew, the meaning of the verb "to hear" is of course "to obey" and this force of the expression is inherent also in the words of Jesus in the text of the gospels. This passage from the Torah would later be a proof text used in what was probably one of the greatest controversies in Judaism of late antiquity. It revolved around the question: What is more important, the study of Torah or its observance in the form of good deeds? It is difficult for the modern mind to grasp the controversial nature of this question within the framework of ancient Judaism. Nevertheless the sources indicate that this issue was discussed and debated extensively. The setting for the rabbinic parallel to Jesus' Parable of the Two Builders was very probably connected to this debate.

The origin of this debate has been a matter of scholarly discussion. Graetz suggested that the controversy between study and action (good deeds or observance of the Torah) developed during the Hadrianic persecutions when both were forbidden on the pain of death.[71] However it seems doubtful if this was the source of the issue since both action and study were forbidden. True the decision concerning *pikuach nefesh* and the argument between R. Tarfon and R. Akiva about study and action both occurred in the upper story of Nithza's house in Lydda according to the Talmud (b. Sanhedrin 74a and b. Kidushin 40b). G. Alon has pointed out that R. Tarfon died before the revolt so that the discussion should have occurred before that time.[72] It is worthwhile to quote Sifre Deuteronomy where the debate is described: " . . . R. Tarfon, R. Akiva and R. Jose Hagalili were sitting in the house of Aris in Lydda. This question was put before them: What is greater, study or action? R. Tarfon said, 'Action is greater.' R. Akiva said, 'Study is greater.' Everyone responded and said, 'Greater is study for study leads to action.'"[73] In the Jerusalem Talmud it is accepted that study takes precedence over practice.[74] This approach was widely accepted, as one can read in the Mechilta Derabbi Simeon bar Yochai, "'And they said all that the LORD has spoken we will do and hear' (Exodus 24:7). Because they placed action [עשייה] first before hearing [שמיעה], Moses asked them, 'Is it possible to observe [the teaching of Torah] without hearing?' Hearing leads to action. They repeated, 'We will do and we will hear—we will do what we hear.'"[75] Thus the verse is interpreted as meaning that the Israelites promised to obey whatever they heard. Not all agreed with this interpretation and Chanina b. Dosa (ca. 60 A.D.) felt that one's actions and good deeds must take precedence over study.[76]

Elisha b. Avuyah's parables in Avot Derabbi Nathan illustrates the importance of having good deeds as well as study. The parables seem to suggest that good deeds are more important than study or at least that they must accompany study. A danger was present that some sages might emphasize study to the neglect of practice.[77]

THE TWO BUILDERS

> R. Elisha b. Avuyah said: A man who has good deeds to his credit and has also studied much Torah, to what is he like? To one who builds [a structure and lays] stones below [for the foundation] and bricks above, so that however much water may collect at the side it will not wash it away. But the man who has no good deeds to his credit, though he has studied Torah, to what is he like? To one who builds [a structure and lays] bricks first [for the foundation] and then stones above, so that even if only a little water collects it at once undermines it.[78]

Elisha b. Avuyah's examples and Jesus' Parable of the Two Builders have a number of common elements. I. Abrahams noted, "All authorities are agreed that there can have been no direct, literary borrowing by the later Rabbis from the books of the New Testament."[79] Indeed it seems unlikely that the parables of Jesus or of Elisha b. Avuyah could have directly influenced one another. It seems overly simplistic to consider *only* the question of dates between Elisha b. Avuyah and Jesus or the time of the final compilation of the gospels and that of Avot Derabbi Nathan. Nor should the importance of the time difference be minimized. Nonetheless the parables are too close to one another to be completely independent. However, were Elisha b. Avuyah's parable a secondary development from Jesus' illustration one would certainly expect that the parables would be more similar to one another and for the rabbinic version to betray signs of embellishment. The rabbinic version is shorter and conforms to the other parables in this chapter of Avot Derabbi Nathan.[80] Perhaps it is wise to recognize the fact that there is a third intermediate stage in the transmission of these parallel parables that connects the world in which Jesus operated with the sphere of the parable of Elisha b. Avuyah. Insufficient evidence has survived to speak with absolute certainty about this intermediate stage but it represents a common stream of Jewish thought that links Jesus with the world of rabbinic learning, the love of man and the love of his Creator.

Jesus addresses the problem of hearing and obedience. It is certainly not far removed from the question of study and practice. However the gospel text does not ask which is greater. Jesus challenges his audience to hear his words and obey them. Elisha b. Avuyah on the other hand addresses the necessity of practicing one's teaching. Learning is not a sufficient foundation; one must put study into action. Both sets of examples employ the image of a man building a house that must withstand the water. Instead of sand and stone, Elisha b. Avuyah speaks of one who lays his foundation with stones before building with bricks. The bricks are not suitable for the foundation of the house.[81]

The rabbinic and gospel parables are separated by time but both come from a common milieu and share a similar theme. The preamble in Jesus' Parable of the Two Builders asks for obedience to the words of Jesus. In Luke 6:46 the text ἀκούων μου τῶν λογῶν points to the supreme authority Jesus placed upon his teachings and the urgency of obedience to his message and also demonstrates his high self-awareness.[82] Are there eschatological implications for Jesus' parable or should one seek only a more direct practical application? Should it be connected to a call to repentance in order to enter the kingdom of heaven movement? Could God's reign be realized if one responded to the challenge of the teaching of Jesus? Jesus contrasts the actions of the wise to those of the foolish and his challenge conveyed a current urgency with the reality of the present and should not be pushed into the distant eschatological future. Elisha b. Avuyah's parable develops a similar motif—the two builders lay two different foundations. The application is parallel. The disciple who is obedient and practices what he has learned builds upon a solid foundation and his house will never be destroyed even by powerful currents of water. The motif is quite similar to R. Eleazar b. Azaryah's illustration in Pirke Avot 3:17 which is also derived from the same milieu of Jewish learning.[83] One's wisdom should be exceeded only by one's good deeds. It seems that both the gospel illustration and Elisha b. Avuyah's parable have been formed from the same *Gattung* and are not so distant cousins employing similar images to communicate specific themes. At least both seem to be derived—*either* directly *or* indirectly—from the common heritage of Jewish learning which flourished during the days when the Temple stood. One feels the urgency of the message to respond to the divine call and to build upon the rock.

The Parable of the Laborers in the Vineyard Matthew 20:1–16

The Parable of the Laborers in the Vineyard appears only in Matthew's gospel. It appears after Jesus' saying, "But many that are first will be last, and the last first" (Matthew 19:30).[84] Hence in the context of Matthew's gospel, Jesus is discussing the rewards of discipleship and in many ways the parable contradicts the idea that Jesus' followers who have abandoned all to be his disciples will receive more reward than others (see Matthew 19:29–30; Mark 10:29–31; Luke 18:29–30). If the first are last and the last first then everyone receives the same wage. The parable is cast in the difficult economic conditions where many laborers are without work.[85] The climax of Jesus' parable appears in the explanation of the householder. A number of rabbinic parables contain similar motifs.[86] The interpersonal relationships between a land owner and his hired workers would have been an everyday topic of discussion. As has often been pointed out, after the completion of the refurbishing of the Temple rather than sending 18,000 laborers who worked on the project into unemployment, a measure was taken to insure that they continued to work. Josephus explained, "Moreover, owing to their fear of the Romans, they did not want to have any money that was kept on deposit. Hence, out of regard for the workmen and choosing to expend their treasures upon them—for if anyone worked for one hour of the day, he at once received his pay for this . . ."[87] This generous policy was an early form of welfare and indeed recalls the situation described in Jesus' parable.

In the parable, the householder hires workers and agrees to pay them a denarius for a day's work. Much later in the day he hires other laborers and promises to pay what is fair. At the end of the day he begins to pay the workers from the last to the first. All receive one denarius. The ones who worked all day thought that they would receive more than their original agreement because the householder had paid the other workers a denarius even though they had not labored the entire day. The householder, in his generosity, had paid equal wages to all his workers. What was the original function and purpose of this illustration? It seems to be derived from the better sources of the synoptics even though it was not preserved by the other evangelists. Sometimes the study of common motifs in rabbinic and gospel parables can elucidate the original setting of an illustration and throw light upon its message.

Two parallel parables in rabbinic literature are closely related to Jesus' illustration.[88] Morton Smith has classified one as a parallel of meaning but noted the close connection between Sifra on Leviticus 26:6 (Weiss, 111a) and Matthew 20:14–30.[89] The similarity between Jesus' Parable of the Laborers in the Vineyard and R. Zeira's illustration in the Jerusalem Talmud was so great that Jeremias proposed that the gospel parable was the source of the later rabbinic parable.[90] Smith was referring to the anonymous Parable of the Laborer who Worked Many Days from the midrash Sifra. Jeremias does not refer to the example from Sifra even though it would be considered antecedent to the illustration in the Jerusalem Talmud. In the Jerusalem Talmud, R. Zeira's parable formed part of a funeral eulogy designed to comfort and to explain a very complex question: Why should a young scholar die at the age of twenty-eight before having lived a full life? This illustration was already noted by John Lightfoot (1658) who used it to illustrate Jesus' Parable of the Laborers in the Vineyard.[91] Wünsche also cited the parable as well as the more recent commentator McNeile.[92] In the Jerusalem Talmud, R. Zeira (ca. 300 A.D.) grappled with the question of why the promising young scholar R. Bun bar Chiya died in his youth at age twenty-eight. In answer to this question he offered a parable as an explanation.

THE INDUSTRIOUS LABORER
(j. Berachot 5c, chap. 2, hal. 8)

> To what may R. Bun bar Chiya be compared? To a king who hired many laborers. One of them was extremely industrious in his work. What did the king do? He took him and walked with him the length and width [of the vineyard].[93] In the evening the laborers came to take their wages. But [the king] gave a full wage to [the man with whom he had walked]. The laborers murmured and complained, "We worked all day long, but [the king] has given this one who only worked two hours a full wage like us." The king answered them, "He has done more in two hours than what you did for the entire day!" Thus though R. Bun labored in Torah only twenty-eight years, he studied more than a mature scholar could have studied in a hundred.

The parable is very similar to the gospel text. After noting the similarities between the rabbinic and gospel parables, Jeremias writes, "It raises the question whether Jesus had made use of a Jewish parable and recast it, or whether R. Ze'era used a parable of Jesus, perhaps without being aware of its source. We can assert with a probability bordering on certainty that the priority belongs to Jesus . . ."[94] Both Jesus' parable and that of R. Zeira make use of the motif of the workers in the vineyard. The colorful picture of the workers murmuring about their wages is developed in both parables. In the rabbinic parable, one of the workers is more industrious and does more work in less time than the rest of the laborers. This element is not even alluded to in Jesus' illustration. Nevertheless the time element is present in both, for the industrious worker only did two hours work in the rabbinic illustration and the laborers who were hired late in Jesus' parable did not put in a full day's work. However nothing is said in Matthew concerning the outstanding achievements of the late comers. They simply did not work as long as the others—but received the same wage because of the generosity of the householder. So while there are many similarities, one also encounters striking differences. Jeremias arrives at far-reaching conclusions on the basis of the differences. He concludes, "Thus in this apparently trivial detail lies the difference between two worlds: the world of merit, and the world of grace; the law contrasted with the gospel."[95] However R. Zeira was trying to make a point. The illustration had been adapted to praise the achievements of R. Bun bar Chiya. The parable would hardly have been suitable for the occasion if it did not contain an industrious laborer. Are the differences between the two illustrations formulated on distinct theologies of law and grace? As Montefiore pointed out, both teach merit, grace, and reward.[96] However the differences would be better understood in light of the different contexts and settings of the parables. Furthermore the closely related illustration from Sifra which is parallel to R. Zeira's parable must also be considered.

THE LABORER WHO WORKED MANY DAYS
(Sifra on Lev. 26:5, Weiss, 111a)

> "And I will have regard for you" (Leviticus 26:9). They tell a parable. To what may the matter be compared? To a king who hired many laborers. One laborer was there who had done work for the king many days. The laborers came to take their wages and that laborer was among them. The king said to that laborer, "I will have regard for you. These many laborers have done little work and therefore I will pay them a minimum wage. But you have a great reward which I will add up for you in the future." Thus Israel seeks their reward in the present world from before the Omnipresent. The nations of the world likewise seek their reward from before Him. But the Omnipresent says to Israel, "My children, I will have regard for you. These nations of the world have done only a little work for me, and I will give them a minor recompense. But you have a great reward which I will add up for you in the future." As it was said, "I will have regard for you" (Leviticus 26:9).[97]

The darshan is dealing with the passage from Leviticus, "And I will give peace in the land, and you shall lie down and none shall be afraid; and I shall remove evil beasts from the land and the sword shall not go through your land. . . . And I will have regard for you . . ." (26:6–9). He saw reference to the day in the future when the wild beast will live in harmony with its prey.[98] God will have regard for Israel and the time of recompense will come. Both Israel and the nations of the world will receive their reward. However Israel is like a workman who had faithfully labored for his master many days. Israel's reward is growing and God will calculate their great recompense in the future. In this illustration one again discovers the motif of laborers in the vineyard. Here the laborers do not complain because one worker is promised a greater wage, but like the illustration of R. Zeira in the Jerusalem Talmud the worker is rewarded for his special achievements—in this case because of his many days of service. The two rabbinic parables are more closely related to one another than they are to the illustration from Matthew. Nevertheless all three have employed a similar motif to teach different themes in each individual context.

The idea of merit and reward is contained in all three illustrations. Jeremias seems to have overlooked the main theme of R. Zeira's illustration because he was searching for a great theological difference between grace and merit. Are these parables derived from two very different worlds? Jesus also spoke of man's reward and the parable of the laborers in the vineyard contains the notion that men receive recompense. The idea of measure for measure is not foreign to Jesus of the gospels and a number of passages use the word *misthos.* An interesting text in Midrash Psalms depicts Solomon the wise as asking God, "When a king hires good laborers who perform their work well and he pays them their wage—what praise does he merit? When is he worthy of praise? When he hires incompetent laborers who do not do their work properly and yets pays them their full wage!"[99] Hence the grace of God becomes a central theme in rabbinic thought. Flusser noted the parable attributed to the tana, R. Simeon ben Eleazar (ca. 190 A.D.) which is closely connected to Sifra on Leviticus 26:6 (Weiss, 111a) and the parable of R. Zeira in the Jerusalem Talmud.[100] The parable is introduced by noting that the righteous uphold the world through their good deeds.

THE TWO WORKERS
(Semachot Derabbi Chiyah 3:2)

How do the righteous come [into the world]? Through love, because they uphold the world through their good deeds. How do they depart—also through love. R. Simeon ben Eleazar told a parable. To what may the matter be compared? To a king who hired two workers. The first worked all day and received one denarius. The second worked only one hour and yet he also received a denarius. Which one was more beloved? Not the one who worked one hour and received a denarius! Thus Moses our teacher served Israel one hundred and twenty years and Samuel [served them] only fifty two. Nevertheless both are equal before the Omnipresent! As it is said, "Then the LORD said to me, 'Though Moses and Samuel stood before me'" (Jeremiah 15:1); and thus He said, "Moses and Aaron were among his priests, Samuel was among those who called on his name" (Psalm 99:6); concerning them and others like them He says, "Sweet is the sleep of the laborer whether he eats little or much" (Ecclesiastes 5:12).[101]

Thus Moses and Samuel receive the same reward even though Moses served much longer. The rabbinic parable illustrates that God's grace was extended in equal measure to both leaders who served Israel even though Moses actually achieved more. The reward is secondary to obedience. Antigonus of Soko taught that one must not serve his master in order to receive his reward (Avot 1:3; cf. Samuel the Little's parable in b. Taanit 25b). Another rabbinic parable (with its parallels) illustrates the idea that God did not reveal the reward for observing each particular commandment in order that some laws would not be observed to the neglect of others—but rather God sought man's total obedience to all that he had commanded.[102] Nevertheless one is left with the innovative parable in Matthew's gospel where the laborers are all paid the same wage even though they did not all deserve it. It is difficult to understand the example without knowing its historical context. One may question Matthew's placing of the parable here. But one possible application of the parable could be seen in the tension between the religious and the secular. One aspect of Jesus' ministry was the call of society's outcasts to repentance. He attacked John the Baptist's critics. The publicans and harlots followed John but the outwardly religious refused. God's grace will be extended to the late-comers in the same way as it had been extended to those who had lived righteous lives. Both obeyed the divine challenge and made a commitment even if the late comers received the call at a later time. A similar tension can be detected in Jesus' parable of the Pharisee and the Publican who both go to the Temple to pray (Luke 18:9–14). The outcast's prayer is received because he humbled himself by pleading for God's mercy. The sociological problem of welcoming the person with a bad reputation into the fold is one that exists in many religious circles. In many ways, it has a universal appeal and application. Jesus' parable is designed to illustrate the character of God and his unlimited generosity in giving an equal wage to all. The emphasis is on the grace and generosity of the landowner in contrast to the grumblers who though they received the agreed wage were not generous but had an "evil eye" in regard to the late-comers and in greed demanded more payment for themselves.[103]

R. Zeira's parable was an eulogy at the funeral of his colleague, the parable of the Laborer Who Worked for Many Days in Sifra deals with the final rewards of Israel and the nations of the world, R. Simeon ben Eleazar's parable illustrated divine grace in equal measure to both Moses and the less deserving Samuel, and it may be assumed that a possible context of Jesus' parable spoke of the outcasts receiving their reward. All the parables contain the motif of laborers who work and then have to receive their wage from the owner. They develop somewhat different plots in order to stress different points. The basic story is the same yet the outcome of each of the mini-dramas is different. After all, even murder mysteries have many common elements whether the butler did it or not. Is it productive to search for dependence of one parable on the other?

Instead of searching for dependence, one should study the *Gattung* of the story parable. Would R. Zeira be required to refer to Matthew in order to formulate his Parable of the Industrious Laborer and to provide an eulogy at the funeral of R. Bun bar Chiya? It seems probable that a number of early Jewish parables employed the motifs of vineyard (and/or *pardes*), laborers, master and reward. The theme and plot reflect the historical reality of the period. Money, the workplace, the boss, the foreman, the owner and wage disputes are all elements of an interesting story especially for workers in a time when men stand in the marketplace anxiously looking for jobs for unskilled laborers. The earliest known references to such illustrative parables are those preserved in the gospels. The similar analogies in rabbinic literature indicate that the genre was more widely used. The parabolist could take different motifs and develop his illustration for his own purposes. Jesus' Parable of the Laborers in the Vineyard is innovative and ingenious, as it illustrates God's grace in a minidrama cast in the workplace where a wage dispute is resolved. According to the Jerusalem Talmud, R. Zeira constructed a similar illustration for a specific purpose and the result is an imaginative story that dealt with a very complex religious question. In short the parables are derived from the same milieu and should not be viewed as representing the opposite worlds of merit and of grace as Jeremias proposed. Parables take common situations from everyman's experience and lead the listeners on a collision course with a specific message often concerning man and his relationship to his neighbor and to God. Often they address issues of great depth and complexity but treat them in remarkable clarity and simplicity. The parables of Jesus must be examined in the larger context of the Jewish environment of instruction and education that gave birth to a genre which is not fully paralleled elsewhere.

Notes

1) See especially the chapters on "The Parables and Talmudic Literature" and "The Parables and the Gospels" as well as "The Parables and Their Context."

2) See especially the discussion of Flusser on the history of parabolic teaching, idem, *Yahudut Umekorot Hanatzrut,* pp. 202–209 and also *Die rabbinischen Gleichnisse,* pp. 141–160.

3) These suggestions must remain exemplary, and of course biblical parallels like Nathan's story must also be taken into consideration (2 Samuel 12:1–4). Compare now the historical and literary analysis by David Daube, "Nathan's Parable," *Novum Testamentum* 24 (1982), pp. 275–288. Daube suggested that the illustration may have originally been connected to Saul, Michal and David instead of to David, Bathsheba and Uriah the Hittite (ibid, p. 281). Cf. also the work of H. Lockyer, *All the Parables of the Bible* (London: Pickering and Ingles, 1976), pp. 27–122. One is hard pressed to accept Lockyer's definition of a parable; nevertheless he has brought together a helpful collection of sayings and examples from the Old Testament.

4) B. Perry, *Babrius and Phaedrus* (Cambridge, Massachusetts: Harvard University Press, 1975), pp. xii–xiii.

5) Schwarzbaum, *The Mishle Shu'alim (Fox Parables) of Rabbi Berechiah Ha-Nakdan,* p. xix.

6) J. Jacobs, "Aesop's Fables among the Jews," *The Jewish Encyclopedia,* vol. 1, pp. 221–222. Jacobs writes, "Of about thirty fables found in the Talmud and in midrashic literature, twelve resemble those that are common to both Greek and Indian fable; six are parallel to those found only in Indian fable (Fables of Kybises); and six others can be paralleled in Greek, but have not hitherto been traced to India. Where similar fables exist in Greece, India, and in the Talmud, the Talmudic form approaches more nearly the Indian, whenever this differs from Greek."

7) See Schwarzbaum, *The Mishle Shu'alim (Fox Parables) of Rabbi Berechiah Ha-Nakdan,* pp. 163–167, Perry, *Babrius and Phaedrus,* p. 50, Jacobs, p. 221 and Flusser, *Die rabbinischen Gleichnisse,* pp. 52f. See the conclusion to the beautiful story about R. Simeon b. Eleazar, Avot De rabbi Nathan, ver. a, chap. 41; b. Taanit 20b; Kallah Rabbati 7:1 and cf. b. Sanhedrin 105b–106a and Derech Eretz Rabbah 4:1 (Higger, vol. 1, pp. 125f).

8) Thus Flusser, *Die rabbinischen Gleichnisse,* pp. 52f. See the preceding note.

9) Exodus Rabbah 5:21 (Shinan, p. 179), Tanchuma, Vaera, 6 (Buber's edition 4) and also quoted as Tanchuma in the Yalkut, vol. 1, remez 176. See Bacher, *Die Agada der Palästinensischen Amoräer,* vol. 3, p. 439 and idem, *Agadat Amore Eretz Yisrael,* vol. 3, part 3, pp. 33–34. Compare some of the similar elements and motifs in "The Wolf and the Shepherds" (Perry, p. 515), "The Lamb who gives himself to the Shepherd instead of the Butcher" (Perry, p. 518) and "The Sheep who Prefers to be Sacrificed as to be the Wolf's Dinner" (Perry, p. 173).

10) Genesis Rabbah 64:10 (Albeck, p. 712, Soncino translation, p. 580) and P. Fiebig noted the fable, idem, *Rabbinische Gleichnisse* (Leipzig: J.C. Hinrichs'sche Buchhandlung, 1929), pp. 19–20. See especially Schwarzbaum, *The Mishle Shu'alim (Fox Parables) of Rabbi Berechiah Ha-Nakdan,* pp. 51–56 where he discusses Rabbi Berechiah's fable of "The Wolf and the Crane."

11) Schwarzbaum notes, " . . . Rabbi Joshua Ben Hananiah, who in the year 118 A.D. tried to calm and pacify an assembly of Palestine Jews at Beth Rimmon who were embittered by an abrogation of the promise of the Emperor to rebuild the Temple. Just as Cyrus the Great employed a fable in order to teach the Ionian and Aeolian Greeks an adequate lesson (cf. Herodotus I 141), or just as the well-known (fictitious) Roman, Menenius Agrippa, used a fable as a political weapon, in order to convince the plebians of their error when they went on strike and refused to collaborate with the patricians (cf. Livy II 32, 9–11), so, according to the old *Midrash Genesis Rabbah,* LXIV 10, did Rabbi Joshua Ben Haraniah. He availed himself of the old fable (current in Indian oral tradition long before it was incorporated into Jataka No. 308. . . ."

12) See notes 10 and 11 above. Schwarzbaum has cited the Indian version as the earliest (Jataka 308, H.T. Francis and E.J. Thomas, *Jataka Tales,* Bombay, 1957, pp. 136–137). In the Indian parallel the bird places a stick in the mouth of the lion to ensure that the lion will not snap shut his powerful jaws when the bone has been removed (Schwarzbaum, *Mishle Shu'alim (Fox Parables) of Rabbi Berechiah Ha-Nakdan,* pp. 52–53). See also Babrius, "Dr. Heron's Fee" (no. 94, Perry, pp. 115–116) and Phaedrus, "The Wolf and the Crane" (no. 1.8, Perry, p. 201 and cf. Perry, p. 451, no. 156).

13) See the expanded version of Jotham's fable in *The Biblical Antiquities of Philo,* XXXVII:2ff, trans. M.R. James (New York: KTAV, 1971), pp. 185f. Compare also the fable of the lion and the beasts in the forest, *The Biblical Antiquities* XLVII:4–6 (James, pp. 207–208).

14) The story appears in the Tosefta and has many parallels, tos. Yom Hakipurim 1:12 (Lieberman, p. 224 and see idem, *Tosefta Kefshutah,* part 4, pp. 735–736). Lieberman suggests that the R. Zadok who appears in the text might possibly be identified with the Pharisee Saddok who is mentioned in Josephus, *Ant.* 18:3–4 (thus Lieberman, *Tosefta Kefshutah,* p. 736; this is also the opinion of Hyman, *Toldot Tannaim Veamoraim,* vol. 1, p. 201, but the suggestion is by necessity conjectural). The story also appears in tos. Shebuot 1:4; Sifre Numbers 161 (Horovitz, p. 222); j. Yoma 39d, chap. 2, hal. 2; b. Yoma 23a and cf. m. Yoma 2:2. In the Mishnah the story has been altered and instead of being

stabbed, the priest breaks his leg. The other parallels are very similar one to the other and the story ends with the same basic conclusion, "The father of the young man came and found him still in convulsions. He said: 'May he be an atonement for you. My son is still in convulsions and the knife has not become unclean.' [His remark] comes to teach you that the cleanness of their vessels was of greater concern to them even than the shedding of blood." See the book by G. Cornfeld, *The Historical Jesus* (London: Macmillan, 1982) in which Flusser collaborated with Cornfeld, "The fastidious care over the application of the rules of purity around the Temple's precincts assumed such exaggerated forms as to call for a critical observation to the effect that 'the impurity of knives was considered a greater sin than the shedding of blood' (*Sifre,* Num. 35:34). The facts related in this connection can be compared to the story of the Good Samaritan (Luke 10:29–36)" (ibid, p. 58).

15) See J. Mann, "Jesus and the Sadducean Priests: Luke 10:25–37," *Jewish Quarterly Review* 6 (1914), pp. 415–422 and preceding note. Mann connected the wounded man in the parable with the laws concerning a dead man found without someone to bury him *(met mitzvah).* The *nomikos* who asked Jesus the question for which the parable was the answer could then be identified as a Sadducean priest who rejected the Pharisaic teaching concerning the *met mitzvah.* Mann reasoned that the priest and the *levite* thought that the man was dead, but refused to bury him as the oral interpretation of the law required (see m. Nazir 7:1 b. Nazir 43b, j. Nazir 56a chap. 6, hal. 1, as mentioned in Jos. *Contra Ap.* 2:29, 211 and see Mann, p. 418). A Sadducee would have rejected the oral law and passed the dead man with a clear conscience. However the parable states that the man was "half dead" which may be a Greek rendering of the Hebrew word *goses,* meaning that he was in agony and would probably die (cf. b. Kidushin 71b; b. Gitin 28a, Billerbeck, vol. 2, p. 182). The priest and Levite would be required to help a dying man who was in agony even if they risked becoming ritually unclean when he died (cf. Semachot 1:1, Higger, p. 97). In any case the priest and the levite passed the wounded man and a Samaritan, an enemy of the people helped him. It should be kept in mind that the Samaritans also had similar laws concerning ritual cleanness and contact with the dead, and like the Sadducees, the Samaritans rejected the oral law. Specialists in Samaritan beliefs during the period should be consulted on the questions pertaining to the Samaritan laws of uncleanness.

15a) See the discussion of this point by K. Bailey, *Through Peasant Eyes,* p. 52, "The Samaritan, by allowing himself to be identified, runs a grave risk of having the family of the wounded man seek *him* out to take vengeance upon him. . . . An American cultural equivalent would be a Plains Indian in 1875 walking into Dodge City with a scalped cowboy on his horse, checking into a room over the local saloon, and staying the night to take care of him." Bailey's analogy probably exaggerates the point. Nonetheless by helping the dying man, the Samaritan placed himself at great risk, not only by possible implication in the crime and revenge from family, but also from the apparent danger of the criminals who attacked the helpless man and left him to die.

16) See note 14 above.

17) See Mann, note 15 above.

18) In the similar story about R. Eleazar ben Shamua, the sage treated the shipwreck victim with great honor and provided him with clothing, food and money (Ecclesiastes Rabbah 11:1). This action proved to be of advantage later when the shipwreck victim turned out to be the king. Compare also the story about Abba Tachnah who risked what he owned in order to help a man who was afflicted with boils who lay at the side of the road (Ecclesiastes Rabbah 9:7; see also the story of Nachum Eish Gimzo in j. Peah 21b, chap. 8, hal. 9). Of course the example of the Good Samaritan is told as a parable and it seemed to emphasize that one must love even one's enemies. In order to understand what a neighbor is, one must be a neighbor. Cf. notes 14 and 15 above and see also Flusser, *Die rabbinischen Gleichnisse,* pp. 70f.

19) Cf. for instance the second century A.D. papyrus letter from the wayward son Antonis Longus to his mother Nilus, in Adolf Deissmann, *Light from the Ancient East* (Grand Rapids: Baker Book House, reprint, 1980), pp. 186–191.

20) Plato, *Republic,* 8,554,B (Paul Shorery, *The Republic,* Harvard University Press: Cambridge, Massachusetts, 1980, vol. 2, pp. 274–275 and see note c on p. 275). Cf. also the parallels in A. Otto, *Die Sprichwörter der Römer* (Hidesheim: Georg Olms, 1965), p. 60 and compare Romans 2:19 with Matthew 15:14 and Luke 6:39. The author expresses his thanks to David Flusser who called his attention to these references.

21) Interestingly Luke (6:39) refers to the proverb as a *parabolē* and this reflects his understanding of the term in Luke 4:23.

22) See the Hebrew text, M. Segal, *Sefer Ben Sira Hashalem* (Jerusalem: Bialik Foundation, 1972), p. 125. Segal connected the text in Ben Sira to Matthew 7:13 (ibid, p. 127).

23) M. Stone, *The Testament of Abraham* (Missoula: Society of Biblical Literature, 1972), p. 25 and see the new critical edition of the text, F. Schmidt, *Le Testament grec d'Abraham* (Tübingen, J.C.B. Mohr, 1986), p. 128. Cf. Charlesworth, *The Old Testament Pseudepigrapha* vol.

1, p. 888 (trans. E.P. Sanders). See Sanders' notes on the text. He correctly noted the connection of the theme of the two ways in the Testament of Abraham with the Didache 1:1 and Sifre Deuteronomy 53. Sanders observed, "The verbatim agreement between this passage and Mt 7:13f., however, is marked. . . . The compact and balanced form of Mt could hardly have been derived from TAb [Testament of Abraham]; and in view of other evidence of verbatim agreement between TAb A and the NT, the dependence of the former on the latter here seems indisputable" (ibid).

24) Stone, pp. 72–75.

25) K. Lake, *The Apostolic Fathers,* vol. 1, p. 308 and see the Latin version, H. Lietzmann, *Die Didache* (Bonn: A. Marcus und E. Weber's Verlag, 1912), p. 3. See Flusser, *Yahadut Umekorot Hanatzrut,* pp. 235–252 and see also J. Licht, "An Analysis of the Treatise on the Two Spirits in DSD," *Scripta Hierosolymitana* IV (Jerusalem: Magnes Press, 1965), pp. 88–99.

26) Charlesworth, *The Old Testament Pseudepigrapha,* vol. 1, p. 152 (trans. F.I. Andersen).

27) The Manual of Discipline 3:17–21, J. Licht, *Megilat Haserachim* (Jerusalem: Bialik Institute, 1965), pp. 91–93 and A.R.C. Leaney, *The Rule of Qumran and Its Meaning* (Philadelphia: Westminster, 1966), pp. 36–56. One should note the parallelism between the two spirits and the "ways of light" and the "ways of darkness." See the beginning of the next section of the Manual of Discipline (4:2), "These are their ways in the world . . ." See also A. Dupont-Sommer, *The Jewish Sect of Qumran and the Essenes* (New York: Macmillan, 1955), pp. 118–130 who noted that the two spirits are mentioned in Zoroastrian thought (quotations from the Gathas, in the Avesta, Yasna 45:2 and Yasna 30:3,4,5,10,11; Dupont-Sommer, ibid, pp. 118–119). Here it is not possible to enter into all of the implications of the relationship between the Essene world view, Paulinism and the teachings of Jesus, but cf. Flusser, "The Dead Sea Sect and Pre-Pauline Christianity," *Scripta Hierosolymitana* (Jerusalem: Magnes Press, 1965), vol. 4, pp. 215–266.

28) Testament of Asher 1:3f *(duo hodous)* Charlesworth, *The Old Testament Pseudepigrapha* vol. 1, p. 816–817 (trans. E.P. Sanders) and de Jonge, *The Testaments of the Twelve Patriarchs,* p. 135.

29) Testament of Judah 20:1f *(duo pneumata)* Charlesworth, *The Old Testament Pseudepigrapha* vol. 1, p. 800 (trans. E.P. Sanders) and de Jonge, *The Testaments of the Twelve Patriarchs,* p. 73.

30) John T. Fitzgerald and L. Michael White, *The Tabula of Cebes* (Chico: Scholars Press, 1983), pp. 84–87. See the discussion in, E. Klos-

termann, *Das Matthäusevangelium* (Tübingen: J.C.B. Mohr, 1971), pp. 68–69.

31) Sifre Deuteronomy 53 (Finkelstein, pp. 120–121); Midrash Hagadol on Deuteronomy 11:26 (Fisch, p. 241); Midrash Tannaim on Deuteronomy 11:26 (Hoffmann, p. 45); Yalkut Hamachiri on Proverbs 24:19; Yalkut vol. 1, remez 875. See the mention of the two ways in the continuation of the passage in Sifre Deuteronomy 54 (Finkelstein, p. 122); Midrash Tannaim on Deuteronomy 11:28 (Hoffmann, p. 46), on Deuteronomy 13:16 (Hoffman, p. 70); Midrash Hagadol on Deuteronomy 11:28 (Fisch, p. 243) on Deuteronomy 13:16 (Fisch, p. 280) and cf. Mechilta Derabbi Ishmael on Exodus 14:29 (Horovitz, pp. 112–113, Lauterbach, vol. 1, pp. 248–249) and Mechilta Derabbi Simeon bar Yochai on Exodus 14:29 (Epstein, p. 68).

32) See S.C.E. Legg, *Novum Testamentum Graece Secundum Textum Westcotto-Hortianum Evangelium Secundum Matthaeum* (Oxford: Clarendon Press, 1940), on Mt. 20:28. Cf. B. Metzger, *A Textual Commentary on the Greek New Testament* (New York: United Bible Societies, 1975), p. 53. The text has been discussed by J. Jeremias, *The Unknown Sayings of Jesus* (London: SPCK, 1958), pp. 6–7. Jeremias views Matthew 20:28 as a secondary variation of Luke 14:8–10.

33) Ibid. The introduction in Matthew, "But seek to increase from that which is small, and from the greater to become less," is a floating logion styled on similar sayings (Mt. 20:27, 23:11, Mk. 10:44, 9:35, Lk. 22:27, 9:48). It is designed to connect the passage with the preceding pericope. In the Matthean addition, no marriage is mentioned. The people are only invited to dine and compare a number of early witnesses in Luke 14:8 where the mention of the wedding does not appear. One notices a number of differences in the wording between the Matthean addition and Luke 14:8–10. For example, Luke employs the words *prōtoklisian, entimoteros* and *keklēmenos, keklēkōs* in comparison to the Matthean addition which has *exechontas topous, endoxoteros* and *deipnokletōr.* In Luke 14:8, both the eminent guest and the host come and ask the less important guest to move to a lower place. However in the Matthean addition it is only the host who approaches him. In any case the text is closely related in Matthew's context, and T.W. Manson correctly noted, "The fact that it was interpolated just there is itself evidence that the parable was rightly understood in the early days of the Church," idem, *Sayings,* p. 279.

34) See note 21 above. Cf. Jeremias, *Parables,* pp. 20 and 192 and Marshall, *Luke,* p. 581. It is doubtful if the word *parabolē* should be translated as table manners in this text as suggested by Jeremias and Marshall.

35) See Billerbeck, vol. 1, p. 916; C.G. Montefiore, *Rabbinic Literature and Gospel Teachings* (New York: KTAV, 1970), p. 353 and Jeremias, *Parables,* pp. 191–193. More recently Fitzmyer has asked whether the New Testament may have influenced rabbinic thought (idem, *Luke,* vol. 2, p. 1047).

36) Leviticus Rabbah 1:5 (Margulies, pp. 16f). Compare also the words of R. Jose in Avot Derabbi Nathan ver. a, chap. 11, ver. b, chap. 22; Ben Azai in Avot Derabbi Nathan ver. a, chap. 22, and also ver. b, 33; R. Tanchuma in Exodus Rabbah 45:5; b. Erubin 13b; Tanchuma Vayikra 1 (Buber's edition, 2); Yalkut, vol. 1, remez 427, vol. 2, remez 961. Both sayings are attributed to Hillel in "Midrash Hallel" *Bet Hamidrash* A. Jellinek (Jerusalem: Wahrmann, 1967) vol. 5, p. 91. In Midrash Hallel the parallel comes as an interpretation of Psalm 113:5–6 and is attributed to Hillel, "My self exaltation is my self-humiliation, [my self humiliation] is my self-exaltation. Thus Hillel used to say, Ascend below and descend above." Cf. Letter of Aristeas 263, Swete, *An Introduction to the Old Testament in Greek,* p. 589. Charles, *The Apocrypha and Pseudepigrapha of the Old Testament,* vol. 2, p. 117.

37) On the midrashic interpretation of the verse citation from Psalm 113:5–6, see Margulies' note, Leviticus Rabbah, vol. 1, p. 17. See also preceding note for the parallels and cf. Bacher, *Die Agada der Tannaiten,* vol. 1, p. 5 and see note 6, idem, *Agadot Hatannaim* vol. 1, part 1, pp. 4–5, note 6.

38) Avot Derabbi Nathan, ver. a, chap. 25, ver. b, chap. 33 and cf. Exodus Rabbah 45:5; Yalkut Shimeoni vol. 1, remez 227, vol. 2, remez 961 and Tanchuma Vayikra 1 (Buber's edition, 2) where the passage is interpreted midrashically concerning the proverbial humility of Moses by the Amora R. Tanchuma. In the Letter of Aristeas (187) the distinguished guests are all seated according to their age (Swete, *An Introduction to the Old Testament in Greek,* p. 583, R.J.H. Shutt, "Letter of Aristeas," Charlesworth, ed., *The Old Testament Pseudepigrapha,* vol. 2, p. 25).

39) See note 36 above and Avot Derabbi Nathan, ver. a, chap. 11, ver. b. chap. 22; see the English translation, A. Cohen and I. Brodie, *The Minor Tractates of the Talmud* (London: Soncino Press, 1971), p. 68 and A. Saldarini, *The Fathers according to Rabbi Nathan a Translation and Commentary* (Leiden: Brill, 1975), 136–137, cf. notes 6 and 7.

40) Avot Derabbi Nathan, ver. a, chap. 11 and see the preceding note.

41) Sifre Deuteronomy 48 (Finkelstein, p. 113) and compare the parallel in Sifre Deuteronomy 41 (idem, p. 87). See also b. Nedarim 62a. In the parallel (Sifre Deut. 41) no mention of sitting in a prominent seat is

made; however the text employs the phrase " . . . in order that I would be called Rabbi . . ." and cf. Matthew 23:7. Thus in the parallel, instead of the word Sage, the word Rabbi appears. In its earlier meaning, the term *rav* referred to a lord or master and not to a rabbinical teacher of great learning (cf. Antigonus of Soko's words in Avot 1:3).

42) Sifre Deuteronomy 48 (Finkelstein, p. 114); Mishnat R. Eliezer, chap. 13 (H.G. Enelow, ed., New York: Bloch Publishing, 1933, p. 246); b. Nedarim 62a; the saying is anonymous in Masechet Yirat Chet chap. 2 (Higger, *Masechtot Zeirot,* Jerusalem: Mekor, 1970, pp. 75 and 83); Masechet Derech Eretz (Higger, vol. 1, p. 74). The text is discussed by Bacher, *Die Agada der Tannaiten,* vol. 1, p. 48, note 2 (idem, *Agadot Hatanaim,* vol. 1, part 1, p. 37, note 6). Cf. Avot 4:5.

43) Avot 2:8, Bacher, *Die Agada der Tannaiten,* vol. 1, pp. 25–26, (idem, *Agadot Hatanaim,* vol. 1, part 1, p. 19).

44) A. Wünsche, *Erläuterung der Evangelien* (Göttingen: Vandenhoeck & Ruprecht's Verlag, 1878), p. 458.

45) Ibid, p. 281. See the early parallel saying in Ahiqar 8:60, "If [yo]u wis[h] to be [*exalted*], my son, [*humble yourself before Shamash*], who humbles the [*exalted*] and [*exalts the humble*]" (J.M. Lindenberger, "Ahiqar," Charlesworth, *The Old Testament Pseudepigrapha,* vol. 2, p. 505).

46) See tos. Sucah 2:2ff and Lieberman's comments on the text in *Tosefta Kefshutah,* p. 854.

47) Derech Eretz Zuta chap. 9, and see the text prepared by A.J. Tawrogi, *Derech Erez Sutta* (Königsberg: E. Erlatis, 1885), p. 50 and cf. also with Higger, *Masechtot Derech Eretz,* vol. 1, pp. 131, 146, his English translation, vol. 2, pp. 52 and 55.

48) H.A.W. Meyer, *Critical and Exegetical Handbook to the Gospel of Luke* (Peabody, Massachusetts: Hendrickson, 1983, reprint of 1884 English edition, first German edition 1832), p. 442.

49) Jeremias, *Parables,* pp. 192–193.

50) Marshall, *Luke,* p. 583.

51) Fitzmyer, *Luke,* vol. 2, p. 1047.

52) Much of the material for consideration of this complex and sensitive question has been collected by T. Herford, *Christianity in Talmud and Midrash* (New York: KTAV, 1975) and cf. with the remarks of R. Abahu who lived in Caesarea about the time of Origen (j. Taanit 65b, chap. 2, hal. 2; Exodus Rabbah 29:5). Of the church fathers, only Jerome ever makes mention of the rabbis by name (Jerome, *Commentariorum in Esaiam* 8, 11–22, LXXII, p. 121; quoted by, A. Klijn and G. Reinink, *Patristic Evidence for Jewish-Christian Sects,* pp. 220–221).

53) Avot Derabbi Nathan, ver. a, chap. 11, ver. b, chap. 22; Midrash Hallel, *Bet Hamidrash,* vol. 5, p. 91 and see notes 36 and 38 above. See also Ahiqar 8:60, op. cit., note 45.

54) Ibid. It is easy to minimize the importance the sages placed upon humility and the proper approach to a life of industrious and productive study. Cf. the words of the Amora R. Joshua ben Levi who speaks about God the One on high who humbled Himself by descending to Mount Sinai to give the Torah to Moses (Pesikta Rabbati 21, Friedmann, p. 102a).

55) Luke 1:52 and cf. 1 QM 14:11 and see Flusser, "The Magnificat, the Benedictus and the War Scroll," *Judaism and the Origins of Christianity* (Jerusalem: Magnes Press, at the press).

56) See Jeremias, *New Testament Theology,* pp. 9ff.

57) See note 36 above. See especially, Flusser, "Hillel's Self-Awareness and Jesus" *Immanuel* 4 (1974), pp. 31–36.

58) Avot Derabbi Nathan ver. a, chap. 24, ver. b, chap. 35 and compare the English translations, Cohen and Brodie, *The Minor Tractates of the Talmud,* vol. 1, p. 119, J. Goldin, *The Fathers according to Rabbi Nathan,* p. 103 and Saldarini, *The Fathers according to Rabbi Nathan,* ver. b, p. 205. See Billerbeck, vol. 1, p. 469 and cf. Bacher, *Die Agada der Tannaiten,* vol. 1, pp. 432–433, idem, *Agadot Hatannaim,* vol. 1, part 2, pp. 141–142.

59) For bibliographical material cf. A. Segal, *Two Powers in Heaven* (Leiden: Brill, 1977), pp. 9ff. and D. Halperin, *The Merkabah in Rabbinic Literature* (New Haven: American Oriental Society, 1980), pp. 2f.

60) See Marshall, *Luke,* p. 81, who correctly saw the term as a reference to Jesus' messianic task. Fitzmyer, *Luke,* vol. 2, p. 644, attributes it to the "early community." See also the additional note at the conclusion of the article, Brad Young and David Flusser, "Messianic Blessings in Jewish and Christian Texts," in Flusser's book, *Judaism and the Origins of Christianity* (Jerusalem: Magnes, at the press).

61) Flusser has prepared an entire reconstruction of the passage which is most certainly correct, idem, "Two Anti-Jewish Montages in Matthew," pp. 39f. Nonetheless I do have one reservation concerning Flusser's placement of Matthew 7:21, "Not everyone who says to me, 'Lord, Lord,' shall enter the kingdom of heaven, but he who does the will of my Father who is in heaven." He positions it at the beginning of the passage concerning the eschatological judgment. Here it would be suggested that it is possible that this logion originally introduced the parable (as in Luke 6:46f) and set the stage for the contrast between the wise who hear and obey and the foolish man who built his house upon the

sand. The passage concerning the future eschatological judgment which also teaches against the dangers of a cult of personality would have started with the Hebraic phrase, רבים יאמרו לי ביום ההוא, from Matthew 7:22 πολλοὶ ἐροῦσίν μοι ἐν ἐκείνῃ τῇ ἡμέρᾳ (see Flusser's comments on the meaning of the passage and its reinterpretation in Matthew, ibid).

62) Thus also Harnack, *Sayings,* p. 72, " . . . the text of Matthew for the most part deserves the preference."

63) Flusser, *Yahadut Umekorot Hanatzrut,* pp. 169ff.

64) Cf. Harnack, *Sayings,* p. 74.

65) See the words of R. Eleazar b. Azariah in Avot 3:17. Cited also by Billerbeck, vol. 1, p. 469.

66) Cf. Wünsche, p. 110.

67) Harnack, *Sayings,* p. 73.

68) See Flusser, "Two Anti-Jewish Montages in Matthew," pp. 39–43 and note 61 above.

69) See note 82 below.

70) See the words of Chanina ben Dosa, Avot Derabbi Nathan ver. a, chap. 24, Avot 3:9, and cf. b. Nidah 70b.

71) See the discussion of G. Alon, *The Jews in their Land in the Talmudic Age* (Jerusalem: Magnes, 1984), p. 499 and H. Graetz, *Geschichte der Juden von den ältesten Zeiten bis zur Gegenwart* (Leipzig: Verlag von Oskar Leiner, 1908), vol. 4, pp. 155, and 428–430. Cf. also with b. Sanhedrin 74a and with note 3 on page 502 of the Soncino translation of the Talmud. See also Chaim Ryans, *Torah Umoser* (Jerusalem: Mosad Derav Kook, 1954), pp. 66–87. It may be asked whether Josephus was acquainted with the question concerning action and study in some form or another. At least he says that Moses combined both systems, the one which involves learning and the other which puts things learned into practice in one's everyday existence, idem, *Against Apion,* 2.16–17 (171–174). See Safrai, "Chasidim Veanshe Maaseh," pp. 144f.

72) Alon, *The Jews in their Land,* vol. 2, p. 499.

73) Sifre Deuteronomy 41 (Finkelstein, p. 85), j. Pesachim 30b, chap. 3, hal. 7; j. Chagigah 76c, chap. 1, hal. 7; b. Kidushin 40b.

74) Ibid. See Alon, *The Jews in their Land,* vol. 1, pp. 88–89, vol. 2, pp. 498–500 and Urbach, *The Sages,* vol. 1, pp. 606–610.

75) Mechilta Derabbi Simeon bar Yochai on Exodus 24:7 (Epstein, p. 221); Midrash Hagadol on Exodus 24:7 (Margulies, p. 554) and cf. Kasher, *Torah Shelemah,* on Exodus 24:7, vol. 19, p. 262.

76) Avot Derabbi Nathan, ver. a, chap. 24, Avot 3:9. See the work of Safrai concerning the Chasidim, idem, "Teaching of Pietists in Mishnaic Literature," *Journal of Jewish Studies* 16 (1965), pp. 15–33 and see

also G. Vermes, "Hanina ben Dosa," *Post-Biblical Jewish Studies* (Leiden: Brill, 1975), pp. 178–214.

77) Cf. with the story about R. Simeon bar Yochai who leaves study in order to visit the ill. When he finds a sick man cursing God, R. Simeon told him that he should be praying for help instead of cursing. The ill man asked that his ailment be transferred to R. Simeon. R. Simeon replied that he deserved such treatment because he left study in order to occupy himself with "worthless matters." Thus visiting the sick was not as important as the study of Torah. See Avot Derabbi Nathan, ver. a, chap. 41, and especially Schechter's notes where the better text is cited; the text is explained by Urbach, *The Sages,* vol. 1, pp. 606–607 and see vol. 2, p. 964, note 83.

78) See note 58 above.

79) Abrahams, *Studies,* vol. 1, p. 92.

80) In version a of Avot Derabbi Nathan, this chapter (34) preserves a collection of the heretic R. Elisha ben Avuyah's teachings which are marked by metaphors and parables. The teaching materials would be representative of the sage before he became a heretic and the lively style of his examples may be compared to that of R. Meir, R. Elisha ben Avuyah's disciple. A number of these sayings are partially paralleled in the preceding chapter and are attributed to others. Here it would seem that version a of Avot Derabbi Nathan (34) better captures the original vividness of the illustrations attributed to R. Elisha ben Avuyah than the parallels, and cf. Finkelstein, *Mevo Lemasechtot Avot Veavot Derabbi Natan* (New York: The Jewish Theological Seminary of America), pp. 79–80.

81) See Flusser, *Die rabbinischen Gleichnisse,* pp. 102–103.

82) The phrase "my words" in Matthew 7:24, 26 and Luke 6:47 requires careful examination. Flusser has convincingly demonstrated that the expression was secondarily proliferated in the texts of the synoptics apparently during the redaction stage of the compilation of the gospel texts (i.e. in the Synoptic Apocalypse, Luke 21:33; Mark 13:31; and Matthew 24:35, "Heaven and earth will pass away but my words will not pass away," see Flusser, *Die rabbinische Gleichnisse,* pp. 99f). In the Synoptic Apocalypse the expression "my words" probably replaced another phrase like, "the words of the Law" or more likely "the words of God" or even "the word of God" (see Flusser, ibid, p. 100 and cf. Luke 11:27). The situation in the present texts (Matthew 7:24,26 and Luke 6:47) is complex. Flusser pointed out that the theme of the passage opposes a personality cult mentality where those who call Jesus Lord do not live up to the requirements of God's will. Hence the expression "my

words" seems very incongruous in a text that places precedence of doing the will of God over calling Jesus "Lord, Lord" (cf. Flusser, ibid, pp. 98–100 and see note 109). Any solution to the entire question has to be based to a certain extent upon conjecture because both the texts in Matthew and in Luke have been revised. At least one sees the secondary addition *toutous* in Matthew 7:24 and 26 which was an attempt to connect the parable with the Sermon on the Mount and Luke's text (6:47) also betrays signs of redaction. The idiom "my words" only occurs in the first introductory phrase of Luke's parable (6:47) and the good Hebraic saying "he who hears and does not do them" occurs in the second text (6:49) which avoids the redundancy found in Matthew " . . . who hears *these words of mine* and does them . . . who hears *these words of mine* and does not do them . . ." (Matthew 7:24,26). Here three possible solutions to this problem will be considered. First: it is possible that originally the first text contained a reference to the "word of God" as in the story of the woman who pronounced a blessing upon Jesus to which he responded, "Blessed rather are those who hear the word of God and keep it!" (Luke 11:27). Then the reference may have been to the "word of God" or even to the "words of God." Second: it is also possible that the object was understood and not referred to directly. The text then would read, "Everyone who hears and does—to what is he like?" or "Everyone who hears and does is like . . ." This reflects the good Semitic text of Luke 6:49, "But he who hears and does not do them is like . . ." Third: it is also possible that the first text contained the expression "my words" and that this text gave rise to the secondary proliferation of the phrase in other contexts (the Synoptic Apocalypse and Matthew 7:26). The second text most surely did not contain a reference to "my words" as the version of Luke suggests (Luke 6:49). However in any event, whether the text contained the expression "my words" or "the word of God" it seems that Jesus would be referring primarily but certainly *not* exclusively to his teaching. Could Hillel the Elder have made a similar statement (cf. David Flusser, "Hillel's Self-Awareness and Jesus," *Immanuel* [1974] 4, pp. 31–36)? After somewhat revising his earlier view, Flusser preferred the second option presented here (private communication and compare idem, *Die rabbinische Gleichnisse,* pp. 99f). Why should it shock us to hear Jesus speak about the supreme authority of his words? The sages felt that their instruction was an actualization of the scripture and that they were teaching the approach to life and man's relationship between his neighbor and his Creator. They considered their teachings authoritative. The gospel passage shows that Jesus strongly objected to those who would attempt to promote a "cult of personality" by proclaiming him Lord (or messiah) without living up to the requirements of discipleship and doing the will of God.

83) See parallel, Avot Derabbi Nathan, ver. b, chap. 34. On R. Eleazar ben Azaryah's figurative sayings, see also Bacher, *Die Agada der Tannaiten,* vol. 1, pp. 221, idem, *Agadot Hatannaim,* vol. 1, part 1, pp. 166–167 and cf. Herford, *The Ethics of the Talmud,* pp. 92–93 and Taylor, *Sayings of the Jewish Fathers,* vol. 1, p. 75 and pp. 21–22.

84) See also Mark 10:31 and cf. Matthew 20:16; Luke 13:30. The enigmatic saying from the gospels was in circulation and has appeared in the Oxyrhynchus Papyri (654,3) and the Gospel of Thomas (logion 3, Guillaumont, *et al,* pp. 2–5) as well as a variation of it in the Epistle of Barnabas 6:13. See H.G.E. White, *The Sayings of Jesus from Oxyrhynchus* (Cambridge: University Press, 1920), pp. 15–17 and cf. Fitzmyer, "The Oxyrhynchus *logoi* of Jesus and the Coptic Gospel according to Thomas," *Essays on the Semitic Background of the New Testament* (Missoula: Scholars' Press, 1974), pp. 379ff.

85) See Jeremias, *Parables,* p. 139.

86) See the important discussion of Montefiore, *Rabbinic Teachings,* pp. 285–299.

87) Josephus, *Ant.* 20:219–220 (during the time that Agrippa II was curator of the Temple by order of Claudius Caesar, and cf. Avigad, *Discovering Jerusalem,* p. 94 and see also Schürer, revised and edited by G. Vermes and F. Millar, *The History of the Jewish People,* vol. 1, p. 476). The similarity between Josephus' account and the parable has often been noted by commentators. Thus, Gundry, *Matthew,* pp. 396–397.

88) J. Berachot 5c, chap. 2, hal. 8, Leiden Manuscript, Scal. 3, Jerusalem reproduction, Kedem, 1971, vol. 1, p. 21 (parallels in Songs of Songs Rabbah 6:2 and Ecclesiastes Rabbah 5:11); and Sifra on Leviticus 26:6 (Weiss, 111a). See also Johnston, "Parabolic Interpretations attributed to Tannaim," p. 256. Cf. Shocher Tov on Psalm 37 (end) and Midrash Hallel, A. Jellinek, *Bet Hamidrash,* vol. 5, p. 91. See also Meir Ayali, *Poalim Veomanim,* pp. 164–167.

89) M. Smith, *Tannaitic Parallels to the Gospels* (Philadelphia: Society of Biblical Literature, 1951, corrected reprint, 1968), pp. 50–53 and 135.

90) Jeremias, *Parables,* pp. 138–139. Jeremias spoke concerning the parable from j. Berachot 5c, chap. 2, hal. 8. Smith arrived at an entirely different conclusion in regards to the parallel parable in Sifra on Leviticus 26:6 (Weiss, 111a). He suggested that an earlier version of the rabbinic parable was already known to the audience for whom the gospel illustration (Matthew 20:14–30) was intended, Smith, *Tannaitic Paral-*

lels, p. 52. On the conditions of workers and their relationship to the landowner, see the excellent work of Meir Ayali, *Poalim Veomanim* (Jerusalem: Yad Letalmud, 1987) and especially, pp. 5–42.

91) Lightfoot, vol. 2, pp. 266–267.

92) Wünsche, *Erläuterung der Evangelien,* pp. 234–235 and McNeile, *The Gospel according to St. Matthew* (London: Macmillan, 1915, reprint Grand Rapids: Baker, 1980) p. 285 and cf. Billerbeck, vol. 4, p. 493.

93) My friend Menachem Rubin suggested that the Hebrew phrase ארוכות וקצרות refers to the length and the width of the vineyard. Jastrow translates the phrase as meaning *"in all directions"* (vol. 1, p. 116) but Rubin's suggestion makes better sense. The word image created is one of the owner and the industrious worker walking together back and forth across the rows of the length and the width of the field watching the others work. This action was strikingly unconventional. The owner might walk with an *aris* but certainly not a common worker (cf. Ayali, *Poalim Veomanim,* p. 42 and pp. 43–62).

94) Jeremias, *Parables,* pp. 138–139.

95) Ibid, p. 139.

96) See note 87 above.

97) Sifra on Leviticus 26:5 (Weiss, 111a), see also Smith, *Tannaitic Parallels,* p. 51 who discussed the difficulty of the correct translation of the Hebrew word *panah.* Here the basic meaning of the word from Leviticus has been retained. The idea seems to be that God will turn to them and thus show his regard for them. This translation may not be the most literal but it seems to convey the correct meaning of the Hebrew text.

98) This was the view of R. Simeon but R. Judah said that the beasts of prey would be removed from the earth. For R. Judah's opinion, see also Mishnat R. Eliezer, chap. 4 (Enelow, p. 87, and cf. the metaphorical application to the nations of the world). Compare Midrash Hagadol on Leviticus 26:6 (Steinsaltz, p. 733–734), Masechtot Derech Eretz (Higger, vol. 2, p. 248) and see also Kasher, *Torah Shelemah* on Leviticus 26:6, vol. 34, pp. 159ff.

99) Midrash Psalms 26:3; Yalkut Machiri on Psalm 26:4 (p. 87b) and see Flusser, *Die rabbinischen Gleichnisse,* pp. 97–98. Compare also the parables in "Midrash Hallel," A. Jellinek, *Bet Hamidrash* (Jerusalem: Wahrmann, reprint 1967), vol. 5, p. 91: "A parable. To a king who hired many workers and among them one who was lazy. When he came to give them their wages, he paid them all the same amount. But the Holy One blessed be He is not like this. He rewards each man according to his

deeds, as it was said, 'I the LORD search the mind and try the heart, to give to every man according to his ways, according to the fruit of his doings.' (Jeremiah 17:10)." See Flusser, *Yahadut Umekorot Hanatzrut,* pp. 180–181 and cf. Ayali, op. cit. note 88 above.

100) Flusser, *Yahadut Umekorot Hanatzrut,* pp. 175–177.

101) Semachot Derabbi Chiya 3:2 (Higger, pp. 220–221). See the partial parallel parable by R. Chanina in Tanchuma, Ki Tisa 3.

102) See the section on the decalogue in Pesikta Rabbati 23–24 and the Parable of the Orchard (Friedmann, p. 121b) and parallels Midrash Hagadol on Exodus 20:12 (Margulies, pp. 422–423); Deuteronomy Rabbah 6:2 (Lieberman's edition, p. 103); Tanchuma, Ekev 2 (Buber's edition 3); Shocher Tov 9:3. The inferior parallel from Deuteronomy Rabbah 6:2 was discussed by Montefiore, *Rabbinic Literature,* pp. 288–289. In Midrash Proverbs (16, Buber's edition p. 41b) a parable is attributed to R. Jose Hagalili which describes a king who stationed himself in the tower of his orchard and watched the workmen. In the application of the parable, God who is unseen rewards those whom he watches and finds to be good workers and punishes the others. See parallel in Semachot Derabbi Chiyah 3:6 (Higger, pp. 222–223).

103) Also compare the conversation of the landowner with the disgruntled laborers in Matthew 20:13–15 to Avot 5:10.

PROPHETIC TENSION AND THE TEMPLE: "THE PARABLE OF THE WICKED HUSBANDMEN"

The Parable of the Wicked Husbandmen (Matthew 21:33–46; Mark 12:1–12 and Luke 20:9–19) is situated after the Question of Authority in all three of the synoptics and thus was understood to have been told on the Temple mount. Only Matthew inserts the Parable of the Two Sons in between the Question of Authority and the Parable of the Wicked Husbandmen. However this is a unique Matthean text and it does not change the setting of the parable but rather intensifies the friction between Jesus and the Temple authorities. At least the Parable of the Two Sons criticizes the hearers for not believing John the Baptist (Matthew 21:32).[1] The Parable of the Wicked Husbandmen itself is cast as an affront to the scribes and the high priests in Luke (20:19) and to the Pharisees and high priests in Matthew (21:45) who perceived that the illustration was directed against them. In Mark's context, Jesus was walking in the temple and was confronted by the "chief priests and the scribes and the elders" (Mark 11:27; cf. Matthew 21:23; Luke 20:1). On location within the Temple precincts, the high priests and the leadership of the Temple complex, who received their positions and support either directly or indirectly from, or collaborated with, Rome, were very likely the intended opponents in the source of the synoptics.[2]

The parable describes a land owner who tried to collect the produce from the tenants of his vineyard. The synoptics employ the Greek term γεωργοί which is probably a translation of the Hebrew word אריסים which designated tenants, who unlike common laborers might actually take over the land in the absence of an heir.[3] These wicked tenants refuse to pay. When the owner of the vineyard sends his servants to collect, some of them are cruelly mistreated and/or murdered. Finally he sends his only son, reasoning that the tenants will show him more regard. The climax of the conflict in the parable is reached when the wicked tenants kill the son of the owner of the vineyard. What will happen to the wicked sharecroppers who kill the son of the householder and the heir to the vineyard? Then the son is compared to a foundation stone—though it was rejected, it becomes the chief cornerstone. Many approaches have been advanced to interpret the parable. Certainly the historical context and situation of the Jewish people in the first century was largely forgotten by Christian interpreters, who allegorized the parable and often viewed it as a symbolic portrayal of Israel's rejection.

The change of audience from first century Jews in the land of Israel to Gentile Christians was decisive. Jesus' relationship to his people was denigrated. Jesus was portrayed as attacking the Jews as a whole and teaching that they had been replaced by the church. Thus Irenaeus allegorically interprets, "For inasmuch as the former [the Jewish people] have rejected the Son of God, and cast Him out of the vineyard when they slew Him, God has justly rejected them, and given to the Gentiles outside the vineyard the fruits of cultivation."[4] Irenaeus viewed the parable as teaching the repudiation of the Jewish people as a whole and its replacement by the church. Little effort had been made to re-evaluate this position, when in 1905 the well-known textual scholar H.B. Swete wrote, "The Jewish rulers were in fact His murderers, though they were compelled to leave the execution in the hands of Gentiles . . ."[5] At least Swete noted the difference between the "Jewish rulers" and the Jewish people as a collective group. Nonetheless it is sometimes difficult to understand why New Testament exegetes are so oblivious to the fact that Jesus was a Jew living under the yoke of Rome and struggled in the same circumstances alongside his countrymen. Jesus maintained solidarity with his people. Not surprisingly, therefore, the Parable of the Wicked Husbandmen has become one of the most controversial texts of the entire gospel tradition. Not a few exegetes have viewed the parable as a secondary allegory invented by the church which was added at a later time.[6] Others have argued that the story accurately reflects the historical situation of the land of Israel in the first century.[7] As has already been noted, the strict Jülicherian approach which claims that Jesus could not have employed points of comparison between the mashal and the nimshal that may include a member of allegorical features in a parable needs reconsideration and modification.[8]

The Greek text of the parable as it has been preserved in the synoptics presents a number of linguistic problems.[9] It is doubtful if the original language of the source of the parable can be recovered. Nevertheless the agreement in wording between the three evangelists (see also Gospel of Thomas, logia 65–66) as well as the independent qualities of each of their versions of the parable makes it possible to look for an underlying source for the text which can properly be viewed as being derived from the better source materials of the synoptics. Nevertheless evidence of redaction in the Greek stage of the parable is patent. Nonetheless the redactive stage of the parable and its tendency toward allegorization should not be interpreted as meaning that the text is an invention of the early church.[10] Is it so far-fetched to view the gospel texts as foretelling the prophet's death in Jerusalem? At least the idea that Jesus was aware of his impending death and that Jerusalem was going to be destroyed seems to be embedded in the gospel tradition at the earliest stages of its development.[11]

In the previous section a number of parallel rabbinic parables were studied in light of their gospel counterparts. Here a number of rabbinic parables which contain common motifs, similar structures and parallel applications will be examined. These parabolic illustrations can be useful when one considers the questions of allegory and setting. But first one must study the original form of the gospel illustration. In this text a number of revisions have been implemented by the evangelists and their redactors.

The Parable of the Wicked Husbandmen

Are the textual differences between Matthew, Mark and Luke best understood as deviations from Mark by Matthew and Luke? At least a number of the salient features of Luke's text caused T. Schramm and A.T. Cadoux to search for another source that would have been used for Luke's version of the parable in order to explain the differences in his version.[12] If one searches for the Semitic background of the parable it becomes clear that each one of the three evangelists preserves better texts at some points by comparison to their parallels and that at other points their narrative betrays signs of stylizing. For instance, all three of the evangelists have fashioned their own introductions to the parable (Matthew 21:33 see his characteristic *allēn parabolēn;* Mark 12:1 see plural form of *parabolē;* and Luke 20:9). Most probably all of these preambles are the results of each evangelist's editorial activities. Moreover Luke's text only alludes to the allegory of the vineyard in Isaiah 5:1ff. By way of contrast, both Mark and Matthew quote the verse. Not surprisingly Matthew's citation preserves the word order of the Septuagint somewhat better than Mark.[13] However it is unlikely that Luke would have deleted these details if they were contained in his source. Luke's allusion to the Old Testament passage here is more original than its quotation by Mark and Matthew.

Another puzzling question appears when one considers the use of the word *agapētos* in the parable. Because the term does not appear either in Matthew or the Gospel of Thomas (logion 65), a number of scholars have suggested that it is a Christian allegorization of the sonship of Jesus and thus refers to the vineyard owner's son—Jesus—as his "beloved" son.[14] However the Greek term *agapētos* is not necessarily to be interpreted as a reference to the "beloved" but is the standard Greek translation of the Hebrew word יחיד.[15] The meaning in Hebrew entails not merely the idea of beloved but also—perhaps quite significantly—his *only* son. In fact this is the main definition for the word in Hebrew. C.H. Turner has demonstrated that this meaning of the term was also understood in Greek.[16] Moreover Mark seems to have understood the term in this way (cf. ἕνα εἶχεν, vs. 6). One should not hastily decide that Luke and Mark are allegorizing the parable because it is possible that Matthew has abbreviated his source on this point. It is difficult to understand why Matthew would have omitted the word *agapētos,* but anyone who feels that he can always logically explain why the evangelists made certain changes in the redaction stage of the gospels is mistaken. At least Matthew seems to have made other innovations in the text of the parable. At any rate, the term presents no linguistic problems. Moreover, the owner's *only* son is required for the plot of the story. Oriental society placed an emphasis on children, and it would have seemed unusual for a man to have only one son. If the tenants wanted to do away with the heir in order to take over the vineyard, it was imperative that the hearers of the parable would understand that the son was indeed the heir and the only heir of the property.

In addition, Matthew speaks of the householder's servants in the plural. Both Mark and Luke retain the singular. Matthew contains plural servants in comparison to the synoptic parallel in other contexts, and it seems that he recognized that the parable was referring to the prophets.[17] Therefore he felt that the plural form was more suitable. Matthew secondarily added πλείονας τῶν πρώτων (21:36). Although Luke employs the singular he adds the detail, "the third one," which was the climax of the gradation leading up to the sending of the only son.[18] Certainly the versions of Mark and Luke which retain the sending out of individual servants is preferable to Matthew who has envoys of servants. In Matthew two groups of servants are sent which may have resulted from his editiorial activities. Both Mark and Luke have three individual servants who are sent to the wicked tenants before the owner of the vineyard decides to send his son. Mark embellishes the story further by saying, καὶ πολλοὺς ἄλλους οὓς μὲν δέροντες οὓς δὲ ἀποκτέννοντες (Mark 12:5).

In correspondence with Matthew's two envoys, the Gospel of Thomas (logion 65) contains two sendings of individual servants which preceded the sending of the son. The threesome of the story as preserved by Luke and Mark has a claim to originality. However even before the discovery of the Gospel of Thomas, Dodd had already theorized that originally the parable contained two sendings and climaxed with the third when the vineyard owner decided to let his son tend to the matter.[19] Scholars were quick to claim that this fact proved that the Gospel of Thomas was based upon earlier sources than the synoptics.[20] Nevertheless such a conclusion based on this evidence alone seems premature.

Snodgrass observed that syr^{s} omitted Mark 12:4 and that both syr^{s} and syr^{c} contain only two sendings of servants in Luke's version.[21] The version of the parable preserved in the Gospel of Thomas is more concise than the synoptics. Nonetheless the authenticity of a number of the features of the Gospel of Thomas' version is questionable. For instance, he describes the owner of the vineyard as "a good (χρηστός) man" and when he tells how the first servant was beaten he elaborates, "a little longer and they would have killed him. The servant came, and he told it to his master." Then in what seems to be similar to a Lucan soliloquy, one reads, "His master said: 'Perhaps he did not know them.'" One may wonder why Thomas refers to "them" in the plural when only one servant had been beaten in the preceding context. Could this indicate that he was acquainted with Matthew or another version which referred to the servants in the plural? The parable ends with one of Thomas' favorite sayings, "Whoever has ears let him hear," and a shortened form of the stone saying is attached (logion 66). Of course secondary conclusions and embellishments appear in the parables of the gospels. Nevertheless to claim a high degree of originality for the Gospel of Thomas remains somewhat problematic. At least the two sending outs of servants is preserved in syr^{s} and syr^{c} and also corresponds to Matthew.[22] Moreover, the reference in the Gospel of Thomas to the son without the descriptive term *agapētos* already appears in Matthew. To sum up the evidence, the threesome which describes the sending out of three individual servants which prepared the way for the sending of the son is probably closer to the original sequence of events in the story.

In Luke's version the vineyard owner's slaves are never killed. The treatment of the householder's servants in Matthew and Mark recalls the persecutions of the prophets as well as the passion of Jesus. Certainly the murder of the servants by the wicked husbandmen is secondary. At least the plot of the story is much more realistic and successful if the servants are only beaten and sent away without being murdered. The plot of the parable is designed to lead up to the death of the son. The hearers are invited to attempt to decide what will happen. At least an illustration which portrays a father who would send his son to a band of murderers lacks the subtlety of a good story and thus it seems reasonable that Luke's version is more original in this detail. However in Luke the performative *ek* has been added to the verb *apostellō* which is due to Lucan style.

The element of shock, moreover, which is embedded in the story should not be overlooked. The sending of the servants and their brutal treatment was intended to build up to the unexpected action of the owner of the vineyard. The factor of surprise was carefully developed in the parable. As Marshall pointed out the soliloquy in the parables is a characteristic of Luke and it may be questioned whether or not Luke's version has been expanded.[23] Nonetheless his text can be reconstructed into colorful Hebrew which may well reflect the original language of the parable: ויאמר בעל הכרם. מה אעשה? אשלח להם את בני את יחידי אותו יכבדו.[24] At any rate the transition between the envoys of the servants who were beaten to the sending of the vineyard owner's son was certainly an unanticipated turn in the story that would have surprised the audience. They would have reasoned that the father had unnecessarily endangered his son. The hearers are thinking: If these tenants did not accept his servant, then why would they honor the vineyard owner's son?

The reaction of the wicked husbandmen was predictable. If the servants had only been beaten and not murdered as suggested above, then the hearers' attention was drawn to the question of whether the tenants would go to such extremes. Would they murder the son? The Greek texts of the evangelists are very similar on this point. The husbandmen's reasoning can be reconstructed into idiomatic Hebrew and the Greek text preserves the Semitic syntax, הנה היורש נהרוג אותו ולנו תהיה הירושה (Luke 20:14; Mark 12:7; Matthew 21:38). Then Matthew and Luke describe the killing of the son which preceded his body being thrown out of the vineyard. Mark says that first he was killed and then was thrown out of the vineyard. A number of commentators have suggested that Matthew and Luke changed the original order to conform more closely with the crucifixion of Jesus which occurred outside the city.[25] But this is by no means certain because they may have wanted to take the son outside the vineyard in order to cover up their crime. The motif emphasized that the vile tenants were so corrupt that they would not even provide the son a grave or burial and thus left his body exposed to the elements and to the beasts of prey. At this point Matthew adds the editorial comment ὅταν οὖν ἔλθῃ ὁ κύριος τοῦ ἀμπελῶνος (Matthew 21:40). Mark and Luke simply ask the question, "What will the owner of the vineyard do to them?" (Luke 20:15 and Mark 12:9). Matthew's text (Matthew 21:40) probably reflects Mark's and Luke's (or their common source's) use of the word ἐλεύσεται in the answer to this question, "He will come and destroy those tenants, and give the vineyard to others" (Luke 20:16 and Mark 12:9). At this point Matthew's text has the crowd answer Jesus. It employs the Greek words *kakous kakōs* which are secondary to Mark and Luke. All three evangelists say that he will give the vineyard to others. However this becomes a point of departure for Matthew. He adds, " . . . to other tenants who will give him the fruits in their seasons" (Matthew 21:41; compare Mark 11:13). Moreover he develops this idea further when he comments, "Therefore I tell you the kingdom of God will be taken away from you and given to a nation *producing the fruits of it*" (Matthew 21:43). The declaration does not appear in the other evangelists and has far-reaching implications concerning how Matthew or his final revisor interpreted the parable.[26]

The Vineyard and the Tenants

Hence it seems that Matthew or more likely his redactor interpreted the vineyard as being representative of the kingdom of God. For him, the point of departure, "He will come and destroy the tenants, and give the vineyard to others," referred to the fact that his circle had replaced Israel. But it seems highly improbable that the vineyard represented the kingdom of God in the parable. The interpreter must take care not to search for allegorical representation where none is warranted. The parable is based in part on Isaiah 5:1ff, but the vineyard is primarily a part of the stage. The parable deals with the sharecroppers of the vineyard and their relationship to the owner. Their first transgression is that they refuse to turn over the fruits of their labors to the owner. On the Temple mount, Jesus' parable seems to deal with the leaders of the priests and thus Flusser connected it to the corrupt leadership.[27] It is precarious to go beyond this theme and look for an allegorical meaning for the vineyard—be it the kingdom of God (as in Matthew), the people, the Temple, the Judaism of the day, the leadership, the land of Israel or some other allegorical interpretation. None of these interpretations may be imposed upon the parable by its context. The parable addresses the action of the wicked tenants, and the vineyard is of secondary importance.

Was the parable a prophetic warning to the leadership of the Temple? Was it an attempt to point out the corruption of the priests in view of the national threat presented by the Romans? As is well known, the priests who were largely composed of Sadducees and who were the overseers of the Temple worship earned sharp criticism for themselves from a number of quarters.[28] The Testament of Levi provides an example of some of the criticisms leveled against the priests; compare these excerpts, "For your father, Israel, is pure with respect to all the impieties of the chief priests. . . . For what will all the nations do if you become darkened with impiety? You will bring down a curse on our nation, because you want to destroy the light of the law which was granted to you for the enlightenment of everyman. . . . Therefore the sanctuary which the Lord chose shall become desolate through your uncleanness, and you will be captives in all the nations. . . ."[29] Interestingly Josephus reports that four years before the war, during a time of peace and prosperity, a peasant named Jesus the son of Ananias began to cry out in the streets and warn about the terrible fate of Jerusalem.[30] He shouted out both "against Jerusalem and the sanctuary" and the Roman authorities finally flogged him to the bone. He did not complain to his tormentors but simply responded to every blow with the cry, "Woe to Jerusalem!" He was declared insane and released, but he continued to wail throughout the intervening years until he was killed during the war. Josephus gives this account, "For while going his round and shouting in piercing tones from the wall, 'Woe once more to the city and the people and to the temple,' as he added a last word, 'and woe to me also,' a stone hurled from the *ballista* struck and killed him on the spot." The incident related by Josephus occurred sometime after the Jesus of the gospels, and was certainly much closer to the time of the destruction of the sanctuary; however it provides further evidence of an existing popular antagonism directed against the beautiful Temple precinct which was operated by authorities who did not always live up to everyone's expectations of holiness and purity. Moreover a number of gospel passages like the cleansing of the Temple and Jesus' saying, "No stone will be left upon another," indicate that tensions existed between Jesus and the priestly establishment which controlled the Temple complex. One may ask—if at least by implication if not by direct association—whether the Roman authorities who gave the priests their position would not also be connected to some of these sayings?

Matthew (or the final reviser of the gospel) interpreted the parable differently. For him the vineyard represented the kingdom of God which was to be uprooted from the Jewish people and transferred to a new nation (ἔθνος) which would replace Israel. Matthew 21:43 is paralleled neither in Mark nor in Luke. The verse betrays a notion peculiar to Matthew. Only in Matthew's gospel does one discover the phrase "sons of the kingdom" (Matthew 8:12 and 13:38). Matthew writes that the patriarchs will sit in the kingdom of God, "while the sons of the kingdom will be thrown into the outer darkness; there men will weep and gnash their teeth" (Matthew 8:11–12). The close parallel in Luke does not use the phrase "sons of the kingdom" even though the wording is quite similar. Here Matthew has referred to the Jewish people as "the sons of the kingdom" who will be thrust into outer darkness while Abraham, Isaac, and Jacob recline in the kingdom of heaven. However in the other Matthean passage that mentions the "sons of the kingdom" one finds an entirely different meaning. It appears in the interpretation of the Parable of the Wheat and the Tares (Matthew 13:24–30, 36–43). Both the parable and its interpretation are unique to Matthew. The explanation of the parable, which seems to have been written originally in Greek, turns the example into an allegory. The good seed represents the "sons of the kingdom" and the tares are to be identified with the "sons of the evil one" (Matthew 13:38). Thus in Matthew's second employment of the term, the "sons of the kingdom" appear as the righteous instead of the Jewish people. At the first examination, these two passages from Matthew seem to contradict one another and appear to be mutually exclusive. However in Matthew 21:43 both meanings are alluded to and appear together as a cohesive unit. According to Matthew, the kingdom will be taken away from the Jewish people, the evil sons of the kingdom, and then transferred to a new nation (Matthew 21:43). The new "sons of the kingdom" will produce the fruits of it. All of these verses and the ideology behind them belong only to a few select verses in Matthew's gospel. It appears to come from the stage of the final redaction of the evangelist, because Matthew is otherwise very positive toward the Jewish people as well as the law.[31] Certainly Paul would not have accepted this radical approach (cf. Romans 9:4–5). In the Parable of the Wicked Husbandmen his terminology obviously refers to the wicked tenants who refused to give the produce to the owner of the vineyard. Matthew 21:43 refers to a nation in the singular and could quite probably be connected to Matthew's (or more probably the gospel's final reviser's) circle. Flusser has pointed to some remarkable evidence that suggests that such a group which viewed itself as Israel's heir and replacement actually existed—and he connected their theological ideas to Matthew's final redaction.[32] The only other alternative is to view the kingdom as representing the corrupt leadership of the Temple who cooperated with the Romans against their own people.

In short it becomes very difficult to argue for the originality of Matthew 21:43, "Therefore I tell you the kingdom of God will be taken away from you and given to a nation producing the fruits of it." Would Mark and Luke have had any scruples about preserving this logion if it had appeared in their source(s)? The verse in the parable which says that the vineyard will be given to others may have originally alluded to the impending destruction of the Temple (Matthew 21:41; Mark 12:9; Luke 20:16). As has been seen, Matthew allegorically connected the vineyard to the kingdom of God and thus distorted the message of the parable.[33] Matthew's secondary interpretation and application of the Parable of the Wicked Husbandmen had far-reaching implications.[34] But what was the original thrust of the parable?

The Son and the Stone

When the Matthean embellishments of the parable are removed, two themes emerge. First, a hint at Jerusalem's fate comes to light which involves the death of the vineyard owner's son, and, second, Jesus makes a strong claim that displays his high self-awareness and a consciousness of his unique task. Of course the second thrust which emerges from the stone saying is true only if the logion is deemed original and appears in its proper context. Would the parable make sense without the stone saying from Psalm 118:22? It does appear here in all three of the synoptics as well as in the Gospel of Thomas.[35] The reference to Psalm 118:22 adds a note of triumph which completes the parable. The connecting phrase in Matthew 21:42a with *grafais* in the plural is preferable to Mark 12:10a *(grafēn)* and Luke 20:17a *(gegrammenon)*. In Hebrew the text would read, אמר להם ישוע הלא קראתם בכתובים.[36] Then comes the citation from Psalm 118:22. But how would the verse be interpreted in the context of the parable? More likely the stone would be connected to an individual as a personification of the son rather than to the people as a collective group (ἄλλοις from the preceding verse), but naturally the triumph of the stone is that of the people as well. However according to Jewish interpreters, the Psalm was a Psalm of David and could easily have been understood as making a poetic reference to the circumstances of David's exaltation in spite of his humble beginnings as a shepherd. In Midrash Hagadol (cf. Midrash Tannaim), the Psalm is related to David.[37] Samuel came to Jesse in order to anoint the future king from among his sons. But David was not even called in from tending the sheep even though he too was a son of Jesse. The darshan explains that David was despised (מאוס) in the eyes of his father. However the midrash explains in a way similar to a Pesher from the Dead Sea Scrolls that David in the end was chosen to rise to power, "'The stone which the builders rejected has become the head of the corner' (Psalm 118:22), 'the builders' [referred to in the verse] are Samuel and Jesse, [and the words] 'has become the head of the corners' refers to [David], the greatest of all kings."[38] Whether this or a similar interpretation of Psalm 118:22 was contemporary with Jesus is impossible to know from the available evidence. However such an interpretation could have arisen at any time and it seems likely that the Psalm of David was connected to David's life, for though he was despised, he rose to greatness. Furthermore as David Flusser pointed out,[39] the idea that David the rejected one was exalted above his more handsome brothers was already reflected in a Pseudo-Davidic Psalm. The antiquity of the Psalm has been affirmed by its discovery in the Dead Sea Scrolls.[40] David recounts how he was chosen, "Smaller was I than my brothers and the youngest of the sons of my father, So he made me shepherd of his flock. . . . He sent his prophet to anoint me, Samuel to make me great; My brothers went out to meet him, handsome of figure and appearance. Though they were tall of stature and handsome by their hair, the Lord God chose them not. But he sent and took me from behind the flock and anointed me with holy oil, And he made me leader of his people and ruler over the sons of his covenant." Here no reference is made to Psalm 118, and the apocryphal text ascribed to King David is closely related to the scripture passage 1 Samuel 16:1–13. However it demonstrates the popular idea of how the despised shepherd boy was chosen to become the leader of the people.

The reference in the gospel parable to Psalm 118:22 has strong overtones that further describe the prominence of the son. As noted above, the verse is cited in all three evangelists but verse 23, "this was the Lord's doing, and it is marvelous in our eyes," does not appear in Luke and was probably added by Mark and Matthew. The son has become the cornerstone. Luke as well as a number of good manuscripts of Matthew contains the somewhat enigmatic saying, "Every one who falls on that stone will be broken to pieces; but when it falls on any one it will crush him" (Luke 20:18 and Matthew 21:44). One is either broken to pieces *sunthalō* or crushed into powder *likmaō*. Which is preferable? One thing is clear—the stone remains. But even if it appeared in his source(s), Mark may have deleted the saying because of its puzzling nature. He also completed the quotation from Psalm

118:23, " . . . this was the Lord's doing and it is marvelous in our eyes," which would have broken the connection to the stone saying. The logion is attested in some manuscripts of Matthew. Was it added to Matthew because of the parallel in Luke? Not only does Matthew complete the quotation from Psalm 118 like Mark but he also was intent on changing the emphasis of the parable by the addition, "Therefore the kingdom of God will be taken away from you . . ." (Matthew 21:43). Hence it would have been natural for Matthew to delete the stone saying.[41] It seems doubtful that Luke would have invented the logion.

The imagery of the saying recalls the passage in Daniel which describes the stone that destroys Nebuchadnezzar's statue (Daniel 2:34–35, 44–45).[42] Billerbeck cites a parallel saying from Esther Rabbah, "If a stone falls on a pot, woe to the pot! If a pot falls on a stone, woe to the pot! In either case woe to the pot!"[43] In the context of Esther Rabbah, the tanna R. Simeon ben Jose ben Lakunya compared the people of Israel to rocks. Both Psalm 118:22 and Daniel 2:45 are cited. So the meaning of the saying in the midrash is related to the ultimate triumph of the people.[44] Though Israel is attacked, in the end they will emerge victorious. Billerbeck also cited Tanchuma where the amora Resh Lakish interpreted the stone of Daniel that destroys the statue, as portraying the King Messiah's triumph over the kingdoms.[45] Did similar interpretations exist at the time of Jesus? The meager evidence precludes a definitive answer. More importantly, if original, what meaning would Jesus have attached to the images of the stone? One thing seems relatively clear—the steadfast stone will survive and overcome all opposition.

One should compare the thrust of the parable to Jesus' lamentation over Jerusalem, "O Jerusalem, Jerusalem, killing the prophets and stoning those who are sent to you! How often would I have gathered your children together as a hen gathers her brood under her wings, and you would not! Behold, your house is forsaken. And I tell you, you will not see me until you say, 'Blessed is he who comes in the name of Lord!'" (Luke 13:34–35 and Matthew 23:37–39). The heartfelt lamentation employs the metaphor of a hen who gathers her brood under its wings. The opportunity of response to the proclamation of the messengers is always available and indeed is urgent. The reference to the house forsaken seems to be connected to the decadent spiritual state of the Temple. The prophetic warnings have not been heeded. The citation of Psalm 118:26 has obvious implications which are not so distant from the references to the son and the rejected cornerstone in the Parable of the Wicked Husbandmen. Jesus views himself as one of those who had been sent. Could the challenge of Jesus and his call to repentance be understood as an effort to avert national disaster (cf. Luke 19:41–44)?

The passion predicitions clearly foretell the death of Jesus, and it should not seem far-fetched that Jesus may have anticipated his fate which was not so uncommon as can be seen by the death of John the Baptist and Roman reaction to other outstanding independent religious figures of the period.[46] In many ways, he was crucified because he was Jewish. The Romans had crucified thousands of Jews and zealously maintained a policy of suppressing Jewish messianic hopes and especially popular movements.[47] Whether the words of Caiaphas the high priest, " . . . it is expedient for you that one man should die for the people, and that the whole nation should not perish" (John 11:50), are historical cannot be determined, but they did become prophetic, albeit not in regard to Jesus and his movement. Not many years after Jesus' execution the Romans' policy of suppression was implemented and the Jewish people were crushed and dispersed in part because of their messianic expectations and another popular movement. The climax was reached during the Jewish revolt, spearheaded by Bar Kochba who was widely believed to embody the long awaited deliverer.[48]

One thing is certain—it seems highly doubtful if anything inherent in Jesus' teachings which were very close to the pharisaic line would have caused legal proceedings against him. The period was characterized by theological diversity and controversy. The differences in teaching between Hillel and Shamai were marked with more conflict and friction than any differences which might exist between Jesus and Johanan ben Zakai, for example. In short, the historian would do better to search for political rather than theological motives when considering possible reasons for the betrayal and execution of Jesus under Pontius Pilate. However the question of responsibility for Jesus' fate is not the main issue of the parable, and it is tragic that a parable of Jesus has been used to disinherit his people and also to prove collective responsibility for his death. Ironically, in a short period of time the Christians would assume the role played by the wicked tenants in the parable and begin to persecute Israel and try to disinherit Jesus' own people in an effort to claim all their divine prerogatives for themselves.[49] The work of Matthew's final revisor which reflected the ideology of his circle contributed to the distortion of Jesus' message. Hopefully it has been clearly seen that this is a late secondary development far removed from the historical Jesus. The parable tells of the fate of the son and it may well be Jesus' first public disclosure concerning his death as well as his ultimate triumph. The gospels portray Jesus as predicting his death to the disciples privately. In the context of the parable the son figure has a very special prophetic role and probably would be correctly connected to the son of David or a Messiah figure. The stone rejected by the builders becomes the cornerstone. The triumph of the stone is the triumph of Jesus.

Matthew and Luke both mention the chief priests (and see the context in Mark 11:27 and parallels). However all three of the synoptics refer to crowds who supported Jesus and prevented his outnumbered opponents from arresting him. Matthew speaks of the Pharisees and the chief priests and Luke refers to the scribes and the chief priests. Both specify the chief priests, and this is suitable for the context within the Temple precinct. A number of scholars may argue that Matthew and Luke have adapted their texts for the setting, but it should not be surprising that the opponents of Jesus would be mentioned here. In any case, the Parable of the Wicked Husbandmen illustrates the tension between Jesus and the authorities in charge of the Temple complex. In addition, the reference to the stone from Psalm 118:22 and the son character in the parable portray Jesus' self awareness. The parable could be considered an example of what Jeremias (following E. Fuchs) referred to as the "veiled christological self-attestation of the historical Jesus" which is inherent in some of the parables of Jesus.[50]

The Romans as well as the Sadducean priests may well have

deemed such claims as being dangerous to the political status quo. But a number of questions remain unanswered. Would a parable of this kind be considered an affront to the Jewish people as a whole? Jesus was certainly not alone in his sharp criticisms of the corruption of the priests and he would not ignore their opposition to his movement. Nonetheless Jesus by no means cast off his people. The triumph of the stone must be viewed as a victory for the entire nation. Here one must also ask whether the Parable of the Wicked Husbandmen is an illustration *sui generis.* How could the motifs employed in the parable function to teach new themes in other contexts? Are the shocking elements of the involved plot from this parable unique to the gospels? Too often the comparative study of rabbinic and gospel parables has been limited to parallels without considering the form and structure of parabolic teaching. An examination of a number of rabbinic parables promises to throw light on the hermeneutical questions regarding the relationship between the motifs, theme and context of the parables in the world of Jewish thought.

The Parable of the Wicked Husbandmen and Its Rabbinic Counterparts

The tannaitic midrash, Sifre Deuteronomy preserves an anonymous parable which contains a number of parallel motifs.[51] The text deals with Deuteronomy 32:9, "For the LORD'S portion is his people, Jacob his allotted heritage." Instead of a vineyard one finds a field.

THE FIELD AND THE KING'S SON (Sifre Deuteronomy 312)

> "For the LORD'S portion is his people" (Deuteronomy 32:9). A parable. To a king who owned a field and rented it to tenants. These tenants began to steal from it. Then he took it away from them and rented it to their children. But they turned out to be more wicked than the first tenants. Therefore he took it away from them and rented it to their children's children but they still were more wicked than the first tenants. A son was then born

> to the king! The king said to the tenants, "Get out of my [field]. I will not allow you to stay in it—give me my portion so that I will be able to make it known [as mine]. Thus when our father Abraham came into the world, dross [פסולת] issued forth from him—Ishmael and the sons of Keturah. When Isaac came into the world dross issued forth from him also—Esau and the myriads of Edomites who were more wicked than the first ones [Ishmael and the sons of Keturah]. Finally Jacob came and dross did not issue forth from him for all his sons were honest. As it is said, "Jacob was an [honest] man, dwelling in tents (Genesis 25:27). From whence does the Omnipresent make known his portion? From Jacob as it is said, "For the LORD'S portion is his people, Jacob his allotted heritage" (Deuteronomy 32:9). Further he says, "For the Lord has chosen Jacob for himself" (Psalm 135:4).

The parable also appears with some slight variations in the Midrash Hagadol (cf. also Midrash Tannaim) on Deuteronomy 32:9,[52] where the fact is stressed that in contrast to Abraham and Isaac, no dross or refuse [*pesolet*] Issued forth from Jacob but all his offspring were righteous men [*tzadikim*].[53] Sifre Deuteronomy employs the term *kesherim* to describe Jacob's children. The text in Midrash Hagadol has adopted the term "my land" *artzi* instead of the more subtle language of Sifre Deuteronomy. The interpretation of the field as being the land of Israel probably influenced the wording in Midrash Hagadol (and cf. Midrash Tannaim).

The basic story of the parable is the same. The king rents his field to wicked tenants who take advantage of their position. After they have robbed the king, he gives the field over to their children in hopes that they will prove to be more worthy caretakers. After they turned out to be worse than the first tenants, the king rents the field to the children of the children of the first tenants. On this detail the parallels in Midrash Hagadol (Midrash Tannaim) are more concise and do not mention the grandchildren of the first tenants. These grandchildren of the original workers are also a disappointment being more evil than the others. The king has a son who is obviously his heir. Naturally the king is pleased to drive the wicked tenants out of his property in order to turn it over to his son. The application of the parable returns to the theme of Deuteronomy 32:9, "For the LORD's portion is his people, Jacob his allotted heritage." The son is identified with Jacob who is viewed as being synonymous with the people of Israel. The references to Ishmael and the sons of Keturah and also to Esau and the Edomites contrast peoples who were considered to be enemies of Israel with Jacob the chosen. The midrash goes on to say, "We do not know if the Holy One blessed be He chose Jacob or if Jacob chose the Holy One blessed be He." The derashah continues and concludes that although Jacob responded, it was actually God who chose Jacob.

The application of the parable says that Jacob was worthy: "Jacob was a quiet man [תם], dwelling in tents" (Genesis 25:27). The darshan seems to have understood the Hebrew word *tam* as meaning innocent or even honest. He was worthy as his righteous offspring indicates. The Septuagint translated this Hebrew term from Genesis 25:27 with the somewhat uncommon Greek word *aplastos.* This word does not appear elsewhere in the Septuagint.[54] When used as an adverb the term can carry the sense of "without disguise" and is used as the opposite of "mythical" in Plutarchus and thus seems to have the connotation of being true.[55] In the Aramaic Targums the passage was rendered גבר שלים, meaning a man complete or perfect in good works (see Jubilees 35:12).[56] In all events Jacob, who was somewhat of a crafty business dealer in the biblical account of the patriarchs, is praised here as the respresentative of the people who was chosen by God. The application of the parable relates the wicked tenants to the dross or refuse *(pesolet)* that issued forth from Abraham and Isaac has a number of parallels in rabbinic literature.[57] Later on in Sifre Deuteronomy it is attached as the conclusion to yet another parable.[58] The application appears in both the Targumim as well as in Pesikta Rabbati.[59] It may be ventured that the parable here in Sifre Deuteronomy preserves the more original context of this tradition as it describes the election of Jacob.

The Parable of the Field and the King's Son has often been

noted as a parallel to the Parable of the Wicked Husbandmen.[60] Indeed a number of similar motifs appear: the owner of the vineyard is paralleled by the king, the field is reflected by the gospel illustration's vineyard, and both parables contain wicked tenants and the son figure. However the similarities stop here and one discovers an entirely different application for the rabbinic parable. In contrast to the gospel parable, the son figure is not killed and in fact it is the son who takes over the field and replaces the wicked tenants.[61] The intensity of the tension between owner and sharecroppers achieved in Jesus' parable has been greatly alleviated in the Parable of the Field and the King's Son. At least the king does not send envoys of servants who are mistreated and the son's life is never in danger. The rabbinic parable describes more or less a simple case of theft. The son in the gospel parable is related to an individual and in the rabbinic parable he loosely represents Jacob and more specifically the people of Israel. In fact most frequently when the son is employed in rabbinic parables, he represents Israel. A similar parable connected the household steward *(ben bayit)* to King David so that the son figure—in this case the household steward—was personified as an individual and not as a collective.[62] The citizens of the city rebel against the king's household steward, who is identified as King David. At any rate the fundamental underlying plot to the parables and the motifs which appear in the texts are closely related. Nevertheless the differences are equally impressive. While the literary forms are connected, both parables have quite divergent applications in the different contexts in which they function to communicate two diverse themes.

In Seder Elijah, a parable is attributed to R. Jose Hagalili (ca. 120 A.D.) which in many ways is more closely related to the gospel Parable of the Wicked Husbandmen than the preceding example from Sifre Deuteronomy.[63] Seder Elijah contains very few attributions. Therefore when the midrash does ascribe a parable or a saying to a particular sage there is every reason to believe that the compiler of Seder Elijah was using what he considered to be a reliable source. The attribution therefore seems to have more credibility. In this section of Seder Elijah, materials are attributed to a number of authorities. To the present writer's knowledge, R. Jose's parable has no other exact parallel in rabbinic literature.

THE KING'S SON AND THE WICKED GUARDIAN
(Seder Elijah, p. 150)

R. Jose Hagalili used to say, they told a parable. To what may the matter be compared? To a human king who had to travel to a distant country across the sea. He desired to entrust his son into the hands of a wicked guardian. His friends and servants told him, "Do not entrust your son to the wicked guardian!" But the king ignored the advice of his friends and servants and entrusted his son into the hands of the wicked guardian. What did the guardian do? He rose up and destroyed his city, burned his house with fire and slew the king's son with the sword! After many days the king came and saw his city—destroyed and desolate. He saw his house burned and his son slain by the sword. He began to pluck his hair from his head and beard and cried out with a loud lament, "Woe to me! How [foolishly] and [senselessly] I have acted in my world because I have entrusted my son into the hands of a wicked guardian!" And thus also with the Holy One blessed be He—the prophets spoke before him, "Master of the universe, do not entrust your inheritance your children into the hand of Nebuchadnezzar the wicked who hates the Holy One blessed be He!" He did not take the advice of Asaf and the prophets and entrusted his children into the hands of Nebuchadnezzar the wicked. What did he do? He rose up and burned Jerusalem, destroyed the Temple and exiled Israel into Babylon. The Holy One blessed be He said, "I only commanded that wicked one to subdue my children to the words of the Torah. But he has gone way too far beyond the limits of justice." As it is said, "Now these are the nations which the LORD left, to test Israel by . . ." (Judges 3:1). "Now therefore what I have here, says the LORD, seeing that my people are taken away for nothing?" (Isaiah 52:5).

The motifs of wicked tenants and vineyard do not appear in R. Jose's illustration. However he tells a story of a king, his son, his city, a wicked guardian and the king's counselors. The parable deals with the theme of theodicy in light of the great sufferings of Israel and the desctruction of Jerusalem. The prophets are said to have warned the Holy One as did the friends and servants of the king in the parable, but who could have conceived that the wicked guardian would have so drastically overstepped all limits of his commission by murdering the king's son and destroying the city. The parable paints the picture of God lamenting the destruction of Jerusalem, the death of so many from the people of Israel and the subsequent cruel exile. While the context of the story illustrates the actions of Nebuchadnezzar, one cannot help but see a relationship between the parable and the tragic history of the Jewish dispersion at a later time. At least it is reasonable to assume that such a universal theme would have been applied to other historical situations.

The shock element of the gospel Parable of the Wicked Husbandmen appears in the brutal and cruel killing of the vineyard owner's son. The motif is by no means atypical in rabbinic parables.[64] Likewise in the Parable of the King's Son and the wicked Guardian, the audience is shocked—first because the king entrusted his son into the care of the wicked guardian and second because the son is murdered. Not only is his son killed by the sword but his city is desolated and his house is burned with fire. Immediately the audience was able to connect these images with the nimshal and visualize Jerusalem and the Temple in ruins. The son of the king is the people of Israel who are slain by the enemies of the Holy One. But the Parable of the Wicked Husbandmen illustrates the death of Jesus as the nimshal of the son of the owner of the vineyard. His death was that of a prophet—but in the parable this stone which was rejected by the builders was destined to become the chief cornerstone. While Jesus alluded to his future sufferings and the fate of Jerusalem and attested to his special prophetic task, R. Jose's parable tried to answer the question concerning God's action: How can a God who loves his children allow them to suffer the devastation of their way of life and then to be exiled? The sufferings of Israel had a deeper significance. The purpose was to bring Israel into obedience and observance of the Torah. The higher aim justified the drastic measures taken to achieve the goal. However the parable vividly describes God's identification with the sufferings of his people in anthropomorphic images. But the suffering that the people were forced to endure exceeded the justifiable limits of God's plan. The enemies of Israel are to blame and not God. The instrument God chose to chastise his people went beyond the divinely set boundary and caused much more suffering than was permitted. Thus R. Jose's parable explains the divine purpose in the midst of Israel's suffering.

The drama portrayed in these rabbinic parables, which are similar to the Parable of the Wicked Husbandmen, all stress a specific theme and retain a special function.[65] In the Parable of the King's Son and the Field, the son inherits his father's property which was abused by the wicked tenants. The son is connected to Israel. In R. Jose's parable, the son is killed by the wicked guardian to whom the king had entrusted his son. Again the son is representative of the people of Israel. However in this example their sufferings are discussed as the text deals with the theme of theodicy. In Sifre Deuteronomy the son's special status as the one who receives the field from the wicked tenants is the main thrust of the story. In Midrash Psalms, the household steward is persecuted by the citizens of a province until the king settles matters. The household servant is identified with King David and not a collective group. Also in the Parable of the Wicked Husbandmen, Jesus employs similar motifs and characters. He combines the motifs to create a setting for the drama and then casts the characters into their roles in the mini-play. The underlying structure is very similar. In act one, the owner of the vineyard entrusts his property into the care of the wicked tenants. In act two the envoys of his servants are mistreated. The plot thickens in act three as the owner of the vineyard decides to send his son to the wicked husbandmen. The conflict is created as the tenants murder his son. Finally the application of the parable is made and one sees how the son, represented by the stone, overcomes opposition and then the parable's theme and function in the context of the gospel text are made evident. In the same way the rabbinic parables describe different scenes from a drama and then reveal the theme and function of the illustration. The same motifs function to teach similar but different themes in the context of the colorful teachings and preachings of Israel's sages.

In actuality, the parable has been misnamed. The designation of the "Parable of the Wicked Husbandmen" emphasizes the nefarious acts of the tenants. Moreover the title, "The Parable of the Vineyard," equally misses the controlling idea of the story and has the tendency to give way to a misplaced ecclesiastical interpretation which claims that the church has replaced historical Israel. The vineyard is secondary to the son. When one reflects on the final week of Jesus' ministry before his passion, and then hears the story about the vineyard, the tenants, the son and the stone, it becomes clear that Jesus is speaking about his future fate. While according to the synoptics, he tried to prepare the disciples for what would happen to him in Jerusalem, this parable is the first allusion made to his death in public ministry. Hence the parable would probably best be named, "The Parable of the Only Son."

Notes

1) See M. Lowe, "From the Parable of the Vineyard to a Pre-Synoptic Source," *New Testament Studies* 28 (1982), pp. 257–263. Lowe has suggested that the son who is killed in the parable originally referred to John the Baptist and not to Jesus. He bases his theory in part on the arrangement of the synoptics, and postulates that one can see a *"Baptist Sequence"* which consisted of 1. Cleansing of the Temple, 2. Question about Authority, 3. The Parable of the Two Sons, 4. The Parable of the Great Supper, 5. The Parable of the Wicked Husbandmen, 6. The Stone Saying. No one would contest that Jesus mentions the work of John in at least two of these pericopes, but what is John's connection to the Cleansing of the Temple? The sequence theory is moreover based strongly upon Matthew's arrangement as well as some reorganization for the sake of the hypothesis. However the Question about Authority and the Parable of the Two Sons deal with John's movement and especially his call to repentance and men's response to that call—not his tragic death. Josephus says that John was executed for political reasons by Herod Antipas, and it is difficult to understand how the Parable of the Wicked Husbandmen could illustrate Antipas' action (see note 43

below). Nonetheless Lowe's theory is a very attractive one. Though rejecting the theory, Fitzmyer has referred to it as "ingenious" (idem, *Luke,* vol. 2, p. 1278). It would somewhat alleviate the tension between Jesus and the Jewish Temple authorities of his day. However when one carefully studies the text, the historical context, and listens to the message of the parable, it requires more powers of the imagination and textual maneuvering to cast John the Baptist into the story than to recognize that the nimshal of the son cannot be anyone other than Jesus himself, the "only son." For other interpretations of the son figure see notes 6 and 7 below.

2) Flusser has discussed the composition of the Temple committee and has noted the similarities between the gospels and Josephus, *Ant.* 12:142. See Flusser, *Jesus,* p. 120 and note 210.

3) David Flusser first pointed out to me the connection between *geōrgos* and *aris* and its significance for the parable (private communication). Compare the use of the word *arisim* in Sifre Deuteronomy 312 (Finkelstein, p. 353). For the definition of *aris,* see now, Meir Ayali, *Poalim Veomanim* (Yad Letalmud: Jerusalem, 1987), pp. 36–42.

4) Irenaeus, *Against Heresies* 36:2, *The Ante-Nicene Fathers,* vol. 1, p. 515. See also the very important work, Heinz Schreckenberg, *Die christlichen Adversus-Judaeos-Texte und ihr literarisches und historisches Unfeld (1.–11. Jh.)* (Bern: Peter Lang, 1982), pp. 119–121.

5) H.B. Swete, *The Gospel according to St. Mark* (London: Macmillan, 1905), p. 270. Compare also M.J. Lagrange, *The Gospel according to Saint Mark* (London: Burns Oates and Washbourne, 1930), p. 124. Lagrange does not even make a distinction between the Jews and their leaders but writes, "The Messiah had resolved to warn the Jews of the consequences of the crime which they were about to commit and which was to cause an outpouring of the divine wrath" (ibid). R.T. France has gone so far as to enlarge the scope of the parable to include the Judaism of Jesus' day, "But the wording [Mt. 21:33 and parallels] is modelled in some detail on Isaiah 5:1–2. There God condemns Israel's failure in the picture of a vineyard which yielded no returns; here Jesus condemns contemporary Judaism in similar terms. The Jewish nation which now refuses the overtures of God's son is only repeating the failure of the Israel of Isaiah's day; only now the failure is more disastrous, and the condemnation final, as the rest of the parable shows" (idem, *Jesus and the Old Testament,* Grand Rapids: Baker Book House, 1971, pp. 69–70).

6) Cf. Jülicher, *Gleichnisreden Jesu,* vol. 2, pp. 385–406; R. Bultmann, *The History of the Synoptic Problem* (Oxford: Basil Blackwell, 1963), p. 177 and W.G. Kümmel, *Promise and Fulfilment* (London:

SCM, 1981), pp. 82–83 and idem, "Das Gleichnis von den bösen Weingärtnern," *Aux sources de la tradition chrétienne: Mélanges offerts à M. Maurice Goguel* (Paris: Delachaux et Niestlé, 1950), pp. 120–131. Kümmel writes, "Therefore this parable can only be considered to be an allegorical representation of salvation-history until Jesus' coming" (idem, *Promise and Fulfilment,* p. 83). Kümmel maintained that no Jew from the first century would have connected the son figure with the messiah (idem, "Das Gleichnis von den bösen Weingärtnern," pp. 129–131 and compare idem, *Promise and Fulfilment,* p. 83). See also Marshall, *Luke,* pp. 726–727 and Fitzmyer, *Luke,* vol. 2, pp. 1278–1279.

7) One can note an increasing tendency to accept the parable as authentic but the interpretations attributed to it remain quite diverse. See, for example, Dodd, *Parables,* pp. 93–98; Jeremais, *Parables,* pp. 70–77; M. Hengel, "Das Gleichnis von den Weingärtnern Mc 12, 1–12 im Lichte der Zenonpapyri und der rabbinischen Gleichnisse," *Zeitschrift für die neutestamentliche Wissenschaft* 59 (1968), pp. 1–39; J. Crossan, "The Parable of the Wicked Husbandmen," *Journal of Biblical Literature* 90 (1971), pp. 451–465; Jane and Raymond Newell, "The Parable of the Wicked Tenants," *Novum Testamentum* 14 (1972), pp. 226–237; J.A.T. Robinson, "The Parable of the Wicked Husbandmen: A Test of Synoptic Relationships," *New Testament Studies,* 23 (1974–75), pp. 443–461; M. Lowe, op. cit, note 1.

8) In the preceding sections, a number of points of comparison between the illustration and the illustrand have been noted in both gospel and rabbinic parables. The strict application of the one point approach advocated by Jülicher certainly has not solved all the hermeneutic questions. Jane and Raymond Newell were very happy to note " . . . what the one point of comparison must have been" (idem, "The Parable of the Wicked Tenants," pp. 236–237). However not all will agree with them that the Parable of the Wicked Husbandmen is an anti-Zealot parable designed to warn the Zealots that if they attempt to take unclaimed land away from the authorities, it will cause Roman reprisals. Nor is it convincing that the illustration attacks the violent methods of the Zealots though Jesus certainly opposed violence (ibid, pp. 236–237).

9) Compare M. Hengel, "Das Gleichnis von den Weingärtnern Mc 12, 1–12 im Lichte der Zenonpapyri und der rabbinischen Gleichnisse," pp. 7f, note 31 where he discusses some of the Semitisms of the text, and see also Robinson, "The Parable of the Wicked Husbandmen," pp. 452–454. An attempt to reconstruct the Hebrew *Vorlage* of the text would have to remain to some degree conjectural.

10) See F.C. Burkitt, "The Parable of the Wicked Husbandmen," eds.

P. Allen and J. Johnston, *Transactions of the Third International Congress for the History of Religions* (Oxford: Clarendon, 1908), vol. 2, pp. 321–328. Burkitt pointed out that if the early church was formulating an allegory concerning Christ in the parable, the narrative would most probably also contain an allusion to the resurrection. See also Taylor, *Mark,* p. 472.

11) These issues are very complicated in New Testament scholarship and in many ways are in need of review. Cf. Jeremias, *New Testament Theology,* pp. 257–286; E.P. Sanders, *Jesus and Judaism,* pp. 71–76; Flusser, *Yahadut Umekorot Hanatzrut,* pp. 253–274; idem, "Jesus and the Sign of the Son of Man," *Judaism and the Origins of Christianity* (at the press). No doubt the scholarly debate will continue, but Jesus seems to have felt his prophetic task as he spoke concerning Jerusalem's fate, and these utterances should not be relegated to the early church.

12) The question has been discussed by Fitzmyer, *Luke,* vol. 2, p. 1278 who treats the theories of T. Schramm, *Der Markus-Stoff bei Lukas: Eine literarkritische und redaktionsgeschichtliche Untersuchung* (Cambridge: Cambridge University Press, 1971), pp. 150–167 and A.T. Cadoux *The Parables of Jesus: Their Art and Use* (London: James Clarke, 1931), p. 40, who both maintained that Luke employed another source besides Mark. Robinson observed, "None of Luke's rewriting appears to show the influence of Mark or vice versa, unless the use of ἀγαπητόν betrays assimilation"; idem, "The Parable of the Wicked Husbandmen," p. 461. It should also be noted that it can be dangerous to decide textual questions solely or primarily on the basis of a theory concerning a solution to the synoptic problem. Robinson's suggestion is worth heeding on this point, "On the view we are urging, the most original form of the material may at any given point be found in any one (or two) of the three gospels. We do not have to force it to fit a theory of over-all priority. We can test it at its several points, as we have been doing with this sample [the Parable of the Wicked Husbandmen], and judge accordingly" (ibid, p. 458).

13) Gundry, *Matthew,* p. 425.

14) It has been suggested that the idea of the "beloved son" in the parable has been derived from the baptism or the transfiguration of Jesus where the term *agapētos* also appears. However care must be taken to study the gospels synoptically and a number of important manuscripts of Luke do not contain the word *agapētos* in either the baptism or the transfiguration, and see *The New Testament in Greek the Gosepl according to St. Luke* (Oxford: Clarendon Press, 1984), p. 68 on Luke 3:22 and p. 205 on Luke 9:34. The manuscript evidence is cited there. Nonethe-

less the editors accepted the word *agapētos* in both texts. However it is highly questionable whether the word *agapētos* originally appeared in either of these texts in Luke. At the baptism, Luke's text was harmonized with Matthew and Mark. Anti-adoptionists may have played a role in the preservation of the tradition (cf. with H. Greeven's revision of A. Huck's synopsis, *Synopse der drei ersten Evangelien,* Tübingen: J.C.B. Mohr, 1981, p. 18, where Greeven has retained Huck's text which certainly seems to be the correct reading). The rule of *lectio difficilior* should be applied. At the transfiguration, the strong attestation for Luke's version of "This is my Son, my Chosen" should not be so easily adapted to the versions of Mark and Matthew. It was natural for scribes to harmonize the texts.

15) In a preliminary version of the work at hand, I championed the text of Matthew and claimed that Luke and Mark had added the term *agapētos.* After a discussion of the material with David Flusser, a reevaluation of the evidence and new facts, it became clear that Luke and Mark preserved the parable more faithfully on this important fact. Flusser's comments were very helpful in consideration of this matter. As is well known, the Hebrew word *yachid* was normally translated by the Greek word *agapētos* in the Septuagint (see Hatch and Redpath, *Concordance,* vol. 1, p. 7). In the Psalms it is also employed to translate the Hebrew word *yadid.* The Hebrew meaning of the word *yachid* is "only" and seems to have also retained the connotation of "beloved" (see especially Genesis 22:2, *agapēton* in LXX; Proverbs 4:3 *agapōmenos;* and Judges 11:34, *monogenēs* in LXX). Compare the Parable of the King who Spoke Harshly to His Only Son (Song of Songs Rabbah 6:1 on Song of Songs 5:16) and the Parable of the King and his Only Daughter (Numbers Rabbah 12:8; Exodus Rabbah 52:5; Song of Songs Rabbah 3:11; Tanchuma, Pekudei, Buber's edition 8; Pesikta Derav Kahana 1:3, Mandelbaum, p. 7, the word *yachid* is missing, but see also the critical apparatus; cf. Sifra on Lev. 9:11, Weiss, 44c, where the context is mentioned but the parable does not appear). In 4 Baruch 7:26 Israel is referred to metaphorically as God's *only son,* "For (it is) just as (when) a father has an only son and he is handed over for punishement . . ." (S.E. Robinson, "4 Baruch," Charlesworth, *The Old Testament Pseudepigrapha,* vol. 2, p. 423).

16) See C.H. Turner, "Ο ΥΙΟϹ ΜΟΥ ΑΓΑΠΗΤΟϹ" *The Journal of Theological Studies* 27 (1926), pp. 113–129. After careful consideration of the evidence, Turner observed, "But the assertion may safely be hazarded that when ἀγαπητός is used in connection with υἱός, θυγατήρ, παῖς, or similar words, no Greek of pre-Christian times would have hes-

itated in understanding it of an 'only child', or would for a moment have thought of any other meaning as possible" (ibid, p. 117). Turner's observation was further confirmed by A. Souter, "ΑΓΑΠΗΤΟϹ" *Journal of Theological Studies* 28 (1927), pp. 59f. Souter noted another passage from Plutarch (*De amicorum multitudine* pp. 93 F, 94 A) which demonstrates that *agapētos* was understood as one's only son. Compare also Philo's mention of the τὸν μόνον καὶ ἀγαπητὸν αἰσθητὸν υἱὸν (*De Ebrietate* 30–31). The passage is discussed by C.H. Dodd, *The Interpretation of the Fourth Gospel* (Cambridge: Cambridge University Press, 1958), p. 67. My thanks to David Flusser who called my attention to these important studies.

17) Cf. Matthew 22:4,6,8,10.

18) See especially Flusser, *Die rabbinischen Gleichnisse,* pp. 304f.

19) Dodd, *Parables,* pp. 96–97.

20) See Dodd, ibid, note 22. See also Robert Grant and Noel Freedman, *The Secret Sayings of Jesus* (London: Collins, 1960) who wrote, "The parable [logion 66], like the preceding two, is derived from the synoptic gospels . . ." (ibid, p. 162). Cf. with W. Schrage, *Das Verhältnis des Thomas-Evangeliums zur Synoptischen Tradition und zu den koptischen Evangelienübersetzungen* (Berlin: Vergal Alfred Töplemann, 1964), pp. 137–147.

21) K.R. Snodgrass, "The Parable of the Wicked Husbandmen: Is the Gospel of Thomas Version the Original?" *New Testament Studies* 20 (1974), p. 143. Snodgrass writes, "Syr[s] omits Mark xii.4 so that only two servants precede the 'many others' and the sending of the son. Likewise, syr[s], which is not extant for Mark, omits the sending of the third servant in Luke xx.12 . . . Syr[s] does record the sending of the third servant in Luke, but it is evident that the text has been tampered with since it follows neither the Lukan style as the preceding verse nor the Lukan sequence" (ibid). Snodgrass also noted the work of W. Schrage, *Das Verhältnis des Thomas-Evangeliums zur Synoptischen Tradition und zu den koptischen Evangelienübersetzungen,* p. 140 who maintained that Thomas was acquainted with the canonical tradition and found agreements between Thomas and the Coptic, Sahidic and Bohairic versions. See Schrage's introduction, ibid, pp. 2–11. Cf. also note 23 below.

22) See preceding note. The evidence from syr[s] for Luke 20:11 is based upon Snodgrass' conjecture that the text has been altered.

23) Marshall, *Luke,* p. 730. Of course the owner of the vineyard speaks to himself also in both Matthew's and Mark's versions of the parable. Has Luke enlarged it? Cf. the Gospel of Thomas (logion 65) which

adds the statement of the master, "Perhaps he did not know them," after the return of the servent who was beaten.

24) The Greek word ἐντραπήσονται, which appears in all three of the synoptics (Matthew 21:37; Mark 12:6; Luke 20:13), presents some difficulty. A similar meaning is reflected in Luke 18:2 and see Bauer, *A Greek-English Lexicon,* p. 269. The question that must be asked is whether this term represents an original part of the text from the Hebrew *Vorlage* of the parable or if it was added later during the Greek redaction of the gospels. Here the text has been literally retranslated into Hebrew. However if the word is original it may have been derived from a Hebrew idiom like, את פניו יקבלו.

25) John 19:17 and Hebrews 13:12f, and see Jeremias, *Parables,* p. 73.

26) See also notes 4 and 5 above.

27) Flusser, *Yahadut Umekorot Hanatzrut,* pp. 426–427 and idem, *Jesus,* p. 94.

28) See L. Gaston, *No Stone on Another* (Leiden: Brill, 1970), pp. 112–128. See tos. Menachot 13:21 (and the *baraita* in b. Pesachim 57a) where the rods and blows of the fists from the priestly class are mentioned. See especially the important discussion of this passage by J. Jeremias, *Jerusalem in the Time of Jesus* (Philadelphia: Fortress Press, 1981), pp. 194–197. Compare also the use of force by the priestly families to take the skins from the Temple storage (tos. Zebachim 11:16–17 and b. Pesachim 57a). Lieberman has pointed out that the Temple guard was composed of Romans (see, tos. Pesachim 7:14 and especially *Tosefta Kefshutah,* vol. 4, pp. 614–615). This has been discussed by Flusser, "Who is it that Struck You?" *Immanuel* 20 and reprinted in *Judaism and the Origins of Christianity* (at the press), see note 7.

29) Testament of Levi 14:2–15:1 (Charlesworth, *The Old Testament Pseudepigrapha,* vol. 1, p. 793, trans. Kee; de Jonge, *Testaments of the Twelve Patriarchs,* pp. 41–43; de Jonge's English translation, Sparks, ed. *The Apocryphal Old Testament,* pp. 533–534 and cf. M. Stone, *The Testament of Levi,* Jerusalem: St. James Press, 1969, pp. 106–113). The text has at least one interpolation and betrays some redaction. Its importance will be determined to a certain extent by its provenance. See also J. Greenfield and M. Stone, "Remarks on the Aramaic Testament of Levi from the Geniza," *Revue Biblique* 84 (1979), pp. 214–230. Could the remarks concerning the law (Test. Levi 14:4–6) possibly be connected to the controversy pertaining to the oral interpretations of the law which were rejected by the Sadducees? Other explanations of the text are feasible. In any case, the cult of the Temple was strongly criticized in a num-

ber of circles during the period and the prophetic utterances of Jesus which speak about the Temple's fate should not be considered secondary additions of the early community after the fact (see preceding note). A more important question is encountered when one asks if the authorities viewed Jesus and his movement as a danger as portrayed in John 11:49ff. See also Flusser, *Jesus,* pp. 94f.

30) Josephus, *War,* 6:300–309. Interestingly the well-known sage who flourished at a later time but witnessed the destruction of Jerusalem had the same name, R. Joshua b. Chananyah (Jesus, from Joshua, son of Ananias).

31) Cf. E.L. Abel, "Who Wrote Matthew?" *New Testament Studies* 17 (1970–1971), pp. 132–152; L. Gaston, "The Messiah of Israel as Teacher of the Gentiles" *Interpretation* 29 (1975), pp. 24–40; Flusser, "Two Anti-Jewish Montages in Matthew," *Immanuel* 5 (1975), pp. 37–45; M. Lowe, "From the Parable of the Vineyard to a Pre-Synoptic Source," p. 261. See notes 4 and 5 above. It should also be noted that Paul would strongly disagree with the approach of the Matthean reviser; Romans 9:4–5; 11:29.

32) Flusser, "Matthew's 'Verus Israel,'" *Judaism and the Origins of Christianity* (at the press).

33) A rabbinic parable illustrates the kingdom theme. One should contrast it to the Parable of the Wicked Husbandmen which is designed to stress the wickedness of the tenants. In Sifre Deuteronomy 305 (Finkelstein, p. 324) a parable speaks about how Moses was sad that instead of one of his own sons or one of Aaron his brother's sons, Joshua would assume leadership of the people after Moses, "A parable. To what may the matter be compared? To a human king who had a son who was not worthy to reign. He took the kingdom from him and gave it to his beloved son. . . ." Here the illustration is clearly connected to the leadership of the people. But the vineyard should not be allegorized in Jesus' parable as it greatly stresses the wickedness of the tenants and their actions against the owner of the vineyard and his son. Another comparison of Israel to the vineyard based upon Isaiah 5:1ff appears in Seder Elijah (7) 8 (Friedmann, p. 43). See also Hengel, "Das Gleichnes von den Weingärtnern," pp. 16–19. Another interesting parallel to this theme appears in Sifre Numbers 117 (Horovitz, pp. 134–135) where a parable is used to describe the rebellion of Korah. The parable speaks about a special household servant who was given a field by the king. But because his ownership was not certified, his property was claimed by another. The conflict was resolved when the king made a covenant with his servant. The Aaronic priesthood was challenged by Korah but God made

it clear who would serve as priests (see also W. Bacher, *Die Agada der Tannaiten,* vol. 1, pp. 248f).

34) Cf. notes 4 and 5 above.

35) Robinson rejects it; cf. "The Parable of the Wicked Husbandmen," pp. 450f.

36) This was observed by Flusser.

37) Midrash Hagadol on Deuteronomy 1:17 (Fisch, p. 32) and see also Midrash Tannaim on Deuteronomy 1:17 (Hoffmann, p. 10). The text is partially paralleled in the Yalkut Machiri on Psalm 118:28. In the Yalkut, David is relegated the position of a slave and has to tend the sheep. His father, brothers and Samuel repudiate him, but he rises above them all. One cannot help but note what may be a word play between the words builders, stone, son and sons. Compare also the mnemonic rendition of David's praise by his father Jesse, his brothers, Samuel, and finally all of them together in b. Pesachim 119a (parallels in Yalkut Shimeoni, vol. 2, remez 873 and the Aramaic Targum to Psalm 118:22), cited by Billerbeck, vol. 1, p. 867. Cf. also Exodus Rabbah 37:1.

38) Ibid. The author's gratitude goes to Flusser who discovered this source from Midrash Hagadol and saw its connection to the stone saying in the parable.

39) Private communication.

40) See J.A. Sanders, *Discoveries in the Judean Desert of Jordan IV the Psalms Scroll of Qumran 11* (Oxford: Clarendon Press, 1965), pp. 48–56. Sanders further discusses the Psalm and the various suggested translations of the Hebrew version in idem, *The Dead Sea Psalms Scroll* (Ithaca: Cornell University Press, 1967), pp. 93–103. A similar Pseudo-Davidic Psalm has been discussed by Safrai and Flusser who maintain that the text originated from the days of the Second Temple period (ca. 140 B.C.), a view accepted also by John Strugnell. In this Psalm appear the Hebrew words פינה ממואסה אשר מאסו הבונים העלית לראש מעל כל האומים. The wording reflects Psalm 118, and see David Flusser and Shmuel Safrai, "Shire David Hechitzoneyim," *Sefer Zikaron Layehoshua Grintz* (Tel Aviv: Kibbutz Hameuchad, 1982), p. 84 and p. 92. One should also compare the parable concerning King David cited in note 62 below. The notion that David was exalted from his humble task as shepherd (as also was Moses) is reflected in the later midrash Exodus Rabbah 2:3 (see Shinan's critical edition, vol. 1, pp. 106–107).

41) Flusser suggested that the stone saying was deleted by Mark and Matthew because after they had made their revisions at the end of the parable, a reference to the stone would have been detached from their immediate contexts (private communication). Manson viewed it as a

separate saying, idem, *The Sayings of Jesus,* p. 322. See also Metzger, *A Textual Commentary on the Greek New Testament,* p. 58. The saying is appropriate for the context of the parable and further emphasizes the ultimate triumph of the stone.

42) See Marshall, *Luke,* p. 732, and Fitzmyer, *Luke,* vol. 2, p. 1286. Certainly the theme of judgment is also contained in the saying. See also Mirjam Prager, "Israel in the Parables," *The Bridge* vol. 4 (1961–1962), p. 64. The idea of the "testing stone" (Isaiah 8:14) became important in early Christian thought (cf. 1 Peter 2:5–6) and see Flusser, "From the Essenes to Romans 9:24–33," *Judaism and the Origins of Christianity* (at the press).

43) Esther Rabbah 7:10 and see Billerbeck, vol. 1, p. 877. On R. Simeon ben Jose ben Lakunya see Hyman, *Toldot Tannaim Veamoraim,* vol. 3, pp. 1189–1191.

44) Ibid.

45) Tanchuma, Buber's edition, Terumah, 6. See the parallel to Resh Lakish's statement in Midrash Daniel on Daniel 2:34 (Lange and Schwartz, p. 26).

46) Consider the circumstances of John the Baptist's death according to Josephus, *Ant.* 18:116–119; cf. with Josephus on Theudas the false prophet, *Ant.* 20:97–99; Judas the Galilean and note that even his two sons were crucified and the Temple was "ravaged by the enemy's fire through this revolt"; *Ant.* 20:100–102, 18:3–10, 23–25, *War* 2:118, 433f, 7:253f; cf. Acts 5:35–36 and see also the report about the Egyptian, *Ant.* 20:169–172, *War* 2:261–263; cf. Acts 21:38. See Jackson and Lake, *The Beginnings of Christianity,* vol. 4, pp. 60–61, pp. 276f. Compare also M. de Jonge, "The New Testament," eds. S. Safrai and M. Stern, *The Jewish People in the First Century,* vol. 1, p. 42.

47) See preceding note. On the crucifixions of the Jewish people, cf. Josephus on Quintilius Varus, *Ant.* 17:295–296, Schürer, revised, *History,* vol. 1, p. 332; Ummidius Quadratus, *Ant.* 20:130, Schürer, ibid, p. 459; Florus, *War,* 2:306; Schürer, ibid, p. 485; Titus, Life, 75 (420–421); see also the description, *Ant.* 12:256. See also Paul Winter, *On the Trial of Jesus* (Berlin: Walter de Gruyter, 1961), pp. 62–66.

48) Cf. G. Alon, *The Jews in their Land in the Talmudic Age* (Jerusalem: Magnes Press, 1984), pp. 592–637 and S. Safrai, *R. Akiva Ben-Yosef Chaiyav Umishnato* (Jerusalem: Bialik Institute, 1970), pp. 29–33. See also the critical analysis of Peter Schäfer, "Rabbi Aqiva und Bar Kokhba," *Studien zur Geschichte Theologie des rabbinische Judentums* (Leiden: Brill, 1978), pp. 65–121 and the condensed English version, idem, "Rabbi Aqiva and Bar Kokhba," William Green, ed., *Approaches*

to Ancient Judaism (Chico: Scholars Press, 1980), pp. 113–130 and his book, idem, *Der Bar Kokhba-Aufstand* (Tübingen: J.C.B. Mohr, 1981), pp. 55–68.

49) Cf. notes 4 and 5 above.

50) Jeremias, *Parables,* p. 230, note 1 and E. Fuchs, "Bemerkungen zur Gleichnisauslegung," *Theologische Literaturzeitung* 6 (1954), cols. 345–348.

51) Sifre Deuteronomy 312 (Finkelstein, p. 353), Midrash Tannaim on Deuteronomy 32:9 (Hoffmann, p. 190), Midrash Hagadol on Deuteronomy 32:9 (Fisch, p. 703) and Yalkut Shimeoni, vol. 2, remez 289. See Billerbeck, vol. 1, p. 874 and Flusser, *Jesus,* p. 94; and cf. Hengel, "Das Gleichnes von den Weingärtnern," pp. 17–18.

52) Midrash Hagadol on Deuteronomy 32:9 (Fisch, p. 703) and Midrash Tannaim on Deuteronomy 32:9 (Hoffmann, p. 190).

53) On the unworthy seed of dross, compare also Sifre Deuteronomy 31 (Finkelstein, pp. 49–50), 343 (Finkelstein, p. 397); Pesikta Rabbati 39 (Friedmann, p. 165a); Midrash Psalms on Psalm 118:20; Targum Yerushalmi on Genesis 49:2, the Frag. Targum on Genesis 49:2 (Klein vol. 1, p. 65, vol. 2, p. 117) and also Targum Neophyti on Genesis 49:2.

54) For other Greek translations of the Hebrew word see E. dos Santos, *An Expanded Hebrew Index for the Hatch-Redpath Concordance to the Septuagint* (Jerusalem: Dugith, 1976), p. 221.

55) H.G. Scott Liddell and R. Scott, *A Greek-English Lexicon* (Oxford: Clarendon, 1968), p. 190.

56) This translation is uniform in Targum Neofiti according to M. McNamara, *The New Testament and the Palestinian Targum to the Pentateuch* (Rome: Biblical Institute Press, 1978), p. 63.

57) See note 53 above.

58) Sifre Deuteronomy 343 (Finkelstein, p. 397) and see note 53 above.

59) See note 53 above.

60) Billerbeck, vol. 1, p. 874 and Fiebig, *Rabbinische Geichnisse,* pp. 10–11.

61) See the parable in Sifre Deuteronomy 305 (Finkelstein, p. 324) and discussed in note 33 above.

62) Midrash Psalm 24:2 (Buber, p. 102a), Yalkut Machiri on Psalm 24:2 and Yalkut Shimeoni vol. 2, remez 675. See Braude, *The Midrash on Psalms,* vol. 1, pp. 336–337, "Another comment. *To David, A Psalm. The land is the Lord's* (Ps. 24:1): A parable of a king who had a retainer [*ben bayit*] in a certain city. The inhabitants of the city honored him because they knew that he was the king's retainer; and whenever he came

to the king, the king also honored him, so that he was honored here as well as there. When the king gave up his city, however, its inhabitants began to rebel against the king's retainer, so that he had to return to his king. But later, when the king reclaimed his city, and when, as before, the king's retainer began to go about in the city, its inhabitants honored him again as the king's retainer. Thereupon the king said: 'When I gave up my city, you rebelled against him! Was he not my retainer then, even as he is my retainer now? Yet only now do you again honor him.' The king is the Holy One, blessed be He; and the city is the Land of Israel; and the king's retainer is David, king of Israel. . . ."

63) Seder Elijah (30) 28 (Friedmann, p. 150). Compare also the parable in j. Sanhedrin 28b, chap. 10, hal. 2. It is attributed to R. Chunya in the name of R. Laazar and contains the motif of a teacher-guardian who starves the king's son to death. Compare also the rabbinic parables which depict the emissaries of the king as being mistreated and sometimes killed, Ziegler, *Die Königsleichnisse des Midrasch,* p. xlvi, Genesis Rabbah 41:2 (Albeck, pp. 402–403); Ruth Rabbah, Petichta 6 (Lerner, p. 26); Leviticus Rabbah 11:7 (Margulies, pp. 231f) and Esther Rabbah, Petichta 11. See also P. Culbertson, "Reclaiming the Matthean Vineyard Parables" (unpublished paper), p. 34. For the shocking motif of killing the workman see also Midrash Proverbs on Proverbs 16 (R. Jose Hagalili) and compare the parallel in Semachot Derabbi Chiya 3:6 (Higger, pp. 222–223, there attributed to Rabbi).

64) See the sources cited in the preceding note.

65) See notes 51, 61, and 62 above. Cf. also with note 33.

JESUS, THE JEWISH PEOPLE AND THE INTERPRETATION OF THE PARABLES

The inadequacies of past hermeneutical approaches to the parables of Jesus become clear when the parables are studied as a literary genre related to their rabbinic counterparts. As has been observed, the church fathers allegorized the parables of the gospels in order to adapt them to their own purposes which were usually far removed from the historical Jesus. In the modern period, Jülicher attacked the allegorization of the parables and has influenced two generations of scholarship by claiming that the parables have only one point and no allegorical elements. Dodd and Jeremias have based their approaches upon a renewed awareness of the eschatological thrust of Jesus' proclamation of the kingdom of God. However their emphasis upon the eschatological content of Jesus' teaching has minimized other aspects of Jesus' message like prayer and repentance. In spite of a few lone voices, the relationship between gospel parables and their rabbinic counterparts has been minimized and often ignored.

The fact that New Testament scholars have often ignored rabbinic parables comes as no surprise.[1] Few New Testament exegetes have been equipped with the minimal linguistic and critical tools that are necessary for the scientific study of rabbinic literature. Most learn about the world of Israel's sages through secondary works like Billerbeck's commentary which is by no means free from bias. Jülicher deemed rabbinic parables as allegorically inferior and secondary to those of Jesus. The present work has attempted to study parabolic teaching from a different approach. The parable should be examined as an entity in itself. The parables of Jesus should be studied in the larger framework of similar parabolic teachings. The closest analogies to the parables of Jesus are those from rabbinic literature.[2] In fact the story parable as it appears in the gospels and rabbinic literature, though somewhat similar to a few select biblical passages and fables, is not fully paralleled elsewhere and seems to be an inner Jewish accomplishment from the Second Temple period.

A parable often has various levels of understanding which are connected with a change of audience and a new context. In the first level, the parable was designed to be told as a story or an illustration. From this stage, the parable was preserved in a text. At this level of understanding, the parable sometimes was reinterpreted. This can be seen in the gospels. The Parable of the Wicked Husbandmen was reinterpreted by Matthew or his final redactor to teach that Israel had been replaced by a new nation.[3] In Luke the Parable of the Pounds was understood to address the question of the delayed parousia.[4] In Sifre Deuteronomy the same illustration could be employed to teach two different themes in two different contexts.[5] In gospel research it is important to seek the first level of understanding and endeavor to hear Jesus speaking to his contemporaries.

In many ways rabbinic parables can be useful in this task. Sometimes they provide collaborative information concerning aspects of Jewish culture and custom. Since they are derived from the same literary genre, one can see how different motifs and components can be combined in different parables in order to teach relevant truth. The form and structure of many rabbinic parables is paralleled in the texts of the gospels. Although some rabbinic parables have been used in exegesis, one discovers a usage in homiletical teaching where the story parable becomes a rhetorical device that can treat delicate themes like theodicy or complaint against God as well as more universal themes like repentance, God's compassion, forgiveness both between man and his fellow and between God and man. The parable can breathe new life into old themes by presenting them in innovative and imaginative ways that informed, educated and inspired the hearers.

Many questions remain unanswered. The process of compiling the synoptic gospels in Greek was much different than the way in which rabbinic texts were preserved. Nevertheless as has been seen, one finds a remarkable similarity between gospel parables and those of the rabbis. This fact does not account for the time span between the composition of the various texts of rabbinic literature and the compilation of the gospels. It is easy to say that all the rabbinic texts are late and therefore have no relationship to the gospels. This extreme approach does not bring the researcher closer to a solution. If one studies only Ben Sira in order to understand Judaism in late antiquity, he will certainly have a different understanding of the Jewish religion during the period than if he only studies the Temple Scroll. While George F. Moore's claims concerning "normative Judaism" paint a distorted picture, rabbinic literature can provide valuable insights into early Jewish teachings of the first century especially when they are corroborated by other earlier sources like the gospels. Extreme caution must be taken in analyzing the evidence critically and historically. All pertinent literary parallels to rabbinic texts must be carefully examined. The common motifs and parallel ideas contained in both rabbinic and gospel parables closes the gap somewhat and brings Jesus into closer contact with his people. It helps to recreate something of the possible Jewish environment in which he operated.

Instead of trying to hear Jesus preach to his contemporaries and illustrate the meaning of his message in parables, too often past approaches to the story parables have sought to discover a reason for sharp conflict and for the rejection of Jesus. In a recent book, John Drury writes, "The meaning of most parables is tied into a past and particular historical crisis: the emergence of the Christian religion out of the Jewish, and the task of self-definition which it imposed."[6] Why are the parables of Jesus the point of departure for the "emergence of the Christian religion out of the Jewish"? Our study demonstrates that the parables come from a time when Jesus was very much a part of the Jewish world. Though Drury may not have intended to do so, his approach suggests that a conflict between the Christian and Jewish religions was the product of the parabolic teachings of Jesus. However a close comparison between the parables of Jesus and those of the Jewish sages shows that the themes of Jesus' parables are often quite similar to those of their rabbinic counterparts. When

Eduard Schweizer discusses the Parable of the Prodigal Son, he felt that he had discovered one of the reasons for the crucifixion of Jesus. He claims, "Who but Jesus would have the authority to assume the role of God. . . . Those who nailed him to the cross because they found blasphemy in his parables—which proclaimed such scandalous conduct on the part of God—understood his parables better than those who saw in them nothing but the obvious message, which should be self-evident to all, of the fatherhood and kindness of God, meant to replace superstitious belief in a God of wrath."[7] Schweizer seems to be saying that the Jewish people nailed Jesus to the cross and that his parables were rightly interpreted as blasphemy. Here one must take issue not only with an historical inaccuracy but also with the claim of Jesus' blasphemy. The Parable of the Prodigal Son would not have been considered blasphemous, but it further illustrates the powerful and liberating theme of forgiveness between man and his fellow as well as between God and man which was an integral part of Jewish piety in many circles during the period and is not unlike rabbinic parables. A misunderstanding of early Jewish thought and parabolic teaching will surely lead to questionable results.

The story parable in the gospels as well as in rabbinic literature is a live drama with a specific function. Any connection between the mashal and the nimshal must be imposed upon the parable in the context by the storyteller. Moreover, one can tentatively conclude that rabbinic literature can provide clues concerning the original setting of Jesus' parables. He was a dynamic parabolist among his own people. Like Jesus, the rabbis often employed the parable to teach relevant truths that had far-reaching moral implications concerning man's relationship to his fellow and also to his Creator. Thus parabolic teaching should be viewed more correctly as a close point of unity between Jesus and his contemporaries rather than one of division.

Notes

1) See G. Vermes, *Jesus and the World of Judaism* (London: SCM Press, 1983), pp. 74–88. Indeed this is the one of the main problems with K. Bailey's works, i.e. little attention has been given to the Jewish con-

text and to rabbinic parables. Nevertheless Bailey's hermeneutical principles are basically sound (idem, *Through Peasant Eyes,* pp. xxii–xxiii).

2) See N. Perrin, *Jesus and the Language of the Kingdom* (Philadelphia: Fortress, 1973), pp. 95–96, "The rabbinical parables to which Fiebig pointed not only stood in closer cultural proximity to Jesus—and, what is probably even more important, to the early Christian communities using the parables—they were also closer to the parables of Jesus in literary form and function." On the problem of the later date of rabbinic materials, perhaps it is worthwhile to cite the warning of Charlesworth, "conversely, late writings must not be ignored in a search for ideas possibly characteristic of Early Judaism; these documents frequently preserve edited portions of early Jewish writings" (*The Old Testament Pseudepigrapha,* vol. 1, p. xv). Of course Charlesworth speaks about later Christian works which are based upon earlier Jewish sources (but cf. his similar statements concerning rabbinic literature, ibid, pp. xxvi-xxvii). Nonetheless, in a similar way later rabbinic parables can be useful in the interpretation of the parables of Jesus and sometimes are derived from much earlier sources than the texts in which they appear.

3) Matthew 21:43.

4) Luke 19:11–27 and see parallel Matthew 25:14–30, Mark 13:34.

5) Sifre Deuteronomy 19 (Finkelstein, p. 31) and 356 (Finkelstein, p. 424) and parallels, Midrash Tannaim on Deut. 1:21 (Hoffmann, p. 11); Midrash Hagadol on Deut. 1:21 (Fisch, p. 34) and compare Midrash Lekach Tov on Deuteronomy 1:21.

6) John Drury, *The Parables in the Gospels* (New York: Crossroad, 1985), p. 6. Charles Smith wrote, "Jesus used parables and Jesus was put to death. The two facts are related and it is necessary to understand the connection . . ." idem, *Jesus and the Parables* (Philadelphia: Westminster Press, 1948), p. 17. Quoted by J. Petuchowski, "The Theological Significance of the Parable in Rabbinic Literature and the New Testament" *Christian News from Israel* 23 (1972), p. 81.

7) Eduard Schweizer, *Jesus* (London: SCM Press, 1971), pp. 28–29. See also the critical remarks of E.P. Sanders, *Jesus and Judaism,* pp. 39–40.

SELECT BIBLIOGRAPHY

Primary Sources, Editions and Translations

Aland, K. *Synopsis of the Four Gospels.* New York: United Bible Societies, 1971.

Avot Derabbi Natan, ed. S. Schechter, Wien, 1887.

Ben-Ḥayyim, Z. ed. *The Book of Ben Sira Text, Concordance and an Analysis of the Vocabulary.* Jerusalem: Hebrew Language Academy, 1973.

Bialik, Ch. and J. Rabnitzki. *Sefer Haagadah.* Tel Aviv: Dvir, 1973.

Braude, W. G. *The Midrash on Psalms* (in two volumes). New Haven: Yale University Press, 1958.

———. *Pesikta Rabbati* (in two volumes). New Haven: Yale University Press, 1968.

———. *Pesikta-de-Rab-Kahana.* Philadelphia: The Jewish Publication Society, 1975.

———. *Tanna Debe Eliyyahu.* Philadelphia: Jewish Publication Society, 1981.

Charles, R.H., ed. *The Apocrypha and Pseudepigrapha of the Old Testament* (in two volumes). Oxford: The Clarendon Press, 1977.

Charlesworth, J.H., ed. *The Old Testament Pseudepigrapha* (in two volumes). Doubleday: New York, 1983–1985.

Codex Vatican 31 Sifra, Eliyahu Rabbah and Eliyahu Zutta. Jerusalem: Makor, 1972.

Cohen, A. and Israel Brodie, eds. *The Minor Tractates of the Talmud* (in two volumes). London: Soncino Press, 1971.

Danby, Herbert. *The Mishnah.* Oxford: Oxford University Press, 1977.

Epstein, I., ed. *The Babylonian Talmud* (in thirty-five volumes). London: Soncino Press, 1935–1978.

Freedman, H., ed. *Midrash Rabbah* (in nine volumes). London: The Soncino Press, 1951.

Freidlander, G. *Pirke de Rabbi Eliezer.* New York: Hermon Press, 1981.

Gaster, T. *The Dead Sea Scriptures.* New York: Anchor Books, 1976.

Goldin, J. *The Fathers according to Rabbi Nathan.* New York: Schocken Press, 1974.

Greeven, H. *Synopse der drei ersten Evangelien* (13th revised edition of Huck's synopsis). Tübingen: J.C.B. Mohr, 1981.

Guillaumont, A., H. Peuch, G. Quispel, W. Till and Y. 'Abd al Masiḥ, eds. *The Gospel according to Thomas.* Leiden: Brill, 1976.

Haberman, A. *Megillot Midbar Yehuda.* Israel: Machbarot Lesifrut Publishing House, 1959.

Herford, T. *Pirke Aboth the Ethics of the Talmud: Sayings of the Fathers.* New York: Schocken Books, 1975.

Hertz, J.H. *The Authorised Daily Prayer Book.* New York: Bloch Publishing Company, 1959.

Huck, A. *Synopsis of the First Three Gospels.* Oxford: Basil Blackwell, 1968.

Josephus (in nine volumes). ed. and trans. H.J. Thackeray. Oxford: Harvard University Press, 1978.

Knibb, M.A. and E. Ullendorff. *The Ethiopic Book of Enoch.* Oxford: The Clarendon Press, 1978.

Licht, Jacob. *Megilat Hahodayot.* Jerusalem: The Bialik Institute, 1957.

———. *Megilat Haserachim.* Jerusalem: The Bialik Institute, 1965.

Lohse, E. *Die Texte aus Qumran.* Munich: Kösel Verlag, 1981.

Masechtot Derech Eretz (in two volumes, Hebrew text and English translation). M. Higger, ed. Jerusalem: Makor, 1970.

Masechet Semachot. ed. M. Higger. Jerusalem: Makor, 1970.

Mekilta Derabbi Ishmael, eds. H.S. Horovitz and Ch. Rabin. Jerusalem: Wahrmann Books, 1970.

Mekilta Derabbi Ishmael. ed. M. Friedmann. Wien, 1870.

Mekilta Derabbi Ishmael (in three volumes, Hebrew text with English translation). ed. and trans. Jacob Lauterbach. Philadelphia: Jewish Publication Society, 1976.

Mekilta Derabbi Shimeon Bar Yochai. eds. Y.N. Epstein and E.Z. Melamed. Jerusalem: Hillel Press, 1980.

Midrash Bereshit Rabbah (in three volumes). eds. Ch. Albeck and J. Theodor. Jerusalem: Wahrmann Books, 1980.

Midrash Devarim Rabbah. ed. S. Liebermann. Jerusalem: Wahrmann Books, 1974.

Midrash Echa Rabbah. ed. S. Buber. Wilna, 1899.

Midrash Hagadol (in five volumes). Jerusalem: Mosad Harav Kook, 1975.

Midrash Lekach Tov (on the Pentateuch). ed. S. Buber. Wilna, 1880.

Midrash Lekach Tov (on Ruth). ed. S. Bamberger. Mainz, 1887.

Midrash Lekach Tov (on Song of Songs and Lamentations). ed. A.W. Greenup. London, 1908–1909.

Midrash Mishle. ed. S. Buber. Wilna, 1891.

Midrash Rabbah (in eleven volumes, on the Torah). ed. with commentary by Moshe Mirkin. Tel Aviv: Yavneh, 1977.

Midrash Rabbah (in two volumes). Wilna, 1887.

Midrash Rut Rabbah. ed. M. Lerner. Doctoral Dissertation at the Hebrew University, 1971.

Midrash Seder Olam. ed. D. Ratner. New York: The Talmudic Research Institute, 1966.

Midrash Shemot Rabbah. ed. A. Shinan. Jerusalem: Dvir, 1984.

Midrash Shemuel. ed. S. Buber. Krakau, 1893.

Midrash Shir Hashirim. ed. Eliezer Halevi Grunhut. Jerusalem, 1897.

Midrash Shir Hashirim Rabbah. ed. Shimshon Donski. Israel: Dvir Publishing, 1980.

Midrash Tanchuma. ed. S. Buber. Wilna 1885.

Midrash Tanchuma. Warsaw, 1879.

Midrash Tannaim. ed. D. Hoffmann. Berlin, 1908.

Midrash Tehilim. ed. S. Buber. Wilna, 1891.

Midrash Vayikra Rabbah (in five volumes). ed. M. Margulies. Jerusalem: Wahrmann Books, 1970.

Mishnah (in six volumes). ed. Ch. Albeck. Jerusalem: Bialik Institute, 1978.

The Mishnah of R. Eliezer. ed. H.G. Enelow. New York: Bloch Publishing Co., 1933.

The New Testament in Greek the Gospel according to St. Luke. Oxford: Clarendon Press, 1984.

Novum Testamentum Graece. ed. S. Legg. Oxford: Clarendon, Matthew 1940, Mark 1935.

Perry, B.E. *Babrius and Phaedrus.* London: Heinemann, 1975.

Pesikta Derav Kahana. ed. B. Mandelbaum. New York: The Jewish Theological Seminary, 1962.

Pesikta Derav Kahana. ed. S. Buber. Lyck, 1868.

Pesikta Rabbati. ed. M. Friedmann. Wien, 1880.

Philo (in ten volumes and two supplementary volumes). eds. and trans. F.H. Colson and G.H. Whitaker. Cambridge: Harvard University Press, 1981.

Pirke Derabbi Eliezer. ed. David Luria. Warsaw, 1852.

Saldarini, A. *The Fathers according to Rabbi Nathan (Abot de Rabbi Nathan Version B).* Leiden: Brill, 1975.

Sanders, J.A. *Discoveries in the Judaean Desert of Jordan IV the Psalms Scroll of Qumran Cave 11.* Oxford: The Clarendon Press, 1965.

Schmidt, F. *Le Testament grec d'Abraham.* Tübingen: J.C.B. Mohr, 1986.

Seder Eliyahu Rabbah. ed. M. Friedmann. Jerusalem: Wahrmann Books, 1969.

Segal, M. *Sefer Ben Sira Hashalem.* Jerusalem: Bialik Institute, 1972.

Sifra. ed. J.H. Weiss. Wien, 1862.

Sifra (incomplete, two volumes in print with the rest of the text in preparation). ed. L. Finkelstein. New York: The Jewish Theological Seminary of America, 1984.

Sifra (incomplete). ed. M. Friedmann. Breslau, 1915.

Sifra or Torat Kohanim according to Codex Assemani LXVI. L. Finkelstein, ed. New York: The Jewish Theological Seminary of America, 1956.

Sifre Al Bemidbar Vesifre Zuta. ed. H.S. Horovitz. Jerusalem: Wahrmann, 1966.

Sifre Debe Rav. ed. M. Friedmann. Wien, 1864.

Sifre Devarim. ed. L. Finkelstein. New York: The Jewish Theological Seminary of America, 1969.

Sparks, H.F.D. *The Apocryphal Old Testament.* Oxford: Oxford University Press, 1984.

Talmud Babli. Wilna Edition: Tel Aviv, reprint, 1970.

Talmud Jerushalmi. Krotoshin Edition, 1866.

Talmud Yerushalmi. Venice Edition, 1523–1524.

Talmud Yerushalmi (based upon the Leiden Manuscript, Scal. 3, from 1334, published in four volumes). Jerusalem: Kedem, 1971.

Taylor, C. *Sayings of the Fathers* (in two volumes). Cambridge: Cambridge University Press, 1877.

Torah Shelemah (thirty-eight volumes). ed. M. Kasher. New York and Jerusalem, 1951–1983.

Tosefta. ed. M. Zuckermandel. Wahrmann Books: Jerusalem, 1937.

Tosefta (in thirteen volumes). ed. with commentary, S. Lieberman. New York: The Theological Seminary of America, 1955–1977.

Vermes, G. *The Dead Sea Scrolls in English.* Penguin Books: Baltimore, 1962.

Yalkut Hamakiri. ed. A.W. Greenup. Jerusalem, 1968.

Yalkut Hamakiri. ed. S. Buber, Berdyczew, 1899.

Yalkut Hamakiri. ed. Y. Shapiro. Jerusalem, 1964.

Yalkut Shimeoni. Wilna, 1898.

Literature on the Parables

Baasland, E. "Zum Beispiel der Beispeilerzählungen zur Formenlehre der Gleichnisse und zur Methodik der Gleichnisauslegung." *Novum Testamentum* 28 (1986), pp. 190ff.

Bailey, K.E. *Through Peasant Eyes More Lucan Parables their Culture and Style.* Grand Rapids: Eerdmanns, 1980.

———. *Poet and Peasant.* Grand Rapids: Eerdmanns, 1976.

Cohen, Chaim. "Eduiyot Akadiyot Chadashot Legabe Hamuvan Vehaetimologiyah Shel Hamunach 'Mashal' Bamikra." Benyamin Oppenheimer, ed. *Sefer Zikaron Layehoshua Grintz.* Tel Aviv: Kibbutz Hameuchad, 1982.

Crossan, J.D. "The Parable of the Wicked Husbandmen." *Journal of Biblical Literature* 90 (1971), pp. 451–465.

Daube, David. "Nathan's Parable," *Novum Testamentum* 24 (1982), pp. 275–288.

Dodd, C.H. *The Parables of the Kingdom.* Glasgow: William Collins Sons and Company, 1961.

Feldman, A. *The Parables and Similes of the Rabbis Agricultural and Pastoral.* Cambridge: Cambridge University Press, 1927.

Fiebig, Paul. *Altjüdische Gleichnisse und die Gleichnisse Jesu.* Tübingen: J.C.B. Mohr, 1904.

———. *Die Gleichnisreden Jesu im Lichte der rabbinischen Gleichnisse des neutestamentlichen Zeitalters.* Tübingen: J.C.B. Mohr, 1912.

———. *Rabbinsiche Gleichnisse.* Leipzig: J.C. Hinrichs'sche Buchhandlung, 1929.

Flusser, David. "Mishle Yeshu Vehameshalim Basifrut Chazal." *Yahadut Umekorot Hanatzrut.* Tel Aviv: Sifriyat Poalim, 1979.

———. *Die rabbinischen Gleichnisse und der Gleichniserzähler Jesus.* Bern: Peter Lang, 1981.

Funk, R. "Poll on the Parables," *Forum* (March 1986), pp. 54ff.

Guttmann, T. *Hamashal Batekufat Hatannaim.* Jerusalem: Abir Yaakov, 1940.

Hengel, Martin. "Das Gleichnis von den Weingärtnern Mc 12:1–12." *Zeitschrift für die neutestamentliche Wissenschaft* 59 (1968), pp. 1–39.

Hunter, A.M. *Interpreting the Parables.* London: SCM Press, 1972.

Jacobs, J. "Aesop's Fables Among the Jews." *The Jewish Encyclopedia.* vol. 1, pp. 221f.

Jeremias, Joachim. *The Parables of Jesus.* London: SCM Press, 1981.

———. *Rediscovering the Parables.* London: SCM Press, 1966.

Johnston, R.M. "Parables among the Pharisees and Early Rabbis," Appendix in, J. Neusner, *A History of Mishnaic Law of Purities Part XIII: Miqvaot.* Leiden: Brill, 1976, pp. 224ff.

———. "Parabolic Interpretations Attributed to Tannaim."

Unpublished Doctoral Dissertation: Hartford Seminary Foundation, 1977.

Jones, G.V. *The Art and Truth of the Parables.* London: SPCK, 1964.

Jülicher, A. *Die Gleichnisreden Jesu* (in two volumes). Tübingen: J.C.B. Mohr, 1886–1910, reprinted, Darmstadt: Wissenschaftliche Buchgesellschaft, 1963.

Kissinger, Warren. *The Parables of Jesus a History of Interpretation and Bibliography.* Metuchen: Scarecrow Press, 1979.

Kümmel, W.G. "Das Gleichnis von den bösen Weingärtnern (Mark. 12.1–9)." *Aux sources de la tradition chrétienne: Mélanges offerts à M. Maurice Goguel.* Paris: Delachaux & Niestlé, 1950, pp. 120–131.

Linneman, Eta. *Parables of Jesus.* London: SPCK, 1977.

Linton, Olof. "Coordinated Sayings and Parables in the Synoptic Gospels." *New Testament Studies* 26, 1980. pp. 139–163.

Little, James. "Parable Research in the Twentieth Century I. The Predecessors of J. Jeremias." *The Expository Times* 87 (1975), pp. 356–360.

———. "Parable Research in the Twentieth Century II. The Contribution of J. Jeremias." *The Expository Times* 88 (1976), pp. 40–43.

———. "Parable Research in the Twentieth Century III. Developments since J. Jeremias." *The Expository Times* 88 (1977), pp. 71–75.

Lowe, M. "From the Parable of the Vineyard to a Pre-Synoptic Source." *New Testament Studies* 28 (1982), pp. 257–263.

Mann, Jacob. "Jesus and the Sadducean Priests: Luke 10.25–37." *Jewish Quarterly Review* 6 (1914), pp. 415–422.

Newell, Jane E. and Raymond R. "The Parable of the Wicked Tenants." *Novum Testamentum* 14 (1972), pp. 226–237.

Noy, Dov. "Mishle Melakim Shel Rashbi." *Machanayim* 53–54 (1961), pp. 73–87.

Oesterley, W.O.E. *The Gospel Parables in Light of their Jewish Background.* London: SPCK, 1936.

Perrin, Norman, "The Modern Interpretation of the Parables of Jesus and the Problem of Hermeneutics." *Interpretation* 25, (1971), pp. 131–148.

Petuchowski, J. "The Theological Significance of the Parable in Rabbinic Literature and the New Testament." *Christian News from Israel* 23, (1972), pp. 76ff, and also "A Panel of Commentary on Petuchowski's Discussion of the Parable." 23 (1973), pp. 144ff.

Robinson, J.A.T. "The Parable of the Wicked Husbandmen: A Test of Synoptic Relationships." *New Testament Studies* 21 (1974–75), pp. 443–461.

Sanders, J.T. "The Parable of the Pounds and Lucan Anti-Semitism." *Theological Studies* 42 (1981), pp. 660–668.

Scott, B. "Essaying the Rock," *Forum* (March 1986), pp. 3ff.

Snodgrass, K.R. "The Parable of the Wicked Husbandmen: Is the Gospel of Thomas Version the Original?" *New Testament Studies* 20 (1974–75), pp. 142–144.

Stein, Robert. *An Introduction to the Parables of Jesus.* Philadelphia: Westminster, 1981.

Stern, D.M. "Interpreting Parables: The Mashal in Midrash with Special Reference to Lamentations Rabba." Unpublished Doctoral Dissertation: Harvard University, 1980.

Thoma, C. "Prolegomena zu einer Übersetzung und Kommentierung der rabbinischen Gleichnisse." *Theologische Zeitschrift* 38 (1982), pp. 514–531.

Thomas, C. and Simon Lauer, *Die Gleichnisse der Rabbinen Erster Teil Pesiqta deRav Kahana (PesK).* Bern: Peter Lang, 1986.

Via, Dan Otto. *The Parables.* Philadelphia: Fortress Press, 1980.

Wallach, L. "The Parable of the Blind and the Lame." *Journal of Biblical Literature* 65 (1943), pp. 333–339.

Winterbotham, Rayner. "Christ or Archelaus?" *Expositor* 8th series, 4 (1912), pp. 338–347.

Ziegler, Ignaz. *Die Königsgleichnisse des Midrasch beleuchtet durch die Römische Kaiserzeit.* Breslau: Schlesische Verlags-Anstalt, 1903.

General Sources and Bibliography

Abel, E.L. "Who Wrote Matthew?" *New Testament Studies* 17 (1971), pp. 138–152.

Abrahams, I. *Studies in Pharisaism and the Gospels* (in two volumes). New York: KTAV, 1967.

Allen, W.C. *The International Critical Commentary according to S. Matthew.* Edinburgh: T. and T. Clark, 1977.

Alon, G. *The Jews in their Land in the Talmudic Age* (in two volumes). Jerusalem: Magnes, 1980–1984.

———. *Jews, Judaism and the Classical World.* Jerusalem: Magnes Press, 1977.

———. *Mechkarim Betoldot Yisrael* (in two volumes). Israel: Hakibbutz Hameuchad, 1978.

Ayali, M. *Poalim Veomanim.* Jerusalem: Yad Letalmud, 1987.

Bacher, W. *Die Agada der babylonischen Amoräer.* Frankfurt: Verlag von J. Kauffmann, 1913.

———. *Die Agada der palästinensischen Amoräer* (in three volumes). Strassburg: Karl Trübner, 1892–1899 (translated into Hebrew by A. Rabinovitz, idem, *Agadat Amore Eretz Israel.* Jerusalem: Dvir, 1926).

———. *Die Agada der Tannaiten* (in two volumes). Strassburg: Karl Trübner, 1890–1903, reprinted Darmstadt: Wissenschaftliche Buchgesellschaft, 1965 (translated into Hebrew by A. Rabinovitz, *Agadot Hatannaim.* Jerusalem: Dvir, 1919).

———. *Die Exegetische Terminologie der jüdischen Traditionsliteratur* (in two volumes). Leipzig, 1899–1905, reprinted, Darmstadt: Wissenschaftliche Buchgesellschaft, 1965 (translated into Hebrew by A. Rabinovitz, *Erche Midrash.* Carmiel: Jerusalem, 1970).

———. *Tradition und Tradenten.* Leipzig: Buchhandlung Gustav Fock, 1914, reprinted, Berlin: Walter de Gruyter and Co., 1966.

Bauer, Walter. *A Greek English Lexicon of the New Testament and Other Early Christian Literature.* revised and augmented by F.W. Gingrich and F.W. Danker, Chicago: Chicago University Press, 1979.

Ben-Yehuda, Eliezer. *Milon Halashon Haevrit Hayashanah Vehechadashah.* Jerusalem: La'am Publishing Company, 1959.

Billerbeck, P. *Kommentar zum Neuen Testament aus Talmud und Midrasch* (in six volumes). Munich: C.H. Beck, 1978.

Bivin, David and Roy Blizzard. *Understanding the Difficult Words of Jesus.* Arcadia: Makor Foundation, 1983.

Black, Matthew. *An Aramaic Approach to the Gospels and Acts* (third edition). Oxford: Clarendon Press, 1977.

Bonner, Campell. "Traces of Thaumaturgic Techniques in the Miracles." *Harvard Theological Review* 20 (1927), pp. 171ff.

Büchler, A. "Learning and Teaching in the Open Air in Palestine." *Jewish Quarterly Review* 4 (1914), pp. 485ff.

Büchler, A. *Types of Jewish-Palestinian Piety.* London: Jews' College Publications, 1922.

Bussmann, W. *Synoptische Studien I-III.* Halle: Buchhandlung des Waisenhauses, 1925–1931.

Buth, R. "Hebrew Poetic Tenses and the Magnificat," *Journal for the Study of the New Testament* 21 (1984), pp. 67–83.

Chajes, Z.H. *The Student's Guide Through the Talmud.* translated and annotated by J. Schachter. New York: Feldheim, 1960.

Dalman, G. *Jesus-Jeshua.* New York: KTAV, 1971.

———. *The Words of Jesus.* Edinburgh: T. and T. Clark, 1902.

Daube, David. *The New Testament and Rabbinic Judaism.* London: Althlone Press, 1956.

Davies, W.D. *The Setting for the Sermon on the Mount.* London: Cambridge University Press, 1977.

Deissmann, A. *Light from the Ancient East.* Grand Rapids: Baker Book House, 1980.

Derrett, J. Duncan M. *Law in the New Testament.* London: Darton, 1970.

———. *Jesus's Audience.* London: Darton, 1973.

Dodd, C.H. "The Fall of Jerusalem on the 'Abomination of Desolation.'" *The Journal of Roman Studies* 37 (1947), pp. 47–54.

Doeve, J.W. *Jewish Hermeneutics in the Synoptic Gospels and Acts.* Assen: Van Gorcum, 1954.

Encyclopaedia Judaica. Jerusalem: Keter Publishing, 1978.

Epstein, Y.N. *Mevo Lanusach Hamishnah.* Jerusalem: Magnes, 1974.

———. *Mevoot Lasifrut Hatannaim.* Jerusalem: Magnes, 1976.

Farmer, W.R. *The Synoptic Problem.* New York: Macmillan, 1964.

Fitzmyer, J.A. *The Anchor Bible the Gospel according to Luke* (in two volumes). New York: Doubleday, 1981–1985.

Flusser, David, "Blessed are the Poor in Spirit." *Israel Exploration Journal* 10 (1960), pp. 1–13.

———. *Jesus in Selbstzeugnissen und Bilddokumenten.* Hamburg: Rowohlt, 1968 (a poor translation into English was published by Herder and Herder in 1969).

———. "A New Sensitivity in Judaism and the Christian Message." *Harvard Theological Review* 61 (1968), pp. 111–118.

———. "Some Notes to the Beatitudes," *Immanuel* 8 (1978), pp. 37–47.

———. *Judaism and the Origins of Christianity.* Jersualem: Magnes, (at the press; as editor of the volume, the present author has been able to make use of the work prior to its publication).

———. "Die konsequente Philologie und die Worte Jesu." *Almanach auf das Jahr des Herrn 1963.* Hamburg, 1963.

———. *Yahadut Umekorot Hanatzrut.* Tel Aviv: Sifriyat Poalim, 1979.

Gaston, L. "The Messiah of Israel as Teacher of the Gentiles." *Interpretation* 29 (1975), pp. 24–40.

Gerhardsson, Birger. *Memory and Manuscript: Oral Tradition and Written Transmission in Rabbinic Juddaism and Early Christianity.* Lund: G.W.K. Gleerup, 1964.

Ginzberg, L. *Genizah Studies* (in three volumes). New York: Jewish Theological Seminary, 1928.

Grinz, Jehoshua. "Hebrew as the Spoken and Written Language of the Second Temple." *Journal of Biblical Literature* 79 (1960), pp. 32ff.

Gross, M. *Otzar Haagadah* (in three volumes). Jerusalem: Mosad Harav Kook, 1977.

Gundry, Robert H. *Matthew.* Grand Rapids: Eerdmans, 1982.

Harnack, A. *The Sayings of Jesus.* New York: Willians and Norgate, 1908.

Hawkins, J. *Horae Synopticae.* Oxford: Clarendon Press, 1909.

Heinemann, I. *Darche Haagadah.* Jerusalem: Masada, 1970.

Heinemann, J. *Agadot Vetoldotehen.* Jerusalem: Keter, 1974.

———. *Derashot Batzibor Batekufat Hatalmud.* Jerusalem: Bialik Institute, 1982.

Heinemann, J. and Dov Noy, eds., "Studies in Aggadah and Folk-Literature." *Scripta Hierosolymitana* vol. 22. Jerusalem: Magnes Press, 1971.

Hyman, A. *Toldot Tannaim Veamoraim* (in three volumes). Jerusalem: Boys Town Jerusalem Publishers, 1963.

———. *Torah Haketubah Vehamasorah* (in three volumes). Tel Aviv: Dvir Publishing Company, 1979.

Jastrow, M. *A Dictionary of the Targumim, The Talmud Babli and Yerushlmi, and the Midrashic Literature.* Jerusalem: Hillel Press, no date.

Jeremias, Joachim. *New Testament Theology.* London: SCM Press, 1981.

———. *Unknown Sayings of Jesus.* London: SPCK, 1964.

Kilpatrick, G.D. *The Origins of the Gospel according to St. Matthew.* Oxford: Clarendon Press, 1946.

Klausner, J. *Jesus of Nazareth.* New York: Menorah, 1979.

Klostermann, E. *Das Lukasevangelium.* J.B.C. Mohr: Tübingen, 1971.

———. *Das Matthäusevangelium.* J.B.C. Mohr: Tübingen, 1975.

———. *Das Markusevangelium.* J.B.C. Mohr: Tübingen, 1971.

Kosovsky, B. *Otzar Lashon Hatannaim Lemekilta Derrabi Ishmael.* New York: Jewish Theological Seminary of America, 1965.

———. *Otzar Lashon Hatannaim Lasifra.* New York: Jewish Theological Seminary of America, 1967.

———. *Otzar Lashon Hatannaim Lasifre Bemidbar Vedevarim.* New York: Jewish Theological Seminary, 1971.

Kosovsky, Ch. *Otzar Lashon Hamishnah.* Tel Aviv: Massadah Publishing Company, 1967.

———. *Otzar Lashon Hatalmud.* Jerusalem: The Ministry of Education and Culture Government of Israel, 1971.

———. *Otzar Lashon Hatosefta.* Jerusalem: Bamberger and Wahrmann, 1932–1961.

Kosovsky, M. *Otzar Lashon Talmud Yerushalmi* (incomplete). Jerusalem: The Israel Academy of Sciences and Humanities, 1979.

Lagrange, M.J. *The Gospel according to Mark.* London: Burns Oates and Washbourne Ltd., 1930.

Levy, J. *Chaldäisches Wörterbuch über die Targumim und einen grossen Theil des rabbinischen Schriftthums* (in two volumes). Leipzig: Verlag von Gustav Engel, no date.

———. *Wörterbuch über die Talmudim und Midraschim* (in four volumes). Darmstadt: Wissenschaftliche Buchgesellschaft, 1963.

Liddell, H.G. and Robert Scott. *A Greek English Lexicon.* Oxford: The Clarendon Press, 1968.

Lieberman, S. *Greek in Jewish Palestine.* New York: Feldheim, 1965.

———. Hellenism in Jewish Palestine. New York: The Jewish Theological Studies, 1962.

Lindsey, R.L. "A Modified Two Document Theory of the Synoptic Dependence and Interdependence." *Novum Testamentum* 6 (1963), pp. 239–264.

———. *A Hebrew Translation of the Gospel of Mark.* Jerusalem: Dugith, 1979.

Lowe, M. "The Demise of Arguments from Order for Markan Priority." *Novum Testamentum* 24 (1982), pp. 27–36.

Mann, Jacob. "Changes in the Divine Service of the Synagogue due to Religious Persecutions." *Hebrew Union College Annual* 4 (1927).

Manson, T.W. *The Sayings of Jesus.* London: SCM Press, 1977.

———. *The Teachings of Jesus.* Cambridge: Cambridge University Press, 1959.

Margulies, M. "Labaiyat Kadmuto Shel Sefer Eliyahu." D. Cassuto, J. Klausner, and J. Gutmann, eds. *Sefer Asaf.* Jerusalem: Mossad Derav Kook, 1943.

Marshall, I. Howard, *The Gospel of Luke.* Grand Rapids: Eerdmans, 1979.

McNeile, A.H. *The Gospel according to St. Matthew.* Grand Rapids: Baker Book House, 1980.

Metzger, Bruce. *A Textual Commentary on the Greek New Testament.* New York: United Bible Societies, 1975.

Montefiore, C.G. *Rabbinic Literature and Gospel Teachings.* New York: KTAV, 1970.

———. *The Synoptic Gospels* (in two volumes). New York: KTAV, 1968.

Moore, G.F. "Christian Writers on Judaism," *Harvard Theological Review,* 14 (1921), pp. 197ff.

———. *Judaism in the First Centuries of the Christian Era* (originally published in three volumes). New York: Schocken Books, 1975.

Moulton, J.J., ed. *A Grammar of New Testament Greek* (in four volumes). Edinburgh: T. and T. Clark, 1978.

Moulton, W.F. and A.S. Geden. *A Concordance to the Greek Testament.* Edinburgh: T. and T. Clark, 1978.

Nathan ben Zechiel. *Aruch Completum* (ed. A. Kohut). Vienna, 1926.

Neirynck, F. *The Minor Agreements of Matthew and Luke against Mark.* Leuven: Leuven University Press, 1974.

Neusner, Jacob. *Judaism the Evidence of the Mishnah.* Chicago: Chicago University Press, 1981.

———. ed. *The Study of Ancient Judaism* (in two volumes). New York: KTAV, 1981.

Perrin, Norman. *Jesus and the Language of the Kingdom.* London: SCM Press, 1979.

———. *The Kindgom of God in the Teaching of Jesus.* Philadelphia: Westminster, 1963.

Plummer, Alfred. *An Exegetical Commentary on the Gospel according to St. Matthew.* London: James Clarke, no date.

———. *The International Critical Commentary on the Gospel according to S. Luke.* Edinburgh: T. and T. Clark, 1977.

Riesenfeld, Harald. *The Gospel Tradition.* Fortress Press: Philadelphia, 1970.

Safrai, Shmuel, M. Stern, D. Flusser, and W.C. van Unnik, eds. *The Jewish People in the First Century* (in four volumes). Amsterdam: Van Gorcum, 1974–1987.

Safrai, Shmuel. *R. Akiva Ben Yosef Chaiyav Umishnato.* Jerusalem: Bialik Institute, 1970.

———. "Avodat Yom Hakiporim Babet Hamikdash Bayame Bayit Sheni." *Machanayim* 49 (1961), pp. 121ff.

———. *Eretz Yisrael Vechachameyah Batekufat Hamishnah Vehatalmud.* Israel: Hakibbutz Hameuchad, 1983.

———. "Chasidim Veanshe Maaseh." *Tzion* (1985), pp. 134–154.

———. "Teaching of Pietists in Mishnaic Literature." *Journal of Jewish Studies* 16 (1965), pp. 15–33.

Sanday, W. *Studies in the Synoptic Problem.* Oxford: Clarendon Press, 1911.

Sanders, E.P. "The Argument from Order and the Relationship between Matthew and Luke." *New Testament Studies* 15 (1968–1969), pp. 249–261.

———. *Jesus and Judaism.* London: SCM Press, 1985.

———. *The Tendencies of the Synoptic Problem.* Cambridge: Cambridge University Press, 1969.

Schäfer, Peter. *Der Bar Kokhba-Aufstand.* Tübingen: J.C.B. Mohr, 1981.

———. "Rabbi Aqiva und Bar Kokhba." *Studien zur Geschichte Theologie des rabbinische Judentums.* Leiden: Brill, 1978, pp. 65–121.

———. "Rabbi Aqiva and Bar Kokhba." William Green ed. *Approaches to Ancient Judaism.* Chico: Scholars Press, 1980, vol. 2, pp. 55–68.

Schechter, S. *Aspects of Rabbinic Theology.* New York: Schocken, 1961.

Schlatter, A. *Der Evangelist Matthäus.* Stuttgart: Calwer Verlag, 1959.

Schreckenberg, Heinz. *Die christlichen Adversus-Judaeos-Texte und ihr literarisches und historisches Umfeld (1.–11. Jh.).* Bern: Peter Lang, 1982.

Schürer, E. *The History of the Jewish People* (in six volumes). New York: Charles Scribner's Sons, 1891.

———. revised and edited by G. Fermes, F. Millar and M. Black. *The History of the Jewish People* (in two volumes, third in preparation). Edinburgh: T. and T. Clark, 1974–1979.

Schwarzbaum, Haim. *The Mishle Shu'alim (Fox Fables) of Rabbi Berechiah Ha-Nakdan.* Kiron: Institute for Jewish and Arab Folklore Research, 1979.

Smith, Morton. "A Comparison of Early Christian and Early Rabbinic Tradition." *Journal of Biblical Literature* 82 (1963), pp. 169–176.

Stephenson, T. "The Overlapping of Sources in Matthew and

Luke." *Journal of Theological Studies* 21 (1920), pp. 127–145.

Stoldt, Hans-Herbert. *Geschichte und Kritik der Markushypothese.* Göttingen: Vandenhoeck und Ruprecht, 1977, English translation, idem, *History and Criticism of the Marcan Hypothesis.* Edinburgh: T. and T. Clark, 1980.

Strack, H. *Einleitung in Talmud und Midrasch,* revised by G. Stemberger. Munich: C.H. Beck, 1981.

Strack, H. *Introduction to the Talmud and Midrash* (this English translation was done before Stemberger's revision). New York: Atheneum, 1978.

Streeter, B.H. *The Four Gospels a Study of Origins.* London: Macmillan, 1953.

Swete, H.B. *The Gospel according to St. Mark.* London: Macmillan, 1905.

Taylor, Vincent. *The Gospel according to Mark.* Grand Rapids: Baker Book House, 1981.

Urbach, E.E. *The Sages their Concepts and Beliefs* (in two volumes). Jerusalem: Magnes Press, 1975.

Vermes, G. *Jesus the Jew.* Glasgow: Fontana, 1977.

———. *Jesus and the World of Judaism.* London: SCM Press, 1983.

———. *Post-Biblical Jewish Studies.* Leiden: Brill, 1975.

INDEXES

PRIMARY SOURCES

Hebrew Scriptures of the Old Testament

Apocrypha

New Testament

The New Testament Apocrypha

Pseudepigrapha

Dead Sea Scrolls

Rabbinic Literature

Minor Tractates of the Talmud

Midrashim

I. Al-Nakawa

Maimonides, Moses (Rambam)

Philo of Alexandria

Josephus

Fathers of the Church

Greek and Latin Authors

Other Sources

SUBJECT AND NAME INDEX

INDEX OF PARABLES, SIMILES AND FABLES

ABOUT THE AUTHOR

Brad H. Young has lived and studied in Israel for ten years. He holds a B.A. degree with a major concentration in the Greek New Testament and a minor in the Hebrew Scriptures from Oral Roberts University, an M.A. degree with a major concentration in early Christianity and a minor in early Judaism, and a Ph.D. from Hebrew University. He has lectured in the Comparative Religions Department at the Hebrew University as well as at the Institute of Holy Land Studies. Dr. Young's unique background and educational experiences provide many insights to the parables of Jesus and their original Jewish context.

THEOLOGICAL INQUIRIES:

Serious studies on contemporary questions of Scripture, Systematics and Moral Theology. Also in the series:

J. Louis Martyn, *The Gospel of John in Christian History: Essays for Interpreters*

Frans Jozef van Beeck, S.J., *Christ Proclaimed: Christology as Rhetoric*

John P. Meier, *The Vision of Matthew: Christ, Church and Morality in the First Gospel*

Pheme Perkins, *The Gnostic Dialogue: The Early Church and the Crisis of Gnosticism*

Michael L. Cook, S.J., *The Jesus of Faith: A Study in Christology*

Joseph F. Wimmer, *Fasting in the New Testament: A Study in Biblical Theology*

William R. Farmer and Denis M. Farkasfalvy, O.Cist., *The Formation of the New Testament Canon: An Ecumenical Approach*

Rosemary Rader, *Breaking Boundaries: Male/Female Friendship in Early Christian Communities*

Richard J. Clifford, *Fair Spoken and Persuading: An Interpretation of Second Isaiah*

Robert J. Karris, *Luke: Artist and Theologian: Luke's Passion Account as Literature*

Jerome Neyrey, S.J., *The Passion According to Luke: A Redaction Study of Luke's Soteriology*

Frank J. Matera, *Passion Narratives and Gospel Theologies: Interpreting the Synoptics through their Passion Stories*

James P. Hanigan, *Homosexuality: The Test Case for Christian Sexual Ethics*

Robert A. Krieg, *Story-Shaped Christology: The Role of Narratives in Identifying Jesus Christ*